GOVERNMENT & DEMOCRACY in AUSTRALIA
2e

Ian Cook dedicates this book to his sisters, Jeanette Black, Robyn Copper, and Carolyn Cook.

Mary Walsh dedicates this book to her mother, Josina Renders, whose strength and courage is an inspiration. Thanks for always being there.

Jeffrey Harwood dedicates this book to Sankari and to his parents, Rod and Val, for all their love and support.

GOVERNMENT & DEMOCRACY in AUSTRALIA

2e

OXFORD
UNIVERSITY PRESS
AUSTRALIA & NEW ZEALAND

OXFORD
UNIVERSITY PRESS
AUSTRALIA & NEW ZEALAND

253 Normanby Road, South Melbourne, Victoria 3205, Australia

Oxford University Press is a department of the University of Oxford.
It furthers the University's objective of excellence in research,
scholarship, and education by publishing worldwide in

Oxford New York

Auckland Cape Town Dar es Salaam Hong Kong Karachi
Kuala Lumpur Madrid Melbourne Mexico City Nairobi
New Delhi Shanghai Taipei Toronto

With offices in

Argentina Austria Brazil Chile Czech Republic France Greece
Guatemala Hungary Italy Japan Poland Portugal Singapore
South Korea Switzerland Thailand Turkey Ukraine Vietnam

OXFORD is a trademark of Oxford University Press
in the UK and in certain other countries

Copyright © Ian Cook, Mary Walsh and Jeffrey Harwood 2009
First published 2004
Second edition published 2009
Reprinted 2009

Reproduction and communication for educational purposes

The Australian *Copyright Act 1968* (the Act) allows a maximum of one chapter or
10% of the pages of this work, whichever is the greater, to be reproduced and/
or communicated by any educational institution for its educational purposes
provided that the educational institution (or the body that administers it) has
given a remuneration notice to Copyright Agency Limited (CAL) under the Act.

For details of the CAL licence for educational institutions contact:

Copyright Agency Limited
Level 15, 233 Castlereagh Street
Sydney NSW 2000
Telephone: (02) 9394 7600
Facsimile: (02) 9394 7601
E-mail: info@copyright.com.au

Reproduction and communication for other purposes

Except as permitted under the Act (for example, any fair dealing
for the purposes of study, research, criticism or review) no part of this
book may be reproduced, stored in a retrieval system, communicated or
transmitted in any form or by any means without prior written permission.
All enquiries should be made to the publisher at the address above.

National Library of Australia Cataloguing-in-Publication data

Cook, Ian, 1960–
Government & democracy in Australia / Ian Cook, Mary Walsh, Jeffrey Harwood.
2nd ed.
9780195561715 (pbk.)

Includes index.
Bibliography.

Democracy—Australia.
Australia—Politics and government.

Walsh, Mary.
Harwood, Jeffrey.

320.994

Edited by Bette Moore
Cover design by Caitlin Ziegler
Text design and typeset by Kerry Cooke, eggplant communicatiions
Proofread by Greg Alford
Indexed by Russell Brooks
Printed in Hong Kong by Sheck Wah Tong Printing Press Ltd

Table of Contents

List of Boxes — vii
List of Questions Explored — ix
Glossary — xi
Preface — xix
How to Use This Book — xxi
Structure of the Book — xxiv
Introduction: Government and Democracy — xxxi

PART I:
Government in Australia — 1

1. The Constitution — 3
2. The Legislature — 21
3. The Political Executive — 38
4. The Judiciary — 56
5. The Governor-General (Head of State) — 76
6. The Bureaucracy — 95

PART II:
Democracy in Australia — 111

7. Federalism — 113
8. Voting — 133
9. Parties — 159
10. Pressure Groups — 182

PART III:
Factors affecting Government and Democracy in Australia — 203

11 The News Media — 205
12 Opinion Polling and Political Marketing — 226
13 Globalisation — 245

PART IV:
Issues for Government and Democracy in Australia — 265

14 Indigenous Australians — 267
15 Ethnic Diversity — 288
16 Citizenship and Australian Identity — 313
17 The Environment and Climate Change — 333
18 National Security and Terrorism — 356

Conclusion — *372*
Bibliography — *374*
Index — *407*

List of Boxes

1.1	Draft preamble proposed by John Howard to introduce the Constitution	18
1.2	*Australia Act 1986*	19
2.1	The passing of legislation: from bill to act	23
2.2	'Welcome to Country' ceremony at opening of Parliament	25
2.3	Senate censure over Iraq	27
2.4	Introduction of the GST	29
2.5	The Committees of Federal Parliament	33
3.1	Hawke and the MX Missiles	46
3.2	Gorton votes against himself	48
3.3	Keating on the backbench	50
3.4	The Rudd Ministry	51
4.1	Reactions to the *Mabo* case	65
4.2	Reactions to the *Tasmanian Dam* case	67
4.3	Michael Kirby and the Commonwealth car controversy	72
5.1	Resignation of the Governor-General	78
5.2	The 1975 Constitutional Crisis	84
5.3	Appointing the Governor-General	87
5.4	A synopsis of the 1998 Constitutional Convention and 1999 Referendum	91
6.1	The creation of the Senior Executive Service	98
7.1	Secession in Western Australia (1933)	125
8.1	Informal votes	137
8.2	Counting votes for the House of Representatives	144
8.3	Counting votes for the Senate	145
8.4	Group voting ticket in the Senate	146
8.5	Election results	148
8.6	Safest and most marginal seats	150
9.1	The Australian Labor Party	161

9.2	The Liberal Party of Australia	163
9.3	The National Party of Australia	167
9.4	The Australian Democrats	169
9.5	The Australian Greens	172
9.6	Independents in the Federal Parliament	178
9.7	Family First Party	178
10.1	Save the Franklin campaign	184
10.2	NFF's fighting fund	193
10.3	Overturning the NT's euthanasia legislation	194
11.1	Media ownership in Australia	213
11.2	Australia's blogosphere	221
12.1	Sample order of questions	230
12.2	Australia's polling agencies	236
12.3	ALP 'It's Time' campaign	239
12.4	Kevin 07	241
13.1	Pro-globalisation	251
13.2	Anti-globalisation	259
14.1	Quality of life for Indigenous Australians	269
14.2	*Little Children are Sacred* report 2007	274
14.3	A short history of the Department of Aboriginal Affairs	275
14.4	A short history of Land Rights for Indigenous Australians	277
14.5	Apology to Australia's Indigenous Peoples	281
15.1	Ethnic diversity in Australia	290
15.2	Patterns of immigration since 1788	292
15.3	The dictation test (White Australia Policy)	295
15.4	Current immigration policy	296
16.1	Australian Citizenship Pledge	318
16.2	The Australian People	319
16.3	Citizenship in Australia 1997–2007	321
16.4	The Australian Citizenship Test 2007	325
17.1	Soil degradation in Australia	335
17.2	Rainfall and water availability	336
17.3	The Kyoto Protocol	344
17.4	UN Framework Convention on Climate Change	347
17.5	Kyoto Protocol targets for selected Annex B countries	349
17.6	The Intergovernmental Panel on Climate Change (IPCC)	350
18.1	Joseph 'Jack' Thomas	359
18.2	Children Overboard	362
18.3	Dr Mohammad Haneef	364

List of Questions Explored

Is the Constitution still relevant to government in contemporary Australia?	12
Is the Constitution still relevant to democracy in contemporary Australia?	15
Is Parliament a waste of time?	24
Who are members of the political executive?	39
What you see: The news media and the Prime Minister	41
Are Prime Ministers as important as they appear?	42
Why have judges been less visible/conspicuous than parliamentarians and members of political executives?	61
Why have judges become more visible/conspicuous?	63
Is increased political visibility on the part of the High Court desirable?	69
When is a Governor-General important?	82
Should Australians choose to elect their Head of State?	86
What are the possible effects of direct and indirect election of the Head of State?	89
Is a federal system a sensible way to organise government and democracy in Australia?	117
Should Australians vote in federal elections?	147
Is Australian politics better off with the two-party system than it would be without it?	170
Are the two parties more similar than they are different?	173
Why are pressure groups important in a representative democracy?	186
Why are some pressure groups more influential than others?	192
Why is the news media so important for government and democracy in Australia?	207
What is the ideal role of the news media?	208
Why do the news media not fulfill an ideal role in government and democracy in Australia?	210
Will the internet improve the situation?	218
Is the extensive use of opinion polling good for government and democracy in Australia?	232

Is there anything new about political marketing?	238
What are the implications of the different understandings of globalisation for government and democracy in Australia?	258
What does policy failure tell us about government in Australia?	269
What does policy failure with respect to Indigenous Australians tell us about democracy in Australia?	276
Can government be effective in a society in which real ethnic diversity exists?	296
Can democracy be effective in a society in which real ethnic diversity exists?	304
Should civic citizenship provide the basis for social cohesion in Australia?	326

Glossary

accountability   Someone is said to be accountable when they can be called to explain and justify (account for) their actions or policies and can be removed from office if they are found to have acted improperly or incompetently.

act, law, legislation, bill   What we often refer to as a law, or piece of legislation, is also referred to as an act of Parliament. A bill is introduced into a House of Parliament (usually the Lower House) and, if it is passed by both Houses and gains the assent of the Governor or Governor-General, it becomes an act of Parliament.

assimilation   When used to refer to the treatment of immigrants, this word describes an attempt to encourage immigrants to become similar to members of the dominant ethnic group in a society.

balance of power   A person or party is said to hold the balance of power when their vote or votes will determine the outcome with respect to any motion put in Parliament. This usually occurs when the major parties control less than half of the votes in a House.

bilateralism   We use this word to describe a situation in which two entities, such as parties, or members of political executives, agree to work together or to accept a particular policy. Members of political executives from two countries sign 'bilateral' trade or diplomatic agreements that commit them to particular trading or defence arrangements.

Budget, supply   In politics, 'budget' is used to refer to an annual financial statement presented to Parliament detailing expected government revenue and expenditure for the following financial year. 'Supply' is used to refer to any legislation introduced in the House of Representatives by members of a Cabinet to provide funds necessary for the business of government.

bureaucracy   We use this word to describe people who advise, support and carry out the wishes of members of political and company executives. Ministers are the political heads of government departments and the rest of the members of their departments can be referred to as bureaucrats.

Caucus 'Caucus' is most commonly used to refer to the formal meeting of parliamentarians belonging to the Australian Labor Party. Caucus is called to appoint people to ministries and other positions and to determine strategies in Parliament.

citizenship 'Citizenship' is used to refer to a legal status accorded to persons who satisfy nationality requirements. In Western societies, this usually includes equality before the law, freedom of speech, the right to own property, and the right to vote and stand for election.

climate change This phrase could be used to refer to any long-term changes in world temperatures and rainfall, but is now more commonly used to refer to those long-term changes in temperatures and rainfall that have resulted from human activity.

coalition When members of two or more parties agree, either before or after an election, to join forces to form and support a Cabinet drawn from their ranks they are said to enter into a coalition.

common law We use this word to refer to the 'law' that emerges from the decisions that judges make. Principles that derive from previous decisions made in higher courts guide, when they do not control, the decisions made by judges in later cases, especially judges who sit in inferior, or lower, courts. We often distinguish between common, or judge-made, and statutory, or Parliament-made, law.

Constitution, conventions, Constitutional Convention We use 'constitution' to refer to a written document that contains most of the rules that control the government of a company or a country. Practices followed for a considerable period because they usefully supplement written rules are referred to as conventions. The Constitutional Conventions, though, were those meetings held to draw up our Constitution.

Council of Australian Governments (COAG) This is a meeting of members of the Federal Cabinet, representatives of the members of state political executives, and representatives of the Australian Local Government Association.

division of powers Power is said to be divided when different powers are formally given to different levels of government. This idea and practice is essential for federalism and the Constitution of a federation must provide some indication of which of the two levels of government will have jurisdiction, or control, over which aspects of people's lives. (Please note that some powers are 'concurrent' in the Australian Constitution, which means that members of parliament of both levels of government can pass laws on these matters—though the laws passed by members of the Federal Parliament will prevail.)

double-dissolution, dissolution When members of a Parliament have served their full term, Parliament is dissolved by the Governor-General, who issues writs for a new election. Normally, the seats of all members of the House of Representatives and half of the members of the Senate will be declared vacant. In a double-dissolution, all members of the House of Representatives and all Senators must seek reelection if they are to return to Parliament. This occurs when there is a deadlock between the two Houses of Parliament and the conditions of s 57 of the Constitution are upheld.

environment This word could be used to refer to our surroundings, but is usually used to refer to our natural surroundings, rather than our built, or artificial, surroundings.

ethnic diversity We say that a society has, or exhibits, ethnic diversity when it contains people who have important cultural differences and does so without evidence of significant tension between the members of the different cultural groups. We are likely to refer to countries in which tension between cultures exists as ethnically divided. We are unlikely to refer to a society with two distinct cultures as ethnically diverse.

ethnicity We use this word to refer to the cultural group with which a person identifies. These cultural groups are marked by differences in language, religion, diet, values and dress.

faction, factional, factionalism A 'faction' is used to refer to a relatively stable group that forms within a political party. It is usually used with respect to the ALP, which has formally adopted a factional structure.

Federal Executive Council All federal Ministers and Parliamentary Secretaries are entitled to participate in the Federal Executive Council, which is presided over by the Governor-General.

Federalism Federal principles, or federalism, lead to the creation of the Australian federation. A federation is a form of political organisation, or political system, in which power is divided between two levels of government. Often the parliaments and political executives at the regional, provincial or state level of government are given power over matters that are closer to home (such as health, education and transport). The parliament and political executive at the central, commonwealth or federal level of government is given power over matters that are further from home (such as immigration, defence and foreign affairs). A federation always has a written constitution at its core because the division of power must be as clear as possible to avoid confusion about and competition over the powers of the two levels of government. A court is required to interpret and apply the written constitution when there are disputes.

franchise, suffrage   These terms are used to refer to the right to enrol and vote in elections, which is accorded to Australians over the age of eighteen.

Gazette, The   In Australia, and other Commonwealth countries, this term is used to refer to an official publication, or journal, in which laws and decisions taken by members of Cabinet are publicised.

Head of State, Governor-General, royal assent   The Head of State of a country is its political representative. A Head of State may play an active part of politics (as in the US) or play a largely symbolic or ceremonial role (Britain and Australia). In Australia, the Head of State is the British monarch. The Governor-General is the representative of the British monarch and is appointed by the monarchy on the advice of the Australian Prime Minister.

High Court   In Australia, this refers to that Court, created under the Constitution, whose judges interpret the Constitution and hear appeals from courts created under the federal and state jurisdictions. It is referred to as the 'highest court in the land' because the decisions of its judges are final.

House of Parliament (bicameral–unicameral)   A House of Parliament is a meeting room or chamber, in which elected representatives sit to pass legislation and to debate important social issues. Like most Australian Parliaments, the federal Parliament has two Houses: the House of Representatives (sometimes called the Lower House) and the Senate (sometimes called the Upper House). A Parliament with two Houses is referred to as a bicameral Parliament, whereas 'unicameral' refers to a Parliament with only one chamber. Queensland is the only unicameral state legislature in Australia.

identity   We use this word to refer to what we think makes us identifiable as a particular person. It usually refers to the things that we believe in, value and regularly do.

integration   In the context of discussions of immigration, this word is used to refer to policies or practices that lead to all people being treated alike and having the same opportunities.

lobby, lobbying   To 'lobby' is to seek to persuade someone to adopt a particular policy. Lobbying is usually used to refer to the actions of agents of pressure groups ('lobbyists') who pursue favourable outcomes from policy-makers.

mandate In politics, members of a political executive who argue that an election result means that the people have given them the authority to govern or to introduce a particular policy claim to have a mandate from the people to govern or to introduce that policy.

Minister, front bench, backbench In a political system, 'Minister' refers to the political head of bureaucratic departments, who are responsible to parliament for their department (sometimes referred to as their portfolio). The front bench refers to the seats in a House of Parliament that are filled by Cabinet members and Shadow Cabinet members. The backbench refers to the seats in which all other parliamentarians from their party sit.

motion of no confidence A motion of no confidence occurs when members of a House of Parliament debate the suitability of Ministers and Cabinet to govern. If a no confidence motion is passed against a Minister or Cabinet, they are expected to resign. This rarely happens in Australia, as Cabinets are supported by a majority of members of the Lower House.

multiculturalism Used to refer to policies adopted by members of political executives that support members of ethnic communities retaining the separation and distinctiveness of their community.

multicultural society Used to refer to a society in which distinct ethnic communities exist and persist because the existence of ethically different communities is accepted and their differences valued.

new public management Used to refer to what was heralded as a new approach to public administration. Advocates of new public management argued that members of political executives should behave more like those in the private sector. They supported selling-off, or privatising, government assets and getting private companies to deliver services that members of political executives, through their departments, once delivered (sometimes called outsourcing).

Parliament, legislature Both the terms 'Parliament' and 'legislature' are used to refer to the institution of government invested with the power of making, amending, and repealing laws.

party, parties, major, minor A group of people who form an association based on their similar views and who present candidates at elections is called a party. A major party is one that can gain sufficient public support to win a majority of seats in the Lower House of Parliament. A minor party is a party that cannot win such a majority.

pluralistic society A society is said to be pluralistic when it is made up of people with different ethnicities, religions, or values. Pluralism, on the other hand, is used to refer to an approach to government in which public policies are the reflection of the pressure that private and independent pressure groups exert on members of political executives.

policy, public policy (monetary and fiscal) 'Policy' is used to refer to a decision made by members of a political party concerning their specific or general goals. Fiscal policy concerns decisions about expenditure and taxation while monetary policy concerns the quantity of money in circulation, the cost and availability of credit, and the composition of national debt.

policy failure We use this phrase to refer to a situation in which a public policy did not achieve the outcomes that its designers and advocates intended it to achieve.

political executive The group of people, usually directors, who determine the objectives and strategies of a company is sometimes referred to as its executive. 'Political executive' is here used to refer to those who determine the objectives and strategies of government. Ministers and Cabinet are the main actors of the political executive. 'Executive' power is sometimes used to refer to the power to execute laws or undertake day-to-day government, but we have not adopted this use in the book.

preferential voting In compulsory preferential voting, voters *must* rank all of the candidates standing for election. In an optional preferential voting system, voters *can* rank all candidates.

private member's bill A 'private member's bill' is introduced into a legislature of parliament by a Member of Parliament acting on her or his own behalf. These bills are introduced either by independents or by a member of a party whose leadership do not wish to commit the party on a particular issue (often associated with issues such as euthanasia, abortion and with certain forms of medical research).

privatisation 'Privatisation' is used to refer to the selling of publicly owned enterprises to the private sector. This is usually done in the belief that the private sector is more efficient than the public sector in delivering services to the community.

proportional representation Used with respect to voting systems to refer to a system in which representatives are elected according to the proportion of the total votes that they, their group or their party, received.

protection   'Protection' refers to economic policies designed to protect local industries from overseas competitors. Protectionist policies include tariffs, which are duties levied on imports, and quotas, to restrict the quantities of a commodity that can be imported.

reading, first reading, second reading, third reading   'Readings' are stages in the passage of bills. A bill is introduced in a first reading, in which little discussion usually takes place. The second reading stage is the most important, as it is at this stage that the merits and specific provisions of a bill are discussed. A bill may be sent to a committee of the House for more careful scrutiny at this stage. The third reading is usually a formality. These procedures are governed by the rules of Parliament, or standing orders, which regulate the procedures and the conduct of business in Parliament.

real ethnic diversity   We use this phrase in this book to refer to significant ethnic differences, such as the differences that can be observed between British-Australians, Indigenous Australians, Italian-Australians, Vietnamese-Australians, and Sudanese-Australians. We treat the differences between Anglo-Australians, American-Australians, Canadian-Americans and New Zealanders as insignificant ethnic differences.

referendum   An opportunity for citizens to register their views through a formal ballot is referred to as 'a referendum'. In Australia most referenda involve attempts to alter the Constitution (see s 128 of the Constitution).

representative democracy   Used to refer to a political system in which the people choose representatives who are to govern on their behalf. Representatives take decisions, make laws, and introduce policies, until they are removed from office in an election. We refer to a system in which the people make decisions, make laws and introduce policies for themselves as 'a direct democracy'.

responsible government   We use this term to refer to a system of government in which members of Cabinet and Ministers have to account for their actions and decisions to the Members of Parliament. The Australian system of responsible government differs from the British (Westminster) system from which it derives because, unlike members of the House of Lords, the members of our upper houses (Senate and Legislative Councils) have been elected and play a greater role in holding members of Cabinet and Ministers responsible, or accountable, for their actions.

rule of law   In politics, we say that the 'rule of law' exists when the power and independence of those who govern are limited by rules that ensure that any decision or action was within the power of those who made it; was made according to correct procedure; and does not violate the basic principles that underpin the political system.

separation of powers 'Separation of powers' refers to a doctrine in which political power is taken to derive from three sources. These are the power to make laws (legislative power); to administer or execute laws (executive power); and the power to interpret laws (judicial power). Separation of powers theory requires that these three forms of power be invested in separate organisations. The separation between legislature and executive is not complete in a Westminster system because members of Cabinet and Ministers are also Members of Parliament.

social cohesion A society is said to be 'cohesive' when its members feel a sense of connection to each other. The more they have in common, or the more points of connection they feel to others, the more social cohesion is said to exist.

two-party system We refer to Australia as having a two-party system even though, technically, three parties, and not two, dominate our government. We tend to treat the Liberal–National Party Coalition as if it is one party, as Cabinets are formed from members of either the Labor Party or Coalition parties and their dominance over Cabinet means that it makes sense to refer to our system as a 'two-party' system.

vertical fiscal imbalance Most of the money collected by members of political executives in Australia is collected at the federal level. Under the Constitution, most of the power to regulate activities and to deliver services in Australia is held by members of state political executives. Those who govern at the federal level have more money than they need to satisfy their responsibilities. Those who govern at the state level have more responsibilities than they have the money to satisfy them. We refer to this situation as one in which a vertical fiscal imbalance exists.

Westminster model, Westminster system The Westminster system is the name given to a form of government that developed in Britain (from which the Australian political system was derived). Westminster is the site of the British Parliament. A Westminster system is characterised by collective and individual ministerial responsibility to Parliament, a Head of State who is not the leader of government, and by an independent judiciary.

Preface

This second edition of *Government and Democracy in Australia* retains much of that presented in the first edition while introducing some important changes. The most important change is that this edition has three authors, whereas the first edition had one author, Ian Cook. Dr. Mary Walsh, from the Faculty of Business and Government at the University of Canberra, and Dr. Jeffrey Harwood, from the John Curtin Institute of Public Policy at the Curtin University of Technology, are the co-authors of this edition. We have all worked together before, so the principles that underpinned the way that chapters were organised in the first edition made sense to all of us. They understand and share my concern with structure and my desire to highlight the structures of arguments, by reducing quotations and references to other works. They too encourage their students to see quotations and references to other works as less important than structure, and this practice is a feature of this edition.

One of the most difficult things for all of us was to continue to avoid using the word 'government' to mean anything other than the activity of exerting control and of directing a group of people (this is sometimes called governance). This was done in the first edition because government is used in different ways which means that it is not always clear to whom we are referring when we use the word and using this word alone often obscures the fact that it is people who are doing things. Governments cannot make laws, introduce legislation, imprison people, or pay them money. People do all of these things and not all of them are those we might refer to as being 'the government'.

Hence, there are two dangers in using the word government as loosely as most people do. First, it implies unity where none truly exists. People in a variety of agencies or institutions are involved in government in Australia, but these people are not acting together, mostly because they have different jobs to do. So instead of saying the government did something, we would be better off if we worked out who actually made the decision and referred to them as the decision-makers.

The second problem with using the word government loosely is that it takes people out of the picture. This is most disturbing when we talk about Australia going to war in Iraq for example. Nobody reading this book, we suspect, was involved in that decision. The decision was made by the members of Cabinet at the time and was opposed by a majority of Australians, including a majority of members of the Senate. Taking people out of the picture by using the word government loosely also takes people's agency away from them. Things happen in Australian politics because people are doing them. People, just like the readers and authors of this book, are making important decisions about the way that we live. It's not the government, it's people; people like us. So, if we choose to take part, let's not blame or applaud the government, let's blame or applaud the people who made the decisions. And when we don't like their decisions, but have done nothing to stop them from making them, then we have to realise that those people made those decisions because other people, like us, did nothing about it.

We have tried to use 'members of Cabinet' and 'members of political executives' instead of 'government' to avoid these problems. There were many moments when we regretted this decision to avoid using the word government loosely and there are places in the book where we have fallen victim to the practice of using it in an unclear and unhelpful way. We apologise for this, but defend ourselves on the ground that the loose and dangerous use of government is hard to avoid because it is so common.

The other changes made in this book are less fundamental than Mary's and Jeff's co-authorship, but they result in a different book from the first edition. First, we decided to remove the chapter on inequality and to include three new chapters. The first is the chapter on the Constitution, with which we begin. In the second of the new chapters, we discuss citizenship in Australia. In the third, we consider the effects on Australian politics of attempts to organise to fight what is often referred to as a global terrorist threat.[1] In making this change, we don't mean to suggest that inequality is not important, but we felt that we had to cover issues associated with citizenship and with terrorism, and this meant that something had to go.

Note

1 UN Press Release SC/7667 Security Council 4710th Meeting (AM) 'UN Action Against Global Terrorist Threat, Strengthened Future Steps Focus Of Security'. Council Debate, Counter-Terrorism Committee Chair Briefs Council http://www.un.org/News/Press/docs/2003/sc7667.doc.htm 20/02/2003

How to Use This Book

ONLINE RESOURCE CENTRE

One of the differences between the first and second editions of this book is that online materials support the second edition. One of the more important changes made relate to those sections of the introduction that were directed to students and to staff. In this edition, these have been removed and modified, and extended versions of them are now available online as part of an extensive Online Resource Centre (www.oup.com.au/orc/cook2e), along with other material. Please visit our URL for a full account of the online material that we provide to support this book.

PRELIMINARY SECTIONS

We have also introduced preliminary sections for each of the chapters in the first two sections of the book. These provide readers with information or ideas that they might find helpful in following the arguments presented in these chapters. They are not, and are not intended to be, complete. They provide material useful for understanding the chapter, but are not enough for a full understanding the aspect of government or democracy in Australia that is the focus of the chapter. Additional discussion has been inserted into many of the chapters and all the chapters have been re-edited, so minor changes have been introduced throughout this edition.

SOME IMPORTANT TERMS

In this edition, we provide readers with the use of certain terms in this book. First, we discuss government and democracy. These terms are important to this book and can be used in a variety of ways. Some discussion of their meanings and how these terms are used in this book might help readers to understand some of the ideas we present (including the suggestion that some tension can exist between government and democracy). Second, we have provided a glossary of terms (see p. xi), preferring to refer to this as a list of ways that these words are used. It might also be read as a list of meanings for this text (that is, a list of stipulated meanings for the terms). The terms which appear in bold in the chapters can be found in the glossary.

The main point that we want to make in this context is that we do not want to provide definitions. Unlike many other examiners, we do not want our students to provide extended definitions of terms that they use. First, this is because a word has either a clear and uncontested meaning or it has a contested meaning. If the meaning is uncontested, then it does not need definition. This is so even when

Comments on using the first person (i.e. 'I')

Many students are told that they should never write in the first person (that is, use the word 'I' in their essays). Why? First, it may be considered overly self-conscious, self-referential, or pretentious. Second, an examiner may be more interested in what others have discovered, written or said than what the author of the essay has to say. The third reason not to use 'I' in essays is that it is redundant. This has some validity. Using phrases such as 'I think', as in 'I think that the sky is falling!', is redundant. 'The sky is falling!' expresses the same idea without the use of 'I'. One response to the question of whether or not to use 'I', then, is that using 'I' makes sense at some points in an essay but not at others. 'I' can be overused, of course, but it can also save a lot of time and words. The points at which it makes most sense is in introductions and conclusions, where we describe and explain our essays to readers. Here I might indicate what I am going to argue (but only if I am making an argument), how I have divided my essay, and how I will use certain words in my essay. One of the problems that arise when writers avoid using the word 'I' is that they might write something like 'This essay argues', rather than 'In this essay I will argue...'. The problem with the latter is that it is anthropomorphic (i.e., it makes things appear human). Essays do not argue. People argue. Avoiding both using 'I' and practising anthropomorphism can be difficult. While using 'I' might be offensive to some readers, practising anthropomorphism both offends against fundamental rules of grammar and diminishes human agency. The fourth and most compelling reason not to use 'I' is that your examiner might hate it. No one will object to your not using 'I', so using it involves taking the risk of annoying an examiner (which can lead to lower marks).

it is hard to give some terms a precise meaning ('weed', for example, is hard to define but, unless it has some special use, we know what people are talking about when they are discussing weeds).

If a word has a contested meaning, such as 'democracy', then the way that word is used may produce different answers to questions that contain it. An answer to the question: 'Is Australia a democracy?' may depend on what we think a democracy is. The different cases that we present may be based upon different meanings of the term and coming to a final position on the question may be determined by what we take to be the more persuasive understanding of the term 'democracy'.

The other reason that we do not like definition sections as preliminaries is that they waste words. Most definition sections do not make a significant contribution to the rest of the essay. Other examiners may take a different view so it is important that students discuss the question of whether definitions must be provided in an essay or oral presentation before they plan their work.

Structure of the Book

This book has eighteen chapters contained in four thematic Parts. The first Part has been devoted to a discussion of important institutions of government in Australia. These are: the Constitution; Parliament; the Prime Minister, Cabinet, and Ministers; judges, particularly justices of the High Court; the Governor-General or Head of State; and the bureaucracy. The second Part covers aspects of democracy in Australia. This Part deals with federalism, voting, parties, and pressure groups. In Part III, we discuss factors that affect government and democracy in Australia. It deals with the news media, opinion polling and political marketing, and globalisation. Part IV contains discussions of issues that arise for Australian government and democracy. These are Indigenous Australians, ethnic diversity, citizenship, the environment, and security and terrorism.

PART I: GOVERNMENT IN AUSTRALIA

The first Part of this book is intended to provide some understanding of institutions that are important to government in Australia. These institutions are the basic elements of Australian politics and are the sites in which policies are implemented and often developed. That is, they represent those points within the political system at which decisions and actions are taken for the community as a whole. While the powers of Parliaments, political executives, judges, and Heads of State are not equal or identical, each plays a role in government in Australia.

The cornerstone of government in Australia is the Constitution. An Act of the British Parliament, the Constitution is not something that most of us think about when it comes to Australian government. Yet it establishes the formal rules that govern our political system, creates the body charged to adjudicate on constitutional disputes (the High Court) and states the means by which the Constitution can be changed. It also provides a framework against which the actions and legislation of the political executive can be challenged (the separation of powers).

Whether Parliament also provides any check against the power of the political executive or is a waste of time is important to the discussion of Parliament in Chapter 2. One of the attributes of the **Westminster system**, which Australians inherited as part of the colonisation process, is that the leading members of the political executive (Prime Minster and all other Ministers) must be Members of Parliament. Indeed, in a Westminster system these leading members of the political executive attain their position because they are supported by a majority of members of the Lower House. This has a profound effect on Parliament's ability to fulfil this function (and is one of the main reasons why Parliament's worth can be questioned).

We discuss the political executive in Chapter 3. In many ways, the political executive is the core of government in Australia. Prime Ministers and their Cabinets constitute the centres of the most important policy-making that occurs in Australian politics. Ministers, including Cabinet Ministers, also play an important role with respect to policy-making within the specific departments for which they are responsible. The policy-making conducted by Cabinet and Ministers is only possible because they are supported by **policy** advisers who work in public service departments. Just as important is the public service's role in policy implementation, for without the public service no policy would become effective. Despite the importance, even centrality, of Cabinet and the public service to government, Prime Ministers receive the lion's share of media coverage and end up appearing to be in control of Australian politics. Hence, in Chapter 3 we ask: 'Are Prime Ministers as important as they appear to be?'

While the system of courts is a central part of government in Australia, they are not the focus of Chapter 4. Instead, the chapter is largely taken up by a discussion of the role of the High Court. This is because the High Court is responsible for interpreting the Constitution, which can be thought of as providing the legal basis for government and democracy in Australia. One of the main issues that arise with respect to the High Court concerns the way that it should approach interpreting the Constitution. Two main alternatives are available to members of the High Court in interpreting the Constitution. The first is to interpret it as if it were a normal legal document; the second is to interpret it in ways that reflect the nature and state of Australian society. The original members of the High Court read the document according to what they took to be the intentions of the men who wrote it. They read it in terms of the type of political system that the writers of the Constitution wanted to create. However, more recently, members of the High Court have read the document according to their sense of the type of society that Australia is. This type of interpretation, combined with their abandoning of the doctrine of *terra nullius*, has resulted in accusations of judicial activism. This has, in turn, brought what we call political visibility to the court. The core question in this chapter concerns whether this increased political visibility on the part of the High Court is desirable.

Chapter 5 has been devoted to a discussion of the Head of State, or Governor-General. While governors-general have rarely been a prominent part of Australian politics, the Governor-General is the Head of State and is given a number of powers under the Constitution. Most governors-general have not used these powers independently and have acted with the advice, really direction, of Cabinet. The notable exception to this was the Constitutional Crisis of 1975. More recently, the position of Governor-General has come under scrutiny due to calls for Australia to become a republic. While a proposal to create a republic was defeated in a referendum in 1999, the issue of whether we should elect our Head of State is discussed in this chapter. This discussion includes a consideration of the effects of the different ways to elect a Governor-General.

Chapter 6 was written against a background of a general negativity, even hostility, among Australians towards bureaucracy and bureaucrats. It begins with an explanation of the creation of modern bureaucracies. Any reflection on the bureaucracy in Australia benefits from a discussion of the reasons for the creation of modern bureaucracies. Most of this chapter is taken up with a discussion of the proposition that less bureaucracy is always better than more bureaucracy. This proposition reflects both the antipathy towards bureaucracy mentioned above and more recent attempts, at both state and federal level, to reduce the size of the bureaucracy.

PART II: DEMOCRACY IN AUSTRALIA

That we live in a democracy, actually a representative democracy, means that these institutions interact with or are affected by citizens. Citizens decide who occupies these positions of institutional power and can have some influence on what these people do. Elections, parties, and pressure groups all represent opportunities for citizens to participate in Australian politics in order to have their interests or views taken into account. We deal with each in Part II, beginning with a discussion of federalism because it is not an institution of government and represents both a way to control the use of power and a specific way to organise citizens.

We have included a discussion of federalism in this Part partly because the core questions addressed in this chapter concern whether a federal system is a sensible way to organise government and democracy in Australia. We placed it after the discussions of the various formal institutions that produce government to show how the practices and informal institutions, in their interaction with formal political institutions, produce democracy. However, the way that Australians are divided by federalism is as important for democracy as it is for government. The questions around which we have organised this chapter are: 'Is a federal system a sensible way to organise government in Australia?' and 'Is a federal system a sensible way to organise democracy in Australia?'

In Chapter 8, we deal with voting. While we think of Australia as a democracy, it is a particular type of democracy: a representative democracy. In the Australian form of representative democracy, voters decide who will represent them in both houses of Parliament (the House of Representatives and the Senate). In doing so, they elect not only lawmakers, but also those who will determine who occupies ministerial positions (and, as a result, Cabinet Ministers and Prime Ministers). This is determined by their vote in the House of Representatives. The Westminster convention, in this context, is that members of the Lower House of Parliament decide who will be in the Ministry. In effect, this means the party that wins a majority of seats in the Lower House. This brings us to voting. Voting can be understood as a privilege and a (democratic) responsibility, yet compulsory voting means that Australians vote not because of their understanding of the issues or their commitment to democracy, they vote because they have to vote. The core question in Chapter 8 is: 'Should Australians have to vote in federal elections?'

Chapters 9 and 10 deal with parties and pressure groups. These represent relatively dynamic aspects of Australian politics. Their dynamism is important, as they can be understood as carriers of ideas, information, and pressure within the political system. Parties are fundamentally important to government and democracy in Australia because they enlist candidates for election and develop policies that may be implemented by members of political executives or that will be part of their election campaigns. Australian politics is divided between the Australian Labor Party and the Liberal Party–National Party coalition. These parties are at the heart of the two-party system. (Technically, of course, it is a one-party and one coalition of parties system, but it is usually referred to as a two-party system.) The core questions in Chapter 9 concerns whether Australian politics is better off with the two-party system than it would be without it and whether the parties are more similar than they are different.

Pressure groups represent even less formal parts of government and democracy in Australia. While some of them are very long-lived, others form around specific problems or issues and can dissipate when that issue or problem is resolved. But they play important roles in ensuring that those in formal political institutions gain some sense of views present in Australian society. They can also be understood to form part of a specific type of political system known as liberal-pluralism or just pluralism. As their names suggest, pressure groups can be seen as vehicles through which pressure is exerted within the political system by groups of people who share similar views and values. Two core questions concerning pressure groups are posed in Chapter 10. The first concerns why pressure groups are important in a representative democracy. The second concerns why some pressure groups are more influential than others.

PART III: FACTORS AFFECTING GOVERNMENT AND DEMOCRACY IN AUSTRALIA

While the institutions, processes, and practices that have been discussed in the preceding Parts are central to the way that government and democracy works in Australia, we do not believe that this is enough to understand politics in Australia. For these institutions, processes, and practices are profoundly affected by the social and technological environment within which they operate. Many factors might have been discussed in this chapter. Three that seem to have the most significant and direct effect on government and democracy in Australia are the news media, opinion polling and political marketing, and globalisation.

No one can doubt that government and democracy in Australia is deeply affected by the news media. Indeed, the news media is sometimes referred to as the 'fourth estate', which is intended to suggest that it is almost part of political process. A central part of its role as a fourth estate is that members of the news media undertake the investigative journalism necessary to discover and expose any maladministration of members of political executives. This view of the media might reflect general dissatisfaction with Parliament's capacity to hold members of political executives accountable for their actions. We have significant reservations about treating the news media as a fourth estate. This led us to consideration of what the ideal role of the news media in Australian government and democracy might be. In Chapter 11, we present and explain our view of an ideal situation with respect to the news media, and then explain why it cannot play this role. We then consider whether the internet will improve the situation and bring us closer to the ideal situation we outlined earlier.

Opinion polling and political marketing are the other factors affecting government and democracy in Australia. Indeed, they may almost be thought to have changed central aspects of the operation of government and democracy in this country. Opinion polling, especially opinion polling enhanced by sophisticated computer technology, provides members of political executives and leaders and strategists within political parties with a much clearer sense of citizens' views than was previously available. At least, properly conducted opinion polls will do so. While the extensive use of opinion polling can be seen to enhance democracy, it can also be criticised for its effects on politics. In this chapter, one of the core questions concerns whether the extensive use of opinion polling is good for government and democracy in Australia. The other question posed in Chapter 12, though we deal with it more briefly, is whether there is anything new about political marketing. Election campaigning may well have always involved candidates and leaders marketing themselves to citizens. The use of sophisticated advertising techniques in election campaigns, however, led us to consider whether something different is now happening.

Globalisation was initially included in this Part because it seemed to be an obvious contextual factor within which government and democracy in Australia operated. Some commentators, however, have argued that globalisation is not a fact, but is an idea that has been used to promote particular political agendas by those involved in government. The result of the doubt about the status of globalisation that this creates led us to discuss the two views of globalisation (as a fact and as an idea used to promote particular political agendas) and their implications for government and democracy in Australia. The question that we ask in this chapter is: 'What are the implications of the different understandings of globalisation for government and democracy in Australia?'

PART IV: ISSUES FOR GOVERNMENT AND DEMOCRACY IN AUSTRALIA

Five issues appear to be important, or potentially important, for government and democracy in Australia. These are Indigenous Australians, ethnic diversity, citizenship and identity politics, the environment and global warming, and security and terrorism. Discussing these issues in the context of government and democracy in Australia may help readers to develop a more comprehensive understanding of Australian politics. It may also assist them to develop a sense of the possibilities and limitations inherent in the Australian political system. Most importantly, it may suggest reasons why government and democracy in Australian requires reform and how it could be reformed.

Indigenous Australians are discussed in the context of policy failure as the focus. The quality of life that most Indigenous Australians experience is generally much poorer than that of other Australians. Indigenous Australians also have shorter lifespans. If we assume that this situation was not deliberately created, then it makes sense to treat this as policy failure. The questions addressed in this chapter relate to what policy failure tells us about government and what it tells us about democracy in Australia.

Ethnic diversity is an issue that provides an opportunity to discuss aspects of and possible limitations to government and democracy in Australia. At least, what we call 'real' ethnic diversity provides this opportunity. While there may be ethnic diversity among British-Australians, the differences between them are insignificant compared to the differences between British and non-British Australians. The fact that Australia seems less attractive to migrants from the United Kingdom and former British colonies suggests that real ethnic diversity may increase in Australia. The core questions of this chapter concern whether government and democracy can be effective in a society in which real ethnic diversity exists.

We discuss the issues that arise with respect to citizenship and identity in Chapter 16. Citizens are an essential part of any democracy, so what citizenship involves is an issue that will arise regularly in a representative democracy. The core question in this chapter is: 'Should citizenship provide the basis for social cohesion in Australia?' Posing and presenting answers to this question allows us to reflect on different conceptions of citizenship and the way that citizenship affects democracy in Australia.

Pollution causing global warming, salination, and the loss of native species constitute some of the most important challenges that we will face in the future. We discuss the proposition that government and democracy in Australia cannot deliver environmental sustainability. If this is correct then it provides a powerful motivation to examine ways of reforming government and democracy in Australia.

We discuss security and terrorism in the final chapter this book. Along with environmental degradation, it is one of the most significant issues with which government and democracy in Australia must deal. First, we discuss the proposition: 'We cannot protect people's rights and freedom and provide for their security'. In discussing this proposition, we present reasons why someone might make such a claim and then comment on these reasons. This leads us to pose and answer the question: 'What conceptions of security characterise the different responses to restricting people's rights to achieve security?'

Introduction: Government and Democracy

The two terms that appear throughout this book are among the hardest to define. These are 'government' and 'democracy'. Difficulties associated with the meaning of government seem to result from the fact that the word is used in very different ways. Three will be discussed below. Government is sometimes used to refer to a Cabinet. It is also used to refer to all the political institutions of a country. Finally, it is used to refer to the control and direction of a society. It is in this last sense that we use the word in this book.

Democracy is hard to define because it can be used to refer to quite different political systems. That democracy is now shorthand for representative democracy means that a democracy might simply be a system in which people elect their leaders. Alternatively, and more in line with ideas of direct democracy, is the view that a democracy is a political system in which the people participate in those forums in which decisions that affect the whole community are made. Between these two meanings is the idea that a democracy is a system in which people shape public policy by voting. Another meaning that seems to fall between the two meanings is the idea that a democracy is a system in which citizens have a continuous influence over the policy-making process within their society. While both of these middle-positions can be taken to be versions of representative democracy, the second is closer to direct democracy than the first.

GOVERNMENT

Cabinet

One of the most common ways in which the word government is used is in conjunction with the name of a Prime Minister or Premier. Thus, we might speak of the Rudd, Howard, Iemma, or Brumby government. One of the reasons that it makes sense to use the word government in this way is that the system we have is one in which Cabinet has a central governing role. So to refer to the government and to mean the Cabinet is a meaningful way to use the word. For there can be no doubt that it is Cabinet that plays a crucial role in determining the policies that shape our lives.

All political institutions

Cabinet is not the only political institution responsible for policy-making and is not the group responsible for policy implementation. Indeed, all political institutions can be understood to play a role in controlling and directing Australian society. Given this, it makes sense to refer to, or more usually complain about, government and mean more than the current Cabinet. In this case, a reference to government can refer to all politicians (even those in the Opposition, minor parties, and independents), bureaucrats, and judges.

Control and direction

Government is not only used to refer to people; it is also used to refer to an activity. Central to this activity are control and direction within a society. Government, in this use, involves producing control within a society and providing the members of society with some collective direction. While this direction might be minimal, a decision to provide minimal direction for a society can mean that other factors, possibly markets, will be relied upon for direction. An important feature of this use of government is that it reminds us that those in government are there to govern the people. To govern a people is to provide them with 'law and order' (please bear in mind that anarchists believe that our view that we need to be governed by those in a central authority is a reflection of our socialisation). Providing law and order may be all there is to government, but we seem to expect a little more than this. For many of us also expect that government is taking us in some collective direction; that is, that government involves creating a certain way of life for a people or a certain type of society. Government may involve massive projects of social reorganisation or it may involve minor tinkering with particular aspects of society in order to achieve minor improvements to society.

DEMOCRACY

Electing and rejecting leaders

Three of the four uses of the word democracy discussed here relate to representative democracy. The simplest use of democracy is to describe a political system in which the people can elect and reject their leaders. While election is important in all uses of the word, democracy can mean more than simply a system in which citizens do more than register support for their leaders. Voters must also be given the opportunity to reject their leaders. In one-party states, such as North Korea or Cuba, voters may vote, but are given only one party for which they can vote. This is not consistent with what most of us mean by democracy and might make the capacity to reject leaders something of a defining characteristic of democracy. Rejected leaders have to be replaced through elections, though, if we are to still call this system a democracy.

Influencing important decisions by voting

Treating a democracy as a system in which people can elect and reject their leaders provides too narrow an application of the term for some people. When they refer to a country as a democracy, they mean a country in which people have the ability to influence important decisions taken on their behalf. In this case, voting can be seen as an essential part of allowing the people to influence important decisions. A democracy, in this use, is a system in which voting goes some way to ensuring that leaders have an idea about the people's wishes with respect to important decisions that will be taken during their term of office. This might be augmented by occasional referenda, but this is impossible when an important decision that was not raised during an election needs to be made quickly.

Continuous influence on the decision-making process

Seeking the people's input at specific moments, like elections and referenda, will only satisfy some people that a political system is a democracy. For them, a democracy is a system in which the people exercise continual influence over the decision-making process, so that all decisions that are made can be understood as reflecting the will of the people. That this might be difficult to achieve does not prevent it from being a defining feature of a democracy. It may well mean that few countries might be said to have democratic political systems, but this reflects the difficulty of achieving democracy (even in a representative democratic system).

The main issue that arises in this context relates to whether people actually have to exert continuous influence on decision-making processes, or simply be continuously able to exert influence on the decision-making process. The problem with the latter position is that people may not exert their influence and, by not doing so, may have no input into decisions taken on their behalf. This is no problem for those for whom democracy is simply about electing leaders and having the opportunity to provide input on policy directions at elections. The more that you believe that a democracy is a system in which people are actively involved in the policy-making process, the less you will be satisfied with potential, but not actual, involvement by the people.

Direct participation in decisions

The view that people need to be involved in the collective decision-making process may lead to a rejection of the view that a representative democracy deserves to be called a democracy. For the view that the people ought to be involved in important collective decisions can lead to the conclusion that they need to be directly involved in making these decisions. A democracy, in this use, refers to a system in which the people are directly involved in making decisions that affect their communal lives. One of the more recent expressions of this idea can be found in the literature and practices of deliberative democracy. While these theories may not result in all citizens being involved in collective decision-making, the idea that people should be involved in making the decisions that fundamentally affect their lives is basic to theories of deliberative democracy. The most important thing to note here is that recent interest in theories of deliberative democracy reflects concerns about a lack of democracy, which here means popular participation in collective decision-making, in representative democracies.

PART I

Government in Australia

The Constitution

LEARNING OBJECTIVES

- Understand what the Constitution is, how it emerged, what it says and doesn't say, the implications of this, and the difference between the separation of powers and the division of powers
- Have a general understanding of key sections of the Australian Constitution
- Be able to consider whether the Constitution is still relevant to government in contemporary Australia
- Be able to consider whether the Constitution is still relevant to democracy in contemporary Australia

INTRODUCTION

The Constitution is the foundation of Australia's political system. The Centenary of Federation in 2001 caused many Australians to take greater interest in the relevance of the Constitution to contemporary Australian political culture. At this time, there was a great deal of discussion and debate about whether Australia should become a republic. The Australian people were asked at a referendum whether they would like to have an Australian Head of State elected by a two-thirds majority of Parliament. Australians rejected this proposal. According to some commentators, they rejected it because they wanted to elect their Head of State and Australia would now be a republic if Australians had been given this option. Whatever the merits of this view, the Constitution did become important to Australians at this time, yet there seemed to be little ongoing interest in Australia's Constitution and its relevance to contemporary Australian political culture.

This chapter is in four parts. The first part provides a preliminary discussion of the Australian Constitution. Here we explain what the Constitution is and how it emerged in 1901. We overview the founding principles of Australia's Constitution and examine what the Constitution says and what it doesn't say and the implications of this for government and democracy in Australia. In the second part of the chapter, we discuss important sections of the Constitution. The purpose of this part is to familiarise readers with core sections of Australia's Constitution in order to provide them with a way of understanding what the Constitution is and does. In the third part of the chapter, we present the alternative positions available on the question of whether the Constitution is still relevant to government in contemporary Australia. Finally, we present the alternative positions available on the question of whether the Constitution is still relevant to democracy in contemporary Australia.

1: PRELIMINARY DISCUSSION

In this part of the chapter, we explain what the Constitution is and outline how the Constitution emerged in Australia in 1901. To do the first of these things, we overview two ideas that explain important aspects of Australia's Constitution. The first of these is the concept of responsible government; this concept was taken directly from the United Kingdom's Westminster system as part of our colonial heritage. The second is the concept of federalism, which came to us primarily because of the influence of the United States political system on those who devised the Constitution, though they were aware of other federal systems (such as those in Switzerland and Germany). We also explain how principles associated with the **separation of powers** and the division of powers are expressed in the Constitution.

Finally, we look briefly at what the Constitution does say and what it doesn't say and the implications of this for government and democracy in contemporary Australia.

What is the Constitution?

The **Constitution** was created in 1901, as a document entitled *The Commonwealth of Australia Constitution Act*, and is the foundation of government and democracy in Australia. It provides the framework, structure and rules that constitute the basis for the conduct of government at the Commonwealth and state levels.[1] In a liberal democracy, such as Australia, the Constitution provides a formal way of dividing power in ways that prevent those at one level of government from dominating those at the other level, while also protecting individuals from the arbitrary use of power by those who govern them. As well as being influenced by the practices and constitutions of the Australian colonies, the Constitution also blends elements of other constitutional systems, namely the concept of **responsible government** from the United Kingdom and the concept of **federalism** from the United States system of government.

How did the Constitution emerge in Australia?

The idea of creating a Commonwealth of Australia through adopting a formal written Constitution was debated for more than sixty years before it actually happened, and this delay reflected the varied values of the colonial politicians[2] who drafted Australia's Constitution. In the 1890s, Australia was six different colonies whose members were deeply suspicious of the idea of one overarching government.[3] Sir Henry Parkes, the then Premier of New South Wales, was one of the main advocates of the idea of creating a Commonwealth of Australia.[4] People, especially politicians, in the various colonies were cautious about Parkes's motives and were fiercely protective of their own independent and self-governing capacities. There was a great deal of rivalry between people in Victoria and New South Wales, particularly concerning trade and the economy. As well, people in the less populated states were concerned that people in the more populated states of New South Wales and Victoria would attempt to dominate them. What eventually brought them all together were a combination

separation of powers: 'Separation of powers' refers to a doctrine in which political power is taken to derive from three sources. These are: the power to make laws (legislative power); to administer or execute laws (executive power); and the power to interpret laws (judicial power). Separation of powers theory requires that these three forms of power be invested in separate organisations. The separation between legislature and executive is not complete in a Westminster system because members of Cabinet and Ministers are also Members of Parliament.

Constitution, conventions, Constitutional Convention: We use 'constitution' to refer to a written document that contains most of the rules that control the government of a company or a country. Practices followed for a considerable period because they usefully supplement written rules are referred to as **conventions**. The Constitutional Conventions, though, were those meetings held to draw up our Constitution.

of their concerns about defence and immigration and a growing sense of national pride.⁵ The colonies had their own armies, with no national defence whatsoever. A perception that they were threatened with invasion, particularly by the Chinese and powerful European countries establishing colonies in the Asia-Pacific, was also a powerful inducement for those in the colonies to unite as one country. This sense of vulnerability was also evident in their concerns about immigration by people who were not British.

Responsible Westminster government and federalism

The Australian Constitution was influenced by the British Parliamentary system, in which elected Parliaments represent citizens and act as a lawmaking body, which is referred to as the legislature. In this Parliamentary system, citizens do not elect the members of Cabinet directly. Instead, citizens vote for individual politicians who decide who will form the Cabinet, which is comprised of the Prime Minister and senior Ministers. Members of Cabinet must be supported by a majority of those in the House of Representatives, if Cabinet members are to have the laws that they want passed, and they must answer to them for the policies that they introduce. This system is referred to as one of **responsible government**.

Federalism is a political solution for peacefully combining separate and independent communities into a single nation.⁶ In a federal system of government, power is divided between the various levels of government with those who operated at each level of government having autonomy and authority over various governmental functions. Our federal system was influenced by the structure of government that was adopted when the United States of America was created. The Australian Constitution outlines the different roles of the national and State governments in ss 51 and 52.

responsible government: We use this term to refer to a system of government in which members of Cabinet and Ministers have to account for their actions and decisions to the Members of Parliament. The Australian system of responsible government differs from the British (Westminster) system from which it derives because, unlike members of the House of Lords, the members of our upper houses (Senate and Legislative Councils) have been elected and play a greater role in holding members of Cabinet and Ministers responsible, or accountable, for their actions.

federalism: We refer to a political system as federal when two permanent levels of government exist and power is divided between political institutions that derive from and operate at both of these levels.

Separation of powers and division of powers

The separation of powers, in a liberal democracy like Australia, is something that people want when they are concerned that the concentration of power will result in political corruption. In such a system, power is given to separate institutions. These are a legislature, an executive, and a judiciary; with each acting as a 'check and balance' that prevents one of these institutions from having too much power. A separation of powers is introduced, then, to limit the power of all actors in the political system. The division of powers refers to a system in which power is divided between a national, or federal, level of government and a regional, or state, level of governments. In a federal system of government, both levels of government must be protected, so that they maintain their independence and spheres of authority.

What does the Constitution say?

The Constitution of the Commonwealth of Australia is divided into a preamble, eight chapters and a schedule. Chapter One is on the Parliament and is divided into five parts. The titles of these parts are General, The Senate, The House of Representatives, Both Houses of the Parliament and the Powers of Parliament. Chapter One is, by far, the largest chapter of the Constitution, containing sixty of the 128 provisions in the Constitution. Chapter Two is on the Executive Government, Chapter Three the Judicature, Chapter Four is on Finance and Trade, Chapter Five the States, Chapter Six is on New States, Chapter Seven covers miscellaneous matters and Chapter Eight deals exclusively with altering the Constitution.

What doesn't the Constitution say?

The Constitution outlines the formal institutions of government, including the Governor-General, the Parliament, the bureaucracy, and the judiciary. Normal, or conventional, practices are also extremely important to the Australian political system and play a crucial role in ensuring the continuity and predictability of the political process; yet they are not mentioned in the Constitution. When those involved in government continue to follow these informal, but normal, practices we refer to them as following **conventions**. These conventional practices are repeated so often that they have become the way that things are done and help to fill gaps in the Constitution. If these gaps were not filled, government would be disrupted because crucial actors, such as the Cabinet and the Prime Minister, are not mentioned, the effects of political parties is not recognised, and the Constitution is silent concerning the rights and roles of citizens and members of the news media.

What are the implications of what the Constitution says and doesn't say?

Parkin and Summers (2002) have argued that while the Australian Constitution is a crucial formal document, it is important to understand the Constitution as existing within a broader constitutional framework. The formal Constitution provides the framework for understanding the institutions and rules by which those in government govern. It determines who has legitimate authority over the various things that must be governed and provides for the accountability of members of the federal political executive. There are also many practices and informal arrangements that are part of Australia's government and democratic processes, which complement the formal written document. The written Constitution and the conventions associated with democratically governing Australia provide a way of understanding how Australia's political system actually works.[7]

Summary

In the first part of this chapter, we provided a preliminary discussion of the Australian Constitution, explained what the Constitution is and outlined how the Constitution emerged in Australia in 1901. We overviewed the two founding principles of Australia's Constitution, which are the concepts of responsible government and federalism. The separation of powers and the division of powers, as they are reflected in the Constitution, were also outlined. Finally, we looked briefly at what the Constitution does say, what it doesn't say, and the implications of this for government and democracy in contemporary Australia.

QUESTIONS

1. What is the Australian Constitution and how did it emerge?
2. What are the two founding principles of the Australian Constitution?
3. What is the difference between the separation of powers and the division of powers?

2: THE AUSTRALIAN CONSTITUTION

In the second part of this chapter, we provide an overview of important sections of the Australian Constitution. We begin with Parliament, which leads us to consider the concept of a Head of State, a term not explicitly used in the Australian Constitution. We then discuss the sections in the Constitution that describe the role of the Governor-General, the Senate, the House of Representatives, the division of Commonwealth and state powers, what happens when there is disagreement between the Houses of Parliament, the role of the High Court as an umpire in disputes between Commonwealth and state governments, and what Australians need to do to change our Constitution.

Parliament and the Head of State

The legislative power of the Commonwealth of Australia resides in the Queen of Australia (or her representative the Governor-General), the Senate and the House of Representatives (which are referred to in the Constitution as Parliament). Including the Queen, or the Governor-General, in the definition of Parliament is interesting because the Australian Constitution does not mention a Head of State. Most Australians are unaware of the fact that the Queen is part of our Parliament, but the issue of an Australian Head of State did come into prominence in the 1999 republic referendum. Australians rejected the idea of having an Australian Head of State who was elected by a two-thirds majority of Parliament, so the Queen remains part of our Parliament.

Sections 2–6: The Governor-General

We discuss the position of the Governor-General in Chapter 5, so we will merely note here that, according to the Constitution, the Governor-General is appointed by the Queen as Her Majesty's representative in the Commonwealth with powers and functions that the Queen assigns him or her. In reality, the Prime Minister selects the Governor-General with the Queen accepting the Prime Minister's choice. The most controversial Governor-General in Australian history was Sir John Kerr, who infamously sacked members of the Whitlam (ALP) Cabinet in 1975 because they could not get the funds they needed to keep paying for federal government after supply was blocked in the Senate.

Sections 7–23: The Senate

The Senate was created to protect the Australian states and the state level of government as a whole. The Senate is composed of Senators from each state directly chosen by the people of that state. Each state is represented by twelve Senators, and two Senators represent the people of each of the territories; so the total number of Senators is seventy-six. Senators are elected for a term of six years and s 13 of the Constitution requires that, in a normal election, only half of the positions in the Senate will be contested. If a double dissolution occurs, by which both Houses of Parliament are dissolved, all the seats in the Senate must be contested. All matters that are brought before members of the Senate are determined by majority rule with each Senator able to cast one vote. If Senators are equally divided on any issue, the matter will be resolved in the negative.

Sections 24–40: The House of Representatives

Section 24 of the Constitution provides that the House of Representatives must be comprised of members who have been directly elected by the citizens of Australia. The Parliament can make laws to increase or decrease the membership of the House of Representatives, but the number of members in the House of Representatives must be twice that of Senators. Matters that come before the House of Representatives will be decided by a majority of its members, excluding the Speaker. When the members of the House of Representatives are equally divided on an issue, the Speaker can cast the deciding vote.

Sections 51, 52 & 109: Commonwealth/state powers

The Australian Constitution divides power between a national, federal or Commonwealth, level of government and a state level of government. The national Parliament has the power to make laws in the areas specified in s 51 of the Constitution, with state Parliaments having authority in all areas not specifically mentioned in s 51. The powers that are left to state Parliaments are referred to as residual powers. While they might be left over, or residual, they are important powers and give those at the state level the power to provide public services such as schools and, hospitals, correctional services, public housing, parks and the environment, etc. The federal and state Parliaments have concurrent powers that include most of the areas set out in s 51. If there is a conflict in the laws passed by members of the federal and state Parliaments, however, then the law passed by the federal Parliament prevails (this is outlined in s 109 of the Constitution). The Commonwealth Parliament has exclusive powers over defence, immigration, currency, customs and excise, external affairs and Australian territories.

double-dissolution, dissolution: When Members of a Parliament have served their full term, Parliament is dissolved by the Governor-General, who issues writs for a new election. Normally, the seats of all members of the House of Representatives and half of the members of the Senate will be declared vacant. In a double-dissolution, all members of the House of Representatives and all Senators must seek reelection if they are to return to Parliament. This occurs when there is a deadlock between the two Houses of Parliament and the conditions of s 57 of the Constitution are upheld.

Section 57: Disagreement between the Houses of Parliament

The drafters of the Constitution were aware that there might be disagreement between members of the House of Representatives and the Senate. Section 57 of the Constitution provides a way of resolving deadlocks between the two Houses. A deadlock between the two Houses of Parliament can be resolved through a **double dissolution** (i.e., the breaking up, or dissolving, of both Houses of Parliament). If a majority of members in the House of Representatives pass a proposed law, or bill, and a majority of members of the Senate reject or fail to pass this bill, or pass it with amendments that are not acceptable to a majority of members of the House of Representatives, then members of the House of Representatives can return the proposed law to the Senate. If, after a three-month interval, the bill is not passed in the Senate or is modified in a way that is unacceptable to a majority of members of the House of

Representatives, then Parliament can be dissolved and an election called for both the House of Representatives and the entire Senate. If, after an election, the Senate again fails to pass the bill, a joint sitting of Parliament may be called to consider the proposed law. If the joint sitting of Parliament decides to pass the legislation, it becomes law (that is, once it has been ratified by the Governor-General).

Sections 71–80: The High Court

Under the **Westminster** system, power is separated between a legislature, an executive, and a judiciary. If disputes arise because of uncertainty or conflict over the division of powers between the national and state governments, s 73 of the Constitution gives members of the High Court the power to act as an umpire in these disputes and provide a definitive interpretation of the Constitution. High Court judges must resign at seventy years of age and no judge over the age of seventy can be appointed to the Court. On the one hand, High Court judges are understood to be 'above' politics, with their security of tenure enabling them to make impartial decisions. On the other hand, the power that they have in a representative democracy has been questioned by people who are concerned that very powerful actors in the Australian political system are appointed by the members of Cabinet, rather than elected by the people.

> **Westminster model, Westminster system**: The Westminster system is the name given to a form of government that developed in Britain (from which the Australian political system was derived). Westminster is the site of the British Parliament. A Westminster system is characterised by collective and individual ministerial responsibility to Parliament, a Head of State who is not the leader of government, and by an independent judiciary.

Section 96: Financial assistance to states

This section of the Constitution allows members of the federal Parliament to pass laws in which they give money to the states that can only be spent according to terms and conditions imposed by members of the federal Parliament. This was not intended to remain a permanent provision, and applied for the ten years following the establishment of the Commonwealth, but was to remain in force if the Members of Parliament wanted to keep it. Members of federal Parliament continue to use s 96. Commonwealth grants to states under s 96 are known as tied grants because the States must use the financial assistance on terms set by the Commonwealth government (that is, the money can be thought of as tied up or tied to requirements that the Members of federal Parliament impose).

Section 128: Alteration of the Constitution

The Australian Constitution is designed in such a way that it cannot be easily changed by those at either the federal or state levels of government. Any proposal to change, or amend, the Constitution must be put to the citizens of Australia in

referendum: An opportunity for citizens to register their views through a formal ballot is referred to as a 'referendum'. In Australia, most referenda involve attempts to alter the Constitution (see s 128 of the Constitution).

a **referendum**. Those proposals to change the Constitution must be supported by a majority of the members of each of the Houses of Parliament and must be supported in a referendum by a majority of voters *and* by a majority of the voters in a majority of states. This process of change is notorious for making it very hard to amend the Constitution. Since Federation, there have been forty-four referendums and only eight of these have been successful.

Summary

In the second part of the chapter, we provided an overview of important sections of the Australian Constitution. We began with the sections that deal with the federal Parliament and commented briefly on what these provisions meant with respect to Australia's Head of State. We then discussed the effects of the sections in the Constitution that described the role of the Governor-General, the Senate, the House of Representatives, and the division of Commonwealth and state powers. We also explained the process for dealing with disagreements between the majorities in the two Houses of Parliament, the role of the High Court as an umpire in disputes between Commonwealth and state governments and financial assistance to the states. Finally, we explained the process for altering the Constitution.

QUESTIONS

1   What are some of the key sections in the Australian Constitution?
2   What processes are involved in altering the Australian Constitution?

3: IS THE CONSTITUTION STILL RELEVANT TO GOVERNMENT IN CONTEMPORARY AUSTRALIA?

In this part, we present the alternative positions on the question of whether the Constitution is still relevant in contemporary Australia. The arguments[8] to support the view that it is still relevant, i.e., the 'yes' case, are that the Australian Constitution is still relevant to contemporary Australian government because it provides the foundation of our political system and that it remains relevant because it is crucial to creating governments and establishing the values of Australia's political system. The arguments that we present in support of the position that the Constitution is not relevant to government in contemporary

Australia, i.e., the 'no' case, are that the Australian Constitution is outdated and is irrelevant to contemporary government because it doesn't even mention our most vital institutions of government, including the Prime Minister, Cabinet and, with one exception (i.e., s 15), political parties.

Yes case

Yes, because it provides the foundation of our political system
In a fundamental sense, the Constitution is still relevant to contemporary government in Australia because it is the foundation of our political system. The Constitution sets out the roles, duties, and powers of members of Australia's political institutions, delineates authority between those at the different levels of government and provides mechanisms for resolving disputes between those at the different levels of government, which create certainty and stability in Australian politics. The stability and clarity provided by the Constitution ensures that people who are involved in the different levels of government know what their role is and what their relationship with each other should be.

Yes, because Constitutions are crucial to creating governments and establishing the values of the political system
The Australian Constitution is still relevant today because at the most basic level it marks out the powers of state Parliaments and protects the autonomy and independence of the states it creates. This is as important to the Commonwealth government and the state governments now as it was when the Constitution was first created. The existence of federations can only be assured through a written and entrenched constitution, so the continued existence of the Commonwealth and state levels of governments depends on the Constitution, which continues to protect them and give them legitimacy. Without the Constitution, the Commonwealth and state levels of government would not exist. The Constitution is still relevant because without it those who work at the Commonwealth and state levels of government would lack formal political authority over their citizens and would lack the legitimacy that is necessary to enforce their decisions.[9]

No case

No, because the Constitution is outdated
The Australian Constitution was created in 1901 and can hardly be described as relevant to Australian government in the twenty-first century. When the fathers of the Constitution first came together to consider uniting the various colonies in the late nineteenth century, their main concerns were a century away from

the concerns and stresses of government activity in the twenty-first century. The Constitution of 1901 was concerned mainly with establishing the foundations of a federal system in Australia and the role of the judiciary in resolving disputes between the newly created states and the Commonwealth government. It was also concerned mainly with finance and trade, the possibility of new states, and making sure that altering the Constitution would not be subject to the whims of any one level of government. It was designed for people at the beginning of a nation at the beginning of the twentieth century. We are now in the twenty-first century and, while Australia and Australians have changed, our Constitution hasn't.

No, because the Constitution doesn't even mention our most vital institutions of government

The Australian Constitution is not relevant to government in the twenty-first century because it does not even mention our most important institutions of government, such as the Prime Minister, the Cabinet and, for the most part, political parties. The Constitution combines the literal interpretation of its sections with practices referred to as conventions, which are not formally part of the Constitution, but are accepted as important practices that evolved over time and must be repeated to ensure the stability of government in Australia. For example, s 2 of the Constitution says that the Governor-General will be appointed by the Queen, yet the established practice is that they are appointed by the Prime Minister of the day. Section 5 of the Constitution says that the Governor-General will determine when Parliament will sit; yet it is the Prime Minister who decides this in practice. Section 64 of the Constitution says that the Governor-General may appoint officers to administer departments; yet, in practice, the Prime Minister leads the political party with the majority of seats in the House of Representatives and appoints Ministers to their portfolios.[10] The Constitution has not prevented members of federal Cabinet from dominating government in Australia. It doesn't even contain a reference to Cabinet.

Summary

In this part of the chapter, we put forward arguments in support of alternative positions on the question of whether the Constitution is still relevant to government in contemporary Australia. The Yes case comprised arguments that the Australian Constitution is still relevant to contemporary Australian government because it provides the foundation of our political system, and is crucial to creating governments and establishing the values of Australia's political system. The No case comprised arguments that the Australian Constitution is outdated and it is irrelevant to contemporary government because it doesn't even mention our most vital institutions of government, including the Prime Minister, Cabinet and, with one exception, political parties.

QUESTIONS

1. Do you think the Australian Constitution is still relevant to government in contemporary Australia? Why/why not?
2. Which case for the contemporary relevance of the Australian Constitution to government is more convincing?

4: IS THE CONSTITUTION STILL RELEVANT TO DEMOCRACY IN CONTEMPORARY AUSTRALIA?

In this part, we present alternative positions, or cases, with respect to the question of whether the Constitution is still relevant to democracy in Australia. The arguments that we present in support of the Yes case are that the Constitution is still relevant to democracy in Australia because it states that members of the federal political executives are accountable to the citizens who elect them, and because the separation of powers and division of powers ensures that no one level of government powers prevents those at another level from responding to the wishes of their citizens by taking over powers that should belong to that level of government. The arguments that we present in support of the No case are that the Australian Constitution has never been relevant to democracy in Australia and that the Australian Constitution does not protect or provide for a democracy because it doesn't have a Bill of Rights.[11]

Yes case

Yes, because the Constitution ensures that members of the federal political executive remain accountable

The Australian Constitution ensures that the Australian political system remains a system of responsible government. This is vitally important for representative democracy in contemporary Australia because citizens elect Members of Parliament who represent their particular interests and who they can remove in periodic elections, if they feel that these representatives are not representing their interests. The important point is that citizens decide who represents them and hold members of the federal political executive accountable for their policies and actions. While it could be argued that representative government is not democratic enough and that citizens should directly participate in policy-making, the generally accepted view is that this is not feasible, because of the time it would take, the knowledge about governmental procedures it would require, and the number of citizens who would participate. Those in representative political institutions receive their authority to make laws and take decisions on behalf of all Australians directly from its adult citizens. The representative government that is enshrined in Australia's Constitution is highly relevant to democracy in contemporary Australia because it ensures that citizens retain their ability to choose the people who represent them and can hold members of political executives accountable for their actions on behalf of all Australians.

Yes, because the separation of powers and division of powers ensures that no one level of government power usurps the democratic rights of the others

Historically speaking, people in federal liberal democracies, like Australia, have always been concerned about those who operate at one level of government or those who are in one political institution dominating the independence of those who work at another level of government or who are in other political institutions. The Australian Constitution formally separates the legislature, executive, and judiciary as a way of establishing democratic 'checks and balances' on the power of those who govern in Australia. While, under the Westminster system, members of Cabinet and other Ministers are drawn from the legislature, they are still accountable to Members of Parliament and need their support in order to have their legislation passed. Similarly, the federal system of government divides power between those who work at the national or Commonwealth level of government and those who work at the state level in a way that preserves their authority and independence. This is crucial to holding members of political executives accountable for their actions. It is also particularly important at the state level, where powers over issues that are 'closer to home' for people are administered by people who are close, both geographically and culturally, to the people whose interests they protect and promote.

No case

No, because it was never relevant to democracy

The Australian Constitution has no relevance to democracy in contemporary Australia because it has never had any relevance to democracy. Neither citizenship nor democratic practices are mentioned in the Constitution. The Constitution creates institutions of government and the federal division of powers. This has continued today. Most Australians don't know or don't care about what the Constitution says and, even if they did, the Constitution gives them no sense of themselves as active citizens in a democracy. This is because the Constitution is a formal and legal document that has no relevance to them. It is the foundation of our political system, yet it does not promote democratic practices and does not inspire Australians to take an active interest in their political system. Most Australians don't trust politicians and consider politics to be about manipulation, if not lying. They do not see themselves in the Constitution and are more likely to see themselves as consumers for whom markets are crucial, than active citizens in a democratic political system.[12]

No, because it doesn't even have a bill of rights
As well as establishing the rules and functions of the institutions of government, a central aspect of other constitutions is the relationship between the individual and the state and the protection of individuals from the arbitrary powers of government.[13] A core aspect of constitutions generally is to constrain governments and protect individual liberty. This is why constitutions are often associated with limited government. The US Constitution, for example, explicitly protects individual rights from the oppressive powers of those in positions of political power. The Australian Constitution does not mention individual rights; it doesn't even mention citizens and, most importantly, it contains no bill of rights that protects individuals from government power.

Summary

In this part of the chapter we presented the yes and no cases for the question of whether the Constitution is still relevant to democracy in Australia. The Yes case was comprised of two arguments. These were that the Constitution is still relevant to democracy in Australia because it ensures that members of political executives are accountable to the citizens who elect them and because the separation of powers and division of powers it produces ensures that no one at one level of government powers usurps the powers of those at another level and, as a result, prevents their citizens from holding them accountable for their actions. In support of the No case, we presented the argument that the Constitution has never been relevant for democracy and that the Australian Constitution is not democratic because it doesn't have a bill of rights to protect the rights of citizens.

QUESTIONS

1. Do you think the Australian Constitution is still relevant to democracy in contemporary Australia? Why/why not?
2. Which case for the contemporary relevance of the Australian Constitution to democracy is more convincing?

CONCLUSION

The Australian Constitution is fundamental to Australian politics and is central to government and democracy in contemporary Australia. In this chapter, we provided an overview of the Constitution. Other chapters in the book go into more detail about core elements associated with the Constitution, including federalism, the role of the Governor-General, the legislature and the judiciary. The chapter was in four parts. In the first, we provided a preliminary discussion of the Australian Constitution, outlining what it is and how it emerged in 1901. We then overviewed the founding principles of Australia's Constitution and examined what the Constitution says, what it doesn't say, and the implications of this for government and democracy in Australia. In the second part of the chapter, we identified important sections of the Constitution. Our purpose of this part was to familiarise readers with core sections of Australia's Constitution that provide a way of understanding what is in the Constitution. In the third part of the chapter, we presented alternative positions on the question of whether the Constitution is still relevant to government in contemporary Australia. And, in the final part, we presented alternative positions on the question of whether the Constitution is still relevant to democracy in contemporary Australia.

BOX 1.1
Draft preamble proposed by John Howard to introduce the Constitution

With hope in God, the Commonwealth of Australia is constituted by the equal sovereignty of all its citizens. The Australian nation is woven together of people from many ancestries and arrivals. Since time immemorial our land has been inhabited by Aborigines and Torres Strait Islanders, who are honoured for their ancient and continuing cultures. In every generation immigrants have brought great enrichment to our nation's life. Australians are free to be proud of their country and heritage, free to realise themselves as individuals, and free to pursue their hopes and ideals. We value excellence as well as fairness, independence as dearly as mateship. Australia's democratic and federal system of government exists under law to preserve and protect the dignity of all Australians equally, which may never be infringed by prejudice or fashion or ideology nor invoked against achievement. In this spirit we, the Australian people, commit ourselves to this constitution.

Source: Singleton, Aitkin, Jinks and Warhurst, 2003, *Australian Political Institutions*, 7th edn, p. 68.

BOX 1.2
Australia Act 1986

The *Australia Act* was created to bring constitutional arrangements affecting the Commonwealth and the states of Australia into conformity with the status of Australia as a sovereign, independent, and federal nation in its own right. At conferences held in Canberra on 24–25 June 1982 and 21 June 1984, it was agreed that this would be the case. The *Australia Act 1986* terminates the power of the Parliament of the United Kingdom to legislate for Australia, including Commonwealth, state and territory governments.

Source: http://australianpolitics.com

FURTHER READING

Introductory texts

Jaensch, Dean, 1997, 'The Australian Constitution,' *The Politics of Australia*, 2nd edn, Macmillan Education: South Yarra.

Maddox, Graham, 2005, 'Australian Constitutionalism,' *Australian Democracy: In Theory and Practice*, 5th edn, Longman Cheshire: Melbourne.

Parkin, Andrew & John Summers, 2006, 'The Constitutional Framework,' in J. Summers, D. Woodward & A. Parkin, (eds), *Government, Politics, Power and Policy in Australia*, 8th edn.

Singleton, Gwynneth, Don Aitkin, Brian Jinks & John Warhurst, 2006, 'The Australian Constitution,' *Australian Political Institutions*, 8th edn, Pearson Education: Frenchs Forest.

Ward, Ian & Randal G. Stewart, 2006, 'The Constitution and the Rules Governing Governments,' in *Politics One*, 3rd edn, Palgrave Macmillan: South Yarra.

Specialist texts

Attwood, Bain & Andrew Markus, 2007, *The 1967 Referendum: Race, Power and the Australian Constitution*, 2nd edn, Aboriginal Studies Press: Canberra.

Botsman, Peter, 2000, *The Great Constitutional Swindle: A Citizen's View of the Australian Constitution*, Pluto Press: Annandale.

Hague, Rod & Martin Harrop, 2004, 'Constitutions and the Legal Framework,' in *Comparative Government and Politics*, Palgrave Macmillan: Houndmills.

Heywood, Andrew, 2002a, 'Constitutions, the Law and Judiciaries,' in *Politics*, 2nd edn, Palgrave Macmillan: Houndmills.

Williams, George, 2000, *A Bill of Rights for Australia*, UNSW Press: Sydney.

Websites

The Australian Constitution: http://australianpolitics.com

The Australian Electoral Commission: http://www.aec.gov.au

The Constitutional Convention 1998: http://www.aph.gov.au/Hansard/conv/hancon.htm

Notes

1. Students may download a copy of the Constitution from http://australianpolitics.com.
2. There was only one delegate at the Constitutional conventions who was not a politician, James Walker.
3. See 'The Fathers and their Constitution,' in Crisp, L.F. 1965, *Australian National Government*, Longman Cheshire: Australia, pp. 1–39.
4. In a speech by Sir Edmund Barton given in 1901 titled 'Unite yourselves and preserve the union,' Barton says 'it was Sir Henry Parkes who, from the very beginning recognised the potentialities of the great union'. See Warhaft, Sally (2004), *Well May We Say: The Speeches That Made Australia*, Black Inc: Melbourne, p. 20.
5. See Singleton, Aitkin, Jinks & Warhurst (2003, pp. 31–4).
6. See Parkin & Summers (2002, pp. 50–4).
7. See Parkin & Summers (2002, pp. 54–5).
8. Gregory R. Copley, Andrew Pickford & Barry Patterson (2007), *Australia 2050: An Examination of Australia's Condition, Outlook, and Options for the First Half of the 21st Century*, Sid Harta Publishers: Hartwell.
9. See Heywood (2002, p. 298).
10. See 'Constitutional Conventions,' http://australianpolitics.com.
11. See Williams (2000) *A Bill of Rights for Australia*, UNSW Press: Sydney.
12. See Jaensch (1997, p. 22).
13. See Heywood (2002, p. 299).

The Legislature

LEARNING OBJECTIVES

- To understand the bicameral nature of the Australian Parliament and the roles of the House of Representatives and the Senate
- Be able to describe the legislative process in the Australian Parliament
- Comprehend the reasons why some people consider Parliament a waste of time and why others do not

INTRODUCTION

The legislature in the federal Parliament constitutes the public face of Australian government and democracy. Most citizens do not participate in party politics or immediately regard the High Court and its decisions as political; however, they do have some familiarity with proceedings in Parliament. Of course, familiarity does not mean understanding. Nevertheless, what happens in Parliament is reported to citizens daily in newspapers, on radio and television, and on the web. This chapter is in two parts. In the first, we explain a little about Parliaments in Australia. In the second, we provide alternative cases with respect to the question: 'Is Parliament a waste of time?'

1: PRELIMINARY DISCUSSION

Formally, the legislature in federal Parliament is classified as **bicameral**; that is, it has two houses: the House of Representatives and the Senate. Currently, the House of Representatives has 150 members, who are elected by Australian citizens over the age of eighteen, through a system of **preferential voting**. The result is winner-takes-all—the party or coalition with control over the Lower House determines Cabinet's membership.

The Senate was to have been the states' House, a defender of less populous states. During negotiations between the colonies over the form that Australian federation might take, representatives of the states with smaller populations (Western Australia, Tasmania, Queensland, and South Australia) were worried that Parliamentarians who represented their state would be overwhelmed by Parliamentarians from the more populous states (New South Wales and Victoria). To ease their minds, each state was guaranteed six seats in the Senate, which was given the power to review and reject legislation (apart from money bills, such as budgets and supply bills, which they cannot amend or reject—but which they can choose to simply not pass).

The Senate has also been regarded as a guardian against majoritarian lower houses. Whereas the members of the House of Representatives are elected by preferential voting, Senators are elected based on **proportional representation**. This means that candidates from minority parties can be

bicameral: When a Parliament is divided into two houses, or chambers, (that is, legislation must be passed in separate meetings of different groups of Parliamentarians), we refer to it as bicameral.

preferential voting: In compulsory preferential voting, voters *must* rank all of the candidates standing for election. In an optional preferential voting system, voters *can* rank all candidates.

proportional representation: Used with respect to voting systems to refer to a system in which representatives are elected according to the proportion of the total votes that they, their group or their party, received.

elected to the Senate with much less than a majority of the vote and can hold the balance of power. Consequently, the government and the opposition do not always control the Senate and must often negotiate with Senators from the minor parties if they are to pass, amend, or reject legislation.

More recently, we have been reminded that the Senate can act as a 'rubber stamp' for the government of the day. For most of the 1980s and the 1990s, the Senate was seen as pivotal for providing a counter-balance against claims by governments that they had a mandate to implement *all* of their policies. Following the 2004 federal election, representatives of the coalition parties gained control of both Houses of Parliament, and members of the Howard Cabinet faced little opposition to their workplace reforms and the sale of Telstra.

BOX 2.1
The passing of legislation: from bill to act

On its way to becoming an **act** of Parliament, a bill usually passes through the House of Representatives and the Senate in the following way:

i   first, notice that a bill is to be presented is published in the Notice Paper for the next sitting day of the House where the bill will be introduced;

ii   the bill is then read for the first time—the Clerk reads the full title of the bill and copies are circulated among the members;

iii straight after the **first reading**, the bill is read a second time and the member (usually a Minister, except in the case of a **private member's bill**) reads the second reading speech, which sets out the background to the bill and its objectives;

iv   debate on the bill is then adjourned until a later date;

v   the second reading debate resumes and the bill is considered in detail by the House or, in the case of the Senate, by the committee of the whole;

vi   at this point, amendments may be proposed and moved;

vii the bill is then read a third time and passed by the House or Senate;

viii after passing through both Houses, the bill is presented to the Governor-General for Royal assent; and

ix   finally, the act commences after it has been signed by the Minister, approved by the **Federal Executive Council** and its Proclamation published in **the Gazette**.

Note: See also the Glossary for definitions of the terms in bold.

Source: // http://www.pmc.gov.au/guidelines/docs/legislation_handbook.pdf

> **QUESTION**
>
> What is a bicameral Parliament?

2: IS PARLIAMENT A WASTE OF TIME?

Anyone who encounters broadcasts of federal Parliament, either on radio or television, or who sees it on the news won't be impressed by what they hear and see. Basically, federal Parliament (and state Parliaments, for that matter) looks like a waste of time. Part of the explanation is that Parliament is an old men's club in which meaningless rituals are conducted for the amusement of politicians and journalists. Part of the explanation for this is that what we see is only a small and trivial part of what is actually going on. Another part of the explanation is that Parliament has some relatively uninteresting, but absolutely essential functions to fulfil and is not a place of real debate. A third part of the explanation is that Parliament is filled with career politicians and not passionate visionaries.

This leads us to ask the question: 'Is Parliament a waste of time?' This chapter has two sections in which alternative cases (Yes and No cases) will be presented as answers to this question. The first section presents the Yes case and the second the No case. The question can be asked of either federal or state Parliaments, so the discussion is intended to apply to both.

Yes case

The Yes case presented here is based on the view that Parliament is a waste of time because it is full of old, white, middle-class men being 'real men'. These men, when in Parliamentary debates, spend most of their time arguing with and sometimes shouting at each other (with the odd look back over their shoulder to make sure that their mates see how clever they are). They do other things, particularly reading boring speeches to which nobody is listening. So Parliaments are pretty much full of men in combat mode (and because Members of Parliament know that this is what it is, even they start to disconnect from the arguments).[1]

Lots of old, white, middle-class men[2]

The answer to the question of why Parliament is full of men being men is simple. Parliaments are full of men because these are the types of people who get elected. Parliaments are full of men because men keep being elected to Parliament in far greater numbers than women do. Many more men are elected than women because lots more men run for Parliaments than women do. But it is not just full of men; Parliaments are full of old, white, and middle-class men. Parliament does not represent the people and this is the start of it being a waste of time (unless, that is, you are an old, white, middle-class man).

BOX 2.2
'Welcome to Country' ceremony at opening of Parliament

For the first time in its 80-year history, the opening of the (41st) Federal Parliament included a 'Welcome to Country' ceremony conducted by Indigenous Australians. The ceremony was led by Ngambri elder, Matilda House-Williams, whose people have a traditional connection with the Canberra and Yass region. Ms House-Williams, who was accompanied by a didgeridoo player and one of her granddaughters, presented the Prime Minister, Kevin Rudd, with a message stick. 'The message stick,' she said, 'is a means of communication used by our people for thousands of years, that tells the story of our coming together.'

'A welcome to country acknowledges our people and pays respect to our ancestors' spirits who have created the lands,' Ms. House-Williams also told the audience.

'In doing this, the Prime Minister shows what we call proper respect to us, to his fellow Parliamentarians, and to all Australians. For thousands of years our people have observed this protocol. It is a good and honest and a decent and human act to reach out and make sure everyone has a place and is welcome.'

Ms Williams contrasted her welcome to that of the barefoot Aboriginal man police drove away from the opening of the first Parliament in Canberra in 1927.

Source: Phillip Coorey and Mark Davis, 13 February 2008, 'Welcome ritual marks opening of Parliament', *Sydney Morning Herald*, http://www.smh.com.au/news/national/welcome-ritual-marks-opening-of-Parliament/2008/02/12/1202760301385.html; Radio Australia, ABC, 12 February 2008, 'Traditional Indigenous Welcome Opens Australian Parliament', http://www.radioaustralia.net.au/news/stories/s2160003.htm

---

Lots of men being real men (even some of the women)
The fact that more men have run for election to Parliament than women might explain why Parliament is full of men. Answering the question of why Parliamentary debates are marked by men being aggressive, competitive men (or what we are calling 'real' men) is a little more complex. Men may be genetically predisposed to this sort of behaviour. Alternatively, their behaviour is explained as a reflection of their socialisation, which leads many men to act in a combative and aggressive manner.

Another, and more interesting, answer is that this is what Parliamentarians think people want from them. This may be because we have become used to these sorts of politicians and the ways they behave and tend to expect this sort of behaviour. Perhaps we have come to think of leaders as having to display strength and determination, which is evidenced by a capacity for domination. This might explain why some female Parliamentarians can end up behaving as badly as the men behave.[3]

Lots of arguing and contesting

The most obvious manifestation of the aggressive masculinity of Parliament is the amount of arguing and shouting that occurs. Much of the rest of the time is taken up with Parliamentarians reading prepared speeches to which no one is listening. Quite often, the House that they are addressing is deserted. Those moments of greater significance, which include question time,[4] debates on matters of public importance, adjournment debates,[5] and speeches with respect to important bills, such as the budget, are when most of the shouting and arguing take place.

Organising conflict is central to the design of our houses of Parliament, which reflect the British Westminster model. In this model, two groups sit opposite one another. One group is led by the Prime Minister or Premier and her or his Ministers who are supported by a major party or coalition of parties. The Leader of the Opposition and his or her shadow Ministers lead the other group, who are supported by the other major party or coalition of parties.

The Prime Minister and Ministers occupy the position of power in federal and state politics. The Opposition[6] is comprised of people who want these positions. Therefore, we have a Ministry comprised of people who want to hold onto their positions of power and an alternative Ministry who confront them in the hope that they can demonstrate that they should hold those positions. The members of these two groups are positioned on opposite sides of the House. The two sides, then, confront each other and speak at each other across a divide.

The only Parliamentarians left out of this description sit on the crossbenches. These people are independents[7] or belong to minor parties. They will neither be Ministers nor Shadow Ministers and may be freer to speak. That the rest of the House is organised around shouting across a divide, however, makes it unlikely that they will do so. An enormous act of will and self-control would be necessary, if independents and members of minor parties were to resist becoming caught up in the atmosphere of Parliament.

'Battle'

Just as important as the physical division between Cabinet and Opposition is that the teams (Ministers and shadow Ministers) already know which side they are on before they walk into Parliament. Even those who sit on the cross-benches generally know their position beforehand. Strict party discipline ensures that no one's vote is going to be affected by what is said in Parliament.

In a House of Parliament where weaker party discipline exists, such as in the US Congress, a good argument might have some effect. However, having a good argument is rarely important in Australian Parliaments. So there is little point in caring about what is said and much more importance attached to how it is said. For this is how Parliamentarians demonstrate their capacity for leadership. Thus, both sides enter Parliament to take part in a battle in which derogatory comments and snide dismissals are the weapons of choice.

Lots of people not paying much attention

That nobody is paying much attention to what is said is going to affect the quality of debate to be found in a House of Parliament. Most of the important moments in Parliament involve attempts to score points against the other side of the House, which means that there really is no meaningful debate. Debate in Parliament is a ritual that people take seriously simply as a ritual. No one in the House is attempting to persuade. This is the case even when there are independents or minor parties in the Upper House who hold the balance of power in that House. When this happens, the argument and persuasion usually happen before anyone walks into the House.

motion of no confidence: A motion of no confidence occurs when members of a House of Parliament debate the suitability of Ministers and Cabinet to govern. If a no confidence motion is passed against a Minister or Cabinet, they are expected to resign. This rarely happens in Australia, as Cabinets are supported by a majority of members of the Lower House.

BOX 2.3
Senate censure over Iraq

On 5 February 2002 the Senate censured members of the Howard Cabinet and passed a **motion of no confidence** in the Prime Minister, John Howard. These motions were passed because independent senators and senators from the Australian Labor Party, Australian Democrats, and Australian Greens opposed the Cabinet members' apparent willingness to participate in a war with Iraq that had not been supported by the United Nations. The Senate's motion of no confidence had no effect on members of Cabinet. Australia joined a coalition, led by US and British forces, which invaded Iraq on 20 March 2003. The UN did not support this invasion.

Source: http://parlinfoweb.aph.gov.au/piweb//view_document.aspx?TABLE=JOURNALS&ID=88029

Nobody really cares what anyone else is arguing

Parliamentarians know that nobody is going to listen to their argument, even when they think it the most brilliant argument that has ever been put. Your side is going to agree with you. The other side is going to disagree with you. An alternative position, as might be put by an independent or member of a minor party, will be dismissed by the opposing sides in **Parliament** (and most of the time they are really only interested in their Parliamentary vote and not their argument). So, there will be little listening and a lot of talking to no real effect.

Parliaments, in short, are full of men engaging in rituals of battle and aggressive masculinity and are empty of sense. Most of the votes in Parliament are entirely predictable and none of them is affected by anything said in Parliament. None of the debates are real debates and no one in Parliament is listening to what is being said (unless they are looking for an opportunity to interject, to hurl abuse, or cheer for their side). The only exception to this is what is called a 'conscience' vote, in which **party** discipline is relaxed in order to allow the parties to avoid having to articulate a collective policy on some issue that is often too difficult for it to do so. These are rare, however, so Parliaments are basically a waste of time.

> **Parliament, legislature**: Both the terms 'Parliament' and 'legislature' are used to refer to the institution of government invested with the power of making, amending, and repealing laws.
>
> **party, parties, major, minor**: A group of people who form an association based on their similar views and who present candidates at elections is called a party. A major party is one that can gain sufficient public support to win a majority of seats in the Lower House of Parliament. A minor party is a party that cannot win such a majority.

No case

Five reasons to reject the view that Parliaments are a waste of time will be presented. First, Parliaments are sites in which issues that cause division within the community are raised. The ritual may be very important, then, as Parliamentary debates reflect our society in important ways. Second, Parliaments are the only bodies that can pass laws. Third, Parliaments are the only formal contexts within which members of Cabinets and Ministers can be called to explain their actions and inaction. Fourth, Parliamentary committees, at least those created by the Senate, are important for the development of legislation, the **accountability** functions of Parliament, gathering information, and developing expertise on specific **policy** areas among Parliamentarians. Finally, Parliament is important for its intangible effects, as it contributes to the development of political leaders, morale within parties, and the analyses of members of press galleries.

> **policy, public policy (monetary and fiscal)**: 'Policy' is used to refer to a decision made by members of a political party concerning their specific or general goals. Fiscal policy concerns decisions about expenditure and taxation while monetary policy concerns the quantity of money in circulation, the cost and availability of credit, and the composition of national debt.

Socially important debates

The first point that needs to be made about Parliament is that it is a forum in which important issues facing Australian society are raised. The bills[8] that members of Cabinets sponsor reflect their attempts to address the problems that face Australian society. A wide variety of bills come before Parliament and each reflects issues and problems that will have a direct or indirect impact on our lives. We will find Members of Parliament talking about bills that deal with terrorism, the economy, the management of the environment, and the prohibition of particular behaviour (like fraud, theft, prostitution, or drug use). Each of these is going to have a direct or indirect effect on our lives. Budgets are particularly important, as they will affect the cost of living. Every one of these bills reflects important choices about who we are as Australians and how we are going to live.

debates on matters of public importance are not debates, but they do concern matters that are important to the public. Adjournment debates, which are also not debates, allow Members of Parliament to draw attention to issues and problems that they feel might otherwise be overlooked.

Politics is about groups of people choosing directions for all of us, and this is never an easy or simple thing. The issues are sufficiently complex and difficult to make forums, like Parliament, inappropriate for developing a coherent position

> **balance of power**: A person or party is said to hold the balance of power when their vote or votes will determine the outcome with respect to any motion put in Parliament. This usually occurs when the major parties control less than half of the votes in a House.

BOX 2.4
Introduction of the GST

After the 1998 federal election, members of the Howard Cabinet sought to reform Australia's taxation system; central to their reforms was a Goods and Services Tax (GST). The Cabinet was not supported by a majority in the Senate, however, and parliamentarians from the Australian Labor Party declared that they would vote against the bill. Independents and members of minor parties held the **balance of power**, so their votes would decide the outcome. Senior Cabinet members began to negotiate with the Australian Democrats, who were led by Senator Meg Lees. Lees indicated that the Democrats were willing to vote for a GST if members of Cabinet redesigned the bill and removed the GST from non-processed foods. While they argued that the amendment was a mistake, members of Cabinet accepted the compromise on the legislation and the GST was introduced on 1 July 2000.

Source: Kelly (1998a)

on complex and contentious issues. That the positions that emerge in Parliament are preconceived and the decisions largely preordained should not blind people to the fact that somebody is grappling, on our behalf, with these important issues. We might hope that they do so in a more hesitant and less confrontational manner, but maybe we do not really want that. The sort of behaviour we find in Parliaments may be necessary to achieve solutions to difficult problems.

The main question concerns whether you think that issues that are important to members of a society can be resolved by consensus. If you think that consensus is possible, then Parliament is not a place to expect it to occur. If you think that consensus is not possible and that Parliament helps to contain divisions that might otherwise split society, then Parliament simply reflects a society in which people have very different views that cannot be reconciled and a consensus achieved. So the arguing and shouting is one way to prevent more violent forms of political conflict from occurring.

Passing laws

The most important reason that Parliament is not a waste of time lies in its legislative (lawmaking) role. If Australian society and politics can be understood to reflect the rule of law, then an institution within which laws are passed according to certain rules is essential to Australian society. While it is other things, Parliament is that body in which laws are produced. This is important for government in this country which requires the production of laws that will be taken to have authority, both by the people and by those institutions (such as courts[9] and the public service) whose decisions and actions are supposed to reflect these laws. That this is both public and, at least in some ways, reflects the will of the people is important for democracy in Australia. The fact that our representatives make the final decision as to whether or not a bill will come into effect as a law could be understood as an essential element of a democratic system.

Accountability

Another function of Parliaments is that they are bodies in which Ministers are called to explain their actions or account for themselves. Parliament is the forum in which political accountability occurs. Question time (particularly questions without notice) is the main and most visible time at which this takes place.[10] Accountability takes a variety of forms and Parliamentarians play a role in each of them.

In the first instance, accountability represents the overall accountability of the members of Cabinet. In the Westminster system, members of Cabinet must sit in Parliament—usually

accountability: Someone is said to be accountable when they can be called to explain and justify (account for) their actions or policies and can be removed from office if they are found to have acted improperly or incompetently.

in both Houses of Parliament in a bicameral (two-house) Parliament.[11] Cabinet is formed from members of the party or parties that has a majority in the Lower House of Parliament. The leader of Cabinet, the Premier or Prime Minster, sits in the House of Representatives and can be called upon to explain and justify the decisions that members of Cabinet have taken in governing the country. The Prime Minster has a representative in the Senate who can also be asked to account for decisions taken by the members of Cabinet. An extreme response to the view that Cabinets have not acted properly is a motion of 'no confidence' in the members of Cabinet. Members of Cabinet control the majority of votes in the Lower House, so that House is unlikely ever to pass a no confidence motion. If it ever happened, though, the members of Cabinet concerned would be expected to resign.

Cabinet members as a whole are not the only Ministers who are held accountable in Parliament. All Ministers, including those who are not members of Cabinet, can be asked to account for the policies that have been developed within and implemented by their departments. All Ministers can be asked to account for the decisions and actions of members of their departments, though the extent to which they accept responsibility for this has decreased significantly.[12] Often, questions are directed to Ministers in order to embarrass them, and there are occasions when a Minister's response to a question can be later shown to be misleading. Misleading the House, that is, giving answers that the Minister knows or should know to be wrong, is grounds for calling upon a Minister to resign.

Finally, all Ministers can be asked to account for themselves as holders of powerful positions. Basically, positions of power offer opportunities for promoting one's own personal or electoral interests. Parliament, therefore, is also a forum in which Ministers can be questioned about behaviour that might constitute an abuse of their office. Obviously, a Minister found to have abused his or her office is expected to resign. There appears to be some doubt, however, as to whether this is automatic, or whether the Prime Minister will decide whether a Minister who has been found to have abused his or her office has committed an offence serious enough to warrant his or her resignation.

Parliamentary committees

Probably the most important development in federal Parliament has been the creation of an extensive and effective committee system.[13] While you will rarely see a parliamentary committee in action, they are extremely important for a variety of the functions that they fulfil and for their effects on Parliamentarians. There are two types of committees. These are standing committees, which continue through the life of a Parliament and, often, across a number of Parliaments, and select committees, which come into existence to deal with specific issues and policy concerns.

Both types allow their members to develop expertise in a particular aspect of policy or administration. While both Houses of Parliament contain committees of these types, the standing committees created by the Senate have been more important for Parliament's ability to participate more effectively in the development of legislation. They can also increase the level of accountability that Parliamentarians can demand from members of Cabinet and other Ministers when they are not controlled by the party or coalition whose representatives have a majority in the lower house and, as a result, have the majority on committees formed by members of the House of Representatives.

Parliament as a 'testing ground'

Parliament is also important as a testing-ground for people who want to become a Minister, a member of Cabinet, or a Premier or Prime Minister. In this context, some of the most important members of the audience for a Parliamentarian are other Parliamentarians. Performing well in Parliament, which would include performing well in committees, is likely to enhance a Parliamentarian's standing in the party and may well bring that person to the attention of members of their party, as a future Minister, member of Cabinet, or Prime Minister or Premier.

Parliament and party members' morale

Part of the reason that being able to perform well in Parliament is treated as a good sign of a person's ability reflects another consequence of the fact that Parliamentarians are among the most important members of the audience for Parliament. This is the effect the performances of a Prime Minister and Ministers have on morale within his or her party. The confidence of all party members falls when the Prime Minister and other Ministers perform badly in Parliament. Organising and managing Parliament well, on the other hand, will be seen to be a sign of competence and effectiveness on the parts of Ministers and the Prime Minister.

The same is true of Opposition leaders and Shadow Ministers. They have a reduced ability to control Parliamentary proceedings and to take the initiative in Parliament, but their performance is still important. To have successfully engineered embarrassing moments and produced telling criticisms of Ministers, Cabinet, or Premier or Prime Minister, is a sign that the leadership of the Opposition is competent and will be able to conduct an effective election campaign next time around. The main point is that the members of their parties are constantly assessing the leadership provided by the Premier or Prime Minister and Ministers and shadow Ministers. Their performance in Parliament is an essential part of this assessment.

BOX 2.5
The Committees of Federal Parliament (as at 15 January 2008)

Senate Committees

Appropriations and Staffing
Community Affairs
Economics
Employment, Workplace Relations and Education
Environment, Communications, Information Technology and the Arts
Finance and Public Administration
Foreign Affairs, Defence, and Trade
Legal and Constitutional Affairs
Privileges
Procedure
Regulations and Ordinances
Rural and Regional Affairs and Transport
Scrutiny of Bills
Selection of Bills
Senators' Interests

House Committees

Aboriginal and Torres Strait Islanders Affairs
Agriculture, Fisheries and Forestry
Communication, Information Technology and the Arts
Economics, Finance and Public Administration
Education and Vocational Training
Employment, Workplace Relations and Workforce Participation
Environment and Heritage
Family and Human Services
Industry and Resources
Legal and Constitutional Affairs
Members' Interests
Privileges
Procedure
Publications
Science and Innovation
Selection
Transport and Regional Services

Joint Committees

Australian Commission for Law Enforcement Integrity
Australian Crime Commission
Broadcasting of Parliamentary Proceedings
Corporations and Financial Services
Electoral Matters
Foreign Affairs, Defence and Trade
Migration
National Capital and External Territories
Intelligence and Security
Parliamentary Library
Public Account and Audit
Public Works
Treaties

Source: http://www.aph.gov.au/committee/committees_type.htm

The press gallery

One of the most important of the intangible effects of Parliament is on the press gallery.[14] 'Press gallery' refers to those journalists whose primary, if not sole, responsibility is to report on state or federal politics and on state or federal Parliament. These journalists are based in the capital city of each state and in Canberra and are as interested and caught up in political life as Members of Parliament themselves. Much of what goes on in Parliament is directed to the press gallery, for they are the ones who will decide what to report and their analyses of the performance of Ministers, Cabinet, and Premiers or Prime Ministers will influence how we perceive them.

As they are the people who will play a significant role in influencing the political agenda in Australia, journalists in the press gallery are important members of the audience of Parliament. That they also play an important role in the perception of the leadership of the parties reinforces their significance for government and democracy in Australia. A decisive 'win' on the part of a Minster or Prime Minister or, on the other side, an effective campaign to embarrass or frustrate a Minister, will be reported in newspapers and radio and television news programs.

Parliaments are not a waste of time, then, because they fulfil a number of important functions for government and democracy in Australia. The legislative and accountability functions of Parliament have always been important aspects of the formal role of Parliament. Australian Parliaments may not always fulfil these functions in ways that we like, but they are important functions that some institution must perform if government and democracy in Australia can even come close to fulfilling our expectations. That Parliament is also a forum in which debates about important social issues occur is another reason to suggest that Parliaments are not a waste of time. Testing political leaders and influencing journalists in the press gallery are other important, if intangible, functions of Parliament.

QUESTION

Does the press gallery have a positive effect upon people's perception of Parliament?

CONCLUSION

We do not expect that many readers' views on Parliament will change significantly as a result of reading this chapter. Anyone who is not an older, white, middle-class man is likely to experience alienation as a result of the images and sounds that emerge from Parliament. The combative and adversarial aspects of Parliament are distasteful to those who believe in consensus and peaceful resolution of disputes. Certainly, Parliament could be much less violent than it is and having more women might improve things. Any conclusions that might be drawn from what one sees and hears of Parliament, however, need to be considered in terms of the important functions that Parliament fulfils in a Westminster system.

FURTHER READING

Introductory texts

Brennan, Geoffrey & Alan Hamlin, 1998, 'Rationalising Parliamentary Systems', in D. Lovell, I. McAllister, W. Maley & C. Kukathas (eds), *The Australian Political System*, 2nd edn, Longman: South Melbourne.

Carter, John, 1993, *Parliamentary Government in Australia: A Students' Guide to the Commonwealth Parliament*, 2nd edn, Parliamentary Education Office: Canberra.

Craig, John, 1993, *Australian Politics: A Source Book*, 2nd edn, Harcourt Brace: Sydney.

Davis, G., J. Wanna, J. Warhurst & P. Weller, 1993, *Public Policy in Australia*, 2nd edn, Allen & Unwin: Sydney.

Evans, Harry, 1998, 'Can Parliament be Reformed?', in D. Lovell, I. McAllister, W. Maley & C. Kukathas (eds), *The Australian Political System*, 2nd edn, Longman: South Melbourne.

Marsh, Ian, 1995, *Beyond the Two Party System: Political Representation, Economic Competitiveness, and Australian Politics*, Cambridge University Press: Melbourne.

Mulgan, Richard, 1998, 'The Australian Senate as a "House of Review"', in D. Lovell, I. McAllister, W. Maley & C. Kukathas (eds), *The Australian Political System*, 2nd edn, Longman: South Melbourne.

Uhr, John, 1997, 'Parliament', in B. Galligan, I. McAllister & J. Ravenhill (eds), *New Developments in Australian Politics*, Macmillan: South Melbourne.

Specialist texts

Bates, J.N., 1998, 'The Future of Parliamentary Scrutiny of Delegated Legislation: Some Judicial Perspectives', *Statute Law Review*, vol. 19, no. 3, pp. 155–76.

Bolton, Geoffrey, 1998, 'Who Should be in Parliament?', *Legislative Studies*, vol. 12, no. 2, pp. 76–9.

Evans, Harry, 1999, 'The Cost of the Commonwealth Parliament: Amalgamations, Values and Comparisons', *Australian Journal of Public Administration*, vol. 58, no. 1, pp. 106–11.

Hamer, David, 2004, *Can Responsible Government Survive in Australia*, 2nd edn, Centre for Research in Public Sector Management, University of Canberra: Belconnen.
Lindell, G. & Bennett R., (eds), 2001, *Parliament: The Vision in Hindsight*, Federation Press: Annandale.
Uhr, John, 1998b, *Deliberative Democracy in Australia: The Changing Place of Parliament*, Cambridge University Press: Melbourne.
Weller, Patrick, 2004, 'Parliamentary Democracy in Australia', *Parliamentary Affairs*, vol. 57, no. 3, pp. 630–5.
Whalan, D.J., 1991, 'Scrutiny of Delegated Legislation by the Australian Senate', *Statute Law Review*, vol. 12, no. 2, pp. 87–108.

Web sites

Australianpolitics.com: http://australianpolitics.com
Legislative Assembly for the Australian Capital Territory: http://www.legassembly.act.gov.au
Northern Territory Legislative Assembly: http://www.nt.gov.au/lant
Parliament of Australia: http://www.aph.gov.au
Parliament of Australia: The Senate: http://www.aph.gov.au/senate/index.htm
Parliament of Australia: The House of Representatives: http://www.aph.gov.au/house/index.htm
Parliament of Australia: Committees: http://www.aph.gov.au/committee/index.htm
Parliament of Australia: Hansard: http://www.aph.gov.au/hansard/index.htm
Parliament of Australia: Who's Who?: http://www.aph.gov.au/whoswho/index.htm
Parliament of Australia: Parliamentary Services: http://www.aph.gov.au/DPS/index.htm
Parliament of Australia: Parliamentary Library: http://www.aph.gov.au/Library/Index.htm
Parliamentary Library: Information and Research: http://www.aph.gov.au/information/index.htm
Parliament of New South Wales: http://www.Parliament.nsw.gov.au
Parliament of South Australia: http://www.Parliament.sa.gov.au/
Parliament of Tasmania: http://www.Parliament.tas.gov.au
Parliament of Victoria: http://www.Parliament.vic.gov.au
Parliament of Western Australia: http://www.Parliament.wa.gov.au/index.htm
Parliamentary Education Office: http://www.peo.gov.au
Queensland Parliament: http://www.Parliament.qld.gov.au

Notes

1. Poor behaviour by Parliamentarians is one aspect of the Decline of Parliament Thesis. For further information on this thesis, see Lovell et al. (1998, p. 73), Haward (1997, p. 106), R. Smith (1994, pp. 106–9), and Emy & Hughes (1991, pp. 359–65).
2. For information about women in federal Parliament, see http://www.aph.gov.au/library/handbook/historical/women_parl.htm
3. A set of procedures govern the running of Parliament; for more on these, see Jaensch (1994, pp. 231–3) and Summers (2006, pp. 72–6).
4. For more on Question Time, see Summers (2006, pp. 75–6), Haward (1997, p. 115) and Singleton et al. (2006, pp. 155–7).
5. There are several different types of debates conducted in Parliament. For a comprehensive discussion of types of debates and their function, see Singleton et al. (2006, pp. 157–60), and Haward (1997, pp. 115–16).
6. For more on the principle of a legitimate opposition, see Ward & Stewart (2006, pp. 126–7), Maddox (2005, pp. 223–5), and Fenna (2001, p. 69).
7. Lovell et al. (1998, pp. 97–8) and Stock (2006, pp. 274–76) provide useful accounts of the role of independents in federal Parliament.
8. Detailed explanations of the passage of a bill through Parliament can be found in Stewart & Ward (1994, p. 81), Haward (1997, pp. 119–21), and Jaensch (1994, pp. 233–5).
9. Powers are usually separated into executive, legislative, and judicial powers. For further information, see Ward & Stewart (2006, pp. 87–8), Singleton et al. (2006, pp. 131–2), and Lucy (1993, pp. 321–4).
10. One of the problems with question time is that members of the party to which members of Cabinet and other Ministers belong ask around half of the questions. They will not want to embarrass members of Cabinet or other Ministers. Another problem is that the questions that come from the Opposition or from independents or members of minor parties are designed merely to embarrass Cabinet members or other Ministers.
11. For more on bicameralism, see Jaensch (1997, p. 152), Ward & Stewart (2006, pp. 76), Haward (1997, pp. 110 and 112), and Smith et al. (2006, p. 126).
12. For more on the issues surrounding ministerial responsibility, see Summers (2006, pp. 76–7), Lovell et al. (1998, pp. 77–80), and Stewart & Ward (2006, pp. 233–6).
13. For detailed accounts of how the committee system operates in the Australian Parliament, see Haward (1997, pp. 117–18), Singleton et al. (2006, pp. 160–4), and Smith et al. (2006, p. 26).
14. For more on the press gallery, see Ward & Stewart (2006, pp. 201–4), Singleton et al. (2006, pp. 444–6), and Lucy (1993, pp. 169–70).

3

The Political Executive

LEARNING OBJECTIVES

- To know who comprises the political executive of Australian government
- To understand the roles of the political executive
- Be able to identify some of the representations of Prime Ministers in the media
- Appreciate the relative importance of Prime Ministers

INTRODUCTION

The Prime Minister,[1] Cabinet, and Ministers are the focus of most, if not all, media reports on Australian politics. The Leader of the Opposition and shadow Ministers get some attention, but most of the time the media are talking about the decisions, actions, or policies of the Prime Minister, Cabinet, or Ministers. Most of the time, Australian politics seems to be run by the Prime Minister, who starts to look like the central figure of Australian politics.

We begin the chapter by identifying the members of the **political executive** and their formal and informal standing. Then, after a brief discussion of the way that Prime Ministers are represented in the media, we present alternative responses to the question of whether Prime Ministers are really as important as they appear. By considering this question, we hope to shed some light on the operation of the role of the political executive. While this discussion has been devoted to a consideration of the apparent centrality to government of Prime Ministers, it could also be posed at a state level to reflect the apparent centrality of Premiers to government in the states.

political executive: The group of people, usually directors, who determine the objectives and strategies of the company is sometimes referred to as its executive. 'Political executive' is here used to refer to those who determine the objectives and strategies of government. Ministers and Cabinet are the main actors of the political executive. 'Executive' power is sometimes used to refer to the power to execute laws or undertake day-to-day government, but we have not adopted this use in the book.

1: WHO ARE MEMBERS OF THE POLITICAL EXECUTIVE?

The most recent Federal Executive Council was formed when Kevin Rudd and his nominated Ministers and Parliamentary Secretaries swore the Oath of Office in front of the Governor-General, Major-General Michael Jeffrey, on Monday, 3 December 2007. Under s 64 of the Constitution, the Executive Council is comprised of Ministers (including Parliamentary Secretaries) and the Governor-General. Formally, the other members of the Executive Council merely advise the Governor-General; however, under the conventions of the Westminster system the Governor-General does what the other members of the Executive Council tell him to do. Convention also results in the leader of the party or coalition whose members occupy a majority of the seats in the House of Representatives becoming Prime Minister and forming a Cabinet; whereas the Constitution does not even contain the phrase 'Prime Minister' or the word 'Cabinet'. Thus, the core of Australia's federal political executive, the Prime Minister and members of Cabinet, exists because of conventions and has no constitutional standing.

The Prime Minister is the head of the federal government. He chairs meetings of the Cabinet and the full ministry, establishes Cabinet committees, chairs meetings of the **Council of Australian Governments**, and sits in the House of Representatives. The Prime Minister is supported by members of the Department of the Prime Minister and Cabinet.

> **Council of Australian Governments (COAG)**: This is a meeting of members of the federal Cabinet, representatives of the members of state political executives, and representatives of the Australian Local Government Association.

The Cabinet comprises the senior Ministers and is the principal policy-making body in Australia's government. Its members meet regularly to establish policy directions and make other important decisions. Members of Cabinet often work in committees that deal with important issues, such as spending by members of the political executive, national security, and the agenda for sittings of federal Parliament. These committees enable more detailed (and, sometimes, classified) work to be undertaken by the Cabinet Ministers more directly involved in a policy area. For example, a Cabinet committee whose members oversee national security would be chaired by the Prime Minister and comprise the Minister for Defence and Foreign Affairs, the Transport Minister (if she or he is in Cabinet) and, perhaps, the Attorney-General. Cabinet members not only initiate public policy, they also deal with internal conflict among members of the Parliamentary Party. Under the convention of responsible government, all members must either support a decision taken by the members of Cabinet or resign.

The Outer Ministry comprises junior Ministers in policy areas, or portfolios, deemed by the Prime Minister to be less important to the running of the country. On occasion, usually immediately after gaining office and before each session of Parliament, junior Ministers will join their senior counterparts in a meeting of the full ministry. Otherwise, they may report periodically to the Prime Minister for briefings and sometimes attend Cabinet meetings, if their policy area is important to electoral strategy.

Typically, Parliamentary Secretaries provide additional Parliamentary support to a Minister or support the members of Cabinet as a whole. Parliamentary Secretaries are usually promising backbenchers or Senators, who the Prime Minister believes have the potential to become ministers and, maybe, rise to the Cabinet. Some Parliamentary Secretaries, though, are senior backbenchers or former Ministers, who either are no longer considered Ministerial material or who are out of favour with the Prime Minister.

QUESTION

Who are the current members of the political executive?

2: WHAT YOU SEE: THE NEWS MEDIA AND THE PRIME MINISTER

Casual observation of news media coverage of Australian politics would lead to the conclusion that the Prime Minister is the central actor in Australian politics. This impression reflects the amount of attention that Prime Ministers get in the news media.[2] The Prime Minister is by far the most recognisable figure in Australian politics. The Leader of the Opposition is likely to be the next most recognisable politician, but this is because she or he is the alternative Prime Minister.

The fact that the Prime Minister is portrayed as the only person in Australian politics who gets things done is reflected in the way that elections are presented in the news media. Elections become leadership contests in which the Prime Minister vies with the Leader of the Opposition to demonstrate who would make the best leader of the country. The Prime Minister and Leader of the Opposition will deliver policy speeches, televised by most stations, in which they will outline the policies of 'their' party and will usually engage in one or more televised 'debates'. Their faces will appear on posters around all electorates and they will be central to any advertising produced by the major parties.

The presentation of the Prime Minister and Leader of the Opposition as the central figures in election campaigns reflects a number of factors. The first is the extent to which many Australians confuse our Westminster system with the US presidential system.[3] When we think of Prime Ministers as if they are like Presidents, we begin to ignore others in the political system. Another factor that explains the prominence of Prime Ministers is that the policies of the major parties don't seem to reflect radically different philosophies or ideologies and they become hard to tell apart. Their different leaders then become the main way that we can differentiate between the major parties. The third, and possibly the most important factor behind the prominence of the Prime Minister, is that it makes for better 'news' to have two individuals fighting it out for control of Australian government. It is simpler and, as a result, easier to write and talk about and, possibly most importantly, it makes for better and more dramatic images for newspapers and television news programs.[4]

QUESTION

Apart from those factors identified above, what others factors can account for the centrality of the Prime Minister and Leader of the Opposition during election campaigns?

3: ARE PRIME MINISTERS AS IMPORTANT AS THEY APPEAR?

There can be no doubt that the Prime Minister appears to be in charge of government in Australia. The most important question that arises in this context concerns whether Prime Ministers are as important as they appear to be. If Prime Ministers are as important as they appear, then the real nature of government and democracy in Australia is being reflected in the news media. If Prime Ministers are not as important as they appear to be, then the news media misrepresents government and democracy in Australia. The discussion that follows is in two parts. In the first, we present reasons to believe that Prime Ministers are as important as they appear. In the second, we present reasons to deny that Prime Ministers are as important as they appear.

Yes case

In this part, four reasons to accept that Prime Ministers are as important as they appear will be presented. The first simply reflects the amount of media attention that the position attracts. The second is that Prime Ministers have become central to electoral contests. The third reason to believe that Prime Ministers are as important as they appear is their role as the leader of a major party or coalition. The final reason is that they are the leaders of Cabinet.

Lots of media attention

This argument may appear circular, but Prime Ministers are as important as they seem because they are the only ones that voters see, hear, or read about in the news media. The Prime Minister is a highly sought-after interviewee and a press conference at which a Prime Minister will speak is a very attractive event for journalists, editors, and directors of news programs. Almost anything that a Prime Minister does or says is likely to appear in the news media and this makes what they say or do appear important.

The argument presented here is that if enough attention is paid to what Prime Ministers say and enough of the words or time of the media is devoted to reporting what they say, then what they say will have an effect on the rest of us. Not all of us, though, but many of us. In short, Prime Ministers are as important as they appear because appearances are important. Our attention is constantly directed to them and, so, the Prime Minister is the first person who comes to mind when we think about government and democracy in Australia.

At centre of election contests

The moment at which Prime Ministers appear to be particularly important is during elections. Elections could be understood to involve complex choices between significant numbers of policies that will have a variety of important effects on our lives and society. They could be taken to represent decisions about the nature of Australian society and the sort of future that we collectively desire. They could reflect our carefully considered judgments about the abilities of the people who are going to form the Cabinet, which, as we indicated earlier, is the main source of policies among the institutions of Australian politics.

If elections were all of those things, however, they would be very difficult times for voters. Voters would have to assess the implications of the policies that the major parties have presented during each election campaign. Elections would involve complex calculations and a meaningful vote would reflect a careful study and assessment of the issues raised during the lead-up to the election.

Another possibility is that, in an election, voters choose between the different political ideologies represented by the two main parties. Some knowledge of the general principles to which these parties are committed, as reflected in the statements that emerge from their national meetings, would help to make this choice. The history of the two major parties could also be a guide to the sorts of outcomes that we might expect of them if their members were to form the Cabinet. We might also consider whether members of the party will be able to deliver on their core principles.

Our vote, at least in the Lower House, could reflect our assessment of the abilities of our local candidates. We might reflect carefully on our current representative's performance in Parliament and elsewhere. We may be interested in their personal backgrounds, including their life and work experiences. We may be interested in the preselection process to which each of the candidates has been exposed, whether it has been conducted fairly, and whether the process ensures that the best possible candidate has been selected.

Voting could be all of those things, or it could be a choice between two potential Prime Ministers. Our choice will reflect what we see on television, read in the newspapers, and hear on radio. We could choose the candidate who looks or sounds right for the job. We could simply go with a 'gut-feeling'. This simplifies things and lets us get on with our lives. Taking the simplest approach, which most Australians do, means that an election is a popularity contest between the Prime Minister and someone who wants to be the Prime Minister.

Head of party
Outside Parliament

Another reason that Prime Ministers may be as important as they appear reflects their position at the head of the Parliamentary 'wing' of their party.[5] Rising to the position of Prime Minister requires gaining support from senior members in the party organisation. Prime Ministers can use this support to ensure that the party follows policy positions that they support. Most of the people who gain the leadership of their party do so when their party is in Opposition. This means that the Prime Minister will have led her or his party to an electoral victory and this will carry some weight among members of the party. The power of the Prime Minister increases through the application of the oft-quoted principle that Australians do not support parties that are internally divided. Avoiding the appearance of internal division is a strong deterrent to any attempts by members of the Prime Minister's party to resist the Prime Minister's will.

Inside Parliament

That Prime Ministers also have the power to appoint Parliamentarians to the Ministry and to Cabinet provides another source of power for the Prime Minister.[6] While all Prime Ministers will be under pressure to include women and members from as many states as possible in their Ministries and Cabinets, they will be reluctant to appoint anyone who will not support them. The fact that Prime Ministers receive the support of their Cabinet and Ministers means they will be in a very powerful position among the Parliamentarians in their party (and in the coalition of which they may be leaders). All members of the party (or coalition) within Cabinet, the Ministry, and the Parliamentary party will be aware that a failure to support the Prime Minister will be electorally damaging. As a result, they will support the Prime Minister. This puts the Prime Minister in a very powerful position.

    The centrality of the Prime Minister in Australian politics is also a result of the principle that all members of Cabinet must publicly support all the decisions taken in Cabinet. This means that the power of the Prime Minister in Cabinet flows into Parliament. This is important, given that Members of Parliament are supposed to hold members of Cabinet collectively responsible for their decisions and policies. Real problems for the whole process of accountability would result if members of Cabinet were permitted to deny responsibility for a decision or policy on the basis that they did not support it when it was being debated in Cabinet. Everyone in Cabinet, therefore, is presumed to support a policy or decision agreed to in Cabinet. Everyone is bound by the decision, which means that all members of the Cabinet must support the decision in public and in Parliament. This adds to the power of the Prime Minister.[7]

Head of Cabinet

While this source has already been mentioned, the Prime Minister's role as head of Cabinet deserves more careful attention due to the impact it can have on Cabinet discussions. That Cabinet is the central policy-making body means that control over Cabinet represents the possession of significant power. Prime Ministers chair Cabinet meetings.[8] This means that they control the agenda and the discussions that ensue. Not all the issues that might be discussed within Cabinet are discussed there. Time pressures mean that the Prime Minister must choose the issues that will be discussed and the order in which they will be discussed. Anyone who has been in a meeting knows that the order in which issues are discussed, i.e., the agenda, is important. You may not notice the issues that have been left off the agenda, but their omission will be important.

Another point to remember here is that Prime Ministers have a department (Department of Prime Minister and Cabinet) that assists them in maintaining control of Cabinet. This department provides them with advice on the issues that will be discussed in Cabinet, which gives Prime Ministers an advantage in these discussions. The formal role of Prime Ministers as chair of Cabinet meetings then can be understood as an important part of their power.

Another aspect of the formal role of the Prime Minister is that, under normal conditions, the Governor-General takes advice from the Prime Minister as to when an election will be held. While the Governor-General takes advice from the Prime Minister with respect to the appointment of Ministers, it is the power to determine when elections are called that is the most important aspect of the Prime Minister's role as adviser to the Governor-General. The capacity to determine when an election will be held helps Prime Ministers to maintain their position as leader of their party.

Informal power

While the formal powers of Prime Ministers as Head of Cabinet are important, their informal 'power' is also important. The points of view that the Prime Minister expresses will carry significant weight in any discussion in Cabinet. Few members of Cabinet are sycophants who continually pander to Prime Ministers in order to be promoted to even more powerful ministerial positions. Most members of Cabinet are senior politicians who have been 'in the game' for many years and have strong views on many issues. Whether it is worth their while to oppose the Prime Minister on an issue is a calculation that they will make. In most cases, they will decide not to oppose the Prime Minister directly and their criticisms of the Prime Minister's position will be muted.

That Prime Ministers may be interviewed on issues that they have not discussed with the other members of Cabinet may also be a source of their power. Prime Ministers may be called upon, then, to make policy 'on the run' and seek Cabinet approval for a policy after it has been announced. While this may not occur often, only very brave or foolhardy members of Cabinet would make the Prime Minister retract such a policy. The two reasons for this are obvious. It would 'weaken' the Prime Minister in the eyes of voters. It may also damage the careers of those who forced a Prime Minister to retract a policy they she or he had announced.

Important sources of the power of Prime Ministers are their centrality to our perception of Australian politics and our tendency to act as if this is true. This is mainly a result of the way that those in the news media report politics, but it also reflects Australians' reluctance to devote much time or attention to politics. Everyone in the Prime Minister's party, either inside or outside Parliament, will do what the Prime Minister wants. This is necessary to avoid electoral damage to the party and career damage to the individual. This means that Prime Ministers have considerable informal power that allows them to dominate their party and government. That Prime Ministers have a number of formal powers, primarily as head of the Cabinet, means that a strong case can be presented positioning support of the claim that Prime Ministers are as important as they appear to be.

> **Caucus**: 'Caucus' is most commonly used to refer to the formal meeting of Parliamentarians belonging to the Australian Labor Party. Caucus is called to appoint people to ministries and other positions and to determine strategies in Parliament.

No case

We present six reasons to believe that Prime Ministers are not as important as they appear to be. We begin with the argument that this perception has been created by those

BOX 3.1
Hawke and the MX Missiles

In 1981, then US President Ronald Reagan announced an upgrading of the United States' nuclear weapons program. This included the development of at least 100 MX missiles. The MX missile was intended to deliver a 10,335 kiloton nuclear warhead with twice the accuracy of previous missiles. When members of the US military were ready to test the MX missile system, they sought approval from members of the Australian political executive to conduct tests off Australia's coast. Leading members of the Hawke Cabinet, most notably the Prime Minister, the Foreign Minister, and the Defence Minister, announced that they would support Australian assistance in the testing of the MX missiles. Members of the Parliamentary Labor Party, or **Caucus**, responded to an increasingly strong anti-nuclear weapons movement in Australia, however, and forced the Cabinet and Prime Minister to refuse support for any testing of the MX missiles in or near Australia.

Source: Coleman (1985)

in the news media and does not reflect political reality. The second reason is that party organisations contain people who have considerable power, even over Prime Ministers. The next point is that members of Cabinet, and not just the Prime Minister, play a central role in policy formation. Fourth, Ministers have considerable discretion in the day-to-day running of their departments, a discretion that simply could not be overseen by even the most dictatorial of Prime Ministers. A fifth constraint on the power of Prime Ministers concerns their continued reliance on support from the backbench of their Parliamentary party. Finally, the central role that public servants play in government in Australia must be recognised. Public servants are one of the principal sources of policy and advice with respect to the decisions that members of Cabinet and the Prime Minister make, and the day-to-day uses of discretion and judgment on the part of public servants in Australia have continuing and significant effects on our lives.

Media attention creates a false impression

While the news media presents a certain 'reality' about Australian politics, this 'reality' is not an accurate reflection of the way things really are. While television is particularly well suited to reporting Australian politics as if it reflects a presidential system, this does not mean that Australia is actually governed in this way. Nor should the fact that journalists find it easier to report politics as if individuals are more important than processes and systems obscure the role of processes and systems that are essential to government in Australia. In short, Prime Ministers are constrained by a number of features of the political system within which they operate, and are not as central as they appear.

Party organisation

All parties have two parts: a group of people who occupy positions in Parliament and their supporters who provide the organisation that is necessary for policy-making and for preparing for elections. Political parties depend for their existence on volunteers whose commitment to the party is rewarded, in part, by their having input into the policies that those in the Parliamentary 'wing' consider and adopt. The ALP and National Party may be better organised to feed this policy input into the decisions taken by Members of Parliament, but few Parliamentarians in the Liberal Party are likely to ignore the strong wishes of the people whose support they need to win the next election. While the volunteers who support parties may not be dominant in any party, they are important and their views cannot be ignored indefinitely.

Even if the ordinary members of parties can be marginalised and ignored, other members within the party organisation cannot. Every party contains powerful members of the organisation who, more often than not, are directly responsible for Parliamentarians, including Ministers and the Prime Minister, holding their offices. These people may take formal positions (Party Director, Secretary) or they may have more nebulous positions (in which case they will often be referred to in the media as 'powerbrokers').

They will offer advice to Parliamentarians and, in particular, the Prime Minister. Some of them will have an eye on opinion polling and their advice will reflect their reading of these polls. Others will have different reasons for giving their advice. That there are a number of powerbrokers within any party will cause tension within that party and internal wrangling over policy. To believe that any one member of a party who occupies a seat in Parliament would want to lose the support of a powerbroker in the organisation is fanciful. While Prime Ministers may be able to resist a powerbroker's will for some time, they must be careful, and their capacity to resist vanishes when their position is under threat.

coalition: When members of two or more parties agree, either before or after an election, to join forces to form and support a Cabinet drawn from their ranks they are said to enter into a coalition.

BOX 3.2
Gorton votes against himself

After leading the Liberal Party to seven straight election victories in 1949, 1951, 1954, 1955, 1958, 1961, and 1963, Robert Menzies retired from politics in January 1966. The new Liberal Party leader, Harold Holt, led the **coalition** into the 1966 elections, which they won by a landslide. A year later Holt disappeared while spearfishing at Cheviot Beach, Portsea. John Gorton and William McMahon vied for leadership of the Liberal Party and the Prime Ministership. Gorton won due to the support of John McEwen, the leader of the Country Party (National Party), who threatened to leave the coalition if McMahon became the Liberals' leader. Gorton led the Liberal Party to a narrow victory in the 1969 election. A result of this near loss was that McMahon challenged Gorton for the leadership of the party. The votes of members of the Parliamentary Liberal Party were evenly split. Gorton, as the incumbent, cast the deciding vote. He voted for McMahon, as he felt that he needed the full support of the party if he was to be Prime Minister.

Source: http://www.whitlamdismissal.com/background

Role of Cabinet
Another constraint on the power of Prime Ministers comes from within Cabinet itself. Cabinet, as we have suggested, is comprised of senior members of the Parliamentary party who are unlikely to be doormats for a Prime Minister. No

matter how much power Prime Ministers may be able to exercise, they will continue to rely upon the loyalty and support of other members of Cabinet. While Prime Ministers are usually better briefed than other members of Cabinet and may be able to dominate discussion, they still rely upon other members of Cabinet and need them to feel motivated and valued. Crippling members of Cabinet is unlikely to result in effective administration and the creation of a powerful and united political unit. Even if Cabinet can be controlled for a time, Prime Ministers ultimately rely upon support from the other members of Cabinet to prevent Cabinet from becoming dysfunctional.[9]

Role of Ministers

Another factor that needs to be taken into account in the context of a discussion of the importance of the Prime Minister is the fact that Ministers are continuously engaged with their areas of administration, or portfolios. Ministers develop policies and take decisions that cannot be overseen by Cabinet and, as a result, the Prime Minister. Ministers often come to see themselves as experts in their policy area and better placed than their colleagues to know what is required.[10] They may present more contentious issues for discussion in Cabinet, but they cannot be constantly running to Cabinet and the Prime Minister with every policy they intend to pursue. On some occasions, a Prime Minister will have a particular interest in a policy area and be more likely to intervene in decisions taken in that area. Not only will this free other areas from Prime Ministerial scrutiny, it will also occupy time that a Prime Minister might have used for controlling policy in another area.

Backbench

The backbench of the Prime Minister's party, or coalition the Prime Minister leads, will generally be compliant, in order to ensure that a Prime Minister is perceived to be in control of a united party. But there are occasions in which members of the backbench will be moved to call on a Prime Minister to reverse a decision or policy or to take action on an issue upon which she or he has not yet acted. Usually this reflects the response of their electorates to a decision or policy that a Prime Minister has supported or action she or he has failed to take. A 'backbench revolt', as journalists like to call it, will either be met with some modification of policy or a concerted attempt to persuade the backbenchers that the policy, decision, or inaction is necessary.

Public service

The view that Prime Ministers are at the centre of government in Australia fails to reflect the role of the public service as the primary source of policy advice to the Prime Minister and Ministers. The fact that the Prime Minister has a department devoted to facilitating the control of Cabinet and important policy areas means that there is a set of public servants who have a direct input into policy-making. That each of the Ministers also has policy advisers means that all of the decisions that Ministers and Prime Ministers take will have been influenced by these public servants.

This higher-level policy advice is only one of the effects of the public service.[11] Many other aspects of policy are controlled by other public servants who develop policy that is only marginally subjected to the control of Ministers (and, as a result, completely outside the control of Prime Ministers). Even the bureaucrat you might encounter when you visit one of their offices is exercising discretion and, in effect, making policy. This 'micro level' policy-making is also a central part of the policy webs within which our lives are embedded. Indeed, in many ways, these micro policies are more significant for many people's lives than anything that might come from Cabinet or the Prime Minister.

The No case is not about Prime Ministers being unimportant; it is that the Prime Minister is not as important as the media might lead us to believe. This media-generated misrepresentation fails to take into account the constraints that come from within the organisation, the Parliamentary party, and Cabinet. Nor does it take into account the effect of policy advice that originates from within the public service. It also significantly underestimates the effect of every public servant's micro policy-making power on our lives.

BOX 3.3
Keating on the backbench

In June 1991, Paul Keating, who had been Treasurer and Deputy Prime Minister under Bob Hawke, challenged Hawke for the party leadership and the Prime Ministership. Keating lost by 44 votes to 66. He had challenged Hawke because he believed that Hawke had agreed in 1988 that he would relinquish the leadership after the 1990 election. After his leadership challenge failed, Keating resigned from Cabinet and sat on Labor's backbench for seven months. Everyone, and especially those journalists who followed Australian politics, knew that he wanted to be the leader of the party and the country, and was simply biding his time. His presence became a destabilising influence on the Hawke ministry and continued to draw attention away from Hawke and his Cabinet. In December 1991, Keating made another challenge for the leadership and this time he won by 56 votes to 51.

Sources: Karene (1991a; 1991b)

BOX 3.4
The Rudd Ministry (as at 15 January 2008)

Cabinet (3 December 2007)

Prime Minister
The Hon Kevin Rudd, MP

Minister for Education
Minister for Employment and Workplace Relations
Minister for Social Inclusion
(Deputy Prime Minister)
The Hon Julia Gillard, MP

Treasurer
The Hon Wayne Swan, MP

Minister for Immigration and Citizenship
(Leader of the Government in the Senate)
Senator the Hon Chris Evans

Special Minister of State
Cabinet Secretary
(Vice-President of the Executive Council)
Senator the Hon John Faulkner

Minister for Trade
The Hon Simon Crean, MP

Minister for Foreign Affairs
The Hon Stephen Smith, MP

Minister for Defence
The Hon Joel Fitzgibbon, MP

Minister for Health and Ageing
The Hon Nicola Roxon, MP

Minister for Families, Housing, Community Services and Indigenous Affairs
The Hon Jenny Macklin, MP

Minister for Finance and Deregulation
The Hon Lindsay Tanner, MP

Minister for Infrastructure, Transport, Regional Development and Local Government
(Leader of the House)
The Hon Anthony Albanese, MP

Minister for Broadband, Communication and the Digital Economy
(Deputy Leader of the Government in the Senate)
Senator the Hon Stephen Conroy

Minister for Innovation, Industry, Science and Research
Senator the Hon Kim Carr

Minister for Climate Change and Water
Senator the Hon Penny Wong

Minister for the Environment, Heritage and the Arts
The Hon Peter Garrett, AM, MP

Attorney-General
The Hon Robert McClelland, MP

Minister for Human Services
Manager of Government Business in the Senate
Senator the Hon Joseph Ludwig

Minister for Agriculture, Fisheries and Forestry
The Hon Tony Burke, MP

Minister for Resources and Energy
Minister for Tourism
The Hon Martin Ferguson, MP

(continued)

Outer Ministry

Minister for Home Affairs
The Hon Bob Debus

Assistant Treasurer
Minister for Competition Policy and Consumer Affairs
The Hon Chris Bowen, MP

Minister for Veterans' Affairs
The Hon Alan Griffin, MP

Minister for Housing
Minister for the Status of Women
The Hon Tanya Plibersek, MP

Minister for Employment Participation
The Hon Brendan O'Connor, MP

Minister for Defence Science and Personnel
The Hon Warren Snowdon, MP

Minister for Small Business, Independent Contractors and the Service Economy
Minister Assisting the Finance Minister on Deregulation
The Hon Craig Emerson, MP

Minister for Superannuation and Corporate Law
Senator the Hon Nick Sherry

Minister for Ageing
The Hon Justine Elliott, MP

Minister for Youth and Sport
The Hon Kate Ellis, MP

Parliamentary Secretaries

Parliamentary Secretary for Early Childhood Education and Childcare
The Hon Maxine McKew

Parliamentary Secretary for Defence Procurement
The Hon Greg Combet, AM

Parliamentary Secretary to the Minister for Defence
The Hon Mike Kelly, AM

Parliamentary Secretary for Regional Development and Northern Australia
The Hon Gary Gray, AO

Parliamentary Secretary for Disabilities and Children's Services
The Hon Bill Shorten

Parliamentary Secretary for International Development Assistance
The Hon Bob McMullan, MP

Parliamentary Secretary for Pacific Island Affairs
The Hon Duncan Kerr, MP

Parliamentary Secretary to the Prime Minister
The Hon Anthony Byrne, MP

Parliamentary Secretary for Social Inclusion and the Voluntary Sector
Parliamentary Secretary Assisting the Prime Minister for Social Inclusion
Senator the Hon Ursula Stephens

Parliamentary Secretary to the Minister for Trade
The Hon John Murphy, MP

Parliamentary Secretary to the Minister for Health and Ageing
Senator the Hon Jan McLucas

Parliamentary Secretary for Multicultural Affairs and Settlement Services
The Hon Laurie Ferguson, MP

The question of whether Prime Ministers are as powerful as they appear is an important one for government and democracy in Australia. Overstating the power of Prime Ministers obscures the important ways in which power is distributed within our political system. While the overstatement of the power of Prime Ministers may facilitate government, in that it reduces the points of internal resistance with which any Prime Minister must contend, it undermines democracy. If Prime Ministers are not as powerful as they seem, there may be more avenues for influencing policy than may appear.

QUESTION

What factors affect the importance of Prime Ministers?

CONCLUSION

We hope that this chapter has provided some indication of the various elements of the political executive and done so in a manner that was of some interest. As you may know, the various elements of the political executive are fundamental sources of the policies and decisions that affect all of our lives. We may pretend not to be interested in the policies and decisions of political executives, but to be uninterested would be to express no interest in how we live our lives. Understanding what political executives do and attempting to influence what they do is a vital part of a democratic system. The less we know about political executives, the more powerful they become. This may make them better at providing the government that they want to provide, but it will mean that such a government does not reflect the will of the people (as might be expected in a democracy).

FURTHER READING

Introductory texts

Considine, Mark, 1996, 'Market Bureaucracy: The Changing Form of Social Administration in Australia', in A. Farrar & J. Inglis (eds), *Keeping it Together: State and Civil Society in Australia*, Pluto Press: Leichhardt.

Lucy, Richard, 1993, *The Australian Form of Government: Models in Dispute*, 2nd edn, Macmillan: South Melbourne.

Solomon, David, 1988, *Australia's Government and Parliament*, 7th edn, Thomas Nelson: Melbourne.

Weller, Patrick, 1985, *First Among Equals: Prime Ministers in Westminster Systems*, Allen & Unwin: Sydney.

Weller, Patrick, 1998, 'Prime Ministers, Political Leadership and Cabinet Government', in D. Lovell, I. McAllister, W. Maley & C. Kukathas (eds), *The Australian Political System*, 2nd edn, Longman: South Melbourne.

Specialist texts

Considine, Mark, 1992, 'Alternatives to Hierarchy: The Role and Performance of Lateral Structures Inside Bureaucracy', *Australian Journal of Public Administration*, vol. 51, no. 3, September, pp. 309–20.

Keating, Michael, S., 1995, 'The Evolving Role of Central Agencies: Change and Continuity', *Australian Journal of Public Administration*, vol. 54, no. 4, pp. 579–83.

Parker, R.S., 1989, 'The Politics of Bureaucracy', in G.R. Curnow & B. Page (eds), *Politicization and the Career Service*, Canberra College of Advanced Education & NSW Division of the Royal Australian Institute of Public Administration: Canberra.

Sharman, Campbell, 1997, 'Defining Executive Power: Constitutional Reform for Grown-ups', *Australian Journal of Public Administration*, vol. 56, no. 2, June, pp. 107–14.

Stewart, Jenny & Megan Kimber, 1996, 'The Transformation of Bureaucracy? Structural Change in the Commonwealth Public Service 1983–93', *Australian Journal of Public Administration*, vol. 55, no. 3, pp. 37–48.

Weller, Patrick, 1996, 'Commonwealth–State Reform Processes: A Policy Management Review', *Australian Journal of Public Administration*, vol. 55, no. 1, March, pp. 95–110.

Weller, Patrick, 2003, 'Cabinet Government: An Elusive Ideal', *Public Administration*, vol. 81, no. 4, pp. 710–22.

Web sites

Australianpolitics.com: http://australianpolitics.com
Australian Commonwealth Government Entry Point: http://www.fed.gov.au
Australian Federal, State, Territory and Local Governments: http://www.gov.au
Australian Governments' Entry Point: http://www.nla.gov.au/oz/gov
Department of the Prime Minister and Cabinet: http://www.dpmc.gov.au
National Archives of Australia: http://www.naa.gov.au
National Library of Australia: http://www.nla.gov.au

Australian Parliament: http://www.aph.gov.au
Prime Minister: www.pm.gov.au

Notes

1. See Grattan (2000) for details of every Australian Prime Minister.
2. For more information on the Prime Minister and media coverage, see Ward & Stewart (2006, pp. 242–6).
3. The Westminster system is one in which Parliament is supposed to be supreme and in which the government is understood to give effect to the will of Parliament. It does not quite work this way, though, because Cabinet dominates at least the Lower Houses of Parliament. A presidential-style system is one in which the presidency is voted for as a separate exercise from the election of Members of Parliament and the powers of the legislature (Parliament) are more clearly separated from those of the executive (President and his political heads of bureaucratic departments). Agreement between both of these institutions is usually necessary for most important political decisions. For more information on the Westminster, presidential, and the Australian mix of these two systems (the Washminster Mutation) see Fenna (2001, pp. 12–23) and Hughes (1998a, pp. 300–8).
4. Some people might claim that a simple representation of Australian politics might be the only way that people who do not know much about politics can get their heads around it.
5. For further information on the roles of the Prime Minister in Australian government and politics, see Davis (1997b, pp. 53–7), Maddox (2005, pp. 153–9), Jaensch (1994, pp. 261–3), and Singleton et al. (2006, pp. 206–7).
6. Kevin Rudd was the first leader of the ALP to select his Cabinet and other Ministers.
7. For more information on the formal and informal powers of the Prime Minister, see Davis (1997b, pp. 53–7) and Lovell et al. (1998, pp. 75–7).
8. To find out more about the Prime Minister's role in Cabinet, see Fenna (2001, p. 103) and Davis (1997a, pp. 85–100).
9. For more information on Cabinet and Cabinet government, refer to Page (1997, pp. 124–38), Jaensch (1994, pp. 143–5), Lovell et al. (1998, pp. 73–5), Fenna (2001, pp. 101–3), and Maddox (2005, pp. 159–68).
10. For more details on the role of Ministers, see Singleton et al. (2006, pp. 185–187), Wanna (1997, pp. 77–9), and Hawker (1994, pp. 102–4).
11. For more on the roles of the public service, see Hughes (1998a, pp. 333–59), Ward & Stewart (2006, pp. 247–8), Jaensch (1994, pp. 270–86), and Singleton et al. (2006, pp. 219-64).

4 The Judiciary

LEARNING OBJECTIVES

- To grasp an understanding of Australia's common law and federal court systems, and the concept of 'rule of law'
- To understand the role of the High Court in adjudicating matters of constitutional significance to Australia's federal system of government
- Be able to identify the reasons for the traditional 'invisibility' of judges vis-à-vis Parliamentarians and members of the political executive, and the recent increase in their public profiles
- To recognise judicial activism as 'legal realism'
- Consider whether the increased public profile of judges is desirable

INTRODUCTION

That judges play an important role in government in Australia may not always be obvious, but remains true.[1] This is true of both judges of the **High Court** and judges who sit in every other jurisdiction. Magistrates, who are not judges but public servants,[2] are also important to government in Australia. Judges are important because they decide whether and how laws and regulations should be applied. They also oversee the uses of power by Parliaments and members of political executives to ensure that they accord with the formal and informal rules that control the use of governmental power.

High Court: In Australia, this refers to that Court, created under the Constitution, whose judges interpret the Constitution and hear appeals from courts created under the federal and state jurisdictions. It is referred to as the 'highest court in the land' because the decisions of its judges are final.

Judges do not derive their governmental power only from their role in applying laws and regulations, however. They have power of their own, which is reflected in the history of case law, called common law, which they have created. Judge-made law, then, is as much a part of government in Australia as Parliament-made law and is just as important in shaping Australian society. The main questions that arise in this context concern the way that judges have avoided being seen to be fundamentally political and the consequences that an increased recognition of the political nature of judges would have for government and democracy in Australia. We examine these issues in four parts.

In the first, we discuss issues that we feel will help to make sense of the discussion of the role of the High Court that follows. Here we discuss the concept of the '**rule of law**' and explain a little about the judicial systems that operate in Australia. Questions associated with the visibility of judges are discussed in the second part. The main questions concern why judges have not been acknowledged as central to the political process and why this ability to remain politically invisible has declined in recent years. The third part introduces the accusation of 'judicial activism' that is sometimes levelled at the members of the High Court. Accusing judges of being judicial activists is to accuse them of using their role as judges to promote their view of the way that Australian society ought to be. The fourth part is a discussion of the desirability, in the context of government and democracy in Australia, of increased political visibility on the part of members of the High Court.

rule of law: In politics, we say that the 'rule of law' exists when the power and independence of those who govern are limited by rules that ensure that any decision or action was within the power of those who made it; was made according to correct procedure; and does not violate the basic principles that underpin the political system.

1: PRELIMINARY DISCUSSION

Government and democracy in Australia are governed by the principle of the 'rule of law' and it is the Australian judiciary, and particularly the High Court, that is responsible for guaranteeing this rule of law. Understanding rule of law is particularly important for appreciating the High Court's role as the interpreter of the Constitution, but it also affects the expectations that Australians have of their political system. The other feature of the Australian judicial system is that it is effectively two systems. The fact that the High Court is at the peak of both, and that the systems intertwine in other ways, obscures the existence of these two systems.

Rule of law

The idea of rule of law has been around a very long time. Plato, a Greek philosopher who was born around 427 BC and died around 347 BC, explained the idea by identifying two different forms of rule. Some writers refer to these as the 'rule of person' and the 'rule of law' (Plato wrote in ancient Greek, so his concepts have to be translated into English).

'Rule of person' refers to a situation in which a person, or group of people, make political decisions based on their inclinations, feelings, or dispositions. 'Rule of person' exists when any person or group is free to use their position of power according to the principles and processes that they have chosen for that particular situation. Putting it a little crudely, but in many cases this sort of rule is crude, they make it up as they go along and can make it up differently if they happen to like, or dislike, you more than the last person.

'Rule of law,' on the other hand, exists when principles and processes mean that decision-makers cannot alter govern political decisions. The Australian Constitution expresses the rule of law (along with many other things). It expresses the rule of law because the laws, regulations, and other decisions made in legislatures, by members of political executives, and by public sector workers, at both the state and federal levels, must be consistent with the provisions of the Constitution. Interestingly, we think that we could make a good case that the political body that is least governed by rule of law is the High Court dealing with Constitutional cases. Every other body has its actions governed by a set of rules that mean that, while we don't know what the decision will be, we do know the processes and principles that constrain the process of decision-making. Once appeals from the High Court to the Privy Council ceased, the members of the High Court were responsible for determining the principles through which they would interpret the Constitution.

The Australian court systems

There are two court systems in Australia. One of these systems is a hierarchy of courts that produce '**common law**'. Common law is made up of the legal principles that senior judges (that is, judges in higher or superior courts) have used in making their decisions, and that must be followed by judges in lower or inferior courts. Many of these principles relate to interpreting law generally and to applying particular laws (with particular courts created to deal with specific pieces of legislation, such as a Children's Court or a Land and Environment Court). This hierarchy is comprised of a set of state-based judicial hierarchies over which is laid a capacity to appeal to the High Court (which makes that court the highest, or most senior, in the system and its judgments, therefore, have to be followed in all lower courts). The second judicial system in Australia applies laws made by the Commonwealth Parliament and regulations produced by the political executive. The courts that form part of this judicial system include the Family Court and the Industrial Relations Commission. However, the High Court is also the peak of this judicial hierarchy and these lower courts, too, must apply the principles that High Court members produce.

common law: We use this word to refer to the 'law' that emerges from the decisions that judges make. Principles that derive from previous decisions made in higher courts guide, when they do not control, the decisions made by judges in later cases, especially judges who sit in inferior, or lower, courts. We often distinguish between common, or judge-made, and statutory, or Parliament-made, law.

Prior to Federation, and in many ways ever since Federation, Australia was covered, and remains covered, by six different legal systems. All of them derived from the English common law system. A common law system is one in which much of law that operates in a society has been made by judges hearing particular cases. In this system, judges provide detailed written explanations of the principles that they have used in making their decisions (including how they interpret legislation generally and particular pieces of legislation. Important judgments are collected and the principles that are expressed in them are applied when similar cases arise. Statute law, or laws passed by a legislature (i.e., legislation), and regulations, rules created by executive bodies are important. But judges, making decisions by following previous decisions, produce much of the law that exists in Australian society.

The most important rule of common law, then, is that judges have to decide cases according to the principles applied in previous cases in which very similar events occurred (*stare decisis*). The next most important rule is that decisions made in the same jurisdiction are more important than decisions made in a different jurisdiction. This is why we wrote that Australia remains covered by six different legal systems. They are all common law systems, but the different colonies contained different sets of judges who, in part because the law that they produced emerged as a result of hearing particular cases, produced different law.

Judge-made law always interacts with legislation and regulations, so another reason that the law in each colony was different was because a different interaction of common law, legislation, and regulation existed in each colony.

The next most important rule of common law systems is that courts are arranged in a hierarchy. Courts of appeal exist at the higher levels of this hierarchy. We appeal to these courts when we think that a judge, or judges, in a lower court have not applied the right principles (the right case law) or have misinterpreted the principles that they applied. The highest courts at the time of Federation were colonial Supreme Courts. The judges of these courts would make a final decision as to the principles that applied in a particular case and how future judges should apply those principles. This could include reversing previous decisions by changing the principles that, from then on, were to apply in a particular case.

At the bottom of the state judicial hierarchies are Magistrates' Courts. These courts function as courts of fact, in that they often decide whether the facts exist to justify trying someone in a higher court. They are also courts of law, though, as they can make decisions concerning relatively minor criminal and civil matters, give a variety of orders (such as 'restraining orders'), and approve bail and motor licensing applications. District or County Courts are above these courts. Judges in these courts try cases involving offences that attract mid-range penalties. (Juries provide assistance in determining matters of fact and guilt in some of the cases tried in these courts.) Full benches of judges on District or County Courts, usually three to five judges, hear appeals from magistrates' courts and from decisions made by single District or County Court judges. Judges on Supreme Courts sit at the top of the judicial hierarchy and, besides being courts of appeal, try offences that attract the most serious penalties.

Federation resulted in the creation of another jurisdiction, the federal jurisdiction, and the changing nature of the interaction between the state and federal jurisdictions makes their relationship hard to explain in a short section like this. The High Court was the first Australian court. It was responsible for interpreting the Constitution and was set up as the highest court of appeal in Australia (which meant that people could appeal decisions made in their state Supreme Court). The High Court wasn't the highest court in the Australian judicial system, however, as appeals could be made to the Privy Council (a court comprised of British judges) against decisions made in state Supreme Courts and in the High Court of Australia. Appeals to the Privy Council are now close to impossible and the High Court of Australia is now the highest court in the Australian judicial system.

The Federal Court of Australia is the next rung down the Commonwealth judicial hierarchy. It mainly deals with cases arising from laws created by the federal legislature (so the matters it deals with relate to the powers that the Constitution grants to the Commonwealth legislature). The Family Court of

Australia is another part of the Commonwealth judicial hierarchy. The Federal Magistrates' Court was created in 1999 to handle more minor cases. Appeals from the Federal Magistrates' Court go to the Federal or Family Courts.

QUESTIONS

1. What is the 'rule of law'?
2. What are the differences between the common law system and the federal court system in Australia?

2: QUESTIONS OF VISIBILITY

The first question that must be asked concerns the way in which the idea of 'visibility' is used in this chapter. Nobody would suggest that judges should not be seen. Therefore, by visibility we mean that judges are not seen to be actors in a political system. So, visibility could be understood as political visibility. This section begins with a discussion of reasons why judges, particularly High Court judges, have tended to be less politically visible than Parliamentarians and members of political executives. The second part is an examination of reasons why judges, particularly High Court judges, have become more visible in recent years.

Why have judges been less visible/conspicuous than Parliamentarians and members of political executives?

Adjudication not lawmaking

One of the reasons that judges tended to be politically invisible is a result of the distinction that is sometimes drawn between adjudication, or the interpretation of a law, and lawmaking. This distinction relies upon the construction of the role of judges as that of interpreters of law and not the creators of law. Judges, in this construction, are responsible for applying a Parliament-made law to a specific set of facts. The questions for the judge, then, become whether this law applies in the case that is presented for judgment and what consequences derive from applying this law.

Legal positivism/impartiality

The possibility that applying a law requires interpreting that law might create problems in this context; for interpreting involves giving meaning to that law that is a judge's creation. Judges avoid this understanding of their role by claiming that they interpret laws according to their literal meaning, which is sometimes called legal positivism. The idea that being trained for work in the law involves being trained in the ability to get the proper meaning of a set of words is commonplace.

In order to derive this 'right' meaning, judges must not impose their views as to what should happen when making a decision. Judges who have been affected by their preferences, from this perspective, will decide that a law has the effect that they want it to have. The only way to avoid this is for judges to practise impartiality or indifference to the outcome of the cases over which they preside. Not to be impartial would be like university teachers grading student's essays on the basis of whether they agreed with the argument presented in those essays.

In the context of constitutional interpretation

While the appearance of impartiality has generally been important for the work of judges, it became particularly important for the work of judges of the High Court. This was, and still is, because their most politically important decisions concern the meaning of the Constitution and result from power struggles between members of state and federal political executives. High Court decisions, then, are a part of struggles for power. To be seen to make decisions based on a preference for which of these competing bodies ought to have a particular power, rather than on the 'objective' meaning of the provision of the Constitution, would make the High Court itself part of that power struggle.

The members of the first High Court[3] did not act impartially, however, and were conscious of their participation in power struggles. Justices Griffith, Barton, and O'Connor had helped to write the Constitution. Aware that the appropriate division of power between the federal and state governments had not been made explicit, they tried to make sure that their decisions reflected the division of power that they believed was implied in the Constitution. As a result, they introduced two principles to guide their interpretation of the Constitution. These are known as 'implied prohibitions' and 'immunity of instrumentalities'. By applying the principle of implied prohibitions, they sought to ensure that the federal government remained significantly weaker and more limited in its powers than state governments. And they applied the principle of immunity of instrumentalities to ensure that the two levels of government could not interfere with the other's use of power.

The judges who followed Griffith, Barton, and O'Connor continued to apply these principles until 1920 when the judges of the High Court stopped applying these principles and adopted instead the doctrine of legal positivism. The *Engineers' Case*[4] marked the apparent introduction by the High Court of a strict literal approach to constitutional interpretation. The limit to the federal Parliament's use of power, expressed as implied prohibitions, is not in the Constitution, so the High Court had no general principle through which it could limit the federal Parliament's power in this case and all subsequent cases. This decision marked the beginning of a steady increase in the powers of the federal government that resulted from a literal interpretation of the Constitution.

This is despite the fact that one can easily infer, from the way that the Constitution was written, that this was not the intention of most of those who wrote the Constitution and supported Federation. This is understandable. There was, after all, little real pressure to federate and the Constitution had to be supported by people who had been powerful in colonial governments. It would also have to go to a referendum in which voters, who were used to strong colonial governments and were yet to think of themselves as Australians, would vote. Interestingly, the first judges of the High Court were actively political when it came to interpreting the Constitution, in that they consciously sought to protect the relationship between state and federal governments that they desired. As a result, they were prepared to invent doctrines that were not contained in the Constitution in order to create a division of power that was also not specified in the Constitution.

Since then, all judges, and particularly those on the High Court after 1920, did not want to be politically visible and have their decisions questioned, implying that they were imposing their preferred outcomes in making those decisions. To create invisibility, judges participated in the view that judicial decisions were simply the result of the application of the meaning of laws, for which Parliament was responsible, to the specific facts of a case. Using principles associated with legal positivism and judicial impartiality facilitates this appearance.

Why have judges become more visible/conspicuous?

There are three reasons to suggest that all judges, and High Court judges in particular, have become more politically visible. The first, and more important, is the fact that the High Court has handed down some controversial decisions. This has resulted in concern about the ability of these officials, who have not been elected, to shape Australian society and politics. The second reason for an increased political visibility of judges derives from, what seems to be, a greater willingness on the part of at least some judges on state Supreme Courts and the High Court to comment on social issues. Finally, some commentators have even suggested that some members of the High Court have acted as judicial activists, and not legal positivists.[5]

Controversial High Court decisions

The main reason that the High Court has been seen as more politically active reflects the consequences of decisions in the *Mabo* and *Wik* cases.[6] The problems that these decisions caused were a result of the fact that the High Court rejected the doctrine of *terra nullius*, which allowed white settlers to ignore prior occupation of what we now call Australia by Indigenous Australians. The decisions in *Mabo* and *Wik*, which recognised land rights for Indigenous Australians, were a source of significant confusion, if not tension, for many Australians. Some saw these decisions as a threat to Australian society. Land rights for Indigenous Australians, from their perspective, were economic and social threats; an economic threat because they would disrupt pastoral and mining interests, and a social threat because claims were made that land rights could deprive people of their property.

Using position to articulate concerns about Australian society

While most of the current members of the High Court seem less willing to do so, recent members of the High Court were more willing to comment on contemporary social issues than previous members. A search of the APAIS[7] database for former Chief Justice Sir Anthony Mason and current Justice Michael Kirby credits them with a multitude of speeches and articles in which they comment on important social issues. Many of these were delivered or written when the justice was a member of the High Court. This is not a definitive test, of course. Henry Bournes Higgins, for example, was a very active commentator on social issues[8] (but he was on the Court before the *Engineers'* case was handed down), as was Herbert Vere Evatt.

Change in approach to interpretation

Another reason that judges, especially High Court judges, are perceived to be taking a more actively political role is because of a change in approach to the interpretation of the Constitution adopted by the High Court. The high point of this was the Court over which Sir Anthony Mason presided. This Court applied 'sociological jurisprudence' in an interpretation of the Constitution. This involves reading the document in the light of community values. The best examples of this, in our view, are the decisions in the *ACTV* and *Theophanous* cases.[9] In both decisions, the court interpreted the Constitution in terms of a right to free speech that was essential for democracy in Australia. This 'right' is not mentioned in the Constitution, and the Court had to imply its existence in order to reach its decisions.[10] The 'judicial activism' that is understood to be reflected in sociological jurisprudence may be another cause of the increased political visibility of the High Court.

BOX 4.1
Reactions to the *Mabo* case

In the *Mabo* judgment of 3 June 1992, the High Court rejected the application of the doctrine of *terra nullius* in Australia. *Terra nullius* indicates emptiness, and specifically emptiness with respect to law. Where a land was found to be empty of law, the only laws that applied were British laws. The fact that Australia was *terra nullius* meant that law among Indigenous people did not persist after colonisation. If it were not *terra nullius*, the laws of Indigenous Australians would have remained in force after colonisation.

Mabo was a polarising decision in Australian society. That is, it generated very strong positive and negative reactions. Those who reacted positively saw the acknowledgment of prior occupation of Australia by Indigenous Australians as a step towards reconciliation. The High Court's decision on the *Mabo* case, from this perspective, made it easier for Australians to say 'sorry' for past injustices and was a step towards building a unified society. Those who reacted negatively argued that if the Indigenous Australians were acknowledged to have occupied Australia first, they could make effective land claims. These, from this perspective, would extinguish existing pastoral and other leases and force primary industries out of Australia. The other fear was that Indigenous Australians could be entitled to massive compensation for the loss of their traditional lands.

Source: Gordon & Windsor (1997)

QUESTION

Aside from the *Mabo* and *Wik* cases, what are some of the other controversial High Court cases over the past two decades?

3: ON JUDICIAL ACTIVISM AND THE HIGH COURT

Two points need to be made about this notion of judicial activism before the question of whether the increased political visibility of the High Court is a good thing can be discussed. The first is that the High Court has always been politically active. Indeed, High Court decisions have been one of the most important, if not the most important, sources of political change in Australia. Interpreting the Constitution makes the High Court central to politics. If this is true, then the second point becomes important. This is the point that accusation of legal realism may reflect more about the accuser's views on the sorts of principles upon which the Court makes its decisions than it does on the activity of the Court. Indeed, it is sometimes hard to avoid a suspicion that sometimes people accuse the High Court of activism because they do not agree with one of its decisions.

The High Court has always been active

Uniform tax cases

The position that the High Court has always been active seems easy to defend. One of the most important decisions in Australian political history arose in the context of the federal Parliament's introduction of uniform income taxation legislation in the 1940s. Up to that point, the states had collected most of the money raised by taxation. This makes great sense, as under the Constitution, the states have most to do. In the *Uniform Income Taxation* cases,[11] as they have come to be known, the High Court was faced with two important questions. The first was whether the federal Parliament had the power to introduce income taxation at a level that made it hard for those in state political executives to impose their own income tax. The second question concerned whether the federal Parliament could give money that it had raised to the states on the provision that it was spent in exactly the way that the federal Parliament dictated.

The result, if the High Court answered yes to both of these questions, was to give the federal Parliament the power to control many more things than it had the Constitutional power to control. The members of the High Court decided that s 51 (ii) gave the federal Parliament the power to make laws with respect to taxation and it was impossible to argue that a law introducing income taxation was not a law with respect to taxation. They also decided that s 96 gave the federal Parliament the power to give money to the states on whatever terms and conditions it decides.

Griffith, Barton, and O'Connor would have implied a prohibition against this use of s 51(ii), and s 96 to massively extend federal government power. They would have argued that s 96, which is stated as applying for the first decade of the Federation and thereafter until the federal government decided to abandon it, was not intended to allow the federal government to control the way that states spent money to the extent that it might undermine the states as the centres of government in Australia. They might have sought to keep the state governments immune from this attempt by one level of government to reduce the power of another level. They would have objected to the combined use of ss 51 (ii) and 96, as they would have recognised that this would effectively cause a shift of power from state governments, where it was intended by the drafters of the Constitution to lie, to the federal government. The *Uniform Income Tax* cases, then, mark the beginning of a fundamental revision of the nature of the Australian Federation that has occurred without changing the Constitution. This is hard to understand as inactivity on the Court's part.

Tasmanian Dam case

The High Court was also very active in reshaping government in Australia in the *Tasmanian Dam* case. Here, the Court was asked to decide whether federal legislation that prohibited the Tasmanian government from damming a river was valid. The federal legislation resulted from obligations that arose from an international agreement to protect the environment that had been signed by representatives of the federal political executive. The High Court held that the federal Parliament's legislation was valid.

The point here is that the federal government was allowed to do this purely because the Constitution gives it the power to make laws with respect to 'external

BOX 4.2
Reactions to the *Tasmanian Dam* case

During the late 1970s and early 1980s the Tasmanian State Cabinet wanted to increase the state's electricity production by creating a new hydroelectric power station. The Tasmanian Hydro-Electric Commission was authorised to dam the Gordon River just below its junction with the Franklin River. This dam would have flooded a vast area of wilderness that had been listed as part of the world's natural heritage under an international agreement designed to prevent continued destruction of important natural areas. Influenced by anti-dam protestors, the Hawke Labor Cabinet sought to prevent the dam and took the Tasmanian Hydro-Electric Commission to the High Court. There, counsel for the federal Cabinet argued that the fact that a representative of the federal Cabinet had signed an international agreement, which listed the area to be flooded as a protected area, meant that the state could be prevented from allowing the area to be developed or used in a way inconsistent with the agreement to protect the area. The High Court accepted this argument by a narrow majority, four judges to three, and the dam was prevented. This case was the first in which it was held that the federal Parliament's 'external affairs' power could be used to extend Parliament's legislative power.

Source: Blackshield, Coper, and Williams (2001)

affairs' (these are the only words in s 51(xxix)). The Constitution does not give the federal Parliament the power to make laws with respect to dams, rivers, or water. Entering into an international agreement was all that it took to allow the federal government to interfere in what the drafters of the Constitution would have been almost certain to see as a state responsibility. Once again, the federal government was allowed to extend its reach well beyond that intended by the people who wrote the Constitution. Simply giving 'external affairs' its literal meaning did this.

Activism may indicate attitudes to decision-making
While both the *Uniform Taxation* cases and the *Tasmanian Dam* case were important decisions and resulted in a major extension of the power of the federal government, the *Uniform Tax* cases have not been labelled as judicial activism (which seems to be a more recent phenomenon). One possible explanation for this, in our view, is that most Australians accepted the extension of the power of federal Parliament. The income taxation legislation was introduced during World War II and this might have had an impact on its reception. The decision in the *Tasmanian Dam* case could be understood to reflect a perception that the Australian government should not be prevented from entering meaningfully into important international agreements. There can be no doubt that the State Premiers of the time and all others who promote states' rights would have been outraged by the decisions. Yet, their protests did not seem to spark accusations of judicial activism.

There can be little doubt that the decisions in *Mabo* and *Wik* are among the principal causes of the accusation of activism made against the High Court.[12] These decisions do not appear to reflect the views concerning Indigenous land rights among significant parts of the Australian community and a variety of powerful groups within Australian society. Some people might claim that the decisions in the *Uniform Taxation* cases and *Tasmanian Dam* case were obvious reflections of legal positivism, but this does not end the matter. The application of legal positivism made the High Court very active.

Perhaps the question is really about the source of any judicial activism. If it is practised because of principles of objectivity and proper processes of legal interpretation, then we might not see these decisions as judicial activism (despite their effects in transforming Australian politics). If judicial activism is practised because of a dynamic approach to the Constitution that reflects the fact that it operates within a society and ought to be applied in terms of the values that operate within that society, then we might be more willing to acknowledge the political roles of decisions. Our suspicion, however, is that some people accuse the Court of judicial activism when it hands down decisions they do not like.

> **QUESTION**
>
> What is the difference, if any, between judicial activism and legal realism?

4: GOVERNMENT AND DEMOCRACY AND INCREASED VISIBILITY

Is increased political visibility on the part of the High Court desirable?

The basic question concerns whether we want judges on the High Court to acknowledge their importance for politics and to make decisions like people who are involved in politics, rather than like judges who want to obscure their involvement in politics. We have constructed this question in terms of 'political visibility', as we think that the issue concerns whether we want the judges on the High Court to be seen to be as important to Australian politics as they really are.

Two alternative positions are presented in the following sections. The Yes case is that increased visibility makes the Court more democratic, in that it makes members of an important governmental institution aware that their decisions are subject to public scrutiny and comment. The No case is that increased political visibility undermines the capacity of the Court to hand down authoritative decisions.

Yes case

The basis of the Yes case is that increased visibility on the part of the High Court promotes democracy. The assumption here is that democracy is a good thing and if a link can be made between political visibility on the part of the High Court and democracy then it follows that political visibility is a good thing. The argument begins with the point that High Court decisions are extremely important to the form and development of government and democracy in Australia. This means that the High Court is a central part of government and democracy in Australia. Governmental processes need to be visible in a democracy in order for them to maintain their legitimacy. No democrats would be comfortable with the idea that a hidden group of people controls their destiny. Thus, political visibility ensures that the members of the High Court cannot act as if their decisions are free from the exposure to public scrutiny that is an essential part of democracy.

Judges are central to social order, especially High Court judges

Nobody can doubt that decisions of the High Court, with respect to the power of federal and state governments, have transformative effects on government and democracy in Australia. Only a few of the important decisions that the Court has handed down have been mentioned, but these have had profound effects on the nature of Australian politics.

The decisions that the Court has made concerning the Constitution are only part of the role that it plays in government in Australia. For, like all other courts, it functions as part of a judicial system through which social order is maintained. Courts are central parts of the structures of control that function within Australian society. Every decision by a court will have an effect on someone's life. The effect might be minor, but it may also be enormous (consider a life sentence). Due to the fact that Australia does not have a Bill of Rights[13] and must rely on the courts to protect the rights and liberties of citizens, courts have a central role to play in government in Australia.

Judges always have discretion

While judges may wish to conceal their political role behind the claim that they engage in an impartial application of the laws created by Parliaments, this conceals both the extent to which judges apply discretion to those to whom laws are applied and in the precise manner in which a law is applied. No one should be under the illusion that Parliament can so tie judges' hands that they are completely powerless. Lawyers are, after all, among the people most practised in argument and the application of fine distinctions, and judges are highly trained lawyers.

Democracy requires that judges are visible

If judges' decisions shape Australian society, then democracy would seem to require that their decisions are visible to the public. In a democracy, we expect that citizens who are affected by decisions know who made them and why they made them. Citizens must be sure that no decision will be taken that is not subject to scrutiny and, in some cases, responses from other political institutions.

Readers must not assume that any increased political visibility on the part of the High Court, and indeed all other courts, would make judges' decisions open to public control. Political visibility will not result in popular control over courts. The result of a decision by a court, and particularly the High Court, may be that the people will call upon Parliament to introduce legislation designed to overcome the effects of a court's decision (though there are limits to how successful such attempts can be). No members of a court, including the High Court, would act in complete disregard of such a legislative initiative. Especially if they are aware that a refusal to comply would be construed as a failure to acknowledge that the people have spoken about a court's decision through Parliament. The people can only do so, however, if decisions are subject to popular scrutiny. In this case, this means political visibility on the part of the High Court.

No case

The No case is based upon the position that political visibility of the High Court would result in damage to that court. This would undermine the effectiveness of an important political institution and, as a result, would damage government itself. To make the High Court, or any other court, politically visible would make judges apply the law with an eye to the political context within which they were applying this law. This would create problems associated with partisanship, as courts would be open to the accusation that they were taking sides in political debates. This would reduce public confidence in their decisions and mean that their decisions were less authoritative. It would also make appointment to higher courts, and especially the High Court, into political appointments. The damage to the system of government from the political visibility of the High Court, it follows, would be so great as to undermine the system as a whole.

Those in government must maintain legitimacy

If governments need anything, it is the support of the people who are subjected to their power. Legitimacy, as this is sometimes known, is a central element in the stability of a political system. The means by which courts maintain their legitimacy is through the application of legal principles and not political principles. People maintain their faith in courts because they believe that courts are not subject to the effects of judges' values or popular pressure, and that the judges who sit on courts do their job with their eyes firmly on what is legally valid and not on their values or the whims of the people (that's what politicians do).

Too much attention to a political context will result in a loss of legitimacy

For judges to pay attention to their own desires, popular opinion or, more generally, to the political context within which they make their decisions, would result in their decisions being caught up in that context. Most of the decisions concerning the Federal Constitution that come before the High Court involve a political executive, either federal or state or both. Either the ALP or LPA–NPA Coalition will dominate those political executives. If we have a state political executive challenging federal legislation, we may have a direct confrontation between the ALP and the Coalition. The decision of the High Court will almost inevitably satisfy one group and frustrate the other. The only way to avoid being dragged into this political confrontation is to treat the question about the validity of legislation as a legal, and not a political, question.

Judges lose legitimacy if they are caught up in political struggles

If the High Court made decisions based on political arguments it could not avoid being taken as part of a political struggle. To decide that legislation was valid or invalid because of political principles would result in the court being seen to support one set of principles and to deny the validity of another set. To decide that the federal government ought to be able to pass a law because the justices on the High Court thought that this was a good law or because they thought that the federal government ought to have this power would make decisions political decisions. However, to make a decision about the validity of an act of Parliament based on the meaning of the words of the Constitution avoids this entirely.

Judges are only lawyers

The fact that lawyers are trained to interpret laws means that judges can claim significant authority with respect to the interpretation of laws. They are, after all, highly trained lawyers who have become judges because of their ability to interpret laws and make legal arguments. Judges are not appointed[14] due to their commitment to certain political principles or their ability to decide what is in the best interests of Australian society. Everyone else would be distinctly uncomfortable if those who went to the High Court thought that the decisions of the Court would be made on any basis other than their ability to present legal principles. Decisions of the Court would be seen to be political and subject to the particular values of the judges who made the decision.

BOX 4.3
Michael Kirby and the Commonwealth car controversy

In late April 2002 Senator Bill Heffernan accused Michael Kirby, a Justice of the High Court, of gross impropriety. Heffernan was protected in making his accusations by Parliamentary privilege, which protects Parliamentarians from being sued, such as for defamation, as a result of statements that they make in Parliament. His claim was that Kirby, an openly gay man, had used a Commonwealth car to 'trawl for rough trade' near The Rocks in Sydney. The claim was proved to be false and Heffernan was forced to apologise to Kirby, the Senate, and the Australian people. He was also removed from his position as Parliamentary secretary. Heffernan's actions drew the High Court and its judges into politics in a way that was unusual in Australian politics. The High Court is generally protected from such attacks due to a desire to keep it out of the political spotlight. This had begun to break down as a result of a series of controversial decisions, of which *Mabo* was a part. Heffernan's allegations took scrutiny of justices of the High Court in new directions.

Source: Price (2002)

Judges need to be above politics
If their decisions were self-consciously political, then a new set of judges might make a different decision in exactly the same circumstances. Appointments to the High Court would become, as a result, political appointments. If members of the federal political executive were primarily responsible for appointing judges, it would mean that they would be able to influence decisions of the High Court by appointing judges who were seen to be more sympathetic to their party. If decisions about the appointment of judges were based on the political principles that a judge supports, then the fact that judges stay on the bench longer than the members of political executives hold office would enable them to affect political life for a longer time.

QUESTION

Can activist judges sitting on the High Court retain judicial impartiality?

Conclusion

A theme in this chapter has been that all courts are important to government in Australia. The fact that this has come to be more readily acknowledged with respect to the High Court is not simply an acknowledgment of its crucial role in determining the shape and form of Australian politics. High Court decisions concerning the meaning of provisions in the Constitution have always been important. The increased political visibility of the High Court seems more of a reflection of the controversial decisions in *Mabo* and *Wik*, an increased tendency on the part of some justices of the High Court to offer views on important social issues, and the fact that the court has been accused of judicial activism. While the accusation of judicial activism may be a reflection of the accuser's views concerning the decisions handed down by the Court, it does lead to the question of whether any increased political visibility of the High Court is a good thing. This is not an easy question to resolve, however, as there are somewhat persuasive cases that can be developed in support of the alternative positions available on this issue.

FURTHER READING

Introductory texts

Cranston, Ross, 1987, *Law, Government and Public Policy*, Oxford University Press: Melbourne.

Nicholson, Pip, 1998, 'Appointing High Court Judges: Need for Reform?', in D. Lovell, I. McAllister, W. Maley & C. Kukathas (eds), *The Australian Political System*, 2nd edn, Longman: South Melbourne.

Solomon, David, 1998b, 'What's Wrong with the High Court Playing a Significant Political Role', in D. Lovell, I. McAllister, W. Maley & C. Kukathas (eds), *The Australian Political System*, 2nd edn, Longman: South Melbourne.

Zines, Leslie, 1997, *The High Court and the Constitution*, 4th edn, Butterworths: Sydney.

Specialist texts

Blackshield, Tony, Michael Coper & George Williams (eds), 2001, *The Oxford Companion to the High Court of Australia*, Oxford University Press: South Melbourne.

Cass, Deborah, 1998, 'Through the Looking Glass: The High Court and the Right to Political Speech', in A. Thacker (ed.), *Women and the Law: Judicial Attitudes as They Impact on Women*: Proceedings of a Conference Held on 9–10 June, 1993 at Melbourne, Deakin University Press: Geelong.

Cunningham, Helen (ed.), 1997, *Fragile Bastion: Judicial Independence in the Nineties and Beyond*, Judicial Commission of New South Wales: Sydney.

Doyle, John, 1998, 'Do Judges Make Policy? Should They?', *Australian Journal of Public Policy*, vol. 57, no. 1, pp. 89–98.

Hughes, Robert Allan & Geoffrey Leane, 2001, *Australian Legal Institutions: Principles, Structure and Organisation*, FT Law and Tax: South Melbourne.

Krieken, Robert van, 2000, 'From Milirrpum to Mabo: The High Court, Terra Nullius and Moral Entrepreneurship', *UNSW Law Journal*, vol. 23, no. 1, pp. 63–77.

Lane, P.H., 1996, 'The Changing Role of the High Court', *The Australian Law Journal*, vol. 70, pp. 246–51.

Macquarie Reference Series, 1998, *Government in Australia: Key Events in Politics, Law and the Economy*, Macquarie Library: Sydney.

Moffitt, Athol, 2000, 'Judges, Royal Commissioners and the Separation of Powers', *Quadrant*, vol. 45, no. 5, pp. 36–9.

Patapan, Haig, 2000, *Judging Democracy: The New Politics of the High Court of Australia*, Cambridge University Press: Oakleigh.

Solomon, David, 1992, *The Political Impact of the High Court: How the High Court has Shaped Australian Politics, from Federation to Today*, Allen & Unwin: Sydney.

Solomon, David, 1998a, 'The Political Impact of the High Court', in D. Lovell, I. McAllister, W. Maley & C. Kukathas (eds), *The Australian Political System*, 2nd edn, Longman: South Melbourne.

Solomon, David, 1999, *The Political High Court: How the High Court Shapes Politics,* Allen & Unwin: St Leonards.

Twomey, Anne, 1997, 'State Constitutions in an Australian Republic', *Monash University Law Review*, vol. 23, no. 2, pp. 312–30.

Web sites

Australian Legal Information Institute: http://www.austlii.edu.au
Law Web Resources: http://www.library.usyd.edu.au/libraries/law/freeweblaw.html
National Library of Australia: http://www.nla.gov.au
The Federal Court of Australia: http://www.fedcourt.gov.au
The High Court of Australia: http://www.highcourt.gov.au

Notes

1. For more details on the roles of Australian judges and courts, refer to Singleton et al. (2006, pp. 302–4).
2. See http://www.lawlink.nsw.gov.au/lrc.nsf/pages/R38APPENDIXA.
3. For general information on the High Court and its history, see Solomon (1997, pp. 115–20), Maddox (2005, pp. 194–9), Kirby (1997, pp. 514–28), and Lovell et al. (1998, pp. 68–9).
4. For more information on the *Engineers'* Case, see Solomon (1997, pp. 120–4).
5. For discussions concerning legal positivism, judicial activism, and sociological jurisprudence refer to Solomon (1997, pp. 114–19), Lucy (1993, pp. 271–6), Ward & Stewart (2006, pp. 40–8), Craven (1999, pp. 214–24), Galligan (1987, pp. 252–4), and Mason (1998, pp. 158–60).
6. For more information on the *Mabo* and *Wik* cases, refer to Hughes (1998a, pp. 213–34).
7. Australian Public Affairs Information Service (APAIS) is an index of books and articles about, among other things, current affairs, economics, law, and politics in Australia. The National Library of Australia produces it. Your library may subscribe to it and give you access via its catalogue. If you want to find out more about the index, the relevant URLs are http://www.informit.com.au and http://www.rmitpublishing.com.au.
8. See chapter 6 of Cook (1999).
9. Ian Cook acknowledges bias here, as he co-authored a submission to a Senate Inquiry and an article in which he defended the banning of televised political advertising in the weeks preceding a federal election, which was the piece of legislation challenged and overturned, in the *ACTV* case (Ward & Cook 1992). *Australian Capital Television Pty Ltd and The State Of New South Wales v. The Commonwealth of Australia* (1992) 177 CLR 106 F.C. 92/033. *Theophanous v. The Herald and Weekly Times Ltd* (1994) 182 CLR 104 (1994) 124 ALR 1.
10. Information on the High Court finding implied rights in the Constitution can be found in Hughes (1998a, pp. 238–41), Blackshield (1994, pp. 23–57), and Walker (1997, pp. 179–81).
11. For more information on the *Uniform Income Taxation* cases, refer to Solomon (1997, pp. 120–4) and Lehmann (1983, pp. 115–56).
12. The decision in *Members of the Yorta Yorta Aboriginal Community v Victoria* [2002] HCA 58 suggests that the *Mabo* decision may not have been as radical as it appeared to some people to be.
13. For more information on an Australian Bill of Rights, see Hughes (1998a, pp. 235–8).
14. For more information on the appointment of judges, see Lucy (1993, pp. 271–6) and Nicholson (1996, pp. 69–87).

5 The Governor-General (Head of State)

LEARNING OBJECTIVES

- To understand the difference between the head of government and the Head of State
- Appreciate that the role of the Governor-General is mostly symbolic
- To know when the Governor-General is important
- Be able to engage in the debate over whether Australians should be able to choose the Head of State and the different methods for choosing the Head of State

INTRODUCTION

Unless they are embroiled in scandal, governors-general appear infrequently in reports of Australian politics. We see them from time to time, but most of what they do is not readily obvious to us. The main reason for this is that the Governor-General is rarely an important player in politics and, so, there is little reason to pay the office much attention. There are really only two reasons to write about the Governor-General. The first concerns his or her potential power. While this is really only potential, rather than actual power, the power of the Governor-General became important because of what happened in 1975. This was when a Governor-General dismissed a Prime Minister and called an election that this Prime Minister did not want. The second reason that a discussion of the office of Governor-General is worth a whole chapter results from increased interest in electing our **Head of State**, which is what the Governor-General is.

Head of State, Governor-General, royal assent: The Head of State of a country is its political representative. A Head of State may play an active part of politics (as in the US) or play a largely symbolic or ceremonial role (Britain and Australia). In Australia, the Head of State is the British monarch. The Governor-General is the representative of the British monarch and is appointed by the monarchy on the advice of the Australian Prime Minister.

This chapter is in four parts. A discussion of the difference between a Head of State and a head of government comprises the first of these parts. The second deals with what we see of the Governor-General, what we could see of the Governor-General, and what we get from the Governor-General. The main point made here is that governors-general have considerable potential power, but do not use this power and, as a result, do not play a significant role in Australian politics. The third part is a discussion of the one moment in which the Governor-General was important in Australian politics (the Constitutional Crisis of 1975). The question here concerns when the Governor-General is important. Finally, we discuss some questions that arise with respect to replacing the Governor-General with an elected Head of State. The obvious question is whether Australians should elect their Head of State. While we can decide without considering the implications of the different ways to elect a Governor-General, these seem important. This part finishes, then, with a discussion of the effects of direct and indirect election of the Head of State.

1: BACKGROUND

Preliminaries for Governor-General

The distinction that is most important for an understanding of the role of the Governor-General is that it is between a Head of State and a head of government in

BOX 5.1
Resignation of the Governor-General

On 26 May 2003, then Governor-General, Peter Hollingworth, resigned from office. His resignation followed repeated calls for him to stand down from the position. These calls came from those who believed that he had not dealt properly with child sex abuse allegations against a priest for whom Dr Hollingworth had been responsible in his previous role as Anglican Archbishop of Brisbane during the early 1990s. Dr Hollingworth indicated that, while he acted in good faith at the time, he would have acted differently if the circumstances had arisen more recently. He denied that he acted improperly and that the situation required that he should resign.

The Prime Minister, John Howard, supported the Governor-General, who had been appointed on a recommendation to the Queen from a Cabinet in which Howard was Prime Minister. The Prime Minister argued that the Governor-General had fulfilled his role as Governor-General with distinction and that nothing that he had done while Governor-General justified a recommendation to the Queen that he no longer be her representative in Australia. This situation raised important questions concerning the role of Governor-General, and the relationship between governors-general and the Cabinets and Prime Ministers who recommend their appointment. It also demonstrated that some Australians remain unaware of the fact that members of Cabinet do not appoint the Governor-General.

Source: http://www.theage.com.au/articles/2003/05/05/1051987655284.html

---

a Westminster-derived Parliamentary democracy. This is an important distinction because some people argue that the Governor-General is the Australian Head of State, and working out the differences between a Head of State and a head of government might help us to understand what governors-general do, and don't do. Section 61 of the Constitution includes the following statement: 'the executive power of the Commonwealth is vested in the Queen and is exercisable by the Governor-General as the Queen's representative…' This makes it hard to accept the argument that the Governor-General is the Australian Head of State. The Queen has rarely exercised her powers in Australian politics (when in Australia, though, she has ratified legislation passed by the Commonwealth legislature). This means that it makes some sense to think of the Governor-General as practically, or conventionally, the Australian Head of State.

The more important question, for our purposes, concerns what a Head of State is and what he or she does. This brings us back to the difference between a

Head of State and a head of government (or, as we refer to the position throughout this book, head of the political executive). Having all executive powers of the Commonwealth vested in her or him (even if only as the Queen's representative) means that the Governor-General is formally the head of government. However, governors-general do not occupy a position from which they can act like a head of government. They do not sit in Parliament, they do not act as a Minister, and they are not the Prime Minister, as the head of government must be in a Parliamentary democracy.

Yet governors-general are involved in important moments in the administration of Australian society. They can dismiss the Commonwealth legislature and issue writs for new elections. They commission the Ministers and Prime Minister, sign bills that have been agreed to by both houses of Parliament in order for them to become legally enforceable (acts), issue regulations, make proclamations, and appoint federal judges, ambassadors, high commissioners, and other senior government officials. The Governor-General is also the Commander-in-Chief of the Australian Defence Forces. Governors-General, then, have many important roles in Australian politics.

The crucial point to note about governors-general is that they have little, if any, discretion concerning how they use their powers. Under the Constitution, many of the powers that governors-general have been given can only be used in accordance with the advice of Ministers. Apart from the 1975 Constitutional Crisis, all of the governors-general's Constitutional powers have been used in accordance with the advice of Ministers. Ministers, and their Chief, or Prime Minister make the decisions and, in that sense, govern the country. The person who stands at the peak of those involved in the ongoing government of Australia is the Prime Minister, who is the head of government.

The fact that governors-general have little, if any, personal discretion in the use of their powers is crucial to their functioning as Head of State. For, if they represent anything else, governors-general do one of the things that all Heads of State do, they help create a sense of stability and continuity in Australian government and they help to legitimise government in Australia. Governors-General provide continuity because their tenures are unaffected by the electoral cycles that result in the election/appointment of the head of government (in Australia, heads of government (Prime Ministers) achieve their positions because of an election and their appointment by the Governor-General). Governors-General also help to create legitimacy through their involvement in important ceremonies associated with government in Australia.

Legitimacy results from the participation of a non-partisan actor (someone with no association with a political party) who represents the Australian people in opening and closing Parliaments, making proclamations, and appointing people to fulfill significant roles, such as judges and ambassadors. The fact that the people do not elect governors-general means that Australians are less likely to feel some meaningful connection with them or, as some Heads of State are thought to do, to reflect 'the spirit of the nation'.

QUESTION

What is the difference between a Head of State and a head of government?

2: WHAT YOU SEE, WHAT YOU COULD SEE, AND WHAT YOU GET

A large percentage of adult Australians would struggle to name the Governor-General. This is not a result of some failure on the part of the Governor-General. Indeed, the men (they all have been men) who have held the office have not wanted to make a name for themselves, at least not while they held that office. This is interesting, in that the Constitution actually gives the Governor-General quite a lot of executive power and even a little legislative power. Of course, the fact that the Governor-General is not elected and that the office is supposed to mirror the position of the Queen of England means that the Governor-General does not actually use any of the power that technically belongs to the office. These are exercised by members of the federal political executive. Well, this is true most of the time, but that story belongs to the next section.

What do we see?

Their appointment is one of the moments at which governors-general appear to Australians. Otherwise, they do not make much of an impact on the news. We sometimes see them giving speeches and otherwise presiding over important events. Anzac Day parades, Commonwealth Games openings, and Olympics are all places where you might find a Governor-General giving a speech and, probably, shaking some hands. Sometimes, we might see the Governor-General meeting a visiting Head of State, but sometimes the Prime Minister does this.

The most important of the speeches that the Governor-General gives, at least for our purposes, is the one that he delivers for the government. This speech is delivered on the first day that Parliament meets, or sits, after an election. The Governor-General reads a speech that has been prepared by the members of the federal political executive, in which they outline their objectives for their three-year term. Very occasionally, you might find the Governor-General commenting on social issues. This is rare, as the office reflects the role that the Queen plays in British politics. It is a symbolic position that is not supposed to create any political fuss. Doing a good job as a Governor-General, then, might be understood as keeping a low profile.

What could we see?

That we expect the Governor-General to stay out of politics and even social commentary is interesting because, for the most part, Chapter Two of the Constitution appears to give the Governor-General a great deal of power.[1] Governors-General are the Chief of the Armed Forces. The Governor-General decides when elections are to be called. The Governor-General signs bills that have been passed by Parliament, and by doing so turns them into acts. The Governor-General is actually given the powers of a political executive under s 61 of the Constitution. Most of the executive's powers that have been presented as belonging to federal Cabinet, then, could be understood to belong to the Governor-in-Council (i.e., the Governor-General and the Ministers, who must come from Parliament). The Governor-General also appoints Ministers, the political heads of government departments (s 64).

While governors-general have a number of executive powers, they also have some power over the Houses of Parliament. The Governor-General has the power to call for elections to the House of Representatives and half the Senate. The Governor-General may also dissolve both Houses of Parliament, but only under certain conditions (see s 57). The Governor-General must also formally approve all bills that have been passed by the two Houses of Parliament if they are to become laws (s 58).

What do we get?

One of the main reasons that governors-general do not act on their own initiative is that the Constitution specifies that some powers can only be used by the Governor-General in Council. This, in practice, means (s 63) that the Governor-General acts with the advice of Cabinet. Most people involved in politics have interpreted this requirement to act on Cabinet's advice to mean acting under instruction from Cabinet. They then extend this requirement to act as directed by Cabinet to all of the powers of the Governor-General. This interpretation of acting on the advice and the extension of this constraint on the Governor-General to all of the powers given to the Governor-General are, however, conventions.

The result of these conventions is that governors-general do not exercise an independent discretion; they only act according to instructions from Cabinet. No one could object to this. First, this is acceptable because the Governor-General is not elected, and no democracy could sustain a non-elected official wielding such extensive powers. Second, governors-general were not intended to retain actual power. And third, though this may be an extension of the second point, the position was created with that of the Queen of England in mind. The conventional understanding of the position of Governor-General reflects the conventional role of the Queen (this is to remain 'above' politics). These conventions associated with the role of the Governor-General have been applied for most of the history of the Australian Federation, with one major exception.

> **QUESTION**
>
> What are the symbolic aspects of the Governor-General's role?

3: WHEN IS A GOVERNOR-GENERAL IMPORTANT?

On only one occasion in Australian politics has the Governor-General acted in a way that did not reflect the conventional understanding of the role of the Head of State in a Constitutional Monarchy.[2] This was on 11 November 1975, when the Governor-General dismissed a Prime Minister and issued writs, or signed the papers necessary, for a **double-dissolution** election.[3] The simple answer available to the question posed here is that governors-general are important in situations like 1975.

Of course, the role of Governor-General can be understood to be important both in terms of the powers indicated above and for symbolic purposes, as we will discuss in the last part of this chapter. The events of 1975, however, indicate a greater potential for the significance of his or her power because it indicates a problem that is embedded in the Constitution.[4] The problem is that the Constitution allows members of both houses of Parliament to claim to speak on behalf of the Australian people. The Governor-General becomes important when this disrupts government in Australia.

The situation in 1975

The story of the dismissal on 11 November 1975 is a long one and starts in 1974.[5] We do not intend to tell this full story, however, as paying too much attention to the details will obscure the larger issues that arise here. The important point to note is that the short answer to the question: 'When is the Governor-General important?' is 'When the Governor-General acts in disregard of the advice of the leader of the party that controls a majority of votes in the Lower **House of Parliament**'.

A deadlock arose between the two Houses of federal Parliament. This can usually be dealt with through the constitutional provisions of s 57, which allow for a double-dissolution election and, if necessary, a joint sitting of both Houses. There were two problems here. The first was that the bills that the Senate was refusing to pass were 'supply' bills, or bills to approve the supply of money to government departments. Another problem was that the Prime Minister, Gough Whitlam, knew that his party had no chance of winning an election at that time, and he would not advise the Governor-General to call an election for the Lower House and half the Senate. Faced with this situation, the Governor-General, Sir John Kerr, dismissed the Prime Minister and appointed the Leader of the Opposition, Malcolm Fraser, 'caretaker' Prime Minister (Fraser had agreed to take care of government until a double-dissolution election).

House of Parliament (bicameral–unicameral): A House of Parliament is a meeting room or chamber, in which elected representatives sit to pass legislation and to debate important social issues. Like most Australian Parliaments, the federal Parliament has two Houses; the House of Representatives (sometimes called the Lower House) and the Senate (sometimes called the Upper House). A Parliament with two Houses is referred to as a bicameral Parliament, whereas, 'unicameral' refers to a Parliament with only one chamber. Queensland is the only unicameral state legislature in Australia.

Deadlock between Houses of Parliament

By 1975, the Australian Labor Party held a majority of seats in the House of Representatives, but had lost its majority in the Senate and faced a 'hostile' Senate. This is a Senate in which the majority is opposed to the party that controls the Lower House. A hostile Senate is unlikely to pass bills that have been accepted in the House of Representatives.

Those who drew up the Constitution had anticipated this problem and created s 57. Under this section, a bill that has been passed by the House of Representatives and rejected by the Senate and, after three months, passed again by the House of Representatives and again rejected by the Senate can be used as the basis for a double-dissolution election. A joint sitting can be called if the two Houses disagree again, with the result that the House of Representatives will win, as there are around twice as many members of the House of Representatives as there are of the Senate.

One of the problems in 1975, however, was that these were not ordinary bills. They were bills that authorised the supply of money to government departments. There are actually two problems here. Those who drafted the Constitution used the Parliament of Westminster as their model. In the Westminster Parliament, the upper house, the House of Lords, is not elected and, by convention, does not reject or fundamentally alter 'money bills', such as budgets and supply bills. Section 53 of the Constitution reflects, but does not reproduce, this convention. Under s 53, the Senate cannot initiate or amend money bills. Nothing in this section, however, suggests that the Senate has to pass money bills.

BOX 5.2
The 1975 Constitutional Crisis

Tuesday, 11 November 1975 witnessed the most dramatic event in Australian political history since Federation. The Governor-General, Sir John Kerr, dismissed the Whitlam Labor Cabinet and appointed Liberal Party leader Malcolm Fraser as caretaker Prime Minister. The dismissal of the Whitlam Cabinet resulted from the Senate's failure to pass bills that would supply the money necessary for government.

Three conventions, the unwritten 'rules' that help Australian government to function, were broken leading up to and during the Constitutional Crisis. The first convention broken was the rule that Senators who died or vacated their seat during their term of office would be replaced by Senators from the same party as the deceased or retiring Senator (this convention is now part of the Constitution, see s 15). Two Labor Senators were not replaced with members of the party from which they had come. They were Lionel Murphy, who retired from the Senate to become a justice of the High Court, and Bert Milliner, who had died. Losing these two votes cost the Labor Party control of the Senate. The second convention that was not followed was that the Cabinet had to be supported by a majority of members in the Lower House of Parliament (House of Representatives). The third broken convention was that the Governor-General acts only on the advice of the Prime Minister.

Source: http://www.whitlamdismissal.com

The Prime Minister was fully aware that an election would result in his losing office (this view seems to have been borne out by the results in the following election, which was disastrous for the ALP).[6] He refused to advise the Governor-General to call an election, either for the House of Representatives and half the Senate or for all members of both Houses. Instead, he advised the Governor-General to call a half Senate election. The Governor-General refused to accept this advice.

The dismissal

The Governor-General, after being convinced that the situation would not be resolved, dismissed the Prime Minister and appointed the Leader of the Opposition in the House of Representatives to the position of Prime Minister. This appointment was conditional. It was given on the basis of the newly appointed Prime Minister only doing the minimum necessary to keep the government going and not introducing any meaningful legislation or taking any important decisions before an election was held.

There are no prizes for guessing that the decisions to dismiss the Prime Minister and appoint a new Prime Minister were not taken with the advice of the leader of the majority in the House of Representatives. The convention that the Prime Minister would be the person who could control a majority in the Lower House had been observed for so long that nobody thought that it would be broken. Especially the ALP Senators who voted to pass the supply bills that had been blocked in the Senate; they were unaware that they were granting supply to a Liberal–National Party coalition government!

Conflicting voices in Parliament

The most important thing to note from this simplified account of the situation in 1975 concerns the problems that were created when the party that controlled the House of Representatives did not control the Senate.[7] This situation is important because it has been the case in every Parliament between 1975 and 2004. The use of proportional representation in Senate elections and an apparent reluctance on the part of Australian voters to give members of political executives too much power seem to have resulted in a situation in which, apart from 2005 to 2007, the political executive has not controlled the Senate since 1975.

The only thing that has prevented the situation in 1975 from recurring is that the Senate has not blocked money bills. It has blocked other pieces of legislation, but not those that a political executive needs to keep government running. The presence of a hostile Senate means that Parliament speaks with two voices. Both of these voices can be said to represent the will of the Australian people, with the difference being the method by which they are elected.

Even if the Lower House can be claimed to be elected on a more democratic basis, there can be no doubt that the Constitution does not reflect this difference. Senators are elected by the Australian people and, as a result, feel entitled to frustrate the will of members of Cabinet. The independents and minority parties who control the 'balance of power' in the Senate will continue to promise that they will pass money bills. Cabinets must always be appointed from the party that holds a majority in the Lower House, due to the power to initiate money bills that belongs to that House. The conventions and the political reality will only remain in a sort of dynamic tension, therefore, as a result of promises made by politicians.

While we shouldn't ignore the promises of politicians, extraordinary circumstances may lead them to break their promises, and the role of the Governor-General may again become important. Until then, governors-general will act only as directed by members of Cabinet and the powers of the Governor-General will remain potential powers. The position of Governor-General will continue to be symbolic and we will continue to see them occasionally and hear from them even less.

QUESTION

Do governors-general exert substantive influence over government?

4: ELECTING A GOVERNOR-GENERAL

Short of exceptional circumstances like those in 1975, the only time that we will find ourselves discussing the role of the Governor-General is when we discuss the question of electing the Head of State. There are actually two questions embedded in this apparently single question. The first concerns whether we want to change from a Constitutional Monarchy to a Republic. The second concerns how we might elect our Head of State. While these are separate questions, they are usually mixed together in discussions of an Australian Republic.

In the first section of this part, we discuss whether Australians should choose to elect their Head of State. In the second, we discuss different methods for electing the Head of State and consider the likely effects on the office of Head of State of these different methods.

Should Australians choose to elect their Head of State?

The following discussion presents reasons to support or reject the election of a Head of State. The Yes case is presented first. The first point in the Yes case is the position that Australian society has changed and that this means that a Constitutional Monarchy is no longer appropriate to that society. The second is that, even if nothing has changed, we might want to create conditions under which things will change. The final one is that by not electing a Head of State, we leave open the possibility of another Constitutional Crisis.

The first point in the No case is that a Constitutional Monarchy is a tradition in Australia and that traditions need to be preserved. The second point is that the stability of Australian politics could be disrupted by such a change. And the third is that the Governor-General is the only one who could resolve another deadlock between the Houses, which we have done nothing to prevent.

Yes case
A Constitutional Monarchy is no longer meaningful
Australian society is nothing like it was in 1901. Far fewer Australians have any real feeling for or connection with Britain. To have a Governor-General who is the Queen's representative (s 2 of the Constitution) fails to represent the nature of Australian society. A Constitutional Monarchy, then, is neither meaningful to most Australians nor reflects their attitude to themselves and to the rest of the world. To maintain a Constitutional Monarchy would be to neglect their feelings in favour of those of a small minority.

We want to be different
Even if Australian society had not changed fundamentally, to preserve a Constitutional Monarchy would be to ensure that Australia could not pursue its own destiny as an independent country. If Australians are to develop a sense of themselves as a separate and different nation requires developing institutions that are indigenous to this country. A Constitutional Monarchy is not indigenous to

BOX 5.3
Appointing the Governor-General

The Queen, advised by the Australian Prime Minister, appoints the Governor-General. After receiving the Queen's commission, the Governor-General is required to make an Oath of Allegiance and an Oath of Office to Her Majesty and then issue a proclamation stating that the office has been assumed. The Governor-General's appointment is formally at Her Majesty's pleasure. In practice, however, the appointment is usually for five years, although this can be extended if required. The Governor-General's salary is set by Parliament at the beginning of each Governor-General's term in office, and the salary cannot be changed during the appointment. Only the Queen can remove the Governor-General from office, though she will only act on the advice of the Australian Prime Minister.

Source: http://www.gg.gov.au

this country. It is a political structure that belongs to other countries. It is not a part of an independent future, but reflects the preservation of a derivative past. Even if we have not changed, we still want to change, to develop, and to grow as an independent nation with its own political institutions.

1975

The last problem with not moving to elect a Head of State is that it will result in the perpetuation of the role of Governor-General. As we have seen from the preceding discussion of the events of 1975, the Governor-General has the capacity to change the direction of Australian politics. That the Governor-General is only bound by conventions means that the powers that the Constitution gives to the Governor-General are not formally constrained and may be exercised by someone with the political will and the opportunity to do so. We cannot afford to maintain the situation when to do so would place a non-elected person in a position of significant potential political power.[8]

No case

We have traditions to defend

The first reason to maintain the current situation is that it provides a link to the past. The position of Governor-General was created in the very process of developing the Australian Constitution and represents an Australian political tradition. Moving to elect an Australian Head of State would not make us different from most other countries and would actually make us like most other countries. A Constitutional Monarchy in which a Westminster parliamentary system is embedded is unusual in the world. It remains something distinctive and to preserve the traditional structure would be to increase and not diminish the distinctiveness of Australian politics.

Don't destabilise Australian politics

Another reason not to elect a Head of State is that we cannot predict the consequences of such a change. Australian politics has been remarkably stable and we should resist any change that might reduce this stability. A change to the Constitutional structure could produce instability. We cannot predict the sorts of powers that elected Heads of State will claim after their election. An elected Head of State could do this and this would create confusion and unpredictability in the Australian political process. An elected Head of State, for example, might refuse to ratify a Bill because she or he has a **mandate** not to do so.

mandate: In politics, members of a political executive who argue that an election result means that the people have given them the authority to govern or to introduce a particular policy claim to have a mandate from the people to govern or to introduce that policy.

1975
Rather than 1975 presenting a reason to elect a Head of State, it ought to be understood to support the case for not electing a Head of State. We have done nothing to negate the possibility of a re-emergence of the sort of deadlock that emerged in 1975. We do not know what an elected official would do in these circumstances. We could not know that a Head of State who had been supported by the ALP would have acted to resolve the situation. The constitutional deadlock might have persisted for even longer than it did. A quick resolution of the situation only occurred because we had a Governor-General who was not loyal to the party that appointed him.[9]

We hope that readers will consider each of the reasons that we have put forward in support of the alternative positions on this issue. We have no doubt that Australians will be called upon to consider the question of electing a Head of State in the relatively near future. This is not a simple question and will require careful consideration if a sound decision is to be made.

What are the possible effects of direct and indirect election of the Head of State?

Even if we agreed to elect our Heads of State, this is not the end of the matter. Moving to elect a Governor-General would mean that Australians have to decide on a method for their election. Two possibilities exist: direct and indirect election.[10] The nature and implications of each of the two forms for electing a Head of State is discussed in the following sections. The first deals with direct election, the second with indirect election.

Direct election
We are familiar with the direct election of a Head of State from French and Irish Presidential elections. In a direct election voters choose between a group of candidates, using either a preferential system or a first-past-the-post-style system.[11] The main difference from normal elections is that we are electing a Head of State, rather than a head of the political executive. Unless we were trying to reshape the entire political structure, we would elect someone to fulfill a symbolic role. The Head of State might speak out on important social issues, but would not play an active role in the federal political executive. And, we would expect that, in all important governmental matters, they would act only under instruction from the members of the federal political executive.

Possible effects of direct election
New power
One effect of direct election of Heads of State is that a significant portion of Australian voters would have supported them. But, despite this, they would be

expected to simply follow the instructions that they receive from Cabinet. Elections tend to breed politicians. Politicians tend to want power. An elected Head of State might be expected to want some power. While these are only tendencies and possibilities, they are important in the context of any decision concerning the method for electing the Head of State.

Deadlock between Parliament and the Head of State

No matter what general issues arise concerning an elected Head of State, the specific issue raised by the requirement that bills are formally approved by the Head of State cannot be discounted. No bill can come into force, that is become an act, until it has received the assent of the Governor-General. An elected Head of State may be required to assent to a bill to which she or he has moral, intellectual, or philosophical objections.

A Head of State who rejects euthanasia, for example, may be required to sign a bill that legalises euthanasia. This would place that Head of State in a very difficult position. The situation might get decidedly more complicated if that Head of State had explicitly rejected euthanasia when campaigning for the position of Head of State. The possibility of a deadlock between Parliament and the Head of State is likely. Whether this is a problem, though, is another question.

Indirect election

Forms of indirect election: appointment by Parliament

In indirect elections, voters choose representatives who then select the Head of State. The simplest version of this, which was presented in the referendum with respect to electing the Head of State in 1999, is for the Parliament to select the Head of State. This might be done by a joint sitting of the two Houses of Parliament or through negotiation between the major parties that results in one name being presented for approval by Parliament. Alternatively, the Lower House might be given this responsibility, which would mean that members of Cabinet control the appointment (reproducing the current situation with respect to the appointment of the Governor-General, though the Queen would have no role in the appointment).

Forms of indirect election: appointment by a representative assembly other than Parliament

A variety of systems exist for indirect election of the Australian Head of State. Any group of people elected or selected to make this decision would choose the Head of State. Their decision about who would be the Head of State is made on the people's behalf. One approach to indirect election would be a system in which voters elect representatives who meet to choose a Head of State. Another possibility for indirect election is that members of federal Parliament and/or those in state Parliaments would appoint people to an assembly created to elect the Head of State. Yet another possibility is that state and/or federal Cabinets would choose people to participate in such an assembly.

BOX 5.4
A synopsis of the 1998 Constitutional Convention and 1999 Referendum

Pressure to change to a republic reached a peak in the late 1990s with the 1998 Constitutional Convention and the 1999 Constitutional Reform Referendum. The 1999 referendum was the first time that Australians had been presented with a change from a constitutional monarchy, with the Queen of England as the Head of State and Governor-General as her Australian representative, to a republican form of government, with a Head of State elected or appointed by Australian citizens.

The 1998 convention was held between 2 and 13 February, and attended by 152 delegates. Half of them had been elected by postal vote and the other half were appointed by the members of Cabinet. The Australian Republican Movement was the largest group at the convention. Its members supported a minimal model for a republic, in which Parliament would appoint a President to serve as Head of State. This model was supported by a bare majority of conference delegates (seventy-five voted for, seventy-one against, and four abstained). It was the model presented to the voters in a referendum in 1999. The model was rejected by a majority of Australians and by a majority of Australians in each of the states (in only the ACT was a majority in favour of the model).

Source: Webb (2001)

Likely effect of Parliamentary appointment (entrenching power of major parties)

A Head of State chosen by the members of federal Parliament will have received the support of one and probably both of the major parties. This would be so whether or not the process involved the Houses sitting together or separately, as Cabinet would seek support from the Opposition in order to avoid politicising the role of Head of State. The successful candidate, then, would be acceptable to the major parties. This would probably end up entrenching the power of these parties and ensure that the Head of State would not undermine the dominance of the major parties.

Likely effects of appointment by representative assembly (tension between Cabinet or Parliament and the Head of State)

Appointment by a representative assembly that has been chosen by voters would free the Head of State from any direct relationship to the major parties. It might create conditions under which the Head of State could represent a potential check on Cabinet's and Parliament's power. A representative assembly appointed by Members of Parliament would tend to reproduce the effects of selection by Parliament (as the major parties would control the appointments to such an assembly). An assembly appointed by state Parliaments might avoid this and this might prove an interesting forum for making such a decision. Candidates may well receive support from their 'home' state and a variety of deals may be required in order for a candidate to be chosen.

Summary

Australians rejected the proposals put forward in 1999, but the issue will not go away. The question is likely to be revisited as Australian society changes because of the effects of the mass media, immigration, and changing generations. The decision as to whether Australians should support the election of a Head of State is not a simple one. There are sensible arguments that can be put forward to support both change and the maintenance of the current situation. Bound up with this question is the issue of the form of election that is adopted. Direct and indirect election, in its many forms, may have consequences for the Australian political system that may be guessed at, but can never be known, except in hindsight.

QUESTION

What is your preferred method for selecting a Head of State and why?

CONCLUSION

If we can know anything, it is that, for as long as the office exists, the Governor-General is unlikely to play a significant role in Australian politics. Governors-General will be seen and occasionally heard, but will have little effect on Australian politics. Unusual circumstances, such as those that existed in 1975, may well occur, but they will be very rare. The problem inherent in the Constitution with respect to the powers of the two Houses of Parliament remains. It is unlikely to produce the same deadlock as occurred in 1975, however, so the Governor-General may not be faced with such a deadlock. Any move to elect a Head of State may have to be accompanied by some attempt to resolve the problem that the Constitution creates with respect to the powers of the House of Representatives and the Senate. This is only one of the issues to address, for the effects of the different methods available for electing a Head of State must also be considered.

FURTHER READING

Introductory texts

Craig, John, 1993, *Australian Politics: A Source Book*, 2nd edn, Harcourt Brace: Sydney.

Emy, Hugh E., 1978, *The Politics of Australian Democracy: Fundamentals in Dispute*, 2nd edn, Macmillan: South Melbourne.

Hughes, Owen, 1998a, *Australian Politics*, 3rd edn, Macmillan: South Yarra.

Maddox, Graham, 2005, *Australian Democracy in Theory and Practice*, 5th edn, Longman Australia: Melbourne.

Parkin, Andrew, 1997, 'Towards a Republic?', in D. Woodward, A. Parkin & J. Summers (eds), *Government, Politics, Power and Policy in Australia*, 5th edn, Longman: South Melbourne.

Specialist texts

Atkinson, Alan, 1993, *The Muddle-Headed Republic*, Oxford University Press: Melbourne.

Hamer, David, 1994, *Can Responsible Government Survive in Australia*, Centre for Research in Public Sector Management, University of Canberra: Belconnen.

McKenna, Mark, 1994, 'Tracking the Republic', in D. Headon, J. Warden & B. Gammage (eds), *Crown or Country: The Traditions of Australian Republicanism*, Allen & Unwin: St Leonards.

Shiell, Annette & Peter Spearritt, 1993, *Australians and the Monarchy*, Monash University: Melbourne.

Solomon, David, 1998c, *Coming of Age: Charter for a New Australia*, University of Queensland Press: St Lucia.

Winterton, George, 1994a, 'The Constitutional Implications of a Republic', in M. Stephenson & C. Turner (eds), *Australia: Republic or Monarchy?*, University of Queensland Press: St Lucia.

Winterton, George, 1994b, *Monarchy to Republic: Australian Republican Government*, 2nd edn, Oxford University Press: Melbourne.

Web sites

Australian Republican Movement: http://www.republic.org.au
Governor-General of the Commonwealth of Australia: http://www.gg.gov.au
The Australian Monarchist League: http://www.monarchist.org.au
The current Governor-General: http://www.aph.gov.au/Library/handbook/
    41stparl/governor-general.htm
The official web site of the British Monarchy: http://www.royal.gov.uk
The role of the Governor-General: http://www.aph.gov.au/library/gov/ggrole.htm

Notes

1. For more on the powers of the Governor-General, see Republic Advisory Committee (1993, pp. 88–94) and Fenna (2001, pp. 95–6).
2. To find out more about Constitutional Monarchy, see Galligan (1995, pp. 19–21) and Bogdanor (1995, pp. 1–41).
3. Technically, the Governor-General issued writs for the election on the advice of the Prime Minister. The Prime Minister in question, however, was Malcolm Fraser, who did not control a majority in the House of Representatives, but there is no provision in the Constitution that requires the Governor-General to appoint a Prime Minister from the party that controls the majority in the Lower House of Parliament.
4. For a hard copy of the *Commonwealth of Australia Constitution Act* see Lovell et al. (1998, pp. 865–88) or for an electronic copy visit http://www.aph.gov.au/senate/general/constitution/index.htm.
5. For a brief introduction to the Constitutional Crisis refer to Jaensch (1994, pp. 224–47), Parkin & Summers (1997, 1, pp. 14–8), Kelly (1998b, pp. 113–20), and Paul (1998, pp. 121–6). For a more in-depth analysis, see Kelly (1995).
6. The effect on the ALP of having been dismissed, both for the election campaign that the party fought and on the minds of voters, is incalculable.
7. For more on the relationship between the House of Representatives and the Senate, refer to Jaensch (1994, pp. 221–6) and Lucy (1993, pp. 191–212).
8. For more arguments on why Australia should become a republic, see Lucy (1993, pp. 232–5) and Hughes (1998a, pp. 203–6).
9. For more arguments on why Australia should maintain the monarchy, see Abbott (1998, pp. 656–7) and Manne (1998, pp. 654–5).
10. Preferential style would mean the elimination of the candidates with low percentages of votes, with their preferences distributed until only two remained, with one declared the winner. In a first-past-the-post system, voters would simply indicate their support for one of the candidates. The winner would be the person who got the greatest number of these votes.
11. For more details on the methods proposed for the appointment of the Head of State, see Republic Advisory Committee (1993, pp. 64–9, 73–4).

The Bureaucracy

LEARNING OBJECTIVES

- To understand the nature of bureaucracy
- Contrast bureaucracy with the charismatic and traditional forms of bureaucracy
- Be able to comprehend the reasons why some people consider less bureaucracy is better than more bureaucracy and why others do not

INTRODUCTION

bureaucracy: We use this word to describe people who advise, support and carry out the wishes of members of political and company executives. Ministers are the political heads of government departments and the rest of the members of their departments can be referred to as bureaucrats.

The federal and state bureaucracies are, in many respects, the most important institutions of government in Australia. Their importance lies in the fact that most of the **bureaucracy** is that body of people primarily responsible for implementing laws passed by Parliament. Their decisions can have profound effects on our lives. They can often make a final decision about our eligibility for benefits (such as Austudy or Abstudy) or a licence (such as a driver's licence). They may impose fines on us and some of them may even detain or arrest us. While the actions of bureaucrats are governed by legislation or regulations and can be appealed, public servants remain one of the main points of interaction between Australians and their political system. The implementation of policies is not the only way in which the bureaucracy is important, however, as the bureaucracy is also an important source of the policies that affect our lives.[1]

This chapter is in two parts. The first is intended to provide an introduction to bureaucracy. It is recognised as a rational form of authority that can be contrast against more charismatic and traditional forms. The second part discusses the proposition that less bureaucracy is better than more bureaucracy. It is a proposition that reflects the hostility that many Australians feel. In fact, 'bureaucracy' has almost become a colloquial synonym for inefficiency, ineffectiveness, and laziness.

1: BUREAUCRACY AS RATIONAL AUTHORITY

The bureaucracies of Australian government can be understood in terms of the Weberian concept of bureaucracy and managerialism. Arguably, the most important theorist of bureaucracy was Max Weber.[2] He recognised bureaucracy as a means to organise the authority of bureaucrats. Weber identified two forms of authority—charismatic and traditional—against which he contrasted bureaucracy, the rational-legal form of authority. The charismatic form of authority rests with a leader who is in some way exemplary. Authority is transferred to those deemed to be acting in the leader's name and collapses upon the death of the leader. Hence, charismatic authority is inherently unstable.

The traditional form of authority constitutes the authority of oligarchies and families of high standing that have been bedrocks of a society. Charismatic leadership is inherently unstable—leaders die or, in bad times, may loose their charisma. Traditional authority possesses a sense of stability and reliability. High standing in society is taken as proof that one possesses 'the right stuff' and deserves to be obeyed. Moreover, as societies grew, traditional leaders required supporters and assistants to take care of the day-to-day administration of the people and help to make important political decisions. The traditional leaders were, of course, considered the best placed to select their assistants.

In this context, administrative positions were part of the government of society and, as positions of power, could be used to defend the interests of rulers against the people they governed. Administrative positions were, at least in some instances, sources of income for those who occupied them. Tax collectors, for example, collected taxes to pay themselves and then to direct money to central authorities. This meant that administrative positions were used in the interests of the people who occupied those positions.

The rational-legal form of authority—bureaucracy—retains a hierarchical structure, but formalises the arrangements. It recognises that supporters and trusted family members do not necessarily make good administrators.[3] A complex economy requires administrators who can establish and maintain an efficient system of regulation and control over the market. A representative democracy must be accountable to the people and seen to be fair, if it is to retain its legitimacy.

Hence, bureaucracy is governed by rules that ensure that decisions are impartially administered by competent people. Such people are first selected to join the bureaucracy by means of a public examination and rise through the hierarchy on the basis of seniority.[4] This ensures that their administrative skills and expertise in particular policy areas are commensurate with their responsibilities.[5] They are then compelled by law to apply administrative rules equally to all people and not treat their office as a means for promoting self-interests.

Bureaucracy is also a more stable system than previous forms of authority. Administrators hold their positions independent of changes to those in positions of political power. This is particularly useful in the context of representative democratic systems, when members of Cabinets can change every three years. It is also useful given the fact that **Ministers** may lose their position as Minister or be given responsibility for a different department or portfolio. That new Ministers can rely on an experienced group of administrators to help them to develop and implement policy means that effective administration can be maintained.

An even more important aspect of bureaucratic hierarchies is that they provide mechanisms for coordination

Minister, front bench, backbench: In a political system, 'Minister' refers to the political head of bureaucratic departments, who are responsible to Parliament for their department (sometimes referred to as their portfolio). The front bench refers to the seats in a House of Parliament that are filled by Cabinet members and shadow Cabinet members. The backbench refers to the seats in which all other Parliamentarians from their party sit.

and accountability.[6] A higher level oversees each level of a modern bureaucratic organisation. There may be other means by which members of a modern bureaucracy can be called to account for their actions (such as the Administrative Appeals Tribunal[7] or the Ombudsman[8]), but such accounting is required in a hierarchical organisation in which those at lower levels of the administrative organisation must report to those in higher levels.

This characteristic of a modern bureaucracy is particularly important in the context of Westminster-style representative democracies. If a Minister or a member of a Minister's department is found to have made significant errors or misjudgments in developing or implementing policy, Members of Parliament may pass a motion of 'no confidence' in that Minister, who is then expected to resign.[9] The convention is important in this context not because it operates in Australian politics—most Ministers now claim that their departments are too large and complex for them to take responsibility—but because it indicates the chain of accountability. Internal hierarchies provide a means by which junior members of a department must account for their actions to those in higher positions. Those in the highest positions in a department are accountable to the Minister, who then is accountable to Members of Parliament (who will ultimately be judged by the people at elections).[10]

BOX 6.1
The creation of the Senior Executive Service

The public service contains a variety of different levels of jobs, similar to ranks in the military. The Senior Executive Service (SES) was introduced in Australia by the *Public Service Reform Act 1984*. The SES was introduced as a service-wide recruitment and advancement procedure. It replaced the old Second Division, which was managed by the individual departments. The SES brought with it continuity with respect to recruitment and promotion across the Australian Public Service (APS). It also was a means by which the ideas of new public sector management could be spread effectively through the Australian Public Service, as it focused on job flexibility and career mobility. This was something new for a bureaucracy that had traditionally focused on job stability. The SES also helped with the employment of new managers who focused on output or results management instead of input management and line-item budgets.

Source: Renfrow (1995)

In the 1980s, Australian bureaucracies were criticised for being inefficient and ineffective, and there were calls for a '**new public management**'. What followed and now characterises Australian bureaucracies is a managerialist approach to the formulation and implementation of government policies. Departmental heads are appointed by Ministers, rather than by members of a public service board, and are granted greater autonomy and held accountable by performance contracts. Decisions are no longer based solely upon due process, bureaucrats must also consider costs and outcomes; ideally, *measurable outcomes*. Power is further devolved to line managers and those closest to the problem are expected to find solutions without first having to consult their superiors. Markets are considered the best mechanisms for the provision of public services and consequently contracts are awarded to the lowest bidders. Hence, citizens are treated as customers or clients.

new public management: Used to refer to what was heralded as a new approach to public administration. Advocates of new public management argued that members of political executives should behave more like those in the private sector. They supported selling-off, or privatising, government assets and getting private companies to deliver services that members of political executives, through their departments, once delivered (sometimes called out-sourcing).

QUESTION

How did bureaucracy improve the practice of government?

2: 'LESS BUREAUCRACY IS ALWAYS BETTER THAN MORE BUREAUCRACY.'

Negative views, or antipathy, towards the bureaucracy and bureaucrats seems to have become increasingly powerful in Australian society. This hostility has resulted in the view that reducing the size and role of bureaucracy in Australia is an important project for members of the Cabinet and Ministers. This view is expressed in the proposition that 'less bureaucracy is always better than more bureaucracy'. The first section in this part explains this proposition. Articulating problems that may be identified with respect to bureaucracy in Australia is central to an examination of this view because the problems with bureaucracy lead, almost inevitably, to the view that bureaucracy should be reduced and not increased. The second section provides some comments on this proposition. These comments concern the validity of the problems identified with bureaucracy that justify the proposition. They also concern the historical and political aspects of this position (as this view took on particular salience in Australian politics in the 1990s). Finally, the development of a new approach to public administration is discussed. Attempts to reform bureaucracy reflect the hostility towards bureaucracy expressed in the proposition that it needs to be pruned.

The proposition

Before we present the two sections, the point must be made that the proposition is not that 'no bureaucracy is better than any bureaucracy'. While this may be a view among significant elements of the Australian population, it is not a view that merits much attention. Only anarchists[11] believe that societies can operate without government and the various institutions of government. Those who argue for less bureaucracy do not argue for no bureaucracy at all, as most see that some public administration is necessary to provide order and coordination in society. Bureaucracies are needed to provide and maintain defence and policing, to issue licences and other forms of authority for people to act in particular capacities, and to create the necessary social and economic infrastructure (such as roads, ports, lighthouses, scientific research to increase economic productivity, parks, and libraries) that Australia needs.[12] Bureaucracies are also required to ensure that markets operate fairly (by acting against cheating and anti-competitive practices) and to provide support for Ministers.

That few of us are anarchists means that we must accept the necessity of some form of public administration by a group of trained and skilled people. The desire to ensure that bureaucracy is reduced, rather than increased, in size can be understood as a rejection of larger bureaucracies in favour of smaller ones because the larger the size, the more likely that problems will occur. Another reason to reduce their size is that larger bureaucracies create a 'bureaucratic mentality' that undermines their capacity to deliver effective public services. These points will be discussed below.

Larger bureaucracy a problem
Cost

One of the principal objections to larger bureaucracies is that they are expensive to create and operate.[13] Levels of taxation and other forms of revenue raising will increase as the size of a bureaucracy increases. Few people want to pay tax and even fewer want to pay more tax because they believe that keeping money in their pockets enables them to live the sort of life they want to live. Larger bureaucracies mean increased levels of taxation and less bureaucracy means reduced levels of taxation (or, at least, they should do so).

Reduces people's freedom

Another problem that is understood to result from large bureaucracies is that they can result in over-regulation of our lives. As bureaucracies grow, they begin to do more than simply provide a framework of laws and regulations in which we live our lives. The more experts on various aspects of our lives (such as agriculture, health, education, and transport) employed or created within a bureaucracy, the greater the likelihood that we will begin to be advised as to how we should live our lives.

Impedes the capitalist economy

Larger bureaucracies cause two problems for markets. The first is that the taxation necessary to support them may reduce economic activity by drawing money out of productive activities and into non-productive bureaucracy. Another problem is that the existence of extensive systems of administration results in the over-regulation of markets. If free markets are understood to be the most desirable way to organise and operate an economy, then, to ensure the greatest freedom of markets is an important political objective. Bureaucracy is necessary to provide basic infrastructure, to issue licences, and to provide the regulation necessary to prevent or reduce fraud and other forms of unethical economic practices. The tendency, from this perspective, is for the bureaucracy to increase levels of regulation as it increases in size. A free market will be protected if bureaucracy is kept small.[14]

Less efficient than markets

Another problem that has been the basis for calls to keep bureaucracies as small as possible is that they cannot deliver services as effectively as markets can deliver them. Bureaucracies, from this perspective, have no powerful internal pressures to ensure that costs are kept to a minimum and that services are provided as quickly as possible. Indeed, critics of bureaucracies might suggest that the internal pressures are to increase costs and to take more time. From this perspective, roads, hospitals, and schools should be **privatised**. They can be built faster and at a lower cost to taxpayers if private companies competing for this business deliver them. Security on trains and within prisons can also be delivered at a cheaper rate. Indeed, there are few public services that private companies, in a competitive environment, cannot deliver more efficiently than bureaucracies.[15]

privatisation: 'Privatisation' is used to refer to the selling of publicly owned enterprises to the private sector. This is usually done in the belief that the private sector is more efficient than the public sector in delivering services to the community.

Problems with accountability

Another reason to believe that bureaucracy becomes a problem as it increases in size relates to the accountability that modern bureaucracy has to provide within a Westminster system. In theory, Ministers are accountable for all of the actions of the members of the department for which they are responsible. This means that they can be held to account for significant errors of judgment and mismanagement. The convention is that Ministers should resign if members of their department have committed serious mistakes in forming or implementing policy or been delinquent or incompetent. This convention is rarely implemented, indeed in recent years has not been implemented, because the increasing size of bureaucracies means that Ministers have argued that they cannot be held responsible for all of the actions of the bureaucrats in their departments.

While the theory of accountability is indifferent to the size of the department for which Ministers are responsible, the argument can be made that government departments are simply too big for the convention to operate in most instances. If Ministers continue to avoid accountability on this basis, then the accountability of members of public service departments to the people does not exist. The only way to overcome this problem is to reduce the size of departments, so that Ministers are less able to argue that they cannot be held responsible due to size.

A 'bureaucratic mentality'

It can produce a sense of superiority

While the size of bureaucracies creates problems that have led to calls for reducing their size to a minimum, bureaucrats are often taken to have acquired a bureaucratic mentality that affects their capacity to serve the public. Central to this alleged bureaucratic mentality is a dismissive attitude to members of the public who are made to feel inferior as a result of their interactions with public servants. Part of this superiority may derive from the experience and expertise that bureaucrats acquire through their administration in a particular field. All experts are susceptible to feelings of superiority, at least when it comes to the field in which they have expertise. Bureaucrats are no less susceptible to these feelings.

Large bureaucratic organisations have a greater potential for administrators to have much more interaction within their departments than with the members of the public whom they are to serve. The distance that can develop between bureaucrats, especially senior bureaucrats, and the public that they are to serve can exacerbate and may even produce a sense of knowing better and being superior to members of the general public. The larger departments become, the more likely they are to create distance between bureaucrats and the public, which can produce a sense of superiority.[16]

It can foster paternalism/social engineering

This sense of superiority, according to some of those who are critical of large modern bureaucracies, can lead to a belief on the part of public servants that they know more about how we should live our lives than we do. This view can result in the perception that the public needs to be looked after in the way that a father is supposed to look after his children. Larger bureaucratic organisations may be thought to be more vulnerable to such paternalism, because they are designed to do more than simply provide the basic infrastructure of law and regulation required for a relatively orderly society and a market economy.

A sense of superiority can also lead to a desire to cause changes in the way that we live by 'engineering', or moulding, the social environment in order to create a better way of life for people. While a desire to improve the lives of those for whom they are responsible may be thought to be admirable, this is inconsistent with people's rights to live as they please and may well reduce their capacity to think and act for themselves. Another problem concerns the validity of the social engineers' views about how people should live. For there is no reason to believe that social engineers are correct, either in their views about how we should live, or their knowledge of how to achieve such a society. Larger bureaucracies are also much more likely to contain the resources and people who wish to improve or engineer society than smaller bureaucracies that are designed to fulfil a minimal role in society.

It can produce laziness

Another perception of public servants is that they are lazy or seek to avoid hard work. The basis for this is that their job security, which is an essential part of the stability of modern bureaucracies, is seen to result in a lack of stimulation to work harder and more efficiently. With a job for life and an endless task of administration, a modern bureaucrat simply has no reason to work harder and more efficiently. The larger bureaucratic organisations grow, the more difficult it becomes for their members to be monitored effectively and pressure exerted to ensure that they are working as hard and as efficiently as possible.

Summary

The alleged problems of bureaucracy in this section are rarely the basis for an argument that bureaucracy itself should be abandoned. Bureaucracy is an inevitable part of a large and complex society in which problems of social order exist and support for a market economy is required. In short, bureaucracy can be taken to be necessary for effective government in Australia. A large bureaucracy, however, may not be necessary. Indeed, an argument can be made to support the reduction of the size of the bureaucracy. Central to this argument are a variety of problems that are often taken to result from a larger bureaucracy. Larger bureaucracies are expensive, reduce personal freedom, impede the operation of markets, provide services that it cannot deliver efficiently, and create problems with accountability to the people. Larger bureaucratic organisations may also be taken to foster a bureaucratic mentality in which superior bureaucrats treat people like children (or even try to engineer a particular sort of society), and result in lazier, less efficient bureaucrats.

Comments on the proposition

Problems with larger bureaucracies are central to the argument that less bureaucracy is always better than more bureaucracy. This means that the validity of the proposition depends upon the legitimacy of the problems identified. However, this does not exhaust the points that can be made about the proposition because it can also be understood as a historically and politically 'located' proposition. That is, the proposition that less bureaucracy is always better than more bureaucracy was an idea that took on particular intellectual and political salience in the 1980s and 1990s. During this period, the ideas associated with neo-liberalism[17] were in the ascendancy and the anti-government sentiments that are central to this ideology dominated the political agenda. Thus, while we can understand the proposition as a general approach to bureaucracy, we can also understand it as a historically situated political (that is, ideological) position. Finally, the proposition can be understood as the basis for a new approach to public administration, sometimes called new public management,[18] that can be understood as a response to the attack on bureaucracy. The second and third sections may not bear upon the validity of the proposition, but they merit consideration in the context of its discussion.

Comments on the problems identified
Problems with bureaucracy
The problem of cost is not a straightforward one. Whether something costs too much has to be determined by a calculation that takes into account the value of the services delivered. That no one seems willing to pay tax means that Australians are susceptible to the argument that bureaucracy should be reduced as a means of reducing taxation. Whether this is a short-term and narrow position that could lead to social degradation is something that we may not discover until it is too late. At that point, we may want to recalculate the cost of bureaucracy.

The question of whether people want freedom to take responsibility for their own lives also remains an open one. Reducing the size (and therefore role) of bureaucracy in people's lives may force Australians to rely more on their own abilities and initiative and not look to government to resolve their problems. It may not solve problems; or it may do so at very significant cost to everyone.

Cutting off unemployment benefits, for example, might stimulate some people to seek work, but it might lead others to steal.

There can be little doubt that larger bureaucracies impede the operation of capitalist economies. Once again, the question of whether this is a bad thing is less easily resolved. At least some of the regulation of markets in which bureaucratic departments engage is intended to reduce fraud and other forms of cheating (such as price fixing). Some of the regulation is designed to protect workers from being exploited or made to work in unsafe conditions. Those who believe that free markets can damage society may not be overly concerned about impeding the operation of a capitalist economy. Yet the arguments that regulation and other forms of interference in markets cost jobs by making businesses unprofitable cannot be discounted. Defenders of markets are also likely to see them as more efficient means for delivering services. Acquiring evidence to demonstrate the truth of this claim may need to go beyond the drop in prices of government services that have been opened up to competition from the private sector.

There seems little doubt that problems with accountability emerge as the size of bureaucracies increase. Whether these problems can be overcome through the introduction of more effective monitoring agencies, which examine the activities of members of departments, seems an open question, but the problem of accountability seems a significant one. This problem seems particularly acute in the context of holding individual Ministers responsible for the actions of members of their departments because this is a breakdown of what was to be a fundamental principle to ensure accountability to the people.

Problems with a 'bureaucratic mentality'

The various aspects of a bureaucratic mentality criticised above may be acknowledged as potential problems with bureaucracies. Feelings of superiority, laziness, and paternalism are not problems confined to the bureaucracy, however, so their source may be as much the people who join bureaucracies as the nature of the organisations themselves. Whether the perception of bureaucrats as lazy is valid or is a caricature that provides a false impression of them seems open to question. There are enough hard-working public servants to justify the claim that this perception is unfair and expresses a prejudice against bureaucrats.

There seems little doubt, though, that expertise in a field can give rise to feelings of superiority that impede the capacity for public service and can result in paternalism (and even a desire to engage in social engineering). Nor can there be much doubt that a genuine desire to assist people can lead to attempts to change their lives in ways that reflect the values of those providing the help. It is hard for us to criticise people who seek to provide services to the public and whose commitment to this leads to a desire for social engineering. Perhaps this is a reflection of our experiences as teachers, in which indifference to the effects of our teaching on our students is impossible to sustain. Despite our awareness of problems that can emerge in this context, a desire to produce good students is hard to avoid and this can lead into forms of social engineering on our part.

Historical and political aspects

While the ideas that underpin the proposition are not restricted to a particular time and place, they gained significant currency during the 1980s and 1990s. This period was marked by the rise of what is known as neo-liberal ideas. Neo-liberalism can be understood as the re-emergence of classical liberal[19] ideas of government. Central to classical liberal thought was a desire that government play a minimal role in the economy and society. During the 1980s and 1990s, a variety of governments, including Australian Cabinets, adopted neo-liberal political programs. Central to them was a desire to reduce the size of the bureaucracy. This proposition can be understood to express the ideas basic to neo-liberalism and, to this extent, must be understood as the expression of a particular ideology. This need have no effect on the validity of the proposition. However, it may also indicate that a number of presumptions, especially about the consequences of bureaucracy and the efficiency and desirability of markets, reflect this ideology.

New public management theory and the reorganisation and reorientation of bureaucracy

The 1980s and 1990s also saw the emergence of what was presented as a new approach to public administration. New public management was presented as a new way to organise, orient, and motivate bureaucrats. While it was also presented as a means by which the size of bureaucracy could be reduced, it can also be understood as a response to problems that had been asserted of larger bureaucracies. Central to new public management theory was the view that bureaucracies should not take up leading roles in society, instead its members should seek to support and facilitate community-based initiatives that develop in the context of particular needs and problems. Bureaucrats should also be placed in situations where they compete with private providers of services in order to ensure that services are provided in the most cost-efficient manner. Bureaucrats were also called on to become more entrepreneurial and to raise money directly from the users of the services they provided, rather than to rely upon taxpayers' money.[20] These were not the only changes advocated by those who promoted new public management, but they provide some sense of how some of the problems that had been identified with respect to large bureaucracies could be overcome.[21]

The proposition seems to bear a relationship to new public management theory that suggests it has been a principle used to reorganise, reorient, and motivate public servants. Proponents of new public management theory do not have to accept a need to reduce the size of the bureaucracy, but they seem to have done so. The proposition, then, can be understood as a reflection of this new approach to public administration. The fact that it can also be understood to reflect a historically specific set of ideas about bureaucracy does not undermine its validity. It reminds us, though, that such claims are almost always part of particular theories about people and how they ought to live their lives. Neo-liberal ideas present only one view as to who we are and how we should live and the proposition may represent more than simply ideas about bureaucracy. It can represent part of a set of ideas about how we should live. In the same spirit, we cannot assume the validity of the problems asserted about large bureaucracy. These criticisms may reflect unsubstantiated prejudices or real problems with large bureaucracies.

Summary

An examination of the proposition requires us to consider the negative views, which may be prejudices that we have towards bureaucracy. While some of the negative views may be defensible, others may not survive careful examination. Some of the negative views reflect a failure in the organisation of bureaucracy, and not its size. Some of these failures may also be overcome through new approaches to public administration. A discussion of the proposition can serve to remind us that views about the size and role of bureaucracy cannot be divorced from views about the sort of society in which we want to live. Most importantly, however, a discussion of the proposition requires that we engage with a variety of problems that have been alleged to derive from large bureaucratic organisations and the 'bureaucratic mentality' of those who staff these organisations.

QUESTION

Would Australia benefit from having a larger bureaucracy?

CONCLUSION

The reasons for creating a modern bureaucracy ought not to be forgotten in any consideration of the size and role of the federal bureaucracy. The desire for efficient, fair, stable, and accountable public administration remains a legitimate desire. The idea that we can be governed by institutions whose members are motivated by a desire to provide public service can also be taken to be a desirable goal. This does not mean that we can ignore the views of those who object to bureaucracy in general and large bureaucracies in particular. At least some of the problems that are said to result from bureaucratic organisations, and especially large bureaucratic organisations, are real and remain to be solved. If they are real problems and cannot be solved, then it may make sense to argue that less bureaucracy is always better than more bureaucracy.

FURTHER READING

Introductory texts

Boreham, Paul, Geoffrey Stokes & Richard Hall, 2000, *The Politics of Australian Society*, Pearson Education: Frenchs Forest.

Bridgeman, Peter & Glyn Davis, 1998, *Australian Policy Handbook*, Allen & Unwin: St Leonards.

Considine, Mark, 1994, *Public Policy: A Critical Approach*, Macmillan: South Melbourne.

Fenna, Alan, 1998, *Introduction to Australian Public Policy*, Longman: South Melbourne.

Perry, James L. & Kenneth L. Kraemer, 1983, *Public Management: Public and Private Perspectives*, Mayfield Publishing Company: Palo Alto.

Specialist texts

Considine, Mark, 1992, 'Alternatives to Hierarchy: The Role and Performance of Lateral Structures Inside Bureaucracy', *Australian Journal of Public Administration*, vol. 51, no. 3, pp. 309–20.

Keating, M.S., 1995, 'The Evolving Role of Central Agencies: Change and Continuity', *Australian Journal of Public Administration*, vol. 54, no. 4, pp. 579–83.

Parker, R.S., 1989, 'The Politics of Bureaucracy', in G.R. Curnow & B. Page (eds), *Politicization and the Career Service*, Canberra College of Advanced Education & NSW Division of the Royal Australian Institute of Public Administration, Canberra.

Stewart, Jenny & Megan Kimber, 1996, 'The Transformation of Bureaucracy? Structural Change in the Commonwealth Public Service 1983–93', *Australian Journal of Public Administration*, vol. 55, no. 3, pp. 37–48.

Weller, Patrick, 1996, 'Commonwealth–State Reform Processes: A Policy Management Review', *Australian Journal of Public Administration*, vol. 55, no. 1, pp. 95–110.

Web sites

Australian Commonwealth government: http://www.fed.gov.au
APS jobs: http://www.apsjobs.gov.au/
South Australian government: http://www.sa.gov.au
Tasmanian government: http://www.tas.gov.au
Australian Capital Territories government: http://www.act.gov.au
New South Wales government: http://www.nsw.gov.au
Northern Territories government: http://www.nt.gov.au
Queensland government: http://www.qld.gov.au
Victorian government: http://www.vic.gov.au
Western Australian government: http://wa.gov.au/

Notes

1. For more information on modern bureaucracies, see Hughes (1998a, pp. 366–78) and Jun (1986).
2. For more on Max Weber's writings on bureaucracy, see Weber (1996, pp. 80–5).
3. For more on political appointment, see Heywood (2002, pp. 373–4).
4. For more information on merit appointment, see Peters (1995, pp. 90–3) and Jaensch (1992, pp. 183–4).
5. For more on expertise, see Jaensch (1992, pp. 173–4).
6. For more details on accountability, see Jaensch (1992, pp. 187–8) and Peters (1995, pp. 289–326).
7. For more on the Administrative Appeals Tribunal, see Lovell et al. (1998, p. 424).
8. For more on the Ombudsman, see Jaensch (1994, pp. 281–2).
9. For more details on Ministerial responsibility, see Solomon (1984, pp. 21–5).
10. These are not the only conventions that govern the behaviour of Ministers. The need for those in positions of administrative power to devote themselves to the public and not personal interest means that those Ministers who are found to have used their offices to derive benefits for themselves or their families must resign. Ministers who are found to have misled Parliament are also expected to resign. Ministers who are members of Cabinet are also bound by the convention of collective responsibility, which means that they must support all decisions taken by Cabinet (whether they supported that decision or not). Those who cannot do so are expected to resign.
11. For more on anarchists, see Heywood (2002, pp. 60–1).
12. For more information on the role of bureaucracy, see Heywood (2002, pp. 362–5) and Hughes (1998a, pp. 347–50).
13. For more information on the costs of bureaucracy, see Hughes (1998a, pp. 351–4).
14. For more on the bureaucracy and markets, see Considine (1996, pp. 76–9).
15. For more details on privatisation, see Hughes (1998a, pp. 337–8) and Henry (1995, pp. 318–57).
16. For more on the sense of superiority of bureaucrats over the public, see Hughes (1998b, pp. 34–9).
17. For more on neo-liberalism, see Heywood (2002, pp. 49–50).

18 For more information on new public administration or new public sector management, see Hughes (1998a, pp. 379–87) and Wanna (1997, pp. 74–6).
19 For more on classical liberalism, see Heywood (2002, p. 45).
20 For more on the user-pays principle see Wanna (1997, pp. 73–4).
21 Osborne and Gaebler were leading figures of new public administration. For more, see Osborne and Gaebler (1993) and Gaebler (1996). New public administration theory is not without its critics. One criticism was that it leads bureaucrats away from the desire to provide public service; see du Gay (2000).

PART II

Democracy in Australia

Federalism

LEARNING OBJECTIVES

- To comprehend the nature of federalism and its relevance to Australia
- Understand the reasons for the permanence of the Australian system of federalism
- Be able to consider whether a federal system is a sensible way to organise government and democracy in Australia

INTRODUCTION

Most of this chapter is devoted to a discussion of whether a federal system is a sensible way to organise government and democracy in Australia. Although this is a bit of a non-issue, it is a useful way to draw attention to important aspects of the Australian federal system described in the first part of the chapter. The second part presents some reasons to believe that a federal system will remain a permanent part of Australian government and democracy. And, the question of whether a federal system is a sensible way to organise government and democracy in Australia is taken up in the third part of the chapter.

1: PRELIMINARY DISCUSSION

Federalism is a mechanism for sharing powers and responsibilities between members of political executives at a central and regional level. It is characterised by a division of powers, shared sovereignty and financial independence. Federalism requires a written constitution that protects each level of government by ensuring that neither can dissolve the other nor jettison it from the Federation.

With different levels of government come the possibilities of policy overlap and conflict over responsibilities. Traditionally, those at the central level control the currency, tariffs and border **protection**, which affect entire countries. On the other hand, the powers of those in regional government tend to concern local matters, such as policing, education, roads, and housing. Conflict can arise, however, if there is ambiguity over who has responsibility for a particular policy.

The right of each level of government to raise monies and set **budgets** is the third defining characteristic of federalism. Without financial independence, members of political executives effectively lose their capacity to act autonomously and exercise control over their constitutionally assigned jurisdictions.

While Australian federalism is a particular type of federalism, it can be understood and studied in terms of the characteristics identified above. It comprises three tiers of government—federal, state and local—although

protection: 'Protection' refers to economic policies designed to protect local industries from overseas competitors. Protectionist policies include tariffs, which are duties levied on imports, and quotas to restrict the quantities of a commodity that can be imported.

Budget, supply: In politics, 'budget' is used to refer to an annual financial statement presented to Parliament detailing expected government revenue and expenditure for the following financial year. 'Supply' is used to refer to any legislation introduced in the House of Representatives by members of a Cabinet to provide funds necessary for the business of government.

only political executives at the federal and state levels are sovereign. Local government is recognised and represented at the Council of Australian Governments (COAG) meetings, but not mentioned in the Constitution. Members of state political executives create and dissolve local government bodies. The Northern Territory and the Australian Capital Territory are governed in the same way as the states, but their powers were given to them under an act passed by members of the federal Parliament, and can be taken from them by a later act.

The **division of powers** in our Federation is not always clear. Our Constitution gives specific powers to members of federal political executives and gives the rest, the residue, to those at the state level. The Constitution also lists what are often termed the 'concurrent' powers that are shared between the levels of government These include international and domestic trade, taxation, postal services, census and statistics, quarantine, immigration, currency, invalid and old-age pensions, copyright, and defence of the Commonwealth. Technically, members of political executives at both the federal and state levels of governments can pass legislation in these areas; however, the Constitution states that in cases of conflict 'the Commonwealth shall prevail'.

Finally, members of state political executives retain some financial independence; however, this has declined since the High Court ruled in the *Universal Tax* case that members of the federal Parliament can prohibit the members of state political executives from collecting income tax. Although this decision does not prevent members of state political executives from raising funds through land, payroll and gambling taxes, it has produced an ever-increasing **vertical fiscal imbalance** between the federal and state levels of governments. Members of federal political executives have exploited this imbalance by making available specific purpose payments, which impose upon the other levels of government conditions that have to be met if funds will be provided for a specific program. This financial dependence makes increasingly tenuous the idea of Australian federalism.

division of powers: Power is said to be divided when different powers are formally given to different levels of government. This idea and practice is essential for federalism and the Constitution of a federation must provide some indication of which of the two levels of government will have jurisdiction, or control, over which aspects of people's lives. (Please note that some powers are 'concurrent' in the Australian Constitution, which means that members of Parliament of both levels of government can pass laws on these matters – though the laws passed by members of the federal Parliament will prevail.)

vertical fiscal imbalance: Most of the money collected by members of political executives in Australia is collected at the federal level. Under the Constitution, most of the power to regulate activities and to deliver services in Australia is held by members of state political executives. Those who govern at the federal level have more money than they need to satisfy their responsibilities. Those who govern at the state level have more responsibilities than they have the money to satisfy them. We refer to this situation as one in which a vertical fiscal imbalance exists.

> **QUESTION**
>
> What are the characteristics of Australian federalism?

2: THE PERMANENCE OF A FEDERAL SYSTEM IN AUSTRALIA

'Federalism[1] will remain a permanent feature of government and democracy in Australia for four main reasons. The first reason is that Australians are conservative[2] people who won't change their political system. The second related reason is that a move away from federalism will require a change to the Australian Constitution. The third reason is that state politicians will block any attempt to move from a federal system. Finally, federalism will persist because the major parties are organised on a federal basis.

Australians as conservative

Federalism is a permanent feature of Australian politics because Australians don't want to change their political system. They continue to support a federal and two-party system and do not demand major changes to this system. The level of passivity, which is sometimes seen as apathy, among Australians reflects general satisfaction with government and democracy in Australia. This is not the same thing as a satisfaction with politicians, however, who are not particularly respected in the Australian community. The behaviour of politicians is not viewed as a reflection of the organisation of Australian politics, so politicians are blamed for problems in Australian politics and not the system within which they operate.

Constitutional change

Another reason to believe that a federal system is permanent is that moving away from a federal system would require extensive alteration of the Australian Constitution. While one observer[3] has rejected the view that the removal of federalism will require significant constitutional change, there is little support for this position. If ending federalism does require significant constitutional change, then we can be certain that federalism will not end. Australians have been very reluctant to change the Constitution and have never done so when the two major parties divide on the proposal. Leaders of the ALP, at the federal level, have usually been less sympathetic to a federal system. Leaders of the Liberal and National

Parties, however, have consistently supported a federal system (whether they respected federalism in practice is another question). Their opposition would make change impossible.

State politicians

State politicians (including those from the ALP) support a federal system. Their opposition to constitutional change is guaranteed and this opposition alone may be sufficient to prevent it. State politicians will support federalism because their positions depend on preserving this system. If anything, they are more likely to support moves out of a Federation (secession[4]) than any attempt to abolish the system.

Australian parties

Another reason to believe that a federal system will be a permanent feature of Australian politics is that states are central to the way that the major parties are organised. Most Australian parties are a network of branches that peak in state organisations. This is because the parties need to function as state organisations for state elections (so they can organise for elections and generate policies to be presented to voters). The nature of voting for the Senate and the fact that boundaries for the House of Representatives do not cross state borders mean that states are also important for organising federal election campaigns. Thus, the parties contain powerful state organisations whose members see the federal system as an important and necessary part of government and democracy in Australia.

QUESTION

Why is Australian federalism likely to persist long into the future?

3: IS A FEDERAL SYSTEM A SENSIBLE WAY TO ORGANISE GOVERNMENT AND DEMOCRACY IN AUSTRALIA?

From a practical point of view, a federal system will persist whether it makes sense or not. Discussing the question of whether a federal system is a sensible way to organise government and democracy in Australia is simply a means by which important aspects of Australian federalism can be brought to light. It can also be defended on the ground that thinking about Australian government and democracy should also involve imagining the best possible political system.

Our usual approach to such a question would be to divide our discussion into separate sections that covered the arguments that a federal system is a sensible way to organise government and democracy in Australia, and that it is not. We have taken a different approach to presenting alternative positions in this part to illustrate a different approach to answering this type of question.

The following discussion is in two main sections. In the first, we deal with the alternative points of view with respect to whether a federal system is a sensible way to organise government in Australia. In the second, we deal with the alternative points of view with respect to whether a federal system is a sensible way to organise democracy in Australia. The arrangement of each of these sections will be explained below. At this stage, readers are warned that this is a slightly more complex way to organise a response to the question.

Is a federal system a sensible way to organise government in Australia?

This section contains four sub-sections. These deal with the division of power created by federalism, the division of responsibility that results from this division of power, the effects of a federal system on the efficiency of government, and the consequences of the written constitution that is required in a federal system. Each sub-section comprises reasons to accept or reject the view that a federal system is a sensible way to organise government in Australia according to the theme of that sub-section.

Division of power
Yes, because the division of power is a check on government
One argument in support of a federal system is that it requires a division of power[5] which provides a check on governmental power. The Australian Constitution identifies a set of powers that are the federal Parliament's, and some powers that state and federal Parliaments share. The remaining powers go to state Parliaments. Dividing power in such a way ensures that no level of government acquires total control of our lives. Moreover, it means that one level of government cannot act alone to change everyone's way of life (and the chances of two levels of government working together on a controversial matter is small).

No, because the division of power prevents effective government
The division of power in a federal system is also a reason to reject a federal system in Australia. It is designed to ensure that neither level of government

has sufficient power to allow members of the political executive to introduce significant initiatives or reforms. Consequently, it prevents governments from making decisions that have a profound effect on people's lives.

A federal system is also designed to prevent change by denying power to both levels of government. Change will be prevented irrespective of whether those changes have been supported by a majority of voters. A federal system favours those people who do not want to see change, even when these people are in a minority. An extreme version of this position is the view that a federal system entrenches the power of those whose dominant positions derive from existing circumstances. A milder version of this position, which is the one put here, is that a federal system simply prevents significant reform by denying the capacity to govern to both levels of government.

Responsibility

Yes, because it makes sense for different levels of government to have responsibility for different aspects of people's lives

Another reason to support federalism results from the way that it allows different types of power to be given to the different levels of government. The Australian Constitution can be seen as an attempt to set out a set of powers that ought to belong to different levels of government. Not only does it make sense to divide powers between different levels of government, it also makes sense to attempt to divide the powers given to the different levels of government. Ensuring that the different levels of government have different powers means that they can take responsibility for specific aspects of people's lives, so that people can be reasonably confident that certain powers are likely to fall into the hands of those in a particular level of government.

Yes, because it makes sense for responsibility over areas that are more central to people's lives to be given to those who are closer to the people

The way that power[6] is divided in the Australian Constitution provides a further reason to support a federal system. The Australian Constitution can be understood to reflect an attempt to divide powers between state Parliaments, which are closer to the people, and a more remote federal Parliament. Most of the powers given to the federal Parliament in the Constitution concern our relations with foreigners, especially with other governments, and promoting and regulating trade within Australia. While other powers are given to the federal Parliament in s 51, the intention of those behind the introduction of the federal system seems clear from the predominance of provisions with respect to these two matters. The powers given to the federal Parliament relate to important matters. Under normal conditions, however, they are not central to people's lives.

Responsibility for education, health, and transport were left to members of political executives at the state level, which indicates that they were intended to have greater ongoing significance in our lives. This makes sense given that members of state political executives are distributed across the country, whereas the federal level of government emanates from only one place. The physical distance between members of state political executives and most Australians is much smaller than the distance between them and those of the federal political executive. The smaller populations of states relative to the Commonwealth means that those at the state level of government can interact more easily with and better understand citizens of their state.

No, because it creates confusion as to which Parliament has responsibility for a particular aspect of people's lives
One of the problems that derive from a division of power is that it makes our system of government confusing for people. If there is one group of politicians who are known to be in complete political control in a country, then people know who is responsible for making policy and for dealing with problems. They know to whom they should take their concerns and, if they are not satisfied with their response, from whom they should withdraw their support in an election. This is not only a problem for citizens. People in the different levels of government cannot be certain of their powers and the limits of their powers. In the different levels of government, this ambiguity is often used to obscure their particular responsibility for a problem.

Efficiency
Yes, because members of political executives that are closer to the people are better able to identify and satisfy people's needs
Another reason to support a federal system for Australia is that it is more efficient than a system of central government.[7] One aspect of its efficiency derives from the closer relationship that members of political executives at the state level have with their citizens. Members of political executives that are closer to the people better understand their needs, respond more effectively to their interests, and are quicker to react to their concerns than those in a central political executive.

Yes, because members of the different political executives compete with each other to demonstrate efficiency
Another reason to believe that a federal system is more efficient than other systems derives from the competition that develops between members of political executives at the state level and the state and federal levels. Part of this competition revolves around attempts to present themselves as the more effective

government. They compete with respect to their ability to develop solutions to problems or their ability to implement these solutions more effectively than another level of government. This is an almost necessary consequence of a federal system. State Premiers are often quick to publicise a situation in which they have been able to attract an industry, a major employer, or even a sporting event to their state (which usually means that they have been attracted away from another state).

No, because a federal system results in over-government and duplication

A reason to reject the view that federalism is a more efficient system is that it results in over-government and duplication of government agencies. Having more than one level of government means that there are more politicians and public servants than there would otherwise be. It will also result in the excessive growth of government because of 'empire-building' on the part of members of political executives, who wish to see the responsibilities of their level of government increase so that their status increases. It is also because members of political executives at different levels of government will monitor the activities of those at the other level of government. This may simply reflect a legitimate difference of view as to which level of government does and should have power over a particular aspect of people's lives.

No, because of a lack of mechanism for coordinating government

Central to the problems of over-government and duplication is an inability on the part of those at the two levels of government to work together. A federal system creates rivalry and a tendency to obscure responsibility for problems. No force exists within the system to make the two levels of government work together as effectively and as often as possible. One of the main reasons that this does not exist is that those at the two levels of government are more accustomed to competing with and criticising each other than they are with cooperating with each other. Indeed, there is too much political advantage to be gained from competition and criticism for this to be abandoned on a regular basis.

Even where there is cooperation at lower levels of government, Premiers will be prone to seek support by creating a sense that those at the federal level are insensitive to the particular needs of the citizens of their state. They will also invoke 'state's rights'[8] on occasions. State's rights refers to a general right to govern free from interference from those at the federal level of government. Tensions also exist between members of political executives of smaller and larger states[9] (who see their interests as different and who believe that resources are distributed unequally). In short, a federal system creates a degree of mistrust and competition that means that the various governments cannot work together effectively.

Written Constitution

Yes, because a written Constitution is the basis of government

A necessary feature of a federal system is a written Constitution[10] that establishes the powers that will be given to the different Parliaments created under this system. That this document is at the foundation of a federal system means that it cannot be changed by either Parliament. A written Constitution means that a legal document is the basis for government in Australia. This provides certainty and clarity with respect to the basic rules for government and ensures that they cannot be corrupted or ignored by members of political executives.

Yes, because a written Constitution allows the High Court to preside over Australian politics

As a written document, the Constitution requires interpretation. This means that a court, or something like one, must have the final decision as to the meaning of its provisions. Federalism is attractive to those who wish to see a legal body given responsibility for determining the outcomes of contests among those in political executives and Parliaments. Judges are more respected than politicians or public servants; so the central role of judges in a federal system reflects people's faith in judges.

Those who welcome a role for judges in politics may even go so far as to welcome the High Court as the body responsible for adapting the Constitution to the conditions of Australian society. The fact that the principal source of change to the Australian political system has been decisions handed down by the High Court provides support for the view that judges can be relied upon to reflect the needs of society in their judgments. The changes that High Court decisions have introduced to Australian government and democracy reflect changes to Australian society and its people's values.

An increase in the power[11] of the federal Parliament during and after World War II (as a result of the *Uniform Tax* cases) reflected the fact that Australia had become more than merely a limited and loose federal agreement between sovereign colonial Parliaments. The increase in the power of the federal Parliament as a result of a broader interpretation of the external affairs power in the 1970s (in the *Koowata* and the *Tasmanian Dam* cases) reflects most Australians' expectations concerning the power of members of the federal political executive. By protecting the right to free speech (in *Wills*, *Theophanous*, and *ACTV*), judges defended principles that Australians would want defended.

No, because a written Constitution is hard to change

One problem with a federal system, however, is the inflexibility that results from a written Constitution. This is a result of the fact that the Constitution has to be protected from being changed by the independent action of members of state or federal political executives. The Australian Constitution can only be changed by a referendum proposal that receives support from a majority of voters and from a majority of voters in a majority of states. This has contributed to making the Constitution very hard to change. It may not be the only reason that it is hard to change. However, that any change to the Constitution must be supported by federal Parliament will result in a level of resistance to the proposal, as voters will take it to be a grab for power by federal politicians and will not support it.

No, because a written Constitution allows the High Court to determine political outcomes

Another reason to oppose a federal system in Australia is that it will make the group who interprets its Constitution into one of the most powerful bodies in our political system. As was noted above, the members of the High Court have the power to shape Australian politics and society by making some of the most important political decisions in the country. That the High Court has caused a shift in power from the state governments to the federal government (in the *Uniform Tax* cases) and granted Indigenous Australians land rights (in the *Mabo* decision) means that the High Court has too much power. Having a significant amount of power is not a problem when those who possess this power are elected. When those who have it are not elected, however, the system is undemocratic and even dangerous.

Summary

Four features or effects of a federal system have been used as the basis for the discussion presented in this section. Each of these features or effects provided reasons to either support or reject federalism as a sensible way to organise Australian government. The division of power may be taken to control government, or it may be taken to prevent it. The division of responsibility may be taken to ensure that responsibilities were separated and the more important given to the level of government closest to the people. Alternatively, it may be viewed as providing a smokescreen that prevents citizens from finding out who is really responsible for a problem.

Federalism may be taken to make government more efficient, as it means that the level of government closer to the people can better gauge their needs and interests, and because federalism promotes competition between the levels of government and at the state level. On the other hand, federalism might be taken to undermine efficiency because it results in duplication of government agencies and over-government more generally. The written Constitution that is essential for a Federation might be taken to promote certainty and stability in Australian politics. It might also be thought to allow the High Court to adjust the Constitution to make it relevant to changes in Australian society. A written Constitution may also be seen to prevent any significant change to Australian society and to give too much power to a non-elected High Court.

Is a federal system a sensible way to organise democracy in Australia?

While many of its effects relate to government, federalism also has significant implications for democracy in Australia. In this section, we present alternative positions with respect to the question of whether federalism is a sensible way to organise democracy in Australia. We use four issues that bear upon this question. The first two concern the representation of individuals and communities in a federal system. The third relates to the effects that federalism has on the reflection of the popular will in the political decision-making process, and the fourth relates to accountability in a Westminster-style representative democracy.

Representation of individuals
Yes, because it produces greater opportunities for representation

One reason to believe that federalism is a sensible way to organise the representation of individuals is that it produces more opportunities for individuals to choose representatives.[12] Instead of a single choice of who they want to represent them Australians have two choices to make. The fact that Australians often vote for one party or coalition of parties at the state level and another at the federal level is evidence that they can distinguish between those who better represent them at the different levels of Australian government. Hence, the answer is yes because it provides more points of responsiveness within the Australian political system

The existence of federal and state Parliaments also ensures a greater level of responsiveness to demands from individual Australians within the Australian political system. In short, they have two sets of politicians and public servants towards whom they can direct demands. Those who find themselves unable to influence one group of politicians or public servants at one level of government have further opportunities to influence political decision-makers at another level. Indeed, they may well be able to use one level of government to put pressure on the other level. This opportunity would not be available to them in a single-level system of government.

No, because it results in representation fatigue

A federal system is not a sensible way to organise the representation of individuals because it results in representation fatigue (people getting tired of elections). The federal Parliament and most state Parliaments have three-year terms. Apart from the Victorian State Parliament, which introduced fixed four-year terms in 2003, these are not fixed terms, and early elections are common. If most Parliaments only last for two-and-a-half years, then elections may occur every second year. If occasional referenda and local government elections are added to this, then voters are faced with an almost endless process of campaigning and voting. This may produce thoughtless responses to superficial advertising campaigns, which is hardly democracy in action.

No, because it creates confusion among people who do not really understand the political system

Having two levels of government also creates confusion for most Australians, who are not particularly interested in politics and have not developed a deep understanding of our political system. This reflects the complexity of a federal system, in which the division of power is not obvious and is subject to change as a result of High Court decisions. Greater complexity reduces people's capacity to vote meaningfully and to direct their demands to the appropriate level of government. This reduces the level of democracy in a Federation.

Representation of communities
Yes, because states represent meaningful communities

Democracy does not relate simply to the representation of individuals, it also relates to the representation of communities.[13] This is evident in the fact that boundaries for electorates are drawn to reflect, as far as possible, communities of interest. The Australian states have extended histories and different cultures,

BOX 7.1
Secession in Western Australia (1933)

The Western Australian secessionist tradition began in the 1890s, when the Kalgoorlie goldfield miners started a movement to secede from the colony of Western Australia to join the other Australian colonies in a federation. Western Australia's position within the Federation continued to be called into question in that state, however. In 1933, a referendum was held to determine whether Western Australians wanted to secede to become an independent nation within the British Empire. Two-thirds of voters supported the proposal. The result of the referendum was tabled at a meeting of the Joint Select Committee of the British Parliament. The members of this committee rejected the proposal to secede, putting an end to this initiative, but not to the movement. In the 1970s, the secessionists resurfaced in Western Australia, with wealthy businessman Lang Hancock sponsoring a group called the Westralian Secession Movement. This group failed to win seats in the 1974 and 1977 elections.

so they reflect particular communities that could not be represented by anything other than a federal system.[14]

Yes, because a federal system protects those in less populated states
The Australian federal system also promotes the representation of communities by protecting people in the less populated states. Not only do these people have state Parliaments that can represent their collective interests, they also have the Senate, which was intended to provide an equal voice for people in these states. That the Senate has rarely acted as a states' house is not important; that Tasmanians elect as many Senators as Victorians is important. This makes the responses of Tasmanians to the major parties as important as those of Victorians.

No, because the states do not reflect communities
Even if a federal system can provide for the representation of communities, our federal system does not, as states are not communities. Those in urban centres in each state have more in common with each other than they do with country people. Those who live in tropical climates share more in the way of lifestyle and culture than those who live in more temperate climates. Southeast Queenslanders may have more in common with those in northern New South Wales than they do with north Queenslanders. Farmers have more in common with each other than they do with miners, cattle-growers, or wine producers, or those in manufacturing industries. State boundaries rarely reflect these differences and usually cut across them.

No, because it penalises those in more populated states
The Australian federal system does not promote the representation of communities because it protects the interests of people in smaller states. The federal system penalises those who live in more populated states by enhancing the voices of those in the less populated states. A system in which the voice of some people is given greater weight than their numbers require is undemocratic because the representation that a particular community receives should reflect the number of people in that community.

Reflection of popular will
Yes, because it creates two levels of connection between the people and political structures
The idea of a popular (or people's) will begins with the idea that the people have a shared, or collective, interest that they seek to express or promote. Representative democratic theory holds that the collective interest, or perhaps the collective interests of a majority of people, can be represented and promoted by the people's representatives. A federal system provides two avenues and processes through

which the people can speak through their representatives. It provides two sets of representatives who can represent and promote the will of the people. It follows from this that a federal system is more democratic than one that provides only a single connection between the people and their representatives.

Yes, because it gives more responsibility to those governments that are closer to the people and allows them to determine their lives
Federalism is also a sensible way to organise democracy in Australia because it creates a level of government that is closer to the people and, as a result, more likely to express and promote the people's will effectively. One of the main problems that can arise with centralised systems of government is that those at the centre are too far away from and out of touch with the lives, hopes, and ambitions of many people. For most Australians, members of state political executives are much closer and this makes them more likely to contain people who reflect the will of the people than those at a greater physical distance from them.

No, because it divides the people's will
A reason to argue that a federal system is not better able to reflect the people's will than a central system is that it divides the people's will. A centralised system requires one process through which people seek a collective response to social, economic, or political problems. A federal system, on the other hand, creates a situation in which two collective interests may be expressed. People are encouraged to see themselves as belonging to two communities, rather than one, and this makes them less able to express a single will.

No, because it sets one popular will against another popular will
Splitting the popular will is not a problem if the two avenues for expressing popular will express the same will. Our federal system, however, promotes conflict between states and between the different levels of government. It also produces division between the Houses of the federal Parliament that express the two popular wills. Rivalry between people and leaders of different states has long been part of Australian social and political life. Members of state political executives compete with each other to attract people and businesses. Rather than producing an effective expression of a single popular will, a federal system creates division between people. This makes it an ineffective way to express the will of the people.

Accountability
Yes, because there are more opportunities to hold politicians to account
Ensuring accountability is central to representative democracies. Federalism provides more moments at which the people can require that their representatives account

for their decisions and to punish them for misconduct.[15] The most important of these are elections, but other processes include petitions to Parliament, appeals to the ombudsman, and demonstrations of opposition to Cabinet policies. A federal system provides more opportunities to call members of political executives to account for their decisions and to punish them for unacceptable conduct.

Yes, because the different levels of government publicise the failures of the other levels
One of the most important ways in which a federal system produces accountability results from the fact that members of the political executive of one level of government have the resources, knowledge, and ability to reveal failures on the part of those in the other level. Accountability relies on the people being made aware of the actions and inaction of members of political executives. While Parliaments are supposed to provide this accountability, they don't. The fact that another level of government exists that contains skilled and knowledgeable politicians provides greater assurance that the people will be informed of the actions and inaction of members of the political executive of both levels of government.

No, because of confusion with respect to responsibility
A federal system reduces the level of accountability because of the confusion with respect to responsibility that a division of power creates. It may be theoretically possible to distinguish between the roles of the different levels of government in such a way that no one is under any doubt as to who is responsible for a particular policy area. Practically, however, responsibility blurs and members of political executives often use and increase uncertainty as to which level of government is responsible for a particular problem. Few Australians understand the division of power created by the Constitution, so they become confused as to which political executive they should hold accountable for a problem, especially in the case of inaction (for this gives rise to the preliminary issue of who was supposed to act).

No, because of vertical fiscal imbalance in the Australian federal system
The federal level of government now generates far greater revenue than the state level, which has the greater financial responsibilities. This creates a vertical fiscal imbalance that magnifies the difficulties associated with determining who is responsible for problems that arise in Australian society.[16] Members of state political executives, who are formally responsible for a particular problem, often claim that they lack the resources to do something. This problem may be overcome by reducing the level of vertical fiscal imbalance, or even by changing the Constitution, but it remains a problem for democracy in Australia.

Summary

Whether you treat federalism as a sensible way to organise democracy in Australia depends on how you view issues associated with the representation of individuals and communities. Federalism may give individuals more representatives and provide greater responsiveness than a centralised system. Yet it may produce representation fatigue and general confusion among many Australians. Federalism may provide for the representation of state communities and protect people in less populated states. On the other hand, states may not represent communities and federalism may penalise people in more populated states.

Federalism may produce a better reflection of popular will by creating two levels of connection between the people and those who serve them and give responsibility for important matters to those closer to the people. Alternatively, federalism may divide the people and set one expression of the people's will against the other expression of that will. Federalism may make sense because it provides more opportunities to achieve accountability in Australian politics and create conditions in which those at one level of government will expose failures on the part of those at the other level. Federalism might create confusion with respect to responsibility, however, especially in a situation in which vertical fiscal imbalance exists (as it does in Australia).

QUESTIONS

1 Does federalism impede government in Australia?
2 Is federalism consistent with the concept of representative democracy?

CONCLUSION

Federalism is, of course, here to stay. There are too many sources of resistance to change and not enough support for change to overcome this resistance. That we are stuck with a federal system does not mean that it is a sensible way to organise government and democracy in Australia. Understanding the alternative views on this issue may not only deepen our understanding of Australian federalism, but also provide an opportunity to begin some creative thinking about possibilities of change for government and democracy in Australia. If we decide that federalism is not a sensible way to organise our government and democracy, we are faced with the question about what type of system would be.

FURTHER READING

Introductory texts

Burmester, Henry, 1989, 'Federalism, the State and International Affairs: A Legal Perspective', in B. Galligan (ed.), *Australian Federalism*, Longman Cheshire: Melbourne.

Fletcher, Christine, 1998, 'Rediscovering Australian Federalism by Resurrecting Old Ideas', in D. Lovell, I. McAllister, W. Maley & C. Kukathas (eds), *The Australian Political System*, 2nd edn, Longman: South Melbourne.

Galligan, Brian, 1989, 'Federal Theory and Australian Federalism: A Political Science Perspective', in B. Galligan (ed.), *Australian Federalism*, Longman Cheshire: Melbourne.

Galligan, Brian, 1993, 'Federalism and Policy Making', in A. Hede & S. Prasser (eds), *Policy Making in Volatile Times*, Hale and Iremonger: Sydney.

Head, Brian, 1989, 'Federalism, the State and Economic Policy', in B. Galligan (ed.), *Australian Federalism*, Longman Cheshire: Melbourne.

Lovell, David, Ian McAllister, William Maley & Chandran Kukathas (eds), 1998, *The Australian Political System*, 2nd edn, Longman: South Melbourne.

Lucy, Richard, 1993, *The Australian Form of Government: Models in Dispute*, Macmillan: South Melbourne.

Specialist texts

Bennett, Scott, 2006. 'The Politics of the Australian Federal System', *Research Brief*, no. 4. Available at http://www.aph.gov.au/library/pubs/rb/2006-07/07rb04.pdf, last accessed 11 October 2006.

Coaldrake, Peter, 1992, 'Public Servants Serving the Public?: The Drive For Regionalism in the Queensland Public Sector', *Canberra Bulletin of Public Administration*, no. 70, October, pp. 102–4.

Farr, Ian, 1992, 'Regional Coordination at Local Level', *Canberra Bulletin of Public Administration*, no. 70, October, pp. 83–7.

Harris, C.P., 1992, 'Regionalism and Economic Development: Propping up or Strategic Choice—1', *Canberra Bulletin of Public Administration*, no. 70, October, pp. 91–8.

Hollander, Robyn & Patapan, Haig, 2007. 'Pragmatic Federalism: Australian Federalism from Hawke to Howard', *Australian Journal of Public Administration*, vol. 66, no. 3, pp. 280–97.

Painter, Martin, 1998, *Collaborative Federalism: Economic Reform in Australia in the 1990s*, Cambridge: Cambridge University Press.

Parkin, Andrew & Anderson, Geoff, 2007, 'The Howard Government: Regulatory Federalism and the Transformation of Commonwealth–State Relations', *Australian Journal of Political Science*, vol. 42, no. 2, pp. 295–314.

Sargent, John, 1992, 'Regionalism and Economic Development: Propping up or Strategic Choice—2', *Canberra Bulletin of Public Administration*, no. 70, October, pp. 98–101.

Twomey, Anne & Withers, Glenn, 2007, *Australia's Federal Future: Delivering Growth and prosperity*, A report prepared for the Council for the Australian Federation. Available at http://www.dpc.vic.gov.au/CA256D800027B102/Lookup/FederalistPaperAustralia'sFederalFuture/$file/Federalist%20Paper%20Australia's%20Federal%20Future.pdf, last accessed 13 June 2008.

Web sites

Australian Federation full text database: http://setis.library.usyd.edu.au/oztexts/fed.html

Australia's Centenary of Federation: Birth of a Nation, Growth of the Commonwealth: http://www.abc.net.au/Federation/fedstory/home.htm

Australia's Federation: http://museumvictoria.com.au/Federation/

Australian politics: http://australianpolitics.com

Federation of Australia: http://pandora.nla.gov.au/pan/41734/20040809-0000/www.statelibrary.vic.gov.au/slv/refresources/federation/

National Archives of Australia: http://www.naa.gov.au/

National Library of Australia: http://www.nla.gov.au

The Australian Constitution: http://www.aph.gov.au/senate/general/constitution/index.htm

Notes

1. For more information on federalism, see Painter (1997, pp. 194–6), Hughes (1998a, pp. 258–62), Jaensch (1994, pp. 293–4), and Ward & Stewart (2006, pp. 56–8).
2. For more details on conservative theory and conservatism in Australia, see Heywood (2002, pp. 46–50) and Maddox (2005, pp. 334–8).
3. See Craven (1988, pp. 85–121).
4. For more on secession, see Craven (1986, pp. 3–30).
5. For more information on the division of powers, see Painter (1997, pp. 196–7), Jaensch (1997, p. 71), and Singleton et al. (2006, pp. 30–1).
6. For more on the powers of the state and federal governments, see Maddox (2005, pp. 106–11), Hughes (1998a, pp. 268–71), and Singleton et al. (2006, pp. 35–6).
7. For more details on federalism and efficiency, see Maddox (2005, pp. 92–7, 100–3) and Singleton et al. (2006, pp. 99–101).
8. For more information on states' rights, see Summers (2006, pp. 149–50).

9 For more on the tensions between the states and between the state and the federal governments, refer to Maddox (2005, pp. 106–11), Summers (2006, pp. 150–4), and Singleton et al. (2006, pp. 103–5).
10 For more on written constitutions, see Jaensch (1994, pp. 290–1).
11 For more on the increases in federal power, see Maddox (2005, pp. 106–11).
12 For more on federalism and representation, see Maddox (2005, pp. 97–9).
13 For more on communities in Federations, see Maddox (2005, pp. 97–9).
14 For more on the benefits of federalism concerning regional diversity, see Sharman (1980, pp. 160–3).
15 For more information on accountability and federalism refer to Painter (1997, pp. 204–7) and Maddox (2005, pp. 92–9).
16 For more information concerning the fiscal relationships between the state and federal governments (including the vertical and horizontal imbalance), see Painter (1997, pp. 200–4), Summers (2006, pp. 138–46, 148, 149), Hughes (1998a, pp. 275–84), and Gillespie (1994, pp. 64–7).

8 Voting

LEARNING OBJECTIVES

- To recognise that while 'universal manhood suffrage' was introduced in the middle of the nineteenth century, it was not until the 1960s that all Indigenous Australians were granted the same right
- To understand the nature of voting
- Comprehend the reasons for supporting and opposing compulsory voting

INTRODUCTION

Most people associate democracy with voting. A democratic system is now defined as one in which citizens choose their leaders.[1] Most of the time citizens are voting for representatives who make important decisions on their behalf. Voting in a referendum is a more direct form of participation. It is an important part of Australian democracy because it gives the people the opportunity to change rules that shape the way that Australian politics functions. Voting is part of being an Australian citizen and, in Australia, voting is compulsory.[2]

Electoral systems have a profound effect on government and democracy in Australia. They determine who can vote, for whom they can vote, and how they vote. We thought, therefore, that a short history of voting in Australia would provide a useful background to this chapter. The second part of this chapter is devoted to discussions of the theoretical and practical aspects of voting. It begins with a general discussion of voting and finishes with some observations about voting in Australian federal elections. The third part is a discussion of the question: 'Should Australians vote in federal[3] elections?' This question was chosen because compulsory voting causes us to think less often about the reasons we vote than we might and because it provides an opportunity to examine some significant features of Australian government and democracy.

1. VOTING IN AUSTRALIA

Indigenous Australians used other methods for making important decisions, so voting only began after occupation by non-Indigenous peoples. The first voting was conducted in 1840, when councillors were elected to the Adelaide and Sydney City Councils. The first elections for an Australian legislature were held for the New South Wales Legislative Council in 1843. Elections were introduced for the Legislative Councils in Victoria, South Australia and Tasmania in 1850, in 1859 in Queensland and in 1893 in Western Australia. Voting for the federal Parliament began in 1901 (though state laws governed the election, as no federal laws existed).

While the existence of voting is an important indicator of the existence of democracy, the more important questions concern who can vote and for whom they could vote. Only men with £1000 could run for either the Adelaide or Sydney City Councils in 1840 and some of the men who voted were able to cast four votes in the same election. Only men who owned land worth at least £200 or paid rent of £20 per year could vote in the election to the New South Wales Legislative Council. South Australia was the first colony to allow all men over the age of 21 to vote in an election, and did so in 1856. Universal manhood suffrage, allowing all men to vote in elections, was then introduced in all Australian colonies.

Universal suffrage, allowing all people over the age of 21 to vote, was introduced in South Australia in 1895 (making that colony a leader in allowing women the vote). The other colonies followed, with Victoria being the last to do so (women were not allowed to vote in Victorian elections until 1908). The fact that the first federal election was conducted under state laws meant that only women in South and Western Australia voted. Women were allowed to vote under the first federal act governing voting (the *Commonwealth Franchise Act* of 1902). The Whitlam government passed laws to allow people over 18 to vote in 1973.

Indigenous Australians (Aborigines and Torres Strait Islanders) and South Sea Islanders (unless they were New Zealanders) were specifically excluded from voting in 1902. In 1949, however, Indigenous Australians were allowed to enrol and vote if they could do so in state elections (which they could in New South Wales, South Australia, Victoria, and Tasmania—Queensland gave Indigenous Australians the right to vote in 1965) or had been a member of the Australian Defence Forces. All Indigenous Australians were allowed to enrol and vote in 1962. Their enrolment and voting were not compulsory, however, until 1984.

Adults are compelled to enrol and to vote in most Australian elections. Only eighteen other countries enforce compulsory voting (thirteen do not enforce laws that require people to vote). Compulsory enrolment was introduced at the federal level in 1911, but it was not until 1924 that compulsory voting was introduced at that level (it had been introduced in Queensland in 1915, but the other states did not do so until after it was introduced, with South Australia the last state to introduce it in 1942). According to Tim Evans, then Director, Elections Systems and Policy with the Australian Electoral Commission, the fall in voter turnout between 1919 (71 per cent) and 1922 (60 per cent) was the main reason that compulsory voting was introduced.[4]

Ensuring that as close to as many Australians register a preference as to their leaders remains the principal justification for compulsory voting. We think this is more democratic because our legislature and the political executive it elects reflect the will of more Australians than would otherwise be the case. The crucial question, then, is whether voter turnout would decline significantly if voting were not compulsory. Louth and Hill argue that, without compulsory voting, voter turnout would fall 'considerably' and, more importantly, that elections would be less 'socially representative' (i.e., that fewer poorer, Indigenous, and non-Anglo-Australians would vote).[5] Australia may maintain a voting rate in the 70 per cent range, as Britain does, and not fall to the high 30 per cent levels that are common in US presidential elections, but even if voting rates were closer to that in the UK, which does not have compulsory voting, the issue remains as to whether elections would be socially representative.

> **QUESTION**
>
> Would you choose to vote if voting were no longer compulsory? If so, why?

2: SOME THEORIES AND PRACTICES ASSOCIATED WITH VOTING

In Australia, voting is the apparently simple practice of marking pieces of paper. For voting to be properly understood, however, it has to be considered in terms of some fundamental theoretical and practical issues. These cannot be dealt with fully here, but some discussion of these issues seems appropriate. The relevant theory is democratic theory, though the important point to note, in this context, is the way that democratic theory transforms into representative democratic theory. The discussion of practical issues, in the second section, begins with the actual way that voters are divided and votes are counted. The final section applies some of the preceding discussion to voting in the House of Representatives and Senate, finishing with a brief discussion of voting in referenda.

Theory

The main point to note in this section is that representative democracy is the only way to practise democracy.[6,7] The justification for this revision is to make democratic theory more practical. In democratic theory, citizens are actively and continuously involved in decision-making. This is not true of representative democracies. The transformation of democratic theory into representative democracy theory tells us a lot about voting in Australia.

Democratic theory
Government by elites

Two factors explain the development of modern democratic theory (democracy is often associated with the collective decision-making practices used in Athens in 508 BC).[8] The first factor behind the emergence of modern democratic theory is the problem caused by elite rule.[9] Members of elites are selfish. Political elites use their control to protect and promote their interests. They do so at the expense of everyone who is not part of the elite or is out of favour with the elite. Elites are often out of touch with the people, which usually results in corruption and almost always in mismanagement. In short, elite control is a highly unreliable and potentially disastrous form of government.

The other factor is the availability of information and communication technologies. Modern democratic theory, which tends to promote mass participation in politics, requires that citizens can participate in politics. For people to participate in policy-making they need information. The most basic information will concern opportunities to have our voice heard (elections, meetings, rallies, pickets, marches). Citizens also need information about how to participate in elections or at meetings. Finally, to participate effectively in a democracy, a citizen must have some understanding of the issues about which they must make decisions.[10]

People deciding and controlling their destiny
A central feature of modern democratic theory, then, is that the people make political decisions. In Australia, 'the people' usually includes all people over eighteen years of age. They also must be Australian citizens who are not serving extended periods in prison and who have not been declared mentally incompetent. The basic principle here is that the people, or citizens, should be involved in all decisions that affect their lives.

There are a number of reasons why, in democracy theory, citizens must be actively involved in the decisions that govern their lives. One reason is that an elite will govern in its own interests if they are allowed to do so; citizens also have a better idea about what is in their interests, so their involvement in decision-making will lead to better decisions. A third reason to involve citizens in decision-

BOX 8.1
Informal votes

A vote can be declared informal for a number of reasons. A ballot paper is informal if it has not been marked; if it has not received the official mark of the presiding officer; if it has writing on it that identifies the voter; if it has been marked in any way except in the prescribed official manner; if it does not indicate the intention of the voter clearly, and when it is not considered to be authentic. Informal votes are cast for a number of reasons. These include a lack of understanding as to how to correctly vote or as a protest against the party system, the candidates, or the electoral process itself. Since the 1983 federal election, there has been an average of 3.9 per cent informal votes for the House of Representatives and 4.3 per cent for the Senate.

Source: http://australianpolitics.com/elections/informal/

making is that it is good for each individual and for society as a whole. It is good for society because involving citizens in collective decision-making means that those in positions of power are more likely to address other people's interests and to consider a collective interest. It is good for individuals because it allows them to develop skills that they can use in their private and public lives and can help them to increase their self-confidence (or sense of political efficacy).

Direct or participatory democracy

In its fullest form, democracy requires ongoing participation from citizens in all of the important decisions that a community faces. This conception of democracy is usually referred to as direct or participatory democracy. It is called direct democracy[11] because citizens are directly involved in making decisions. It is called participatory democracy because citizens must actively participate in decisions and must do so on a regular basis. This can be taken to be the ideal form of democracy: in part, because it resolves the problems that result from elite domination, and in part, because it seems to be the only way to guarantee that citizens' views will be taken into account when important decisions are made.[12]

Representative democratic theory
Problems with direct democracy

While direct or participatory democracy remains the ideal form of democracy, representative democracy has come to dominate the way that we think about democracy. Some of the justifications for moving from direct to representative democracy are presented in this section. This makes some sense of the relationship between theories of direct democracy and those of representative democracy. Representative democracy is defended as the only way that something like democracy can be achieved because direct democracy requires too many people to be involved in too many decisions that they don't have time to consider.

An important postscript to this discussion, however, relates to the real possibility that modern information and communication technologies can help overcome these problems. Whether we must accept that representative democracy is the only way to achieve democracy, therefore, ought to be treated as a more open question than it is in this section. This issue will not be addressed, though, simply because Australian politics is based upon representative democracy and will remain so. One reason for this is that the major parties will defend the current system.

Too many people

Direct democracy poses significant logistical problems as a system for collective decision-making in Australia. There are simply too many Australian citizens spread too thinly across the country for continuous collective decision-making. No forum exists for our meeting. No method exists for getting us together. The only alternative to this is to break up Australian society into smaller self-governing units, but this won't happen. Indeed, modern nation-states appear to require a territory and population that may make direct democracy logistically impossible.

Too many decisions to make
Even if citizens could be brought together to participate in collective decision-making, a defender of representative democracy might argue that modern government remains too complex to be handled in this way. Modern governments have too many problems to manage and too many demands to deal with for direct democracy to work. Citizens can't be expected to understand all of the issues that arise across all of the areas for which modern governments are responsible. Even if they could be involved on an ongoing basis, citizens cannot be expected to develop sufficient understanding of the issues in, what for most people will be, their spare time.

Too limited a time
Not only do too many decisions have to be made in a representative democracy, these decisions must be made too quickly for representative democracy to work. We might imagine a forum in which all Australian citizens could be brought together. We might imagine an information distribution network that provides all of us with an understanding of the variety of issues with which we have to deal and the information that we need to deal with these issues. We might not be able to imagine, however, that we will be able to digest and respond to this information in time for our response to be meaningful and effective.

Democracy through representatives
These problems with direct democracy were the basis for a modification of democratic theory. Representative democratic theory emerged as a means to overcome problems with direct democracy. Indeed, representative democracy is the dominant conception of democracy, and direct democracy has been reduced to an impossible ideal. A democracy is now a system in which citizens express themselves politically through elected representatives. A rarely examined prerequisite for representative democratic theory, however, is that one person can make decisions on another person's behalf.

The primary purpose of voting is to select representatives who will determine the membership of Cabinet. They will also participate in a legislature, or lawmaking body, that produces the laws that govern our lives. Before the practical issues associated with the election of representatives are dealt with, though, three ideas about what representatives are will be discussed. These ideas provide a useful background for an understanding of the nature and role of representative bodies. The three views of the role of representatives discussed are as mirrors, agents, or trustees of the people.[13]

Representatives as mirrors

Representation as mirroring means that representatives reflect the composition of the community being represented. The idea here is that a representative body is a microcosm, or miniature version, of the community it represents. The justification for this approach is that decisions taken by a representative body ought to reflect the inputs that would be provided if the community as a whole had been involved in the decisions. However, the main question concerns which of the characteristics of 'the people' should be mirrored. The most obvious answer is to mirror demographic characteristics of the community (gender, age, race, and **ethnicity** are the most obvious criteria). Functional representation is another answer to this question. In this version, the attributes of the community being mirrored are the principal economic functions of its members.

> **ethnicity**: We use this word to refer to the cultural group with which a person identifies. These cultural groups are marked by differences in language, religion, diet, values and dress.

Representatives as agents

When representatives act as agents they assemble to communicate the views and carry out the wishes of the people they represent. Representatives have to return to the people they represent regularly to get their views on issues that will be decided by the representative assembly. Decisions taken by representatives as agents reflect the instructions that they have received from those they represent.

Representatives as trustees

A representative acting as a trustee plays such a different role from mirroring or agency that it could be argued that representation is not occurring. In this view, representatives make their own decisions as to how to promote the interests of the community they represent. Representatives do not respond directly to the wishes of their constituency and may be quite unlike them. They are entrusted with responsibility for deciding what is in the best interests of that community and for ensuring that this is achieved. They might even ignore the immediate demands of those they represent in order to promote their longer-term interests. Representatives acting as trustees appeal to this understanding whenever they make unpopular decisions.

Summary

Democratic theory is based on the view that the people who are affected by decisions ought to be the ones who make those decisions. This not only leads to decisions that better reflect the needs and interests of the people, but also ensures that elites do not dominate society through their control over political institutions and processes. A variety of problems make it impossible for all of the people to participate in all of the important decisions made within their community. A result of this was the development of representative democratic theory in which a small group of people met to make decisions on behalf of the people they represent. Representatives were to be chosen within specific communities and were to represent these communities. They may represent them in a variety of ways, each of which has significant consequences for representation. Mirrors act differently from agents, and both act differently from trustees.

Practice

When it comes to a representative democracy, the two main issues to address are how to group voters and how to count their votes. The following section is a discussion of different ways of creating boundaries[14] and the nature of the preference expressed in a vote. The second part is a discussion of the way that voting for the House of Representatives, Senate, and in referenda reflects specific choices about boundaries and the way that votes are counted.

Boundaries and numbers of representatives

Boundaries are not the only way to organise voters. Functional representation, for example, does not use boundaries. In this system, voters are grouped according to the type of work they do and choose representatives for their functional groups. In most representative democracies, though, voters are grouped according to where they live, i.e., their geographical location. Boundaries are drawn around voters who choose representatives for the people in their area (electorate). These boundaries are important in themselves. The number of representatives who are to be elected from within each boundary is also important.

We use boundaries because we believe that where people live significantly affects their interests. Whether this is true will depend, to a considerable extent, on the way that boundaries are drawn. Members of electoral commissions, the groups responsible for drawing up electoral boundaries, try to ensure that boundaries reflect communities of interest. This may not always be possible. One of the problems that electoral commissioners face is that the sizes of the electorates they are asked to create are too great to ensure communities of interest. This problem needs to be considered in terms of the number of representatives who are being elected. Few states, for example, reflect actual communities of interest (whatever Premiers might say). That twelve Senators represent the people in their state, however, may not make this a major problem.[15]

Single member constituencies (description and consequences)

Single member constituencies[16] are electorates in which people within the electorate boundaries elect only one representative. A consequence of this system is that voters feel and are closer to the people who represent them (representatives usually live in the electorate and always maintain a local electoral office). Being a part of the local community gives representatives a sense of local interests and issues and can result in election campaigns that are conducted on local community issues. This reflects the way that boundaries are designed to reflect communities of people with specific interests arising from the local conditions.

A problem with this sort of electorate is that votes can be wasted. Some people's votes will have no real effect, as they will have been directed to unsuccessful candidates or will be more than the 50 per cent of the votes (plus one) a candidate must win to be elected. Getting more than 50 per cent of the vote indicates that candidates are very suitable representatives of their electorate. When it comes to forming a Cabinet, however, the lack of impact of these excess votes may be significant. If enough votes are wasted in this way a party may receive more than 50 per cent of the overall vote, but not win a majority of seats in Parliament and not determine the membership of Cabinet.

Multiple member constituencies and proportional representation (description and consequences)

Multi-member constituencies[17] are electorates in which voters elect more than one representative. A consequence of this system is that representation and responsibility becomes less clear than for single member constituencies. Representatives are elected because of the support of a specific type of voter. They won't deny that they represent specific voters, but they will struggle to see themselves as representing all voters. The fact that multi-member constituencies are often significantly larger than single member constituencies is also important. This means that representatives from multi-member constituencies don't represent specific localities in the way that those who represent single member constituencies do.

An advantage of multi-member electorates is that they reduce vote wastage. Multi-member constituencies require some form of proportional representation. That is, to be elected a candidate requires a specific proportion (a fraction plus one) of the vote. If three representatives are to be elected, then a successful candidate will require one third of the votes plus one vote. There will always be a remainder of votes that were insufficient to provide a candidate with the required proportion (in this case, one-third minus three votes). This will be a much smaller fraction, however, than in a single member constituency (in which, depending on the way votes are counted, close to 50 per cent of the votes may be wasted).[18]

Vote weighting

The final issue that merits attention, in the context of voters, boundaries, and representatives, is vote weighting.[19] Vote weighting occurs when voters in electorates containing fewer voters elect the same number of representatives as voters in electorates with significantly more voters. Votes in numerically smaller electorates, then, are worth more, or carry greater weight, than votes in larger electorates. One of the justifications for weighting votes is that people in rural areas are more sparsely distributed, and electorates that contain the same number of voters as urban electorates would be massive and impossible for a representative to serve. Another argument, once again often presented to defend greater weight for rural votes, is that some regions of a country are more important to its economy or society than other regions. Vote weighting would reflect this importance and ensure that these regions were protected from being overwhelmed by larger numbers of voters in less economically or socially significant regions.

The nature of the preference expressed in a vote for a single member geographical constituency

The next question that arises concerns what a vote in a single member geographical constituency means. While all votes involve the expression of a preference, the exact nature of the preference expressed in a vote can vary. We will discuss this in the context of three different forms of voting: first-past-the-post, compulsory preferential, and optional preferential voting.[20] The view we present in the next section is that each of these forms of voting results in a different position being expressed in a vote.

First-past-the-post system

In first-past-the-post systems,[21] voters express only one thing in their vote. They must choose which of the candidates they most support. In this case, the votes are counted (tallied), and the candidate who gets the most votes wins. Candidates do not have to get a majority of the votes to be elected. A successful candidate will be the one who received more support (votes) than any other candidate. This means that the candidate who is elected will be the person preferred by more people; but not necessarily by a majority of voters.

Compulsory preferential voting

In compulsory preferential voting,[22] voters rank candidates according to the level of intensity of support they feel towards them. In this system, voters are required to express their preferences with respect to all candidates. Those candidates who have received the least number of highest preferences are eliminated and their votes given to the candidates next preferred by each voter. Candidates are systematically eliminated until a candidate emerges who is the least non-preferred by the majority of voters. 'Least non-preferred' may not make immediate sense, but it seems the most appropriate description of what is happening here. Preferences seem to us to work negatively in this system. At the end of the process, voters who despise both major parties end up having their preference for one of these parties used to elect a representative

Optional preferential system

Optional preferential systems[23] are those in which voters do not have to express more than one preference. They are not forced to rank all candidates from most preferred to least preferred. They can do so if they wish, but they can refuse to express any support for one or more candidates. They may express support for only one candidate, because no other candidate appeals to them. This method for counting votes lies somewhere between first-past-the-post and compulsory preferential voting. The winner may not be the candidate who most people prefer. Nor is the winner likely to be the candidate that is least 'non-preferred'. Rather, the successful candidate will be that candidate for whom the greatest number of voters was willing to express some level of support.

BOX 8.2
Counting votes for the House of Representatives

The members of the House of Representatives are elected using a compulsory preferential voting system in single-member electorates, or constituencies. Counting of the vote begins at 1800 hours on polling day and the winning candidate needs to gain 50 per cent + 1 of valid votes. If no candidate has an absolute majority of first preferences, then the candidate with the least number of first preferences is removed and their second preferences are distributed to the other candidates. This process is repeated until one candidate has obtained an absolute majority, or 50 per cent + 1, of the votes.

Source: http://www.aec.gov.au/Voting/counting/hor_count.htm

Voting to elect members to the House of Representatives and Senate

Voting to elect members to the House of Representatives

The system used for voting to select members of the House of Representatives[24] is a combination of single member constituencies and compulsory preferential voting. Single member electorates result in area-specific representation and vote wastage. Compulsory preferential voting allows the Liberal and National Parties to function as a coalition because they can swap preferences. A combination of single member electorates and compulsory preferential voting tends to favour the major parties. For no matter whom they may prefer as a representative, in the end, voters will be forced to express a preference for a candidate from one of the major parties, and it is likely that this preference will be counted.

BOX 8.3
Counting votes for the Senate

Senators are elected using a proportional representation voting system in multi-member electorates. A Senator needs to receive a certain percentage of votes to be elected; this percentage is known as a quota. The quota is arrived at by the following equation: Number of Formal Votes/(Number of Seats + 1) + 1. In a half-Senate election, a quota is 1/7th + 1 (or 14.3 per cent) of the valid votes, and in a full Senate election 1/13th + 1 (or 7.7 per cent).

Any candidate who has achieved the required quota of votes is elected. Most candidates elected in this first round of counting usually have more votes than they required; these surplus votes (Total Number of Votes − Quota = Surplus Votes) are then redistributed among the candidates who have not achieved a quota, starting with the largest surplus. The transferred votes are not considered to be of equal value to first preferences, however, as it is impossible to decide which votes should be transferred and which taken to have elected the Senator whose surplus votes are being transferred. A transfer value for surplus votes is determined by dividing the number of surplus votes by the total number of votes for Senators who have achieved a quota. These transferable votes are then distributed downwards among the remaining candidates. If all of the positions are not filled by this first redistribution, the next largest surplus is redistributed. This process is followed until all vacancies are filled. If all of the surplus and transferable votes have been counted and not all positions have been filled, the candidates with the highest number of votes are elected.

Source: http://www.aec.gov.au/Voting/counting/senate_count.htm

BOX 8.4
Group voting ticket in the Senate

Proportional representation was a very complex voting system before 1984, as voters had to number every candidate on the ballot paper. This could mean indicating preferences for as many as eighty candidates. This complexity led to a high percentage of informal votes. In the 1983 election, the average number of informal votes across the states was 9.9 per cent. Since 1984, however, political parties have been able to register an order of preferences with the Australian Electoral Commission.

A ballot paper is divided into two sections. A '1' placed next to the party's name in the top section indicates that the voter wants his or her votes to be distributed according to the order of preferences registered by that party. The bottom section allows voters to register preferences for all candidates, in whatever way they like. 95.2 per cent of Australian voters used the top section in the 2001 election.

Source: http://www.aec.gov.au/Voting/How_to_vote/Voting_Senate.htm

Voting to elect members to the Senate

Voting for the Senate[25] is based on multi-member constituencies and proportional representation.[26] The main effect of this combination is that it is more likely to result in candidates from minor parties and independents winning sufficient votes to gain seats in the Senate. When neither of the two major parties has a majority in the Senate, independents and representatives of minor parties gain the 'balance of power' in that house. Their votes are required for the passage of legislation and means that they can provide an alternative view in Senate committees. This has contributed to the Senate's capacity to constrain the power of the political executive and to influence the content of legislation.

Vote weighting is also a significant feature of the system for electing the Senate. The Constitution requires that all states have an equal number of representatives. This means that a Tasmanian's vote is worth around 140 times that of a voter in New South Wales.[27] The development of the two-party system has reduced the significance of vote weighting in the Senate, however, as Senators vote as party representatives and not as state representatives. Senators from states with smaller populations do not combine, then, to oppose those from states with larger populations.

Referenda[28]

The other times at which Australians are called upon to vote in federal politics is in a referendum. Referenda can be called to find out what voters know about a variety of issues, such as allowing Aborigines to vote, conscription, determining a retirement age for judges, and choosing our national anthem. Most referenda, though, concern changes to the Constitution. Section 128 of the Constitution requires that changes to the Constitution must be approved in a referendum by an overall majority of voters and by a majority of voters in a majority of states. This is more like direct democracy, but is slightly complicated by the requirement for a double majority.

Australians have been reluctant to alter the Constitution. This is partly because all referendum proposals must be supported, if not sponsored, by Cabinet. Australians, like most other people, are suspicious about the motives of politicians. Voters usually see constitutional changes as attempts to increase the power of the members of the federal political executive. Political executives usually sponsor referendum proposals and this often means that the opposition will call on voters to reject the proposal. Negative campaigns are easier to run and are more likely to appeal to the distrust that voters feel towards politicians. An alternative explanation for the lack of constitutional change is that Australians are conservative.

QUESTION

What is modern democratic theory? In what ways is it evident in Australia?

3: SHOULD AUSTRALIANS VOTE IN FEDERAL ELECTIONS?

This might be considered a surprising question to pose here, as it will lead to the presentation of reasons not to vote. One reason to vote is that Australian citizens will be fined if they don't vote (though if they do not register as a voter they may be hard to find and more likely to escape the $20 or $50 fine;[29] the penalty for failing to register is $50).[30] This is a compelling, and for most of us decisive, reason to vote. So most of us will continue to vote without thinking too hard about why we do it. We present reasons not to vote, in part, to encourage readers to think about why they vote.

Eight reasons why people should vote (the Yes case) are presented first. These are that there is a moral obligation, there is a direct relationship to democratic principles, there are benefits (symbolic, personal, and social) that accrue from voting, and that it helps those who are discontented with the effects that the major parties have on Australian politics because they might be able to get an

BOX 8.5
Election results

House of Representatives: 2004, 2007

Election results	2007	2004
Liberal Party	55	74
National Party	10	12
Country Liberal Party	0	1
Australian Labor Party	83	60
Independent	2	3
Total	150	150

Senate results after the 2004, 2007 federal elections

Election results	2007	2004
Liberal Party	15	17
National Party	2	2
Country Liberal Party	1	0
Australian Labor Party	18	14
Democrats	0	0
Greens (WA)	0	1
Australian Greens	3	1
One Nation	0	0
Harradine Group	0	0
Family First	0	1
Country Labor Party	0	0
Independent	1	0
Total	40	36

Source: http://www.aec.gov.au

independent or member of a minor party elected. Other reasons to vote are the effect voting can have on those who live in marginal House of Representatives electorates, and to stop a candidate from losing their deposit. In this context, we do not discuss the avoidance of a fine as the reason to vote because such a reason needs no elaboration.

Nine reasons are presented in support of the No case. These are that voting is a tiresome chore, people feel resentful about being forced to vote, voting just encourages politicians, elections are really all about spin and not principle, and that all politicians lie. Other reasons not to vote are that political choices are too complex to be dealt with in a single vote (this applies to voters who know little about Australian politics), there is no real choice, at least with respect to the House of Representatives, as candidates from the major parties look and sound the same, and that voting in a safe House of Representatives seat is ineffectual.

Yes case

Moral obligation

Australians should vote in federal elections because we have a moral obligation to do so. Voters are citizens and beneficiaries of the political system. While citizenship is often understood to imply rights, it also ought to be understood to involve obligations or duties. Australians should recognise that, as members of a democratic system, we have an ethical obligation to participate in elections and referenda.[31] Our political system requires little from us and to refuse to undertake this one activity would be a moral failure on our part.

Democratic principle

Voting in federal elections supports and maintains the democratic nature of the society in which we live. If Australians believe that a representative democracy is the best system under which to live, then we ought to support this system by engaging in the one practice that is basic to a representative democracy. To support the right to vote but not engage in the practice of voting is absurd. If someone believes that voting is important, then the only way to demonstrate this is to actually vote.

Symbolic/affective benefits

Voting helps us to feel part of a larger community. Individual life can be an isolated and isolating experience for many people. The act of voting in an election is a moment when individuals can overcome that sense of isolation, and remind ourselves that we are part of, and count in, a greater whole. It is a moment in which we can assert our involvement and know that our actions will be recognised within our community. Voting in an election or referendum may not be much, but it is one of the few acts in which almost all Australian adults participate.

Personal benefits

Voting promotes our personal interests. It provides the opportunity to choose candidates who will represent our electorate in the way that we want it represented. Voting for a representative who comes from a particular party will also allow us to vote for policies that are more beneficial to us as individuals than the policies put forward by the other party. In short, we can use our vote to try to elect candidates who support policies that will improve our personal position.

BOX 8.6
Safest and most marginal seats

The Australian Electoral Commission classifies a seat as marginal, fairly safe, or safe. A seat is classified as marginal if it is held by less than 56 per cent of the vote after the full distribution of preferences. A seat is classified as fairly safe when it was won with between 56 to 60 per cent of the vote after the full distribution of preferences, and safe when it was won with over 60 per cent of the vote.

The ten safest federal seats in Australia before the 2007 election

Safest Federal Seats	Electorate	State	Two Party Preferred	Party
1	Mallee	Vic	74.75	NP
2	Murray	Vic	74.08	LP
3	Batman	Vic	71.32	ALP
4	Grayndler	NSW	71.19	ALP
5	Melbourne	Vic	71.14	ALP
6	Maranoa	Qld	71.05	NP
7	Riverina	NSW	70.85	NP
8	Mitchell	NSW	70.68	LP
9	O'Connor	WA	70.39	LP
10	Barker	SA	69.88	LP

(continued)

The ten most marginal seats in Australia before the 2007 election

Marginal Federal Seats	Electorate	State	Two Party Preferred	Party
1	Hindmarsh	SA	50.06	ALP
2	Kingston	SA	50.07	LP
3	Swan	WA	50.08	ALP
4	Macquarie	NSW	50.47	LP
5	Bonner	Qld	50.51	LP
6	Wakefield	SA	50.67	LP
7	Cowan	WA	50.78	ALP
8	Parramatta	NSW	50.83	ALP
9	Makin	SA	50.93	LP
10	Bendigo	Vic	50.96	ALP

Source: http://www.aec.gov.au/About_AEC/Publications/Newsfiles/2007/131.htm

Social benefits

Voting in federal elections also allows us to participate in decisions that will have profound effects on the nature of society as a whole. In short, we can use our vote to elect representatives who will seek to create the type of society in which we want to live. This is not to the same as voting to create a society in which we will be better off. Some voters support a party even though they will pay more money in taxes than they would under the other major party. They might do this because, even though they will pay more taxes, they believe that Australia will be a better place to live. Australians who believe that crime rates fall when wealth is spread more evenly will support higher taxes for wealthier people, even when they are wealthy. They might decide that staying wealthy, but having to live in a 'gated' community, protected by high walls and extensive security systems, makes no sense. Voting for a party that will promote the sort of society we want to live in, then, is a different reason to vote from voting to promote our own interests.

To get a representative from a minor party or an independent elected

One of the reasons that many people do not want to vote is that they dislike the way that Australian politics works. Australian politics is dominated by the major parties, and one way to express our frustration with the major parties is to support an independent. This is particularly important in voting for the Senate.

The system of proportional representation means that vote wastage is not as high as it is for the House of Representatives. This means that there is a greater chance that a vote will have an effect. By electing representatives from minor parties and independents who can play an active role in controlling and scrutinising the actions of the political executive, we help limit the dominance of the major parties. To put it as the Australian Democrats once did, we can use our vote for the Senate to 'keep the bastards honest'.

We might be in a marginal House of Representatives seat
A sixth reason to vote only applies to voters in marginal House of Representatives electorates. We can predict the result for a large majority of House of Representative seats and this makes voters in the other electorates crucial, as they are likely to determine the result of the election. These are often seats in which the previous winning majority was very small. Some seats have been won by as few as forty votes. Every vote is important in an electorate like that. If you live in one, then your vote is worth casting. You might not be able to influence the overall result, but you could certainly make (or break) someone's political career.

Someone might not lose their deposit
People who want to run for election must get signatures from fifty eligible voters and pay a deposit to the Commonwealth Electoral Commission (in 2008 the amounts were $1,000 for the Senate and $500 for the House of Representatives).[32] The deposit is to deter candidates who are not serious and possibly to cover some of the costs of an election. Candidates who do not receive 4 per cent of the primary votes lose their deposits.[33] Helping candidates to recover their deposits is a reason to vote.

No case

It is a tiresome chore
Having to vote might well disrupt our enjoyment of a fine and pleasant Saturday. Alternatively, we could object to being forced out of our home on a cold, wet, or windy day. Our time is valuable and, for most of us, free time is scarce. Not voting would free us up for more important things, like watching television, going for a drive, reading, or exercising. We can make a postal or pre-poll vote, which will save our Saturday, but we will have to organise them for ourselves (http://www.aec.gov.au/Voting/Voting_Special_Circumstances.htm).

Because we are forced to
Another reason not to vote is that we are required to do so. Not to vote under these conditions is to reject the use of force or compulsion in a democratic society.

Not to vote represents a rejection of any constraint on our freedom to do what we want to do. Nobody likes being told what to do and it is even worse when we are being threatened with some penalty if we do not do it. This is particularly the case when politicians are forcing us to do things. If we live in a democracy, then we should be allowed to choose for ourselves. We should be able to choose not to vote. Not voting, when we are legally required to vote, is to express our commitment to democratic principles.

It just encourages them
Voting might be construed as approving of the political system or of the Cabinet whose party attains a majority of seats in the House of Representatives. As has been discussed, in a system with compulsory preferential voting, we often end up being taken to have given support to a candidate from one of the major parties because our preferences have been exhausted. What might be our final, and reluctant, choice between candidates from the two major parties becomes the choice that will determine which of these candidates wins. We end up being taken to have voted for one of these candidates.

If that candidate's party gains a majority in the House of Representatives, we will be treated as if we gave a mandate to the Cabinet formed by that candidate's party. But all we might be indicating is that we could think of more reasons not to vote for the candidate from the other major party. That this will be taken as support for a Cabinet seems bizarre.[34] Not to vote is the only way to avoid appearing to support a Cabinet formed by a major party that we dislike only marginally less than the other major party.

It's all just 'spin'
A fourth reason not to vote is that elections have become a public relations exercise in which one set of 'spin doctors' opposes another set of 'spin doctors'. Election campaigns become tests of the skills of political advisers, who are employed by the major political parties because of their marketing skills. Elections are marketing campaigns in which Prime Ministers and their parties are sold to the people, like cars. Prejudices, fantasies, and fears are manipulated to make the sale. Voting is like shopping. The principles are the same, and elections become tests of the effectiveness of advertising campaigns.

We have probably been lied to anyway
Another reason not to vote is the likelihood that most of the people standing for election are not telling the truth. Mostly, they are simply not telling us everything, but sometimes they're lying. There are a variety of justifications for withholding information or lying. One is that voters do not really want to hear the truth. We want to be told that there are simple answers for very complex problems. We want

to be told that political executives can actually control what happens in our society. We want to be told that voting matters. Another justification for withholding information or lying is that it is for the greater good of the community.[35] A lie told to keep the other major party out of office is, in this construction, a public service. It is saving us from ourselves. Besides, if members of one party assume that members of the other major party are lying, then they have to counter these lies (perhaps with a lie). Not to vote is to show that we never believe anything that any politician tells us.

The choice is too complex to make in one moment
The sixth reason not to vote is that voting reduces very complex decisions to a single choice. One vote every two to three years is a poor substitute for actually having input into government decisions. Voters are presented with complicated combinations of policies that deal with a variety of problems and issues, and are then given a piece of paper that is going to decide who the political executive is for two to three years. That all we can do is write numbers on that piece of paper increases the absurdity of the situation. Voting is making politics simple when it is complex. Voting, in short, is stupid.

We probably have not considered most of the issues
Even if voting is not stupid, most voters are. Partly because we think that putting a number on a piece of paper could actually represent a meaningful act, but mostly because few of us have given more than a few minutes' serious consideration to the multitude of complex issues raised in any election. That the personal appeal of party leaders can decide the outcome of an election is a clear indication that elections are not about rational choices. Even if we assume that a rational choice is possible, few of us seem to make them. Many of us will, with little reflection, vote for the same party, in election after election. Some of us will vote for someone because they 'look' right. Some of us might even vote for a person because they thought they heard something about how they treat their family. Most of us know so little about what we are doing when voting that it makes no sense to vote.

There is no real choice
Possibly, the only thing that saves federal (and most state) elections from being complete debacles is that no real choice exists, at least when it comes to the Lower House. Compulsory preferential voting means that most of us will end up voting for things staying more or less the same. The differences between the two major parties are so small that we will end up voting for more of the same, no matter which party gets a majority of seats in the House of Representatives. We might vote for an independent who manages to be elected to the House of

Representatives, but he or she is unlikely to be able to do anything because of the control that members of Cabinet exert over the Lower House.

The Senate is only marginally different. Here, independents and minor parties can frustrate members of the federal Cabinet and other Ministers. While we might be sympathetic towards stopping these politicians from getting what they want, stopping a political executive for which you've voted in the Lower House doesn't make much sense. Independents in the Senate have also used their control over the balance of power to do deals that benefit their state.

We are in a safe seat

A final reason not to vote, at least for the House of Representatives, is that we live in a safe seat. There are usually only about a dozen electorates that are crucial to the result in any election. Occasionally, a seat that is not designated marginal changes hands, but this is simply an exception that proves the rule. The other marginal seats will still determine the final outcome. We probably live in a safe seat. Therefore, the chance that our vote will matter is small. Our vote may have some effect in the Senate, but not much.

Summary

We do not want to encourage readers to break the law, so we call on every eligible Australian to enrol and vote. Moral and democratic principles also require that we vote. The benefits that accrue from voting far outweigh any inconvenience that might be experienced. Voting is also the only way to register dissatisfaction with the major parties. The opportunity to influence an election outcome is another important reason to vote. So, we should vote, even though we live in a safe seat or do not understand either the system or the issues. The view that representative democracy is such a pathetic approximation of democratic theory that voting is little more than a farce is not a good enough reason to refuse to vote. Having no choice and being forced to vote are also insufficient grounds to refuse to vote. While concerns with spin and lying are grounds for greater participation and not less. We are not encouraging you to break the law by not voting, but we take no responsibility if you think that the reasons for not voting presented above, are valid.

QUESTION

Does compulsory voting provide a satisfactory basis for representative democracy?

CONCLUSION

Most Australians think they live in a democracy. They believe this because they are not troubled by the way that representative democratic theory bears a limited resemblance to democratic theory. While direct democracy may be more readily available due to new information and communication technologies, representative democracy is likely to remain the dominant understanding and form of democracy. Appreciating the theoretical and practical aspects of the representative democratic system practiced in Australia is important to understanding some of its effects on government and democracy because it has important effects on the nature of voting and the meaning of a vote. Indeed, the representative democratic system has profound implications for any answer to the question of whether we should vote in federal elections. Of course, we argue that all Australians should vote on principle and because this is the means by which they might influence Australian politics.

FURTHER READING

Introductory texts

Chaples, Ernie, 1997, 'The Australian Voters', in R. Smith (ed.), *Politics in Australia*, Allen & Unwin: St Leonards.

Craig, John, 1993, *Australian Politics: A Source Book*, 2nd edn, Harcourt Brace: Sydney.

Farrell, David, 1998, 'The Study of Electoral Systems', in D. Lovell, I. McAllister, W. Maley & C. Kukathas (eds), *The Australian Political System*, 2nd edn, Longman: South Melbourne.

Fenna, Alan, 2001, *Essentials of Australian Government*, Tertiary Press: Croydon.

Goot, Murray, 1994, 'Class Voting, Issue Voting and Electoral Volatility', in J. Brett, J. Gillespie & M. Goot (eds), *Developments in Australian Politics*, Macmillan: Melbourne.

Gray, Gary, 1998, 'The Political Climate and Election Campaigning', in D. Lovell, I. McAllister, W. Maley & C. Kukathas (eds), *The Australian Political System*, 2nd edn, Longman: South Melbourne.

Jaensch, Dean, 1994, *Parliament, Parties and People: Australian Politics Today*, 2nd edn, Longman Cheshire: Melbourne.

Lovell, David, Ian McAllister, William Maley & Chandran Kukathas (eds), 1998, *The Australian Political System*, 2nd edn, Longman: South Melbourne.

McAllister, Ian, 1992, *Political Behaviour: Citizens, Parties and Elites in Australia*, Longman Cheshire: Melbourne.

McGuinness P.P., 1998, 'Practical Protest Against the Compulsory Vote', in D. Lovell, I. McAllister, W. Maley & C. Kukathas (eds), *The Australian Political System*, 2nd edn, Longman: South Melbourne.

Specialist texts

Hinich, Melvin & Michael Munger, 1997, *Analytical Politics*, Cambridge University Press: Cambridge.

Jaensch, Dean, 1995, *Election!: How and Why Australia Votes*, Allen & Unwin: St Leonards.

McNutt, Patrick, 2002, *The Economics of Public Choice*, 2nd edn, Edward Elgar: Cheltenham.

Web sites

Australian Electoral Commission: http://www.aec.gov.au/index.htm
Australian politics: http://australianpolitics.com
Electoral Council of Australia: http://www.eca.gov.au
National Library of Australia: http://www.nla.gov.au

Notes

1. Few of us consider one-party states as democracies. See, though, Macpherson 1966 (esp. pp. 12–34).
2. For more on compulsory voting, see Painter (1997, p. 177), Costar (2006, pp. 190–1), Lucy (1993, pp. 97–9), and Singleton et al. (2006, pp. 278–80).
3. While this discussion, and this chapter, is focused on voting in federal politics, many of the points remain valid with respect to state politics.
4. See Evans (2006, p. 5).
5. Louth & Hill 2005: 34.
6. For more on democratic theory, see Heywood (2002b, pp. 27–71) and Jackson (1997, pp. 32–42).
7. For more on representative democracy, see Heywood (2002b, p. 70) and Jackson (1997, pp. 45–6).
8. See Maddox (2005, pp. 4–9). The reason that we refer to modern democratic theory is that Athenian democratic theory denied participation to women, slaves, and resident aliens and, as a result, reproduced some of the forms of elite rule discussed here.
9. For more on elite theory see Mills (1959, pp. 3–29), Bottomore (1971, pp. 7–23), and Parry (1969, pp. 30–63).
10. We are sorely tempted to try to sneak the ability to read and write into the list of functional requirements for a modern democracy. This could be taken even further, and a capacity to understand the issues that might arise from collective decision-making in a democracy might be added to the requirement for a democracy. These are not functional requirements for a democracy, however, so these temptations have to be resisted. We might note, however, that many of those men who opposed extending the right to vote (franchise) to workers and women did so because they argued that these classifications of people would not be able to make sound judgments. They justified restricting the right to vote to a limited number of men because in their view it would result in better government. Eventually, these men lost the debates, mostly because other men did not share their views, and the franchise was extended.

11 For more on direct democracy, see Heywood (2002b, pp. 70 and 72–3), Jackson (1997, pp. 42–5), and Maddox (2005, pp. 4–9).
12 The latest approach to direct democracy is referred to as deliberative democracy. For more on deliberative democracy, see Dryzek (2000), Wallington & Barns (2001), Uhr (1993), and Pettit (2001). For a discussion of the practicality of deliberative democracy, see Head (2007) and Shelly (2001).
13 For a classic discussion of representation, see Pitkin (1967).
14 For more on electoral boundaries, see Painter (1997, pp. 186–9) and Costar (2006, p. 194).
15 Electoral commissioners are not required to ensure that all electorates contain the same number of voters; though, in federal elections a 10 per cent variation in House of Representative electorates is allowed. Much greater variation is evident in state elections and in voting for Senators.
16 For more on single-member constituencies, see Painter (1997, pp. 178–9) and Lucy (1993, p. 99).
17 For more on multi-member constituencies, see Painter (1997, pp. 178–9).
18 A first-past-the-post system may result in vote wastage of greater than 50 per cent. Preferential voting (sometimes called single transferable vote) can reduce vote wastage. Compulsory preferential voting can reduce it even further. Both may change the nature of a vote, however, as is discussed in this chapter.
19 For more on vote weighting, see Lucy (1993, pp. 100–2).
20 A preferential voting system can also be referred to as a system of single transferable votes (STVs).
21 For more on the first-past-the-post voting system, see Stewart & Ward (2006, pp. 96–8), and Singleton et al. (2006, p. 273).
22 For more on compulsory preferential voting, see Ward & Stewart (2006, p. 105), Costar (2006, pp. 191–3), Lucy (1993, p. 90), and Singleton et al. (2006, p. 274).
23 For more on optional preferential voting, see Costar (2006, p. 193) and Singleton et al. (2006, p. 275).
24 For more on the voting processes and consequences of the House of Representatives, see Painter (1997, pp. 181–2).
25 For more on the voting processes and consequences of the Senate, see Painter (1997, pp. 182–4).
26 For more on the proportional representation voting system, see Ward & Stewart (2006, pp. 99–101), Costar (2006, pp. 194–7), Lucy (1993, pp. 91–2), and Singleton et al. (2006, pp. 275–7).
27 Australian Bureau of Statistics data for June 2004 indicates that the population in Tasmania was 482,236 and New South Wales 6,720,791.
28 For more information on the processes involved in changing the Australian Constitution and on referenda in Australia, see Galligan (1995, pp. 110–32) and Singleton et al. (2006, pp. 57–64).
29 Eligible people who fail to vote may have to pay either $20 if they simply respond to the penalty notice, or $50 if the matter is heard in court (*Commonwealth Electoral Act* s 245 (5C iii) and s 245 (15)). For a copy of the *Commonwealth Electoral Act* of 1918, visit http://www.comlaw.gov.au/ComLaw/Legislation/ActCompilation1.nsf/0/67A68060AFEEC305CA25736A0004B0D7/$file/CwlthElectoral1918_WD02.pdf
30 John Stuart Mill advocated a system of multiple voting. See http://plato.stanford.edu/entries/mill/#13
31 For interesting ideas as to whom we owe this obligation, see Hill (2002).
32 See *Commonwealth Electoral Act* s 170.
33 See *Commonwealth Electoral Act* s 173.
34 We are reminded of the old anarchist slogan that goes something like 'If voting could change anything, it would be illegal'.
35 Members of Cabinet often use this justification, as national security can require that the truth be withheld from the people.

Parties

LEARNING OBJECTIVES

- Understand the roles of political parties and their effects on representative democracy in Australia
- Understand the nature of the two-party system
- Consider whether the two-party system has a positive effect on government and democracy in Australia
- Be able to understand the alternative cases on the question of whether Australian politics is better off with the two-party system than it would be without it
- Be able to consider whether the major parties are more similar than they are different

INTRODUCTION

two-party system: We refer to Australia as having a two-party system even though, technically, three parties, and not two, dominate our government. We tend to treat the Liberal–National Party Coalition as if it is one party, as Cabinets are formed from members of either the Labor Party or Coalition parties and their dominance over cabinet means that it makes sense to refer to our system as a 'two-party' system.

representative democracy: Used to refer to a political system in which the people choose representatives who are to govern on their behalf. Representatives take decisions, make laws, and introduce policies, until they are removed from office in an election. We refer to a system in which the people make decisions, make laws, and introduce policies for themselves as 'a direct democracy'.

Most of this chapter is devoted to a discussion of the two-party[1] system as it operates in Australia. The **two-party system** has dominated Australian federal politics for most of its existence. The major **parties** determine the nature of political debate and what we think is politically possible. Thinking of Australian politics without the two-party system is difficult for most Australians because we have grown up with it. Our concentration on major parties is not intended to suggest that minor parties and independents are not important. Indeed, they are often important because they enhance the capacity to hold members of Cabinet and Ministers responsible for their actions and decisions and can frustrate legislation sponsored by members of the Cabinet. Their roles, however, will reflect the operation of the two-party system.

This chapter has four parts. The first is a discussion of the roles and effects of political parties in **representative democracy** in Australia. In the second part, we introduce the two-party system. We discuss whether Australian politics is better off with the two-party system than it would be without it in the third part. While a two-party system has been fundamental to Australians politics, it is not inevitable. In the final part of the chapter, we briefly examine the question of whether the major parties are more similar than they are different.

1: PRELIMINARY DISCUSSION

Parties in government and democracy in Australia

Parties play important roles in and affect government and democracy in Australia in a variety of ways.[2] They are central to elections and play an important role in policy-making and are also centres of political strategising. They represent career paths and enable people's involvement in causes, as well as simply providing companionship. A final effect of parties has been to entrench men's power in Australian politics.

During elections (letters, advertisements, candidates)
The times at which we are most aware of the major parties is during elections. Members of parties select candidates for seats in the Lower and Upper Houses of Parliament. Parties also channel a massive amount of information to voters about issues and candidates in elections. They provide support to individual candidates (both before and on election day), including fund-raising to support their campaigns.[3]

BOX 9.1
The Australian Labor Party

The Australian Labor Party (ALP) has strong ties to the Australian trade union movement, as it formed as a response to the failure of the 'Great' maritime and shearers' strikes of the 1890s. The ALP is the oldest surviving political party in Australia and sixteen members and eight senators represented it in the first sitting of federal Parliament.

The ALP first won office in 1904, led by J.C. Watson. Three major splits, in 1917, 1931 and 1955, have contributed to the fact that the ALP has only determined the members of the federal Cabinet for a total of thirty-three years.

Source: http://www.alp.org.au/about/index.php

Policy-making

One of the most important roles of party members is to develop policies and to justify them to citizens.[4] Most political parties are organised around a network of branches, which are essentially meetings of members of the party in particular federal electorates. Branches are sometimes a source of new policies. The ideas for policies that their members generate are channelled through larger party meetings, councils, and conferences, in which they are scrutinised and sometimes adopted.[5] Parties provide opportunities for public participation in policy-making that are central to a representative democracy and can facilitate effective government.

The role of branches in policy-making has declined in recent years. This resulted from the fact that other parties have tended to adopt the same practice as that of the Liberal Party which gives their Parliamentarians the responsibility for policy-making. All parties maintain a system in which branches are organised into a policy-making network, but the effect of this network on party policy is now more limited.

Political strategising (organisation)

One of the factors behind the decline in branches as sources of policy is the increased power of party organisations. Party organisations are the administrative cores of parties;[6] they began as part of the support structure for members of parties in Parliament and the organisational nodes of the branch network. More recently, however, they have taken on a more significant role in developing policy and determining electoral strategy. Part of the explanation for this is that members of the party organisation see themselves as better suited to developing electoral strategy. The fact that a federal election is never more than three years away means that they take greater responsibility for leading their party.

Access to and uses of the results from opinion polls they commission have been important to the increased power of party organisers. Opinion polling is now central to any party's chances in an election, and to party organisers who know what the polls indicate. As a result, organisers see themselves as better placed to develop election-winning policies than branch members. Party officials may occasionally be overruled, but this is more likely to be the result of the efforts of Parliamentary leaders than the result of power being exercised from the branch level.

Site of power struggles

Political parties also constitute centres of power. That Australians do not vote for parties whose members cannot hide their internal divisions means that party members work hard to hide the power struggles within their parties. These power struggles are sometimes simply the reflection of the quest for individual power but, more often, they arise from different views as to the best sort of society to live in and how to achieve such a society. Most party members join parties because they believe that the party they join reflects their values. While parties may have core values, they are complex organisations whose members adopt a variety of philosophical and ideological positions. This means that they will often disagree either about what the party stands for or about how the members of a party can achieve its goals.

faction, factional, factionalism: A 'faction' is used to refer to a relatively stable group that forms within a political party. It is usually used with respect to the ALP, which has formally adopted a factional structure.

While few parties have formalised these disagreements as completely as has the ALP,[7] most parties are divided by philosophical and strategic disagreements. Major parties are large and therefore more likely to be divided by these disagreements. The ALP's **factions**, then, have equivalents in the Liberal and National parties. Some members of the Liberal Party[8] believe in completely free markets, whereas others believe that markets must be controlled to prevent or soften their effects on societies. The National Party[9] divides in ways that reflect the divergent interests of different sectors of the rural community. If we treat the Liberal and National Parties as two wings of the same conservative party, as is implied in the idea that we have a two-party system, we can see them as reflecting a highly organised factional division.

Only some of the struggles for power that occur within parties derive from differences concerning philosophy or strategy, however. Many are simply power struggles. Parties provide a variety of benefits to individuals and these benefits are a source of internal division and struggles for power. Some benefits are primarily symbolic, others are directly economic. Some people like to be in charge. Some people like to be seen to be in charge. Others like to play games of strategy. If individuals believe that being in charge, being seen to be in charge, or 'winning' carries financial rewards, then their membership of a party or their role as a candidate for a party becomes more attractive.

Career paths

An obvious financial reward that parties offer is a career. Some people join parties to obtain jobs and pursue careers. Most are looking for political careers, but not all. Many of the career paths begin with voluntary labour, but they are nonetheless paths upon which at least some people are moving. Larger and more stable parties often contain more meaningful career paths than smaller and less stable parties, which rely almost completely on volunteers.

BOX 9.2
The Liberal Party of Australia

The Liberal Party of Australia (LPA) was formed in 1944. It emerged from a three-day meeting, comprising eighty members from non-Labor political parties, which was hosted by the then Opposition leader Robert Menzies (who led the United Australia Party). The Liberal Party of Australia formed as a reaction against the policies of the Labor Cabinet elected after World War II. Menzies, who is often credited with being the founder of the party, has been the most successful Prime Minister in Australian history. He led the nation and the party from 1949 to 1966.

Source: http://www.liberal.org.au/about/

Involvement in causes

One reason that parties can rely on volunteers is that they give people a forum in which they can promote particular causes or address specific social problems. Whatever views we may have concerning the power of parties, some of their members believe that they can be used to progress change. The Greens are the most obvious examples of this, but all parties provide people with opportunities for trying to improve Australian society.

People seeking company

At the simplest level, parties are just groups of people. Party meetings are opportunities to meet new people and extend social networks. Once we leave school or university, we have fewer opportunities for meeting people. Work provides some opportunities, but there may be limited appeal in socialising with co-workers. Parties are not the only means for developing contacts with others, but we are more likely to meet people with similar political views through a party.

Entrench male domination

Political parties in Australia have also entrenched men's power in government and democracy in Australia.[10] If parties are at the centre of Australian politics, then men are at the centre of Australian parties. That men dominate federal Parliament is a direct reflection of the fact that men predominate among candidates for office. However, men are also the main organisers within the parties, so their non-elected officials also tend to be men. When it comes to the public faces of political parties in Australia, then, it is pretty much men, men, and more men. Certainly, women are active in all Australian parties, but they are much less likely to take up roles that would bring them to the attention of voters. This changed somewhat in 2007, with the appointment of Julia Gillard as Deputy Prime Minister. In fact, Julia Gillard became the first women to take up the position of Acting Prime Minister when the Prime Minister attended the United Nations Conference on **Climate Change** in Bali in December 2007.

Some parties are more receptive to women taking up leading public positions. Minor parties, such as the Australian Democrats and Greens, have been much more receptive to women than other parties. Members of the ALP have tried to overcome the exclusion of women by requiring that one-third of the candidates for 'winnable' seats must be women. Whether this will increase to 50 per cent is not clear; and it

> **climate change**: This phrase could be used to refer to any long-term changes in world temperatures and rainfall, but is now more commonly used to refer to those long-term changes in temperatures and rainfall that have resulted from human activity.

does not addresses problems associated with the exclusion of women within the party organisation. Neither the Liberal Party nor the National Party have adopted formal policies associated with increasing the participation of women in significant positions, either in the Parliamentary parties or in the party organisation.

Summary

Parties are fundamental to government and democracy in Australia. They are central to the selection and presentation of candidates in elections and are the primary sources of the policies presented to voters. Their organisations contain political strategists who play fundamental roles in shaping Australian politics. Parties are sites for power struggles among those who seek political power. They also represent career paths, avenues through which people promote causes, and ways that people can develop and increase their social contacts. Finally, parties, especially the major parties, have been important to men maintaining their control over government and democracy in Australia.

QUESTION

What are some of the important roles played by parties in government and democracy in Australia?

2: THE TWO-PARTY SYSTEM

This part provides a background for the following part in which alternative positions on the question of whether Australians would be better off without the two-party system are presented. We included it because we wanted to draw attention to certain aspects of the two-party system before we considered whether it has a positive effect on government and democracy in Australia. An important aspect of the two-party system is its stability. We engage with this issue after discussing the nature and origins of the two-party system in Australia.

The two-party system

Meaning of 'two-party' system
A two-party system is a political system in which two parties dominate politics.[11] Members of these parties compete for domination of a legislature and Cabinet.

The system is called two-party because both parties can gain control of these institutions. This is most clearly evidenced by the fact that party representatives alternately gain and lose control over the Cabinet and legislature. Only a system in which two parties alternate in their control over major political institutions can be described as two-party.

Origins of the two-party system

franchise, suffrage: These terms are used to refer to the right to enrol and vote in elections, which is accorded to Australians over the age of eighteen.

Tracing the source of the Australian two-party system isn't overly difficult. It is slightly complicated by the fact that its origins derive from changes to the **franchise** and developments in industrial relations. While one preceded the other, their combined effects have contributed to the particular form that the two-party system took in Australia.

Initially, only men who owned relatively valuable property could vote.[12] Over time, the right to vote, or franchise, was extended, so that by the middle of the nineteenth century all men could vote to elect representatives to the Lower House of colonial Parliaments (women were not enfranchised until the end of the century). While voting for representatives to Upper Houses remained more restricted, the extension of the franchise meant that all men were given some political power. Workers were one of the most important of those who benefited from an extended franchise.

The 1890s were also pivotal in the development of the Australian two-party system. The 1890s was both a period of economic downturn and the stage at which worker organisation had reached a level of sophistication that gave workers a sense of their economic and political rights. The tensions that developed within the Australian economy created two divergent sets of economic interests and these subsequently became divergent sets of political interests. These tensions resulted in the 'Great Strikes' of the 1890s and the move to organise a political movement to represent the interests of workers.

When the Great Strikes failed, workers shifted their battle from workplaces to Parliaments. Workers' parties began to develop, so that by the turn of the century they were able to mount effective election campaigns. The ALP had been established before the Australian colonies federated, and it came to dominate the representation of workers in Australian federal politics. It was the formation and practices of the ALP that contributed most to the development of the Australian two-party system.

Support from unions and its political and economic agenda meant that the ALP was a more cohesive party than all preceding parties. People who wanted to represent the party had to commit, or pledge, themselves to supporting the policies and legislation that had been agreed to by party members. By requiring their representatives to follow policies that came from the party, the ALP fundamentally disrupted the ways that the Australian Parliament worked at that time.

Prior to the formation of Labor parties and the ALP, colonial politics was dominated by politicians whose behaviour in Parliament was sometimes coordinated, with, but not governed by, the strict party discipline practiced by Labor parties. A combination of a restricted franchise, the fact that Parliamentarians were not paid, and the nature of the colonial economy and society, meant that Parliament was comprised of wealthy men. Disputes emerged between representatives of rural and urban interests and free traders and protectionists who wanted to develop and stabilise the colonial or federal economy. These disputes, however, were not as fundamental and antagonistic as the division that emerged between representatives of workers and representatives of employers.

The emergence of the ALP as a powerful political force forced changes in the tactics of those who sought to resist its influence. The result was that a two-party system had developed by 1910. A confusing aspect of our system is that three parties form the Australian two-party system: the ALP, the Liberal Party, and the National (previously Country) Party.[13] Ours is a two-party system due to the similarity of values among the members of the Liberal and National Parties and the fact that Cabinets are formed from and supported by either members of the Labor Party or a coalition of members of the Liberal and National Parties. Tensions often emerge between the Liberal and National Parties, but these are no more intense than those between the factions of the ALP. While the National and Liberal Parties are much like factions of the same party, they are also internally divided (in the same way that the factions of the ALP are divided).

BOX 9.3
The National Party of Australia

The Country Party was formed in 1920 from an amalgamation of rural parties and interests. The party has maintained its rural heritage and continues to represent Australians in 'the bush'. The party was renamed the National Party of Australia in 1982. It has influenced federal and state politics through the formation of coalitions with other conservative parties, most notably the Liberal Party of Australia. The exception is the National Party in Queensland, which gathered enough support to govern in its own right, or to dominate a National–Liberal coalition.

Source: http://www.nationals.org.au/About/default.asp

Stability of the two-party system

The two-party system dominates our political imaginations and practices. We struggle to imagine living under anything other than a two-party system. We can think of names for more parties, but we have to go further to re-think the nature of salient political issues and our philosophical differences. This is only one step in moving from a two-party system, however, as a change to the electoral system in Australia would also be required.

Undermining the intellectual/philosophical foundations of the two-party system

An important intellectual support for the two-party system derives from a perception that two-party systems are more stable than multi-party systems. The two-party system has corresponded with a level of stability within Australian politics that is less evident in some multi-party systems. Multi-party systems generally require a level of negotiation and compromise that two-party systems do not. Negotiation and compromise slows down policy-making and policy implementation. Changing our conception of politics, so that we see this different style of policy-making and implementation as normal, is the most important adjustment that we must make, if we are to move to a truly multi-party system.

Undermining the two-party system also requires a fundamental reorientation of the way that Australians think about political issues. The two-party system itself developed around an apparent conflict between the interests of workers (and their dependants) and employers (and their dependants). The two parties, then, may persist because they represent this fundamental and persistent division in Australian society.

The two-party system represents both people and values. Australia's two-party system, for example, may reflect divergent positions on the issue of the role of government. It reflects a division between those who believe that governments should be active and reduce the adverse effects of markets on society (ALP) and those who support a limited role for government and place greater priority on free markets (LPA and NPA—though members of the National Party part company with those in the Liberal Party when rural interests are concerned).

These approaches to the role of political executives are related to different positions about the levels and forms of taxation and on the division of power in our federal system. Historically, the ALP has tended to be a higher taxing and more centralist party than the lower taxing more federalist Liberal–National coalition.[14] However, this may be a misleading construction of Australian politics in today's world, and may not represent actual differences between the parties now.

The electoral system and the two-party system

While our familiarity with and our inability to think beyond the two-party system are important, the electoral system contributes most to the maintenance of a two-party system.[15] An electoral system based on single member geographical constituencies and with compulsory preferential voting is much more likely to produce a two-party system than an electoral system based on multi-member constituencies and proportional representation.

Compulsory preferential voting contributes to the maintenance of a two-party system by forcing voters to rank representatives of the major parties. Compulsory preferential voting may support our form of a two-party system by allowing preference deals that mean that members of the National and Liberal Parties can work together, rather than merge. Moving to either optional preferential voting or first-past-the-post voting might undermine our two-party system. Proportional representation in elections for members of the Lower House is more likely to undermine this system, although this will depend on the size of the electorates being used.

BOX 9.4
The Australian Democrats

The Australian Democrats formed in 1977 when Don Chipp left the Liberal Party because of repeated disputes with the Prime Minister, and leader of the Liberal Party, Malcolm Fraser. Their first federal Parliamentarian was Janine Haines and the party won enough Senate seats to gain the balance of power in the 1980 federal election. Janine Haines became Australia's first female leader of a federal party after Don Chipp's retirement. The Australian Democrats party is unique among the main political parties in Australia, as it is not based on relatively independent state organisations, and its members determine the leadership of the Parliamentary arm of the party. It is also the only political party of note to have been led by women.

Source: http://www.democrats.org.au/about/

QUESTIONS

1 What is the nature of the two-party system?
2 Does the two-party system have a positive effect on government and democracy in Australia?

3: IS AUSTRALIAN POLITICS BETTER OFF WITH THE TWO-PARTY SYSTEM THAN IT WOULD BE WITHOUT IT?

In this part, we present alternative cases with respect to the question: 'Is Australian politics better off with the two-party system than it would be without it?' This was not an easy question to frame, but it reflects concerns about the current validity of the two-party system.[16] This means that the question is understood in terms of contemporary Australian society and politics (though some of the points made below would apply generally).

Five reasons are presented to support each of the positions that can be put in this context. The Yes case begins with one of the most common defences of the two-party system: that it produces stable government. The second reason to prefer the two-party system is that it provides a clear connection between citizens and members of political executives. The third argument is that it reflects the main division within Australian society and, because of this, is more representative of Australian society.

The No case begins with the argument that the two-party system has produced a system in which members of Cabinets are not held accountable. The second point is that an end to the two-party system would produce real debates within federal Parliament, and the third that the two-party system limits the number of talented people who can be included in Cabinet.

Yes case

Produces stable government
The first reason to prefer a two-party system is that it has delivered stable government.[17] The fact that members of Cabinet can rely on the ongoing support of a majority of members of the Lower House of Parliament means that they will hold office until they choose to call an election. Even if they are forced to negotiate with members of the Upper House, who represent minor parties or are independents, they are not seeking to retain support for their Cabinet positions. A multi-party system would mean that members of Cabinets were supported by unstable coalitions of parties. Parliamentarians from the National Party might vote against a particular piece of legislation from a Labor Party Cabinet, but would never threaten to support a Cabinet formed by members of the Liberal Party.

Connections are clearer
Another reason to retain the two-party system is that it provides a clear link between voters and major political institutions. Voters effectively choose the

members of Cabinet because they support the major parties who will take up leading positions in a Cabinet. Parties also link voters and Ministers because Ministers are selected by key decision-makers in their party or coalition. A Cabinet formed from a coalition of minor parties would be harder to make Cabinets and Ministers accountable, as Ministers in this case would answer to the members or leader of their own party and not to the Prime Minister.

Represents the most salient division in Australian society

Another reason to retain the two-party system is that it reflects the most salient division in Australian society. While Australians divide in a variety of ways, the division between workers (and their dependants) and employers (and their dependants) remains the most basic of these divisions. An obvious example of the centrality of this division is wage increases. Employers and their representatives never support wage increases, workers and their representatives always support wage increases. The permanence of this division indicates that it is a fundamental division in Australian society and this is reflected in the two-party system.[18]

No case

Lack of constraint on political executives

The first reason to abandon our two-party system is that it has undermined Parliament's ability to hold members of Cabinet and Ministers accountable for their decisions and actions. The two-party system means that the Lower House of Parliament will never hold the members of Cabinet and Ministers accountable. The number of recent inquiries into corruption among senior members of state political executives and the introduction of codes of conduct and bodies to enforce these codes points to problems with achieving accountability. The two-party system, which gives members of Cabinet a sense of invulnerability, lies at the heart of problems with accountability and corruption.

Serious debates in Parliament

Abandoning the two-party system would also make serious debate in Parliament possible. Parliamentary debates have no meaning because everyone knows how the members of Parliament will vote. The end of the two-party system would mean that the outcomes of any vote would not be predetermined. Members of Cabinet would have to persuade the other Members of Parliament that their performance warranted support for their Cabinet decisions. They would also have to persuade Members of Parliament that the legislation they are promoting is necessary and likely to be effective. In short, members of Cabinet who do not control Parliament would have to take Parliament much more seriously.

Limits pool of talent

Another reason to reject our two-party system is that it limits the pool of people who can be Ministers. The two-party system means Ministers can only be chosen from a little more than half of the House of Representatives and an even lower number of Senators. Another factor is that Prime Ministers gain their positions through various internal party deals that oblige them to appoint particular people as Ministers. The combination of a limited range of available candidates and the way that appointments reflect internal party deals means that no Cabinet or Ministry could ever represent the most able group of Parliamentarians available at the time.

environment/environmental: This word could be used to refer to our surroundings, but is usually used to refer to our natural surroundings, rather than our built, or artificial, surroundings.

BOX 9.5
The Australian Greens

The Australian Greens formed in 1992 when members of the New South Wales, Queensland, and Tasmanian Green Parties decided that a federal body was required to represent those who supported **environmental** sustainability. Like the major parties, the Australian Greens is a federation of individual state parties, so a member of a state Green party is automatically a member of the Australian Greens. The Greens (WA), however, are not a part of this federation of state Green parties and maintain their independence at the federal level. Currently, the best known Australian Greens Parliamentarian is Senator Bob Brown, who entered the federal Parliament in 1996.

Sources: http://www.greens.org.au/; http://wa.greens.org.au/about/; http://www.bobbrown.org.au/

Summary

Moving away from the two-party system could require a change in our understanding of the nature and legitimate form of Australian politics. We might achieve such a change simply by introducing proportional representation. The question, of course, is whether this would be a good idea. Resolving this requires considering whether stability is more important than democracy. We must also consider what we want from Parliament and what we are willing to sacrifice to get it. We will have to decide whether the confusing, though dynamic, aspects of a multi-party system are preferable to the clarity and certainty of a two-party system. We must also decide whether the internal process within the parties that dominate our two-party system provide forums in which real debates occur.

QUESTIONS

1. Is it possible to move away from the two-party system in Australian politics?
2. Would it be a good idea to do so? Why/why not?

4: ARE THE TWO PARTIES MORE SIMILAR THAN THEY ARE DIFFERENT?

Throughout Australia's political history, the major parties have generally represented two different sides of the political divide. The Liberal Party has represented those who support smaller political executives, individual rights and employees, whereas the ALP has represented those who prefer larger and more powerful political executives, communal needs, and workers' rights more generally. However, things seemed to change somewhat in the 1970s, when inflation and unemployment rose at the same time and members of Australian political executives faced new challenges, both domestically and in the international arena. Debate continues about whether the major parties are now more similar than they are different and, in this part of the chapter, we look at arguments for both positions.

They are more similar than different

Three reasons to believe that the major parties are more similar than they are different are put forward in the following sub-section. These are that neither of the major parties would change Australian society in any meaningful way; they both compete to convince Australians that they can manage our economy, and that members of the major parties are now simply the servants of a leader.

Neither provides a meaningful alternative for Australians

Members of both of the major parties are committed to maintaining Australian society as it is. We are reminded, in this context, of an anarchist slogan that went something like 'Don't vote, it just encourages them'. The idea that the anarchists were trying to express in this slogan is that neither of the parties represents a force for real change. However, an important question, in the context of global warming, is whether the major parties can produce the changes necessary to address Australia's contribution to this problem. Members of the Greens are certain that they cannot.

A related problem is that the parties look very much alike. The major parties have similar approaches to selecting candidates, generating policy, and engaging with their constituents. Only the Australian Democrats have employed a different approach to party leadership and policy-making.

Both compete for recognition as better economic managers
Generally speaking, members of political executives believe that ensuring the efficient working of the national economy is their primary responsibility. Members of both parties promote their ability to manage the national economy in explaining why they are fit to govern or retain government. In the 2007 federal election, for example, senior members of the Howard Cabinet presented low levels of unemployment and lower inflation rates as the reasons why they should be re-elected. To counteract this message, then Opposition leader, Kevin Rudd, assured voters that little would change with respect to economic management because he was an economic conservative. The Treasurer of the first Rudd Cabinet, Wayne Swan, has said that controlling inflation was their highest priority for the first eighteen months of their term.

Both are simply vehicles for leaders
Another reason to believe that the major parties are similar is that both are simply support teams for their leaders. For example, we refer to Cabinets by using the leader's name. The leaders of the parties are the focus of election campaigns and voters' preferred Prime Minister is a focus of the media's reporting of elections. The Leaders' Debates have become a regular part of contemporary Australian elections and have reinforced the idea that leaders personify the whole party. The way that politics is reported in the news media makes leaders the public face of their parties and their actions determine the way their party is perceived by voters.

They are more different than they are similar

We present three reasons to believe that the major parties are more similar than they are different in this sub-section. These are that they express different ideologies, they have very different approaches to social policy, and that party members have very different attitudes to our relations with the leaders of other countries.

They have very different political ideologies
One of the main sources of difference between the major parties is that they have been influenced by different ideologies. Members of the Liberal Party have been

deeply influenced by the ideas of liberalism, and in particular classical liberalism. Central tenets of classical liberalism include the belief that people are essentially rational and self-interested. This political ideology also holds the view that people should be protected from interference in their lives by members of political executives, whose role should be limited to supporting an efficient economy and not interfering with market forces.

The other form of liberalism that has influenced members of the Liberal Party and has been more influential among members of the National Party is social liberalism. Social liberalism has been given a few different names, such as new, modern, or welfare liberalism. The main difference between classical and social liberals is that social liberals pay much more attention to the quality of the society in which people live. They believe that real equality of opportunity exists when all people have the same life chances. This means providing resources to poorer families, so that the children in these families receive the nutrition, education, and other things they need to have the same chances in life as children from wealthier families. Social liberal ideas, in short, justify a welfare state. Social liberals are also less willing to believe that markets work properly and fairly and that people are as anti-social or individualistic as classical liberals take them to be.

Social liberal ideas have influenced at least some members of all the major parties. However, they have been most influential in the Australian Labor Party. Historically, the ALP has been perceived, including by some of its members, as a socialist party. The ALP Constitution says that it is a democratic socialist party, but party members abandoned any commitment to socialise industries in 1922. A party that is not committed to members of political executives taking control of major industries on the people's behalf is not a socialist party.

Members of the ALP have a much more positive view of people and see them as social beings that thrive when the best society possible exists around them. Social liberals are less worried about interfering in markets than classical liberals. They seek to spread wealth around more evenly in society, or redistribute wealth, so that everyone benefits (including the wealthy, who may pay higher taxes, but who get to live in a better society). This explains why newly elected Prime Minister Kevin Rudd spoke of returning decency and the 'fair go' back to Australian society.

They have very different views on social policy
Another reason to reject the view that the major parties are similar is that their difference lies in their members' approach to social policy. Generally speaking, members of the Liberal Party of Australia treat social policy as an oxymoron (a contradiction in terms). For them, there is no such thing as 'society', which is

nothing more than a collection of individuals. Most importantly, some of these individuals work hard and some do not. Some deserve to be poor and some do not. The 'deserving' poor are those people who have worked hard, but not succeeded and deserve support. The 'undeserving' poor are those people who have not contributed to society and do not deserve support.

Members of the Australian Labor Party, on the other hand, do not distinguish between the 'undeserving' and 'deserving' poor, because they see people's motivations as being affected by the society of which they are part. As a result, they seek to include and to provide for the entire community when developing social policy. The social policy they produce reflects their belief in society and community, both of which they see as more than just a collection of individuals.

They have very different views on our relationships with allies

A third reason to believe that the major parties are not more similar than they are different is that members of the major parties have very different attitudes to Australia's principal allies. Members of the Liberal and National parties are less critical of, and keener to establish and maintain a strong relationship with the United States. While members of Howard Cabinet were already willing to support the U.S. President, George W. Bush, and other members of his political executive, the attacks of September 11, 2001 led them to seek to strengthen their relationship. They did this by supporting the US in refusing to ratify the Kyoto Protocol on Climate Change and joining the United States and the United Kingdom, in what became known as the Coalition of the Willing, in the 'War on Terror'. They agreed to send troops to help to fight the political leaders of Iraq (and were one of the few to agree to send troops to fight in this war).

Members of the ALP are much more willing to criticise decisions made by members of political executives in the United States. While they are accused of being US-haters, especially by members of the Liberal and National parties, they claim that they want a strong relationship with members of US political executives. They argue that developing a strong relationship with the United States does not entail agreeing with everything they say and do, and claim that the strong relationship between the two countries must be based on respect for their differences. The election of the Rudd Government in 2007 marked a change in the relationship between members of political executives in the USA and Australia. Prime Minister Rudd and the members of his Cabinet moved quickly to show that they would develop their own position and not merely follow the US President and the other members of the US political executive on key issues such as climate change and the war in Iraq.

Summary

We have outlined arguments that support the position that the major parties are more similar than they are different and arguments that they are not more similar that they are different. We have not attempted to provide an exhaustive list of similarities and differences, but to provide a brief overview of some key ones. These similarities and differences impact on the way major parties understand government and democracy and also provide a way to distinguish the major parties in terms of how they would function in government and facilitate democratic processes in the wider Australian community.

QUESTIONS

1. Should the major parties be different? Is this important?
2. Does the apparent convergence of the major parties on some issues imply a threat to the democratic system of government in Australia?

CONCLUSION

Parties play important roles in government and democracy in Australia. The fact that members of all parties provide an invaluable contribution to Australian politics and society ought not to be discounted, if we are to appreciate Australian politics. Devoting most of this chapter to a discussion of the two-party system and a consideration of the question of whether the major parties are more similar than they are different reflects the way that this system has shaped Australian politics. It is not intended to diminish or obscure the important contribution to Australian politics made by members of minor parties. All the parties of Australian politics, however, must be understood in terms of the form and practices associated with a two-party system. This system has shaped our understanding of the nature of politics and the roles of parties themselves. Australia's political system reflects the general principles that underpin a two-party system and the specific developments that created the 'ALP versus LPA/NPA' framework that is the Australian two-party system. Once we have this understanding, we can form our own views about the desirability of this two-party system, which is closely related to the question of whether the major parties are more similar than they are different.

BOX 9.6
Independents in the Federal Parliament

Independents are candidates or Parliamentarians who are not members of a political party. In Australia, where voters tend to vote according to their party allegiances, few independents have sat in Parliament. During the 1990s, however, Australians began to vote consistently for independent candidates, and the number of independents elected to the House of Representatives and the Senate increased. In 1996, for example, there were five independents in the House of Representatives, and two independent Senators. By 2007, though, there were two independents in the House of Representatives and one in the Senate. A willingness to support independents, and minor parties is generally attributed to dissatisfaction among voters with the major parties. In particular, voters have supported independents and minor parties in the Senate, as they did the Australian Democrats, because they see this as a way to keep members of major parties honest. Nick Xenophon, an anti-poker machine Independent from South Australia and Stephen Fielding, of Family First, hold the balance of power in the Senate in the aftermath of the 2007 federal election.

Source: Smith (1997a)

BOX 9.7
Family First Party

Family First came to our attention in the federal election of 2004, when Steve Fielding was elected to the Senate. Family First gained two representatives in South Australia. The top priority of members of Family First was Australian families, and in Parliament their representatives sought to raise issues that were important to families. Its members claimed that the party represented independence, commonsense, and the mainstream values of ordinary Australian families. They believed that parenting is the hardest and most important job in society and that families must have genuine choices about their 'work and life balance' to reduce the number of marriage and relationship breakdowns in Australian society. The party gained no seats in the 2007 federal election, so Stephen Fielding is its sole representative in the Senate. He, with Nick Xenophon, holds the balance of power in the Senate.

Source: http://www.familyfirst.org.au

FURTHER READING

Introductory texts

Ball, Terence & Richard Dagger, 2006, *Political Ideologies and the Democratic Ideal*, Pearson Longman: New York.

Hayden, Bill, 1998, 'End of Ideology Will Lead to More Pragmatic Age', in D. Lovell, I. McAllister, W. Maley & C. Kukathas (eds), *The Australian Political System*, 2nd edn, Longman: South Melbourne.

Jaensch, Dean & David Scott Mathieson, 1998, *A Plague on Both Your Houses: Minor Parties in Australia*, Allen & Unwin: St Leonards.

Lucy, Richard, 1993, *The Australian Form of Government: Models in Dispute*, Macmillan: South Melbourne.

Sharman, Campbell, 1994, 'Political Parties', in J. Brett, J. Gillespie & M. Goot (eds), *Developments in Australian Politics*, Macmillan: South Melbourne.

Vromen, Ariadne & Katherine Gelber, 2005, 'Political Parties', in *Powerscape: Contemporary Australian Political Practice*, Allen & Unwin: Crows Nest.

Warhurst, John & Andrew Parkin, 2000, *The Machine: Labor Confronts the Future*, Allen & Unwin: St Leonards.

Specialist texts

Aldred, Ken, Kevin Andrews & Paul Filing (eds), 1994, *The Heart of Liberalism*, Albury Papers: Mitcham.

Barns, Greg, (2003), *What's Wrong with the Liberal Party?*, Cambridge University Press: Port Melbourne.

Brett, Judith, 2003, *Australian Liberals and the Moral Middle Class: From Alfred Deakin to John Howard*, Cambridge University Press: Port Melbourne.

Daverall, Kate, Rebecca Huntley, Penny Sharpe & Jo Tilly, 2000, *Party Girls: Labor Women Now*, Pluto Press: Annandale.

Faulkner, John & Stuart Macintyre, 2001, *True Believers: The Story of the Federal Parliamentary Labor Party*, Allen & Unwin: Crows Nest.

Hagan, Stephanie & Graham Maddox, 1984, 'The Australian Democrats and the Two-Party System', *The Australian Quarterly*, vol. 56, no. 1, pp. 30–40.

Henderson, Gerard, 1994, *Menzies' Child: The Liberal Party of Australia 1944–1994*, Allen & Unwin: St Leonards.

Maddox, Graham, 1992, 'Political Stability, Independents and the Two Party System', *Current Affairs Bulletin*, vol. 69, no. 1, pp. 20–7.

Moore, Tod, Sandra Bourke & Graham Maddox, 1998, 'Australia and the Emergence of the Modern Two-Party System', *Australian Journal of Politics and History*, vol. 22, no. 1, pp. 17–31.

Web sites

Australian Political Parties List:
http://www.aec.gov.au/Parties_and_Representatives/Party_Registration/
http://www.aph.gov.au/library/intguide/pol/polparti.htm
Australian politics: http://australianpolitics.com
The ALP home page: http://www.alp.org.au
The Australian Democrats: http://www.democrats.org.au
The Australian Greens: http://greens.org.au
The Greens—International home page: http://utopia.knoware.nl/users/oterhaar/greens/intlhome.htm
The Liberal Party of Australia: http://www.liberal.org.au
The National Party: http://www.nationals.org.au
The Tasmanian Greens: http://www.tas.greens.org.au
The Family First Party: http://www.familyfirst.org.au

Notes

1. Most analysts refer to the system as a two-party system because we tend to treat the Liberal and National Parties as if they are the urban and rural wings of the same party. We will discuss both this conflation and its legitimacy later in this chapter.
2. For more on the roles played by political parties in Australia, see Smith (1997a, pp. 165–73), Jaensch (1994, pp. 153–6), Maddox (2005, pp. 252–9), Ward & Stewart (2006, pp. 115–18), and Lovell et al. (1998, pp. 255–8).
3. For information on the role played by political parties during elections, refer to Marsh (1995, pp. 35–8), Bean (1997, pp. 104–8), and Lovell et al. (1998, pp. 270–1).
4. For more details on the role of political parties in the policy process, see Marsh (1995, pp. 39–41) and Singleton et al. (2006, pp. 341–2).
5. The Australian Labor Party includes representatives from unions in these larger policy-making meetings of party members. The Australian Democrats have used a system in which party members are allowed, where possible, to vote on policy issues.
6. For more information on party organisation see Jaensch (1994, pp. 134–5), Singleton et al. (2006, pp. 339–41), and Marsh (1995, pp. 320–3).
7. For more details concerning the Australian Labor Party, see Smith (1997a, pp. 158–60), Jaensch (1994, pp. 122–4), Maddox (2005, pp. 260–77), Hughes (1998a, pp. 107–33), and Ward & Stewart (2006, pp. 153–71).
8. For more details concerning the Liberal Party, see Smith (1997a, pp. 160–2), Jaensch (1994, pp. 124–7), Maddox (2005, pp. 277–8, 289–302), Hughes (1998a, pp. 136–61), and Ward & Stewart (2006, pp. 134–52).
9. For more details concerning the National Party, see Smith (1997a, pp. 162–4), Jaensch (1994, pp. 127–9), and Maddox (2005, pp. 277–89).
10. For more information on the male dominance of Australian politics, see Emy & Hughes (1991, pp. 517–25) and Singleton et al. (2006, pp. 135–6, 181).
11. For more on the history of the two-party political system, see Marsh (1995, pp. 18–29), Jaensch (1994, pp. 119–22), Ward & Stewart (2006, pp. 119–22), and Singleton et al. (2006, pp. 314–16).

12   The first election in Australia was held in 1843 for the Legislative Council of New South Wales. Voting was restricted to men who owned land worth £200 or who paid more than £20 for rent (http://www.aec.gov.au/Elections/Australian_Electoral_History/reform.htm).
13   This is something of a simplification both of the formation and reformations of the Liberal Party, but it is close enough for our purposes.
14   We must always be a little careful about these constructions, as there are a number of commentators who argue that taxation levels in Australia are relatively low.
15   For more information on how the electoral system affects the two-party system, see Bean (1997, pp. 103–4), Ward & Stewart (2006, pp. 97–9), and Lovell et al. (1998, p. 269).
16   See Marsh (1995, pp. 17–44).
17   For more details on the stability of the two-party system, see Bean (1997, p. 103), Jaensch (1994, pp. 77–80 and 93–5), and Singleton et al. (2006, pp. 316–22).
18   For more information on the ideological divide between the major parties in Australia, refer to Jaensch (1994, pp. 142–6), Maddox (2005, pp. 248–59), Singleton et al. (2006, pp. 350–2 and 361–4), and Lovell et al. (1998, pp. 367–9).

10 Pressure Groups

LEARNING OBJECTIVES

- To understand the effects that pressure groups exert upon Australian government and democracy
- Appreciate the significance of pressure groups to representative democracy
- Be able to explain the reasons that some pressure groups are more influential than others

INTRODUCTION

So far, our attention has been on more formal institutions of Australian politics. These are relatively stable and internally regulated organisations that tend to provide fairly predictable outcomes. The only possible exception to this is political parties, but these are sufficiently stable, internally regulated, and have produced sufficiently predictable outcomes to be considered as political institutions. While political institutions are important for the stability and predictability that they produce, they can only work effectively for government and democracy in Australia if they are supported by and interact effectively with less formal social organisations. For it is the interaction between pressure groups reflecting popular interests and political institutions that produces the form of government and democracy in Australian politics with which we are familiar.

This chapter has been divided into three parts. In the first, we discuss the 'public face' of pressure groups in Australia. Pressure groups may be viewed as the basis for distinctive forms of representative democracy, or they may be understood as a means to overcome some of the deficiencies of representative democracies, and especially Westminster-style representative democracies. These two views are discussed in the second part of the chapter. The final part explains why some groups are more influential than others. This is important for two reasons. First, because it bears on the question of whether pressure groups can provide for a more effective representative democracy. Second, because it will contribute to an appreciation of the nature and operation of pressure groups in Australian government and democracy.

1: PRESSURE GROUPS AND THEIR INFLUENCE ON GOVERNMENT AND DEMOCRACY IN AUSTRALIA

Pressure groups are groups of citizens who seek to persuade those in positions of political power to change policies or to develop new policies.[1] That pressure groups are not a formal part of the policy-making process means that their members must attract the attention of those who are in order to promote their cause.[2] This first part discusses the emergence of pressure groups and their **lobbying** of members of political executives, public protesting, and the news media's reporting of these activities.

lobby, lobbying: To 'lobby' is to seek to persuade someone to adopt a particular policy. Lobbying is usually used to refer to the actions of agents of pressure groups ('lobbyists') who pursue favourable outcomes from policy-makers.

The emergence of pressure groups

The issues around which pressure groups operate vary widely. They may form around big issues, such as world poverty or environmental degradation, or smaller scale issues, such as toxic waste in a particular residential area. These issues may affect a billion people or a hundred people. The only thing that can be said of all pressure groups is that they seek to put pressure on members of political executives to highlight an issue or problem that has not been addressed. The 'force' that pressure groups exert does not necessarily correlate with the number of people who support the group, but the weight of numbers is influential in a democracy.

Sometimes pressure groups form for specific purposes. Those that develop to protest against closing a local school may well disappear once that school is kept open or closed down. Others form for more general purposes. Pressure groups that form around environmental issues may participate in policy-making concerning a wide range of issues (from addressing land degradation, stopping logging of native forests, and preventing the introduction of genetically modified organisms). Other groups can become pressure groups when the activity for which they were formed comes under some threat. Members of a softball club, for example, may seek to

BOX 10.1
Save the Franklin campaign

The campaign to save the Franklin River was triggered by the failure to save Lake Pedder in the 1970s, and the Tasmanian Hydro-Electric Commission's proposal to construct a dam on the Lower Gordon River. Three pressure groups joined forces to oppose the dam. These were the Wilderness Society, the Tasmanian Conservation Trust, and the Australian Conservation Foundation. In June 1980, 10,000 people marched through the streets of Hobart in support of saving the Franklin River. Alternative propositions and compromise solutions offered a partial damming. The Legislative Council in the Tasmanian Parliament blocked these solutions, however. In 1982 the Liberal Party won office in Tasmania and legislated for the Franklin Dam to go ahead. Dr Bob Brown, head of the Wilderness Society, called for a blockade of the area. From January to March 1983, blockades impeded the use of machinery, and protestors engaged in various actions to gain further public attention. Many arrests occurred during this period. A turning point in the campaign was the election of the Hawke Labor government in March 1983, as leaders of the Labor Party had committed themselves to saving the Franklin River.

Source: http://www.greenleft.org.au

pressure members of a local council who are planning to redevelop their home ground in a way that would inhibit the club's development.

Lobbying

The members of pressure groups often seek new policy, funding, or legislation. The most obvious people from whom to seek these things are members of political executives. They are the ones who can change policy, supply funds and, if necessary, are best placed to ensure that Parliament passes or changes laws. The members of political executives, especially of Cabinets, are the first people that members of a pressure group will seek to persuade that their position is legitimate. Professional lobbyists[3] are increasingly part of government and democracy in Australia, as pressure groups found that the most effective lobbying came from people with contacts in political executives and the ability to influence them.

Protests

If they fail to get support from members of political executives, then members of pressure groups must seek other ways to increase the pressure on members of political executives. One of the principal ways that pressure groups do this is to seek public support for their cause. Different strategies to achieve this will be adopted depending on the nature of the issue and the people whose support is being sought. Leaflets and posters are ways of getting regular messages to people. Pickets and occupations can help draw attention to problems, but only where those who are responsible for problems can be identified and physically located. Demonstrations, street marches, and rallies are among the most common tactics that members of pressure groups use to gain support and increase their pressure on the members of political executives.

The news media

While protests can be understood as direct appeals to the people, pressure groups are more likely to target members of the news media[4] because of the important role they play in identifying significant and current issues in Australian politics. Members of political executives may have refused to respond positively to pressure group demands because they did not think the issue of sufficient importance to require action. But if those involved in the news media give prominence to an issue in their political coverage, then this could lead to executive action—the issue could then be seen as important and require action. In short, it might be politically damaging not to do anything about it because it has been reported in the news.

The news media is also important to members of pressure groups because of its ability to provide information to a significant number of people. If information can change people's attitudes, then using the news media to disseminate information to people may result in greater support for a pressure group. In many instances, pressure groups deal with issues that involve specialised knowledge. Pressure groups can be a source of this knowledge and, in this way, the news media can be used to ensure that more people receive the information they need to understand an issue (and, hopefully, come to support the pressure group's position).

QUESTION

How do pressure groups seek to influence members of political executives in Australia?

2: WHY ARE PRESSURE GROUPS IMPORTANT IN A REPRESENTATIVE DEMOCRACY?

Through their impact on formal political institutions, pressure groups play an important role in a representative democracy.[5] A positive approach to the role of pressure groups can be found in liberal-pluralist theory. For advocates of liberal-pluralism, pressure group activity has produced a new form of representative democracy (liberal-pluralism). For critics of Westminster-style representative democracies, effective pressure group activity can assist in overcoming problems associated with a lack of responsiveness on the part of members of political executives. From this perspective, pressure groups are a means for reviving democracy by increasing the responsiveness of a Westminster-style representative democracy. These positions are clearly related, however. An understanding of both assists in an understanding of the nature, operation, and potential of pressure groups in government and democracy in Australia.

Liberal-pluralism, pressure groups, and representative democracy

Pressure groups are so important for some people that they have led to a new theory of a democratic system. In this theory, called pluralism or liberal-pluralism,[6] political institutions, and especially political executives, act like a political barometer that responds to the pressures generated by pressure groups.

The amount of pressure a group can direct at members of political executives will determine how successful they will be in achieving their aims. Pluralism seems important here for two reasons. First, it provides some sense of how pressure groups operate in Australian politics. And second, it represents a model for a democratic system that might offer ways to improve government and democracy in Australia.

The following section provides an account of pluralism. It first discusses the liberal principles embedded in pluralism and then explains the way that pluralists have used groups as the basis for their model (rather than individuals, which is central to liberal thought). Groups of individuals with shared interests often find themselves in opposing positions with respect to policy. It is the competition between these groups for influence over a political executive that is not predisposed to favour any group that constitutes the essence of a pluralist system. This competition between pressure groups also makes a pluralist system into a democratic one.

Liberal-pluralism as development from liberalism

Because pluralism theory is sometimes referred to as liberal-pluralism, we will discuss pluralism with some comments about liberalism.[7] While this is putting it a little crudely, liberalism begins with the view that people are self-centred, calculating individuals. That individuals are self-centred, possibly even selfish, has a number of consequences. First, it means that people are not necessarily social. Second, it means that they are concerned primarily with themselves and only subsequently about others. Third, it means that people are pursuing their individual interests. Finally, and as a consequence of all this, people will find themselves in positions where their self-interest results in conflict with others. Sometimes this conflict is a result of competition over scarce resources; sometimes differences in values or principles.

Groups of individuals with shared and often competing interests

Pluralists do not reject a concern with conflict and competition among individuals, but they believe that individuals use groups to further their own ends. While we may be individuals, we share particular interests with many other people, and acknowledge that there are many other people who, at least in one respect, are like us. They may like what we like. They may believe what we believe. No two individuals share exactly the same set of interests or values, so we will tend to share each of our interests, then, with a different group of people. A young, Christian, Aboriginal mother who plays netball, lives in Lucas Heights (Sydney), is an environmentalist, works for a multinational, and smokes marijuana will belong to a variety of groups who share an interest (at least nine in this example).

Just as our interests and values can be like those of other people, they can also be very different. The interests and values of young people seem markedly different from those of older people. The interests and values of Christians are different from non-Christians. Those who live in Lucas Heights may have different interests from those who do not live in a suburb in which a nuclear reactor is located. Those people who use recreational drugs seem to have different values and interests from those who do not.

Groups with opposed interests on policies

Like liberals, pluralists believe that society is characterised by conflict or competition.[8] Neither liberals nor pluralists are concerned about this conflict or competition (as long as it is not violent). They expect this, because of the different interests that people have. Further, they seek to use this conflict in a positive manner. For pluralists this conflict or competition can be an important part of the policy-making process. Pluralists seek a society in which individuals join groups that actively promote their interests and, by directing their energies towards the political executive, participate in a policy-making process that is fundamentally democratic.

Sharing an interest with others is only the beginning of this story. Sharing an interest means little until a group of people act to protect or promote that interest. By actively combining our energies with those who share our interests or ideas, we can increase our capacity to further those interests and ideas. To do this we will have to join groups and work together to achieve our goals. Democracies are particularly amenable to the use of groups because they provide a number of points at which people can register their opinions and contain Parliamentarians who will ultimately have to seek support from voters. Indeed, it is the combination of democratic practices and group activity that characterises pluralism. By combining into groups, individuals can use democratic principles and processes to promote their interests. Democratic principles legitimise individuals using groups to influence political outcomes. Democratic processes provide groups with the ability to promote their interests.

Policy decided as a result of pressure

Pluralism is a theory about policy-making in a truly democratic system. In a pluralist model, members of political executives make policy as a result of the pressure that different groups are able to exert on them. Issues usually give rise to groups whose members have opposed interests. These groups seek to put pressure on members of political executives to force them to develop and implement policies that serve their interests. The political executive reacts to this pressure and develops a policy that reflects the variety of pressures to which it was exposed. The best outcome, from the perspective of those in the political executive, is to develop a policy that reflects all of the views presented to it.

This is not easy. And it is impossible in the case of issues like abortion, where pro- and anti-abortion groups cannot both be fully satisfied. It seems almost impossible with respect to the introduction of genetically modified organisms into Australian agriculture. It seems very difficult with respect to logging old growth forests and immigration. Indeed, few simple solutions exist in a situation in which groups are opposed to each other. In these circumstances, the pressure exerted by all sizeable pressure groups may be reflected in a final policy which does not satisfy anyone.

Reflects weight of opinion

Once all interested groups have been given the opportunity to exert pressure on members of political executives, it is up to them to develop policy. The only requirement that pluralists impose in this context is that the policy that is developed is a fair reflection of the pressure that was exerted. Members of political executives are to exhibit the greatest amount of openness and responsiveness possible. In short, they are not to allow their interests or values that they have as individuals to influence their decision concerning the best policy. Certainly, the members of Cabinet have 'won' an election because of a set of policies and this will constitute grounds for believing that it would be democratic[9] to implement those policies.

These policies can be sufficiently open to allow for further negotiation, however. Many other issues will arise, though, and some policies may be seen as less central to 'winning' than others. These will constitute the grounds upon which pressure group opposition will be most important.

Is democracy in action (within a representative democracy)?

Some readers may be sceptical about the capacity of the members of Australian political executives to resist imposing their values and interests on their policy decisions. But this view may be countered with the argument that the primary self-interest of members of political executives is to remain in office.

The main reason that members of political executives would be open to the influence of pressure groups, from this perspective, is that it will help them to gain support from voters and other Members of Parliament (especially those within their own party). Members of political executives are power seekers who will do whatever it takes to keep their power. Doing what it takes, in this context, is trying to gain the support of as many of the members of competing pressure groups as they can.

To reach a decision that alienates as few voters as possible, the members of a political executive must try to satisfy as many people as possible. If the vast majority of voters desire a specific outcome, then the interests or views of the minority of people who disagree with this may be sacrificed. As the groups become increasingly equal, members of political executives will seek to produce a policy that reflects pressure from all groups. Their goal is a policy that meets some of the needs of as many groups as they can. For many people, a political system in which members of political executives are responsive to citizens' demands is a democracy. Pressure group activity plays a central role in achieving this democracy.

Problems with (Westminster-style) representative democracies

While pluralists have positive reasons to support a form of politics based on pressure groups, problems with representative democracies may be another reason to value pressure groups. From this perspective, pressure groups are important because their involvement in the policy-making process can overcome some of the deficiencies that have developed in representative democracies. These deficiencies include a lack of responsiveness on the part of members of Australian political executives. Another problem relates to the way that political institutions in representative democracies seem to have become less flexible and, as a result, less able to accommodate new interests, new issues, and new generations of voters. It can be argued that this problem is more fundamental than a lack of flexibility. It is an inability on the part of political institutions to allow a different type of society to emerge.

A lack of responsiveness from political executives

Some of the problems associated with a lack of responsiveness on the part of members of political executives have already been encountered in the discussion of the role of Parliament. This lack of responsiveness stems from the inability of state and federal Parliaments to effectively scrutinise the actions and policies of members of Australian political executives and to hold them responsible for those failures. There are other reasons for this. One of these is an increasing professionalisation of politics in which professional politicians, surrounded by professional advisers, create policy that reflects the orientations and values of these professionals.[10] Rather than listening and responding to the desires of the people, these politicians create an imaginary 'ordinary' Australian whose interests they imagine and then seek to satisfy. However, the activities of pressure groups may force them to at least acknowledge the views and values of those outside the professional political elite.

Lack of flexibility of Australian political institutions (including parties)
Another reason for dissatisfaction with the Australian political system arises from its perceived lack of flexibility. Political institutions, from this perspective, become rigid channels that allow only some ideas and values to influence decision-making processes. Most people who are elected to Parliament have had to join one of the main political parties and seek endorsement as its candidate for a specific electorate or Senate seat from the members of a branch of that party. To get endorsement for leading positions within the party requires winning the support of senior members. It may require joining a specific sub-group, or faction, within the party and abiding by the requirements of that sub-group. While there are obvious differences in the way that you get to the top in a party (and Parliament) and the public service or judiciary, they all constitute career paths that 'institutionalise' those who follow them. Those who have been effectively trained by their institution are better equipped to respond than those outside them.

Political institutions suited to a society that no longer exists
This sort of analysis of Australian political institutions can go even deeper to argue that the political institutions of Australian politics do not reflect today's society, but simply repeat a pattern that was created in the late nineteenth century. From this perspective, the two-party system may be understood to represent a division between workers and employers that is no longer the most important division in Australian society.

While the Australian political system might be well suited for resolving conflicts between workers and employers, it is unable to provide any resolution of problems that relate to the unjust treatment of Aborigines, women, and ethnic minorities, or that are associated with environmental degradation and the effects of globalisation. These problems might best be dealt with in a differently constituted political system, but achieving such a system seems unlikely. The best that can be achieved is if pressure groups function within the existing political system to represent those interests that are not well represented in Australian politics.[11] Although this may not be a long-term solution, pressure groups can play an important role in increasing the flexibility of the political system.

Summary

Whether liberal-pluralists or critics of Australian politics are right about pressure groups is less important for our purposes than the political possibilities that pressure groups may represent. In short, pressure groups play an important role in ensuring that interests and values, which might otherwise not be taken into account, are brought to the attention of those in the political executive.

That they lack the rigidity of formal political institutions means that they can provide a more spontaneous and more contemporary vehicle for those people who wish to have their voices heard without having to submit to the demands of formal political institutions. In this way, pressure groups can form another layer of government and democracy in Australia that provides the interface between citizens and their formal political institutions. Pressure groups create new channels for communicating people's interests and values to the political executive. Their ability to operate outside the normal channels of formal politics makes them important for any appreciation of Australian government and democracy.

QUESTION

In what ways does Australian politics evidence pluralism?

3: WHY ARE SOME PRESSURE GROUPS MORE INFLUENTIAL THAN OTHERS?

This part of the chapter discusses reasons why some pressure groups are more influential than others. The short answer to this question is that they are able to generate effective pressure on the members of Cabinet. Effective pressure can either be directly delivered to the members of Cabinet or it can be indirect and delivered to points that can transmit that pressure to members of Cabinets. A discussion of effective pressure will provide an insight into the way that pressure groups work in government and democracy in Australia.

Effective pressure

Amount of force

For a pressure group to be effective, it must develop a sufficient amount of pressure to lead members of political executives to take the values and interests of the members of the pressure group into account. The size of the group is an important factor in this. In a representative democracy in which Parliamentarians and members of Cabinet are sensitive to electoral support, the number of people who support a pressure group will be an important factor in determining whether a pressure group will be taken into account in policy decisions. However, numbers are not the only factor of importance. Force or effectiveness is also determined by the extent to which the demands of a pressure group are consistent with the dominant values of society. Most importantly, it will be determined by the extent to which the demands of a pressure group are consistent with the dominant values of leading members of political executives.

BOX 10.2
NFF's fighting fund

The National Farmers' Federation is among the most important pressure groups that seek to represent the interests of people in rural areas and industries. In 1986, the Federation created a 'fighting fund' to which over $13 million was contributed by Australian farmers and industries that depend on them.

The NFF has been engaged in a number of campaigns, including an attempt to overturn the *Native Title Act* and to resolve the confusion surrounding land rights that was allegedly created by the High Court's *Mabo* and *Wik* decisions.

Sources: http://www.nff.org.au; http://www.greenleft.org.au

Points receptive to pressure (plugs and sockets)

This concern with the 'fit' between the values expressed by members of a pressure group and those who are the targets of this pressure is important. If a political system is envisaged with a number of points at which pressure can be delivered, the crucial factor for the delivery of effective pressure is the 'fit' between the values of the pressure group and those at the point where the group is attempting to direct its pressure.

Think of electricity plugs and sockets as an analogy. Australian sockets require a particular sort of plug. Take those plugs to Hong Kong, for example, and they will not work (because the sockets there are made for a British-style plug). A perfectly good hair dryer, that will work when plugged into the electricity sockets available in Australia, will not dry hair in Hong Kong. An adapter can be bought, however, that will allow a hair dryer to be plugged into a socket in Hong Kong. This might make some sense of the role and importance of lobbyists. However, a lobbyist may not be able to help overcome the problems faced by members of a pressure group who challenge the dominant values of people at the points in the political system where they are seeking to be heard.

The Cabinet as the point at which pressure is to have effect

While a political system contains a number of points upon which pressure can be exerted, they are not of equal importance. In the end, a pressure group is usually concerned with getting members of Cabinet to change a policy or develop a policy where previously they had none. The other points in the political system can be understood to constitute means by which pressure can subsequently be exerted on members of Cabinet.[12] A pressure group that can successfully lobby non-government members of an Upper House to reject a bill developed by Cabinet is delivering a kind of pressure to Cabinet, assuming that these non-government members have a majority of votes. A pressure group that is able to use the High Court to overturn a piece of Cabinet's legislation is also delivering a kind of pressure to Cabinet. Pressure that serves to prevent members of a political executive from acting is a last resort, but remains a strategy for members of a pressure group who have been unable to bring effective pressure to bear on members of Cabinet.

BOX 10.3
Overturning the NT's euthanasia legislation

The *Rights of the Terminally Ill Act 1995* in the Northern Territory allowed terminally ill people to seek assistance from medically qualified people to voluntarily end their lives in a humane manner. The Act allowed such assistance to be given in certain circumstances without penalty to the person rendering the assistance. It also sought to protect against the possibility of abuse of the Act. This legislation was anti-ethical to the principles to which 'Right to Life' groups were committed. An attempt to repeal this Act was undertaken in the NT Assembly by Neil Bell, but it was defeated. The Act was also challenged in the courts, but was upheld by the High Court in August 1996. A private bill to repeal the Act, however, was introduced into the House of Representatives. Kevin Andrews' private member's bill was introduced in December 1996. The Prime Minister, the Deputy Prime Minister, and the Leader of the Opposition supported it. The Andrews Bill relied on provision s 122 of the Constitution, which provides 'that the Parliament may make laws for the Government of any Territory'. The Bill was passed in federal Parliament and approved by the Governor-General. Consequently, the *Rights of the Terminally Ill Act 1995* was no longer in force in the Northern Territory.

Source: http://www.qrtl.org.au; http://www.nt.gov.au

Pressure points within the Cabinet
Premier or Prime Minister

The centrality of the role of the Premier or Prime Minister in Cabinet means that one of the best strategies available to members of a pressure group is to successfully pressure a Premier or Prime Minister to support them. Gaining support from a

Premier or Prime Minister will usually result in a pressure group being successful. This makes the values of a Premier or Prime Minister important, for their values will play a significant role in determining the outcome. There may even be occasions when their values may lead them to refuse to support members of a pressure group who have been able to mobilise significant levels of public support (and which, as a result, threatens to do electoral damage to the party in power).

Cabinet Ministers
Gaining the support of the Premier or Prime Minister is most likely to result in a pressure group being successful in achieving its aims. If members of a pressure group cannot achieve this, then the next most effective strategy is to influence members of that Premier's or Prime Minister's Cabinet. The more support that a pressure group can gain from Cabinet Ministers, especially senior members of Cabinet, the more likely it will be to influence policy. Once again, this influence will not be simply a product of the numbers of people concerned, but will also reflect the extent to which members of Cabinet are sympathetic to the pressure group's values.

Ministers not in Cabinet
Departments that are not headed by members of Cabinet may control some of the issues around which pressure groups organise. Gaining support from a relevant Minister may be very important for the success of a pressure group. Ministers may have some discretion with respect to policy and may use this discretion in a way that members of pressure groups desire. Ministers who are members of Cabinet may also have discretion with respect to an issue that will not come before Cabinet. Cabinet does not control all of the issues that arise for Ministers who sit in it and these Ministers can play an important individual role in determining policy.

Advisers to Ministers (including Premiers and Prime Ministers)
All Ministers (especially Premiers and Prime Ministers) have a number of advisers to develop policy. These advisers play an important role in policy development and in a Minister's general decision-making. To influence them might play a significant role in increasing a pressure group's chances for achieving success. Once again, the values of these advisers will play a role in determining whether they will be open to pressure group influence and willing to pass on in their advice to their Ministers.

Pressure points 'outside' Cabinet
The greatest likelihood of success for the members of a pressure group comes from getting direct pressure to members of Cabinet (or a responsible Minister, if it is not a matter for Cabinet). A failure to do so means that pressure must be exerted indirectly,

via other institutions or actors within the political system. In some instances, the pressure can only be negative, in that it will be exerted on institutions that can only frustrate the will of members of Cabinet. This applies to Parliament, which can call the members of Cabinet and other Ministers to account for themselves and can attempt to block Cabinet-sponsored legislation in the Upper House (assuming that members of Cabinet do not control that House).

This also applies to the High Court, which can overturn legislation promoted by members of Cabinet. Other channels, such as the public service or political parties, might provide conduits that are more positive for pressure groups because they can produce different policies that reflect the interests and values of the members of the pressure groups concerned. The final channels for pressure are not really channels at all, in the sense that they do not lead directly to the members of Cabinet. These include political executives at the state level of government, the people, and organisations like the United Nations. None of these can act directly on members of Cabinet, and are very much last resorts for pressure groups that have failed to 'plug' into other points in the Australian political system.

Public service

The fact that the public service[13] is responsible for much of the policy approved by Cabinets means that seeking to influence the members of a specific department can provide an avenue for influencing policy. Also, some policies generated within Cabinet do not require Cabinet approval, and this may result in a pressure group achieving its ends. However, because most of the issues around which pressure groups develop will be controversial means that they are more likely to go to Cabinet (whose members are sensitive to electoral pressures). But influencing members of the public service, might also influence the advice that Ministers and Cabinets receive from support staff within their department.

Party

Another channel through which pressure can be exerted on members of Cabinet is through their party.[14] While the members of a political executive are influential members within their party, they do not control the party. They cannot simply ignore advice that comes from the party organisation or from meetings, such as national conferences, in which party policy is determined. The members of political executives are not the only significant voices to be heard within a party and a pressure group may seek to influence those other voices. If the party to which the members of a Cabinet belong can be persuaded to adopt a policy that reflects the values and interests of the pressure group, then this will go some way to creating pressure on Cabinet to change policy or to adopt a new policy.

Parliament

While the members of political executives are not particularly answerable to Parliament, Parliament retains some capacity to scrutinise the actions and policies of the members of political executives and to require them to account for their actions. In this way, Parliament can constitute a vehicle for applying pressure on the members of Cabinet.[15] Apart from a capacity to ask questions of Ministers, Members of Parliament also give speeches in which they criticise Cabinet policies. They can table petitions given to them by their constituents in which Cabinet policies are challenged. These actions have little effect, however, apart from bringing issues to the attention of the journalists who report on Parliament.

Much more effective is Parliament's capacity to refuse to pass legislation that has been supported by the members of Cabinet. This capacity only exists when the party or parties to which the members of Cabinet belong do not control the Upper House. In some cases, the votes of as few as two or three members may determine the outcomes of votes in the Upper House. If the members of a pressure group can influence these two or three members, then members of political executives can be prevented from introducing the legislation concerned. Taking this course of action indicates that the members of the pressure group have failed to influence the Cabinet's policy and are left in a situation in which they can only seek to frustrate their will.

High Court

To go to the High Court to seek to invalidate legislation supported by a Cabinet is another, though more negative, form of pressure. The High Court[16] can only invalidate legislation on the following grounds: because it is outside the powers of a state or federal Parliament; because it contravenes an international agreement that has been legitimately ratified by a representative of the federal political executive; or because it is inconsistent with a principle fundamental to Australian democracy. It cannot overturn legislation that a pressure group believes to be bad legislation because it is poorly conceived or based on misguided principles. The High Court can be used to serve a pressure group's larger purpose, but only when members of the High Court have been persuaded by legal arguments that it is valid to do so.

Political executives at the other level

If a pressure group has failed to apply direct or indirect pressure to members of a state or federal Cabinet, then it may seek support from the members of political executives at the other level. Legislation passed by one Parliament might serve to frustrate the policy adopted by Cabinet at another level of government. Alternatively, a lack of cooperation from members of Cabinet at one level might also inhibit the effects of Cabinet policy. Criticism from a Prime Minister or State Premier of actions or policies is unlikely to constitute effective pressure on that Cabinet, but it is a form of pressure. The degree of pressure will diminish significantly if the Premier is not from the same party as the members of Cabinet at the other level.

'The people'

The final group to whom a pressure group can appeal in Australia is the Australian public itself.[17] That the members of Cabinet are conscious of opinion polls and other indications of public support for their policies means that any changes in attitude among large numbers of Australian voters is likely to come to their attention. This will not produce a change of policy on every occasion because the values of members of Cabinet may create resistance to change. It will have an effect, however, and can eventually produce a change of policy.

To gain widespread public support for their position will greatly increase the pressure on Cabinet to change policy or develop policy in an area in which it has been inactive. Protests that have been arranged to attract the attention of those in the news media are intended to fulfil this purpose. The members of a pressure group can do much to achieve their goals by bringing themselves to the attention of as many people as possible and attempting to provide information that will change their attitudes on the issue of concern. Of course, this is a last resort and is only necessary when all other strategies fail.

Summary

Pressure groups seek to put pressure on Cabinet to change policies. The various points discussed above indicate the main targets of pressure group activity. A pressure group can only generate effective pressure if it is able to 'plug into' one or more of the pressure points within the Australian political system. Cabinet is the most important of these. Effective pressure on Cabinet, however, is often determined by the 'fit' between the values of the pressure group and those of the members of Cabinet. If the members of Cabinet are not receptive to direct pressure, then indirect avenues are required. A variety of avenues exist for delivering indirect pressure; some of these, such as Parliament and the High Court, are simply means by which the will of the members of Cabinet can be frustrated. Pressure on the public service or party may result in members of Cabinet deciding to change policy. If all else fails, there is always the people (though this must be considered in the context of problems associated with using the news media to gain public support).

> **QUESTION**
>
> Does the pressure exerted by pressure groups on members of Cabinet necessarily result in positive outcomes for government and democracy in Australia?

CONCLUSION

Successful groups do not require public support, as they have been able to play a significant role in the policy-making process by influencing members of Cabinet directly. While we may associate pressure groups with street marches, pickets, demonstrations, and other forms of protest, it is when they function as part of the policy-making process that they are fulfilling the role that pluralists and critics of the Australian political system expect of pressure groups. It is by this means that they are providing the sort of popular participation in policy-making and flexibility that is associated with a better form of democracy. Their role as vehicles through which the values and interests of groups within Australian society are brought to the attention of the members of Cabinet and those at other points within the Australian political system means that pressure groups can be seen to produce or enhance democracy.

FURTHER READING

Introductory texts

Economou, Nick, 1998, 'Interest Groups and Governments: The Case of Environmental Policy-making', in D. Lovell, I. McAllister, W. Maley & C. Kukathas (eds), *The Australian Political System*, 2nd edn, Longman: South Melbourne.

Gruen, Fred & Michelle Grattan, 1998, 'Managing the Pressure Groups', in D. Lovell, I. McAllister, W. Maley & C. Kukathas (eds), *The Australian Political System*, 2nd edn, Longman: South Melbourne.

Marsh, Ian, 1995, *Beyond the Two Party System: Political Representation, Economic Competitiveness, and Australian Politics*, Cambridge University Press: Melbourne.

Warhurst, John, 1998, 'In Defence of Single-Issue Interest Groups', in D. Lovell, I. McAllister, W. Maley & C. Kukathas (eds), *The Australian Political System*, 2nd edn, Longman: South Melbourne.

Warhurst, John, 1993, 'Changing Relationships: Interest Groups and Policy-making in the 1990s', in A. Hede & S. Prasser (eds), *Policy Making in Volatile Times*, Hale and Iremonger: Sydney.

Specialist texts

Abbott, Keith, 1996, *Pressure Groups and the Australian Federal Parliament*, Australian Government Publication Service: Canberra.

Melucci, Alberto, 1980, 'The New Social Movements: A Theoretical Approach', *Social Science Information*, vol. 19, no. 2, pp. 199–226.

Melucci, Alberto, 1985, 'The Symbolic Challenge of Contemporary Movements', *Social Research*, 1985, vol. 52, no. 4, pp. 789–816.

Melucci, Alberto, 1992, 'What Is "New" in the "New Social Movements"?', *Sociologia*, vol. 26, nos 2–3, pp. 271–300.

Melucci, Alberto, 1995a, 'Conflict and Rule: Social Movements and Political Systems', *Sociologica*, vol. 10, no. 28, pp. 225–33.

Melucci, Alberto, 1995b, 'The New Social Movements Revisited: Reflections on a Sociological Misunderstanding', in Louis Maheu (ed.), *Social Movements and Social Classes: The Future of Collective Action*, Sage: London.

Richardson, Jeremy J., 1993, *Pressure Groups*, Oxford University Press: Oxford.

Smith, Martin J., 1993, *Pressure, Power and Policy: State Autonomy and Policy Networks in Britain and the United States*, Harvester Wheatsheaf: London.

Smith, Martin J., 1995, *Pressure Politics*, Baseline Books: Charlton.

Touraine, Alain, 1985, 'An Introduction to the Study of Social Movements', *Social Research*, vol. 52, no. 4, pp. 749–87.

Touraine, Alain, 1992, 'Beyond Social Movements?', *Theory, Culture & Society*, vol. 9, no. 1, pp. 125–45.

Touraine, Alain, 2004, 'The Subject and Societal Movements', in J.R. Blau (ed.), *The Blackwell Companion to Sociology*, Blackwell: Malden, MA.

Web sites

Australian politics: http://australianpolitics.com
Australian Chamber of Commerce and Industry: http://www.acci.asn.au
Australian Conservation Foundation: http://www.acfonline.org.au
Australian Council of Social Services: http://www.acoss.org.au
Australian Council of Trade Unions: http://www.actu.asn.au
Australian Institute of Petroleum: http://www.aip.com.au
Australian Medical Association: http://www.ama.com.au
Business Council of Australia: http://www.bca.com.au
Evatt Foundation: http://evatt.labor.net.au

Friends of the Earth Australia: http://www.foe.org.au
Greenpeace: http://www.greenpeace.org/international
Gun Control Australia: http://www.guncontrol.org.au
National Farmers Federation: http://www.nff.org.au
The Wilderness Society: http://www.wilderness.org.au

Notes

1. For more information on the different types of pressure groups, see Matthews (1997, pp. 269–71), Heywood (2002, pp. 269–73), Singleton et al. (2006, pp. 409–11), Warhurst (2006, pp. 328–38), Jaensch (1994, pp. 171–4), and Ward & Stewart (2006, pp. 212–17).
2. For more on the strategies employed by pressure groups, see Singleton et al. (2006, pp. 411–13) and Ward & Stewart (2006, pp. 222–4).
3. For more information on the role of lobbying and lobbyists in Australian politics, see Jaensch (1992, pp. 343–4), Maddox (2005, pp. 370–1), Lovell et al. (1998, p. 351), Cullen (1998, pp. 372–3), and Davis et al. (1993, pp. 148–9).
4. For more detail on the interaction between the news media and pressure groups, see Jaensch (1994, pp. 190–8).
5. For more information on how pressure groups affect democracy, see Heywood (2002b, pp. 67–84).
6. For more information on pluralism, see Matthews (1997, pp. 286–8), Heywood (2002b, pp. 78–9, 88–90, 129–30 and 273–5), Gilding (2006, p. 383), Jaensch (1994, pp. 181–5), and Emy & Hughes (1991, pp. 549–71).
7. For more on liberalism, see Heywood (2002b, pp. 43–6, 49–50).
8. For more details on the role that competition plays in liberal-pluralist theory, see Maddox (2005, p. 368).
9. For more information on pressure groups and democracy, see Jaensch (1994, pp. 185–6) and Jaensch (1992, pp. 344–9).
10. Fletcher & Whip (2000) offer an interesting discussion of the professionalisation of Australian politics and the sense of exclusion it may create on the part of some citizens.
11. Some people have argued that the late twentieth century saw the development of new social movements, which reflected the interests of those previously excluded from political processes. Those interested in this idea may wish to consult works by Alain Touraine and Jurgen Habermas.
12. For more information on pressure groups and their interaction with the political executive, see Matthews (1997, pp. 278–9), Jaensch (1994, pp. 176–7), and Matthews (1980, pp. 460–3).
13. For more information on pressure groups and the public service, see Davis et al. (1993, pp. 147–8).
14. For more details on pressure groups and political parties, see Matthews (1997, pp. 282–3), Jaensch (1994, pp. 177–8), and Matthews (1980, pp. 463–5).
15. For more information on pressure groups and Parliament, see Matthews (1997, p. 279) and Matthews (1980, pp. 463–5).
16. For more detail on pressure groups and the High Court, see Matthews (1997, p. 280).
17. For more on pressure groups and the public, see Matthews (1997, pp. 281–2), Jaensch (1994, p. 178), and Matthews (1980, pp. 467–8)

PART III

Factors affecting Government and Democracy in Australia

The News Media

LEARNING OBJECTIVES

- To identify sources of political information
- Understand why information is important for government and democracy
- Be able to consider what role the news media should play
- Recognise the impediments to the flow of information via the news media
- To appreciate the effect of the internet on the news media

INTRODUCTION

Information has always been important to people and societies and it has always been important to politics. Information has been important in all ages and gaining control over the flow of information has been a fundamental political contest. This is part of what we mean when we refer to democracies as 'open' political systems. Openness refers partly to the free flow of information between those in power and the people they represent and serve. Indeed, democracies can only work if citizens have the information they need to participate effectively in the political process. The availability of information concerning the activities and decisions of their representatives is vital to the proper functioning of representative democracies.

After discussing the importance of information for politics in the first part of this chapter, we move to the most important vehicle for the transmission of information about politics in Australia—the mass media—and, more specifically, the news media. The news media is the principal source of information about Australian politics for most, if not all, people. In an ideal situation, as we describe it, the news media would provide information that would allow people to make informed decisions about policy issues and be able to participate effectively in Australian politics. Few people would suggest that we live in an ideal situation. Understanding why we don't, which we then discuss, provides some insight into the workings of the news media in Australia. The final issue addressed in this chapter is whether the internet can overcome deficiencies in this information and opinion.

1: THE NEWS MEDIA

The main sources of information about politics, for most Australians, are newspapers and the television and radio news programs (the news media).[1] Most people get most of their information about political events, issues, and personalities from the news media.

The significance of the news media goes beyond being a source of information, however. Many journalists see reporting on politics as an essential part of the political process. The news media, in this understanding, is a 'fourth estate',[2] or an active and legitimate part of the political process—even a political institution in its own right. Due to its roles, as a disseminator of information, a forum for the airing of opinions, and a 'watch dog' to protect the public interest, the news media is potentially a vital element of democratic politics. But whether the news media fulfils its potential is an important and open question. It may not be fulfilling the roles that would make it a real contributor to Australian democracy.

This chapter is in three parts. Reasons that the news media is important to government and democracy in Australia are discussed in the first part. In the next, we outline an ideal situation in which the news media play a direct and positive role in a representative democracy. The final part discusses the reasons why the news media does not play this role in Australia.

Why is the news media so important for government and democracy in Australia?

The mass media[3] is becoming increasingly enmeshed in our lives and has important effects on how we live as individuals and as a community. Its delivery of news about politics is its most significant role because the news media provides information that is important for the effective functioning of government and for the health of our democracy. While the relationship between parties, pressure groups, and the news media is significant, the relationship between the news media and political executives is the focus of this section. This provides the basis for a discussion of 'fourth estate' theory, which is important for this chapter.

Information from political executives

The news media is one of the main channels through which members of political executives transmit information to the people through press releases and press conferences. Many of their press releases announce policies or decisions that have emerged from Cabinet or a department of the public service. Members of political executives organise press conferences in order to make these announcements and, most of the time, allow journalists to ask questions about them. They also employ former journalists to help them present information in a style that helps working journalists to use it.[4]

Main source of information for voters

The news media is also important as an independent source of information about the activities of members of political executives. In this case, journalists publish information that these politicians may not wish to be widely known. Investigative journalism refers to journalists seeking to provide different information about actions or decisions than the information they receive. Parliaments regularly fail to uncover this information. Consequently, members of the news media play an important role in ensuring that members of political executives are made accountable for their actions and decisions by providing voters with information that they would not otherwise get.

Fourth estate theory

The idea that the news media are participants in democratic processes has been around since the middle of the nineteenth century.[5] In this theory, those in the news media not only inform citizens about the actions and decisions of members of political executives, they question them to find out more. More enthusiastic advocates of this position even see the news media journalists as protectors of the people.[6] Fourth estate theory suggests that the news media have a distinct and crucial role to play in a healthy political system and an even more important role to play in a representative democracy. In this theory, the news media is not simply a supplier of information; it is an active participant, if not an institution, within representative democracy.

What is the ideal role of the news media?

While fourth estate theory has been expressed in a variety of ways,[7] a common theme is that the news media plays a role in achieving the most effective representative democracy possible. The question that arises in this context concerns what we might expect from the news media in an ideal[8] situation (this is one in which the news media fulfilled the responsibilities that fourth estate theory would suggest for them). We provide an answer to this question in the remainder of this section. Our answer is not particularly insightful and requires explanation. It is also long. Here it is: In an ideal situation, the news media provide important information and opinion about issues that are significant for government and democracy. They do so without prejudice, or with multiple prejudices, in order to allow voters to identify issues that are important to them. Voters are then in a position to make up their own minds on these issues and to determine appropriate responses to the actions and lack of action of members of our political executives.

Important information and opinion

In a representative democracy, people must have information about the decisions and actions of their representatives. We also need to know what members of political executives and other politicians think about problems or issues. We might also find it useful to find out what journalists and experts think about the issues and problems we face.

A variety of issues

Many political issues will be important to voters and those in the news media should provide information and opinion about all of them.[9] Vast amounts of information and opinion about a narrow range of issues may result in important issues being excluded from public attention. Some issues are more immediate, such as a decision to close a school, while others are less immediate, but just as important, such as global warming. Journalists, editors, and producers of news programs must ensure that information and opinion is available on all issues and problems.

Significant for government and democracy

Information and opinion is only useful, however, if it concerns matters of importance. In an ideal situation, those in the news media are responsible for ensuring that the information and opinions that they carry relate to issues and questions that are significant for Australian government and democracy. To know that a Prime Minister collects antique clocks is interesting, but we'd rather know what she or he thinks about the role of the Reserve Bank of Australia. Journalists, editors, and producers of news programs must select important information to present to their audiences.

Without prejudice or with multiple prejudices

All of the relevant information must be presented in the news media and no important information can be suppressed. The 'objectivity' of those in the news media is important to them fulfilling their role in providing information to the people. They can't selectively present information in order to lead readers, listeners, or viewers to accept a particular point of view.

Opinions cannot be objective. When it comes to providing opinion, then, the news media must convey a full range of opinions. Not to convey some opinions is to fail to provide citizens with a range of views from which they can develop their own positions. A single outlet may find it difficult to provide the full range of opinions, especially if it is a televised news program. To have a variety of news media outlets is an important part of ensuring that a range of opinions is available to the people.

Allow voters to identify important issues

The purpose of providing information and opinion is to allow voters to identify the issues about which they feel strongest. If every individual is different, then each person will identify a different set of issues as important to her or him. This is why providing information and opinion about a variety of issues is part of an ideal situation. If only a limited range of issues is presented, then this may result in issues that would have been significant to some people not being brought to their attention. This is particularly important if information about representatives or policies would cause voters to change their vote in an election.

Voters make up their own minds

The information that is provided must be presented in a manner that allows people to make up their own minds. We all know about the media's capacity to manipulate our emotions (and, when we go to the movies, we want this). When it comes to the news media, however, we do not want to be manipulated into adopting a particular position on a political issue.[10]

People determine appropriate responses
The final attribute of an ideal situation is that the information and opinions that are presented allow people to work out what they can do. Knowing what's happening, but having no idea as to what we can do about it, does us little good. We need to know what we can do to influence the debates about an issue or problem. We may not be able to do much, but we still want to know what our options are.

Summary
Two points need to be made before we discuss reasons why we do not have the ideal situation. The first is that this is a specific version of an ideal situation. It was presented so that readers would think about what the news media's role should be in government and democracy in Australia. The second point is that an ideal situation cannot exist. But trying to imagine an ideal situation is important because it gives us a measure against which we can assess the news media's performance. Reality can never fully reflect an ideal, but reality can't be improved if we have no idea what we want from those in the news media.

Why do the news media not fulfill an ideal role in government and democracy in Australia?

Three reasons explain why we don't have the ideal situation described in the preceding section. First, most Australians don't want it. Second, we don't have an ideal situation because delivering news is about selling audiences to advertisers. Finally, the nature of media and news media organisations prevents them from fulfilling their ideal role.

We don't want one

A lack of interest in politics
Few Australians are interested in politics. Compulsory voting ensures that most of us participate in politics every couple of years, but that's about it. As Rodney Smith has suggested, even when participation appears high, this reflects Australians' sense of duty, not a commitment to or an interest in politics.[11] An ideal situation does not exist because Australians are not interested in using the news media to identify important issues, to develop their views on those issues, and to acquire knowledge that will allow them to express their views in a manner that is most likely to have an effect on Australian government and democracy. We could go even further to suggest that Australians prefer a misrepresentation of politics in which it is presented as if it is simple and as if the parties are united behind the simple answers presented by their leaders. Most Australians would not have it any other way.

'News' and advertising
News media provide news to attract an audience to sell to advertisers
Even if we wanted it, the news media can't produce an ideal situation because news programs are intended to attract an audience for the advertisements they carry. The 'news' is not provided in order to improve politics, it is provided to attract and keep the largest audience possible. To do this, those responsible for the news media, especially television and radio programs, must keep the news simple and entertaining. Unfortunately, politics is rarely simple or entertaining for most Australians.

'Newsworthiness'
Journalists, editors and producers of news programs select stories that are 'newsworthy'.[12] Reporting the news is about selling an audience to advertisers, so newsworthiness is determined by whether the story will attract the largest audience possible.

The most newsworthy stories involve death or disaster (and, in the case of television programs, deaths or disasters that provide good images). Personal tragedies and triumphs are also prominent in news programs and, we must infer, important to audiences. Heroes and villains also feature regularly. This concern with personalities contributes to the significance of the Prime Minister and explains why elections are usually turned into a battle for control between the leaders of the major parties. Newsworthiness concerns what people want to know about and not what they need to know about.

Agenda setting
Little room for the sort of reporting that might contribute to an ideal situation remains when a considerable portion of the news in newspapers and television and radio programs is devoted to death and disaster, personal tragedies and triumphs, heroes and villains, weather and sport. By selecting a limited number of political issues to report, and as a consequence excluding many others, the news media play an important role in determining the issues that we think are important. This is known as agenda setting.[13] But the agenda will be set by those issues that have newsworthiness, and not necessarily those that are important for government and democracy in Australia.

Audience's limits
Journalists, editors, and producers work hard to report stories that maintain an audience's attention. If thinking is hard work, and it is, then stories that require too much thought will put people off. Thinking about political issues is not interesting or attractive for most Australians. Newspapers or television and radio news programs that cover too many stories at too great a length will lose their audience (as people close their paper or switch stations or channels).

A note on the ABC and SBS
While those in the commercial news media are in search of the largest audience possible, we might think that those in the ABC and SBS are free from these pressures and can contribute to the creation of our ideal situation. This does not follow, however, because those in charge of the ABC and SBS have to justify the billions of tax dollars that are spent on their organisations. Part of their justification will relate to the quality of the programs they air, but they must also attract enough listeners and viewers to be seen to provide a service for which all Australians should pay. Their news programs, therefore, will compete with the commercial news media according to the principles governing the attraction and retention of an audience discussed above.

Summary
The news is simply a product through which media companies attract and retain audiences. Both the selection of stories for coverage and the way in which they are covered reflects this preoccupation with attracting the largest possible audience, not some desire to contribute to improving the quality of government and democracy in Australia. While we acknowledge the efforts of those who pursue journalism as a public service, their efforts run counter to the fundamental principles that govern the news media, and represent a refusal to conform to those principles.

Media organisations

Commercial organisations
The media is a business and this affects the news media. Media organisations are deeply conservative because the businessmen [sic] who own them benefit from the way things are and don't want to radically change Australian society. The values of businessmen, the importance of economic development, and the maintenance of profitability for Australian firms, are made to appear legitimate by those in the media and news media.[14]

Concentration of ownership
The general environment of a business organisation will dampen the enthusiasm of any journalist who is naïve or zealous enough to try to use the news media to promote alternative views (assuming she or he wants to remain a journalist). The fact that the news media are owned by a small number of wealthy businessmen makes it even less likely that they will present a variety of opinions on a variety of issues to the people.

Those who manage news media outlets are usually aware of the values and attitudes of their bosses and, given the limited number of positions for senior managers in the media and news media, are reluctant to do anything that might contradict them. They will do nothing, we can safely assume, to resist the direct orders that media proprietors sometimes pass down to those who edit or produce the news.[15] As Trevor Barr (2000) has pointed out, to increase the number of owners will achieve little. All owners will be business people and their values will be much like those of existing owners of media organisations.

BOX 11.1
Media ownership in Australia

Australian Consolidated Press

(ACP is a subsidiary of Publishing and Broadcasting Ltd, in which the Packer family holds a controlling 35 per cent share.)

The Nine Network

- Subscription TV—25 per cent ownership in Foxtel Pay TV, Crown Casino, and Hoyts Cinemas
- Magazines—*Australian Women's Weekly, Woman's Day, Cleo, Cosmopolitan, Dolly, People, Australian Personal Computer, Australian House and Garden,* and *Wheels.*

John Fairfax Holdings Ltd

- Newspapers—*Age, Sunday Age, Sydney Morning Herald, Australian Financial Review.*

- Magazines— *Business Review Weekly, Personal Investment, Australian Geographic,* and *Shares.*

News Corporation

(The Murdoch family holds 30 per cent of the voting stock.)

- Newspapers—*The Australian, Herald Sun, Sunday Herald Sun, Daily Telegraph, Sunday Advertiser, Courier Mail, Mercury,* and *Northern Territory News.*
- Subscription TV—25 per cent ownership in Foxtel Pay TV
- Festival Records, Mushroom Records (50 per cent)
- National Rugby League (50 per cent)

Source: http://www.aph.gov.au;http://australianpolitics.com/issues/media-ownerership/

Routinised organisations—news sense and presentational style
News media organisations are, in the end, like all organisations. They organise or coordinate a group of people's activities to ensure that they function together, in this case, to produce the news programs or editions of newspapers that they are employed to produce. This requires training people so they can work together

effectively. In this context, young journalists are trained to recognise 'news' and to present it in the way required by their media organisations.

For journalists, the most effective part of their training is the rejection of their story or idea for a story. News media have limited carrying capacity and so an editor or producer will assess a journalist's work to determine whether it ought to be included in an edition of a newspaper or news program. Journalists who have chosen an 'angle' that does not produce the most newsworthy reports possible will have their work rejected. Similarly, they will be rejected if they are not written or presented in the approved manner. Journalists do not choose the same angle to cover a story or write and speak in the same manner because of their genetic makeup; they do so because they have been trained to do so.

Routinised organisations— press galleries

Most journalists have particular areas upon which they report, or have particular rounds. The most important 'round', in this context, is reporting events in and around the federal Parliament. The Canberra Press Gallery,[16] as it is known, is comprised of journalists who come from a variety of media outlets, but group together because they cover the same thing: federal politics in Canberra. Press galleries socialise journalists. This is significant because it often results in journalists from different media outlets covering the same stories in very much the same way. This may be effective in ensuring that all journalists identify and report on 'major' stories, but it reduces both the variety of issues covered and the angles from which they are covered.

Routinised organisations—press secretaries, lobbyists, and advisers to pressure groups use knowledge of routines to manipulate news programs

Those who understand the routinised nature of news media organisations can use this knowledge to their advantage. Members of political executives, especially Ministers, employ former journalists whose knowledge of the news media assists in ensuring that the Minister uses it effectively. A simple example of this is when these former journalists, often referred to as press secretaries, write press releases in the same format as journalists write their stories.[17] This makes it easier for journalists, as it means that they can incorporate passages from these press releases in their stories.

Other techniques that these former journalists use include releasing positive stories on the weekend, especially Sunday, when there is usually less to report. Where possible they will seek to release negative stories when other major stories are breaking. Releasing a story at these times means that it is unlikely to be a lead story in a radio or television news program or appear on the front page of the daily newspapers. Major sporting or community events, like the Melbourne Cup or football Grand Finals, or the Christmas–New Year period, offer predictable opportunities to attempt to ensure that bad news will be buried.

Many of the techniques used by those who understand the routines of the news media relate to televised news programs, as these are the sources of most people's news (and are considered the most reliable of news sources). One technique to reduce the effect of releasing information or making an announcement that will have negative effects is to release this information late in the afternoon, when it cannot be included in the main television news programs. Televised news programs have to be finalised well before they go to air (even live to air reporting has to be organised well in advance). This means that a story released later in the day will have been used in radio news and in newspapers, which could cause television news producers to decide that the story is no longer news when they make decisions about what to include in their program scheduled for the following evening. The opposite will apply to positive information or an announcement that will be well received within the community. Great pains will be taken to ensure that this news is released in time for the main evening television news programs.

A characteristic of radio and television news media programs is that the individual items covered are rarely given more than three minutes. After the newsreader and reporter have had their say, the 'talent', as an interviewee is known, will get little more than ten seconds. Becoming expert at delivering a short 'grab' is an essential skill for a politician and is one that those who have been involved in the news media will understand. Other techniques for controlling television and radio news stories include repeating the same grab as often as possible. Radio and television journalists know that they can only use a short grab and are looking for this. To give them the one that they want will get rid of them, but this is not a good idea if it will produce a negative impression among listeners and viewers. A politician schooled in the principles of radio and television news reporting will work out the required 'grab' and will repeat it until the interview finishes—one of the reasons it will end is that a journalist will be reluctant to use up extensive amounts of tape, which will have to be watched and edited.

Internationally syndicated/nationally networked organisations
Another important feature of news media organisations is that they are usually part of national and international networks. One reason that this is important is that it can mean that the same stories are reproduced across a wide range of news media outlets. There are two aspects to this. The first is that the range of news stories from which editors and producers choose their stories is limited to those produced within the network of which their news outlet is part. The other is that

the story will be governed by the values of the other reporters who filed the story. Wire Services, such as Australian Associated Press (AAP),[18] provide news stories to a variety of news outlets. So there is little regional variation in the stories covered and the ways they are covered.

Male, white, middle-class organisations
News media organisations are also dominated by white middle-class men. The fact that women are now more prevalent in these organisations has not changed the culture that often exists within them (women remain only a third of all journalists).[19] This does not make the news media biased, but the fact that most journalists are white and male has created problems for women and non-whites who want to have their voices heard.

The reporting of the ethnic communities in Australia often conforms to the prejudices of conservative white Australians. Less than one per cent of Australian journalists come from an Asian background,[20] so 'outsiders' report events within Asian–Australian communities. Most journalists come from more privileged backgrounds and have a higher level of education than most Australians.[21] Journalists are also less conservative than the majority of Australians.[22] An Australian Broadcasting Association study suggests that journalists get their sense of newsworthiness from the conversations that they have with other journalists.[23] This means that journalists are not like most other Australians and their approach to the news reflects what they learn from other journalists.

The ideal situation
The role that the news media can play in government and democracy in Australia is limited by the very nature of news media organisations. They are limited because they are predictable commercial organisations that are owned by a small number of businessmen. They are also limited because they are dominated by white middle-class men.

Summary
Many features of news media organisations limit their capacity to play the type of role that some people might expect of them. The notion of newsworthiness plays an important part in limiting the types of information and opinion that the news media make available to voters. The routines and other features of news media organisations also undermine their capacity to play the role they ideally could play (largely because this means that, with the advice of former journalists, members of political executives can control the way they appear in the news media). Most important, however, is the lack of popular demand for a different type of journalism.

Conclusion

The news media play an important role in government and democracy in Australia. They are the main source of information from and about members of political executives. They are also a source of different opinions about political events. For some people, the news media constitutes a fourth estate, which provides an external check on the power of political executives that Parliaments are rarely able to provide. This idea provided the basis for our construction of an ideal situation. In this ideal the news media would provide the type of information that would allow people to make informed decisions about policy issues and be able to participate effectively in Australian politics in order to have their views on these issues taken into account. The nature of the news media makes it impossible to achieve this ideal situation.

QUESTION

Which news media outlets are the principal sources of political information in Australia?

2: THE INTERNET

If the preceding discussion of the nature and operation of the news media is valid, then the news media do not provide the variety of information and opinion that would provide a basis for effective government and democracy in Australia. The next question that arises is whether the internet could improve on this situation. This question is addressed in the affirmative. Rather than present alternative cases, we present and comment on four reasons to believe that the internet will improve the situation.

The first reason is that the internet offers a wide range of sources of information and opinion. This argument can be countered with the contention that the information and opinion conveyed via the internet is not reliable. The second reason to believe that the internet will improve the situation is that it is a cheap and accessible medium, which means that it is a source of information and opinion available to everyone. This can be challenged with the argument that access to the internet requires a combination of hardware, software, and skills that is not available to everyone. The third reason to believe that the internet will make a difference is that it is open to participation from a variety of people from diverse backgrounds. This point can be countered with the claim that the internet is dominated by white, middle-class men and is deeply affected by American multinational corporations. The emergence of a political blogosphere is the fourth reason to believe that the internet can improve the situation. The problem with this blogosphere is that it is dominated by white middle-class men.

At the very least, the internet is an additional space—alongside television, radio, and newspapers—in which to obtain information about politics and to present political ideas. It is rapidly overcoming these 'old media' as the major source of news for people. Online services provided by the ABC, *The Age*, the *Australian Financial Review*, the *Sydney Morning Herald*, and others, as well as exclusively online media, such as *Crikey*, provide up-to-date and developing political stories to peoples' desktops at work, home and school. If members of the political executive give press conferences, door-stop interviews at the entrance to Parliament House or simply issue press releases, they can be reasonably assured that these will receive immediate coverage in one or more of these outlets.

In the past, members of the political executive were the only politicians whose views were reported in newspapers and on television. Copies of speeches and press releases were primarily made available to other politicians, bureaucrats, journalists, and academics, not to the general public. Furthermore, when a politician or civic leader spoke directly to the people in a public forum, such as in a town hall, the size of the audience was limited because many people were unable to attend due to other commitments. Consequently, these speakers were dependent upon journalists attending the forum and reporting events in a favourable way.

Will the internet improve the situation?

Information
Multiple sources of information and opinion
One of the distinctive features of the internet is the range of sources of information and opinion that it offers. Anyone with a networked computer can create a web page, post to a discussion list or bulletin board, participate in a newsgroup, or engage in chat. A web page allows its creator to present information and offer their own views, which derive from their experiences and knowledge. Anyone interested in a particular issue is likely to find a web page that deals with this issue by using a search engine. This means that information and opinion that is not readily available in the news media can be made available to voters online.

Potentially unreliable information and opinion
The main problem with the internet, at least in this context, concerns the reliability of the information presented. Web pages are not subjected to any screening with

respect to the accuracy of the information they present or the motivations of the person offering an opinion. So-called hate sites provide a graphic, if extreme, illustration of the way that the internet is just as effective in disseminating misinformation and ill-informed opinions as it is in providing real information and informed opinions.

Accessibility
Cheap and accessible medium
Another important feature of the internet is its accessibility. Only wealthy people can own a newspaper, radio, or television station, whereas everyone who owns a networked computer can make content available to others. The internet does not impose significant costs on anyone wishing to present information and opinion. Access to the information available on the internet is available to anyone who owns a networked computer, or who can use one in a public library or internet café.

Not as cheap and accessible as is suggested
Claims that the internet is low cost and accessible must be treated with caution. People in many areas in the world do not have the basic infrastructure to gain internet access and a significant number of Australians do not have internet access. This is because access to the internet is not 'free'. First, you need to have access to the hardware and software you need and there is a cost associated with getting them. Even if access to this software is available, specific skills are required to make use of it. The problem is compounded by the fact that those people who lack access to hardware and software or the skills they need to use them are likely to be the people whose interests and opinions are under-represented in Australian society and politics.

Diversity
Not just white, middle-class men
Another reason to believe that the internet will improve the situation is that it provides a means for people other than white, middle-class men to present information and opinions. The internet can carry information from a variety of sources, including from outside sources. That the internet is relatively easy to access allows those who do not belong to the dominant culture in a society to present views on issues that arise in Australian politics. The internet can provide an opportunity for different voices and perspectives to be expressed from those of white middle-class voices that dominate the news media. Outsiders can be provided with alternative sources of information and comment that might lead to a different understanding of a non-dominant culture. Dale Spender,[24] for

example, sees enormous opportunities for women emerging from their increased use of the internet.[25]

Dominated by white, middle-class men (and US multinationals)
The problem with this position, however, is that it ignores the fact that a significant proportion of the voices on the internet are those of white, middle-class men. The internet was created by Europeans and American men and they continue to dominate the internet. This is because white middle-class men are more likely to own the hardware and software and have the skills necessary to access their interest. The internet may be changing, as Chinese has become the language most used on the internet,[26] but those Australians for whom English is a first language will benefit little from information and opinion expressed in languages other than English. The prevalence on the internet of pornography designed to appeal to heterosexual men also makes cyberspace seem to be a place of and for men, and thus, inhibits participation by women.[27]

Political blogosphere

Increase in variety and amount of opinion and information
The emergence of the blogosphere is one of the most important parts, or spaces, of the internet that offers hope for improving the situation in which Australians find themselves. Web logs (blogs) are web pages that people create as a means to express themselves and, in many cases, to share ideas and information with others. The political blogosphere has emerged as a space in which people share ideas and information about local, national, or international politics. The political blogosphere contains a mass of analysis, opinion, rumour, and facts that are not available through the mainstream media. Academics, journalists, and others who can articulate views and share information that they have developed or acquired in their professional capacity have created many political blogs. Other political blogs have been created by people who have achieved their status through the care taken with and quality of the opinions and information they present. So, sources of authoritative and influential opinions and information are available through the political blogosphere that provide content not available through the mainstream news media.

Political blogs have problems
The blogosphere suffers from the same problems as the internet so the same objections as those presented above apply. The quality of political blogs varies and much of the information presented has not been checked for accuracy and

may not be verifiable. Access problems also affect access to political blogs and white, middle-class men produce most of them. Australians appear to have been slower than Americans in the production and use of blogs, so this is still to develop as a source of alternative opinions and information about politics for most Australians. If this is a result of cultural differences, in which Australians are less willing to accept blogs as legitimate sources of opinion and information, then a meaningful political blogosphere will not emerge in Australia.

BOX 11.2
Australia's blogosphere

http://actnow.com.au/	eActivist network: blogs on topical issues, volunteering opportunities, background information on some political issues, membership structure
http://www.ozpolitics.info/blog/	Oz Politics
http://www.pollbludger.com/	Dedicated to polling and poll results
http://www.crikey.com.au/	Controversial commentary on Australian politics. Often based on rumour, lighthearted
http://www.blogotariat.com/	Blogotariat blogs on a range of issues with importance for politics in Australia.
http://www.onlineopinion.com.au	Australia's e-journal of social and political debate
http://www.theaustralian.news.com.au/opinion/blogs/	*The Australian* newspaper's blog
http://www.news.com.au/blogs	Fox news website

Summary

The internet has a number of features that suggest that it could play an important role in helping to overcome the deficiencies in the provision of information and opinion by the news media. The internet is an incredibly rich source of information and opinion. It is also widely accessible, which means that it is available to everyone as a source of information and opinion and as an avenue for expressing their views. This means that it can provide diversity in sources of information and opinion that overcomes the limitations in perspective in the news media. At least these points *might* be true of the internet. It may also be viewed as a source of unreliable information and opinion, involving an expensive and exclusive set of technologies that is largely the plaything of Western (more specifically, American) men.

QUESTION

Does the internet constitute a reliable source of political information?

CONCLUSION

Flows of information are vital to effective government and democracy. One reason for this is that members of political executives must communicate important policies and services to those they govern. The people also need to have some sense of the actions and decisions of those in political executives. This is particularly true in a representative democracy, in which voters will be asked to assess a Cabinet's performance. The principal source of information about members of political executives comes to us via the news media. This makes the news media a crucial part of the environment for Australian government and democracy. The news media may even be viewed as a part of representative democratic processes. However, there are reasons to believe that it cannot play such a role due to the constraints under which it operates and the nature of the news organisations themselves. We may look to the internet as a means to overcome the deficiency in representative democracy that occurs when the media cannot fulfill its role, though we may be looking in the wrong direction.

FURTHER READING

Introductory texts

Lucy, Richard, 1993, *The Australian Form of Government: Models in Dispute*, Macmillan: South Melbourne.

Tiffen, Rodney, 1994, 'Media Policy', in J. Brett, J. Gillespie & M. Goot (eds), *Developments in Australian Politics*, Macmillan: South Melbourne.

Ward, Ian, 2006, 'The Media, Power and Politics', in A. Parkin, J. Summers & D. Woodward (eds), *Government, Politics, Power and Policy*, 8th edn, Pearson Education: Frenchs Forest.

Specialist texts

Bray, John, 1997, 'A Web of Influence', *The World Today*, August/September, pp. 206–8.

Chishti, Muhamad, W.J. Martin & Jack Jacoby, 1997, *Information Technology Enabled Organisational Change: A Survey of Australian Practices*, RMIT Business: Melbourne.

Eggerking, Kitty, 1996, 'Introducing the Media and Indigenous Australians Project', *Australian Journalism Review*, vol. 18, no. 1, pp. 21–4.

Everard, Jerry, 2000, *Virtual States: The Internet and the Boundaries of the Nation State*, Routledge: London.

Ewart, Jacqui, 1997, 'Journalists, Readership and Writing', *Australian Studies in Journalism*, no. 6, pp. 83–103.

Forde, Susan, 1997, 'Characteristics and Values of Alternative Press Journalists', *Australian Studies in Journalism*, no. 6, pp. 104–26.

Graber, Doris, Denis McQuail & Pippa Norris, 1998, 'Introduction: Political Communication in a Democracy', in D. Graber, D. McQuail & P. Norris (eds), *The Politics of News, The News of Politics*, CQ Press: Washington DC.

Henningham, John, 1996, 'Journalists' Perceptions of Newspaper Quality', *Australian Journalism Review*, vol. 18, no. 1, pp. 13–19.

Johnston, Carla, 1998, *Global News Access: The Impact of New Communication Technologies*, Praeger: Westport.

Klotz, Robert, 1997, 'Positive Spin: Senate Campaigning on the Web', *PS: Political Science and Politics*, vol. 30, no. 3, pp. 482–6.

Loo, Eric, 1998, 'Journalistic Representation of Ethnicity', in M. Breen (ed.), *Journalism: Theory and Practice*, Macleay Press: Paddington.

Luke, Timothy, 1991, 'Touring Hyperreality: Critical Theory Confronts Informational Society', in P. Wexler (ed.), *Critical Theory Now*, The Falmer Press: London.

McLean, Iain, 1989, *Democracy and New Technology*, Polity Press: Cambridge.

Patching, Roger, 1998, 'The Preparation of Professional Journalists', in M. Breen (ed.), *Journalism: Theory and Practice*, Macleay Press: Paddington.

Pfetsch, Barbara, 1998, 'Government News Management', in D. Graber, D. McQuail & P. Norris (eds), *The Politics of News, The News of Politics*, CQ Press: Washington DC.

Public Accounts Committee, 1999, *Report on the Role of the Government in an Online Environment*, Report no. 42, State Law Publisher: Perth.

Rash, Wayne, 1997, *Politics on the Net: Wiring the Political Process*, WH Freeman: New York.

Starck, Kenneth, 1994, 'The Case for Intercultural Journalism', *Australian Journalism Review*, vol. 16, no. 2, pp. 11–24.

Stockwell, Stephen, 1999, 'Beyond the Fourth Estate: Democracy Deliberation and Journalism Theory', *Australian Journalism Review*, vol. 21, no. 1, pp. 37–49.

Web sites

Australian politics: http://australianpolitics.com
Australian Broadcasting Corporation: http://www.abc.net.au
Australian Communications and Media Authority http://www.acma.gov.au/
Australian Financial Review: http://www.afr.com
The Australian: http://www.theaustralian.news.com.au
www.news.com.au

Notes

1. We have not included a discussion of talkback radio in this chapter, despite the fact that it seems to have an impact on government and democracy in Australia. Adams & Burton (1997) and Marsden (1999) both provide good insights into talkback radio in Australia.
2. The other three estates, implicitly referred to here, are spiritual leaders (the church), secular leaders (government or the state), and the common people. For more background on the notion of the fourth estate, see Schultz (1998).
3. For more information on the role of the news media in Australian politics, see Lovell et al. (1998, p. 355) and Jaensch (1994, pp. 190–4).
4. For more information on how politicians seek to influence the news media, see Lovell et al. (1998, pp. 335–6) and Ward & Stewart (2006, p. 203).
5. See Kirkpatrick (1998, p. 84).
6. Ibid (p. 83).
7. See Schultz (1998, pp. 23–46).
8. Fourth estate theory as an ideal is also important to Schultz's (1998) book.
9. For more detail on the news media and the political agenda, see Lovell et al. (1998, pp. 356–7), and Ward & Stewart (2006, pp. 192–4).
10. For more information on the influence of the news media, see Jaensch (1994, pp. 197–8) and Smith (1997b, pp. 347–52).
11. See Smith (2001, p. 45).
12. For more details on newsworthiness, see Singleton et al. (2006, p. 170).
13. See Gadir (1982, pp. 13–23).
14. For more information on the issues concerning the media and ownership, see Lovell et al. (1998, pp. 357–60) and Smith (1997b, pp. 333–46).
15. See Bowman (1994, p. 26).
16. For more on the Canberra Press Gallery, see Steketee (1998, pp. 407–17) and Ward & Stewart (2006, pp. 201–4). For a more extended account of the Canberra Press Gallery, see Simons (1999).
17. This style is sometimes referred to as the inverted pyramid, with the first paragraph (top) bearing the greatest significance and information, and the following paragraphs diminishing in importance.

18	See http://aap.com.au
19	See Henningham (1998, p. 337).
20	Ibid (p. 338).
21	Ibid (p. 336).
22	Ibid (p. 339).
23	See Flint (2001, p. 15).
24	See Spender (1995).
25	See also http://womenst.library.wisc.edu/
26	See http://www.glreach.com/globstats/ and http://internet-statistics-guide.netfirms.com/ and http://www.internetstats.com/
27	Readers interested in this issue might be interested in Moser (1996) and Trend (2001).

12 Opinion Polling and Political Marketing

LEARNING OBJECTIVES

- To understand the methods used for opinion polling in Australia
- Appreciate the importance of the survey sample, the wording of questions and the preceding questions
- Be able to discuss whether opinion polling is good for Australian government and democracy
- Comprehend the uses of political marketing

INTRODUCTION

In this chapter, we deal with another important part of the context within which government and democracy in Australia operate. The prominence of opinion polls in reporting on politics and their significance to strategists within political parties means that opinion polls have profound effects on Australian politics.[1] Although we know that members of political executives and other politicians have always engaged in selling themselves, contemporary political marketing seems different and we think that it merits particular attention.

This chapter is in two parts. The first deals with opinion polling. Mostly, we discuss whether the extensive use of opinion polling is good for government and democracy in Australia. Our intention is to encourage reflection on the relationship between democracy and opinion polling. We've devoted the second part to a discussion of the question of whether there is anything new in contemporary political marketing. Opinion polling and marketing are now normal features of Australian politics, so we need to ask questions about them and, through this, to consider their effects on government and democracy.

1: OPINION POLLING

The first of the two sections in this part is a brief introduction to opinion polling. We describe different types of opinion polls and then examine some important aspects of them. A problem with the reports of opinion polls in the news media is that we rarely get enough information about how the poll was conducted. In the second section, we present different points of view on the question of whether the extensive use of opinion polling is good for government and democracy in Australia.

A brief introduction to opinion polling

Types of opinion polls
Face-to-face interviewing
The first opinion polling was by interviewers visiting people's homes to ask them questions.[2] An interviewer would spend from fifteen minutes to an hour working through a series of questions with an interviewee. One of the advantages of face-to-face interviewing is that it allows interviewers to see how people respond to their questions, which might allow them to learn more about their opinions than would otherwise be possible. In face-to-face interviews, however, people respond to the interviewer as much as they do to the questions being asked.

Another of the problems with this sort of interviewing is that it relies on people being at home. Doing an opinion poll during normal working hours will result in more women being interviewed than men. Conducting opinion polls at night will result in the exclusion of some shift workers. Persuading people to let a stranger into their house may also be a problem with this kind of opinion polling. Probably the most important problem with face-to-face interviewing is that it is expensive.

Telephone interviewing

The main alternative to face-to-face interviewing is telephone interviewing.[3] This is much less expensive and is becoming the dominant method for polling. It provides greater flexibility with respect to the times that interviews can be conducted and makes it easier to obtain a representative sample of the population. Telephone interviewing also makes it easier for people to decline to be interviewed, as this is harder to do when interviewers are standing in front of you. While telephone polls exclude those who do not have telephones, this is not the problem it once was. Another potential problem is that we find it easier to lie or misrepresent our opinion on the telephone than we do in a face-to-face interview.

Focus groups

Another technique used to gauge public opinion is the focus group.[4] In this case, a small group of between six and twelve people, who have been selected according to specific criteria, are brought together to discuss issues, parties, or candidates. While a facilitator directs the conversation, the interaction between participants is an important aspect of this form of study. Sometimes these groups are used to check or help to analyse the results from face-to-face and telephone interviewing. The groups might contain a diverse range of people, but usually they are people of similar backgrounds.

This method for ascertaining popular opinion is particularly useful when the views of a specific type of person are required (because they are the target population of a policy or because this type of voter is important to an election result). The moderator or facilitator plays an important role in this method for gauging popular opinion, and problems with the moderator or facilitator can significantly reduce the quality of the information gained. Group effects can also influence the information gathered. The fact that focus groups are small may also limit the inferences that can be drawn from the data gathered from a session.

'Phone polls' and web site visitor polls

So-called phone polls[5] have become a feature of many news media programs. In this case, viewers are asked to call specific numbers to register their views on an issue. A poll conducted by those responsible for a web site, in which they seek to elicit the views of visitors to the site, is similar to this type of poll. Neither of these are reliable forms of opinion polling. We have only included them to make the point that they tell us nothing about popular opinion. At most, they may tell us something about the views of those who watch a certain program on a specific day or visit a particular site during a particular period (or even how well political parties and lobby groups are organised to influence the results of these polls). Self-selected groups are not reliable ways to gauge public opinion. They are a bit of fun, but tell us nothing about what 'the people' are thinking.

Important aspects of opinion polls
The sample
Polls must be conducted carefully if they are to be meaningful reflections of popular opinion. One of the most important aspects of opinion polls is that interviewees must represent the population. To achieve this, the sample of the population whose opinions are surveyed must reflect the population as a whole.[6] Another important aspect of the sample is the number of people who are included in it. If the sample is representative, then the larger the sample the more likely it is that the results of the opinion poll will reflect the views of the population as a whole. The first questions to ask of any opinion poll, then, concern the size and the representativeness of the sample. We need to know how the sample was generated and we need to know how many people were surveyed.

The wording of questions
The wording of its questions can also have a significant effect on the results that are obtained from an opinion poll.[7] Questions that are open to different interpretations may not produce meaningful results. More important, though, is the effect of the particular wording of a question, for this can have a profound effect on the responses that it receives. Knowing the specific wording of the questions used in a particular survey will provide important information to those seeking to interpret the results of an opinion poll.

The question: 'Do Indigenous Australians deserve special treatment to the exclusion of equally deserving non-Indigenous Australians?', for example, would be likely to produce different results from the question: 'Do Aborigines who can demonstrate a close and ongoing relationship to a specific region be given rights associated with religious practices or hunting and fishing?' Similarly, a question that asks respondents to identify the most important issues in an election will be likely to produce different results from one in which respondents are asked to select from a specific set of issues.

The nature of preceding questions
Responses to a question can also be affected by the nature of the questions that preceded it. A specific order of questions may result in a momentum being created that will tend to result in particular responses to the last question in this chain. Consider the following sequence of questions. While the last question in each sequence is the same, responses to it may be affected by the questions that precede it.

BOX 12.1
Sample order of questions

Sequence 1

1. Do you believe that some people deserve different treatment from others?
2. Do you think that government programs designed to promote the interests of women have been effective?
3. Should the government develop more policies designed specifically to address women's interests?

Sequence 2

1. Do you believe that women have the same chances to advance in their careers as men do?
2. Do you believe that women's different needs with respect to childcare and other domestic responsibilities mean that they cannot take advantage of government programs as readily as men can?
3. Should the government develop more policies designed specifically to address women's interests?

The last question in both sequences is the same, but the responses that each question is likely to produce may be very different. Even if we know the wording of a question, we may need to know the questions that preceded it if we are to understand responses to the question fully.

'Background' information provided to interviewee
In some polls, interviewees are provided with background information to help them to make sense of the questions that they are being asked. This background information may have a significant effect on their responses and predispose them to a particular response to the question that follows this information. We may misinterpret the results of a poll in which particular background information has been provided if we don't know what this background information was.

Murray Goot[8] has discussed a situation in which the nature of background information may have been important. He discussed opinion polls conducted after the High Court *Mabo* decision by the Roy Morgan Research Institute[9] and AGB McNair in which quite different responses to the decision were obtained. According to Goot, those interviewed in the Morgan (Gallup) poll were told that the High Court had decided that 'Aboriginal people may be the traditional owners of various land areas of Australia and entitled to be granted or given those various land areas'.[10] Those in the AGB McNair study, according to Goot, were told that the High Court had 'decided that Aboriginal people own land which they have been continually associated with since before European settlement. This does not affect any privately owned land'.[11]

While we cannot be certain that the differences between the background information provided produced the differences in response to the decision, the fact that interviewees in the Morgan poll were more critical of the Court's decision suggests that the background information they were given might have had an effect on their responses to the High Court decision. We can't be sure, but it seems a reasonable inference. We won't be in a good position to interpret the results of these opinion polls, then, if we don't know what background information was provided to respondents.

What was done with 'don't know' responses?
Another important factor associated with results from opinion polls concerns what was done with those respondents who replied with 'don't know'.[12] This is particularly important in the context of opinion polls that are intended to determine people's voting intentions. While respondents may generally wish to reward interviewers with answers, they might find themselves unable to give a definitive answer to a specific question (including for whom they might vote).

Those who answer with 'don't know' may be pushed for their opinion, or 'don't know' responses may be allocated to parties according to the distribution of responses from those who did express an opinion. While distributing 'don't know' responses according to how those who did respond makes some sense, it does tend to combine those with strong preferences with those with weak preferences. The strength of their commitment is important to determining whether voters might change their minds before they cast their vote, or whether they might change their views on an issue after being exposed to further information.

Summary
We usually only see the results of opinion polls. While providing all the information required for a complete understanding of the results of a poll can be difficult, a

full understanding of these results may not be possible without it. The size of the sample is the easiest information to provide and is the information most often provided. Information about what was done with 'don't know' responses is also relatively easy to provide—although it is provided less frequently than the sample size. We are sometimes given the wording of a question for which we are given results. We are almost never told about questions that may have preceded an important question. Nor are we informed of the background information provided to interviewees. Yet al.l of this information is important to the results obtained from a poll.

Is the extensive use of opinion polling good for government and democracy in Australia?

The increasing use of opinion polls by journalists, members of political executives, and strategists within political parties raises the question of whether the extensive use of opinion polling is good for government and democracy in Australia. The Yes case is a series of connected propositions that boil down to the argument that opinion polls are good for government because they allow members of political executives to use popular opinion in developing their policies and determining the effectiveness of their policies. They are good for democracy because they provide members of political executives and those in parties with a direct means for determining the 'will of the people'. The No case comprises four points. The widespread use of opinion polling results in a confusion of popularity with leadership, 'poll following' on the part of the leaders of the major parties, 'horse-race' journalism that provides only superficial coverage of Australian politics and gives undue weight to the views of those who are ill-informed and insufficient weight to the views of those whose opinions are considered and, therefore, of greater value.

Yes case
Democracy is about the people having a role in policy-making and about representatives responding to the will of the people

While democracy may be open to a variety of interpretations and practices, nobody can deny that it is about people being involved in political decision-making. Representative democracy may result in limited opportunities for people to be involved in decision-making, but it still requires involvement from citizens. In a representative democracy, Members of Parliament must respond to the will of the people, and policy-makers within the parties must develop policies that reflect the views and values of citizens.

Opinion polling delivers 'popular will' to the members of political executives and political parties

Opinion polling can be understood, in this context, as a means for communicating the will of the people to members of political executives and policy-makers within political parties. Members of political executives can use results from polls to develop policies and to determine the likely success of government programs. Opinion polling can be used to determine the level of community awareness of specific services and programs that political executives provide and to ascertain their views about them. The more obvious and common use of opinion polls is to determine popular attitudes on policy matters. Leaders of political parties can then use this information in determining their party's policy. They may choose to adopt a different policy from that which is supported by a majority of those surveyed, but they will know that they need to devote considerable energy to changing people's minds.

This diminishes the role of elites in policy-making

To understand the importance of opinion polling in a representative democracy, we need to consider policy-making in the absence of opinion polling. Without access to surveys of popular opinion, members of political executives and political parties will rely upon their own judgments and the views of those close to them in deciding what the people want, what ought to be done to give them what they want, and how the people are responding to policies and programs that have been introduced. Basically, politicians, their advisers within government departments and political parties, and spokespeople of powerful pressure groups will determine public policy. The result will be that a political elite will determine policy. Their distance from the people will mean that they are not responding to the views of the people and politics will not be democratic.[13]

This is good for the people's involvement in politics and the responsiveness of Australian political executives

Ensuring that members of political executives and those in political parties are responding to the will of the people, as is required in a representative democracy, is impossible if they can't accurately gauge popular opinion. Opinion polling, if it is done properly, is a means through which the people's views can be continually sought on major issues that must be considered.

Extensive and regular polling results in members of political executives and political parties remaining informed about the will of the people. A system in which those in positions of political power are regularly confronted with and forced to address the will of the people for whom they are responsible seems a close approximation of a democracy. The widespread use of opinion polls is a means, and may be the only means, by which this can be done. The widespread use of opinion polling, then, is good for government and democracy in Australia.

No case
Confuses popularity with leadership—opinion polls measure popularity
One of the problems with opinion polling is that it often measures the popularity of a leader or party and nothing more;[14] this is particularly evident in those questions that concern whether a respondent believes that a leader is 'doing a good job'. Few respondents are likely to know very much about the sort of job a leader is doing, given how little Australians know about their political system and how dismissive they tend to be of politics in general. If they are reporting anything, it is likely that those who answer this question are responding to a limited exposure to the way that a leader has been reported in the news media. This is a shallow response to how leaders appear in the news media and not a considered analysis of their performance.

One of the most important omissions from opinion polls is any real reflection on the question of what leaders are supposed to do and, therefore, what doing a good job might mean. Occasionally, polls attempt to gauge something of a leader's ability by asking people whether they thought that they would be better off under a particular person's leadership and then whether they supported that leader. This seems to register the fact that some decisions might be necessary, but not popular. This is rare and seems to reinforce the view that a good leader is someone who does things that are good for us. While we might believe that it is a leader's role to persuade people that a decision is necessary, even if it causes problems for them, leaders are more likely to have unfavourable opinion polls presented as if they indicate a failure of leadership.

Another feature of the way that opinion polls reward appearance over substance is that they treat laypeople's perceptions of policies as if they constituted real evaluations of those policies. Once again, a widespread lack of understanding of and knowledge about issues raised within the Australian political system means that popular opinion represents little more than a test of popularity. While this may be a meaningful test, it does not reflect on the viability of policies. Popular opinion may well be in favour of reducing income tax, but there would be little sense in initiating such a policy when people also expect a significant number of services from their government.[15]

To put it bluntly, the narrow and short-term prejudices of a number of uninformed respondents are not a sound basis upon which to judge leaders or policies. This will likely undermine the effectiveness of government and allow democracy to be construed as requiring little understanding of politics or consideration of issues on the parts of voters. Nor does it make sense to think of democracy as requiring nothing from participants; an unwillingness to engage with issues is hard to justify as an acceptable basis upon which citizens participate in politics.

Produces poll-following

All parties contain people who believe that they will do a better job than the current leader. Some of these will desire a leadership position and will seek to position themselves for a leadership challenge. This is an inevitable result of the fact that politics attracts those who seek power and those who consider themselves suited to leadership positions. Therefore, leaders of political parties must be aware of and sensitive to the possibility of a leadership challenge.

One reason that party leaders will be required to follow polls carefully, then, is that a fall in their popularity may leave them vulnerable to a leadership challenge. Parliamentarians, especially those in marginal seats, are very sensitive to opinion polls and a poor result in a poll can make them open to withdrawing support from a leader. Hence, a leadership challenge may be forthcoming, if a leader's popularity has declined or support for the party has declined.

Extensive use of opinion polls also produces poll-following on the parts of leaders. If opinion polls reduce democracies to popularity contests, then a leader's popularity is the primary measure of their suitability for the role. Following opinion polls seems the strategy most likely to maintain a leader's popularity. Unfortunately, the power of the ill-informed and uninterested is magnified as a result of the fact that they are important to a leader holding onto to a leadership position.[16]

Results in horse-race journalism

Leadership is not the only thing that suffers when opinion polls are used extensively. Journalism also suffers, as journalists treat opinion polls as important to reporting on Australian politics. Journalists will be prone to treat opinion polls as important pieces of news because their organisation has paid for the poll. They also treat them as important because opinion polls allow them to comment on the people's perceptions of the leaders and the potential for one of the leaders to face a leadership challenge. The problem with this is that polls can often become the story. Who is ahead and by how much becomes a story in itself.[17]

The problem with opinion polls is that they provide little information as to what is happening in Australian politics. They may reflect the handling of issues by a party leader, but even when they do, they do not reflect much more. Furthermore, they provide little meaningful information about the broader social and political environment within which decisions are taken, and tell us nothing about which issues are likely to be of long-term significance. They do not even

BOX 12.2
Australia's polling agencies

Modern opinion polling began in the United States in the 1930s, when the 'father' of opinion polling, George Gallup, conducted polls. Polls have been conducted in Australia since World War II. There are four main published polls. The Morgan Poll (Roy Morgan Research Centre) was published in *The Bulletin*. Newspoll (Newspoll Research Centre, managed by Sol Lebovich) was published in *The Australian*. The Fairfax papers publish polls conducted by AC Nielsen Consult. Saulwick Polls are presented in the Melbourne *Age* and the *Sydney Morning Herald*. The Galaxy Poll is published in Sydney's *Daily Telegraph* and *Sunday Telegraph*, the Melbourne's *Herald Sun* and the Brisbane *Courier Mail*. The major parties usually engage their own pollsters and are particularly interested in monitoring opinion in marginal seats.

Sources:
http://www.ROYMORGAN.COM.AU/
http://newspoll.com.au
http://www.all.nielsen.com
http://www.galaxyresearch.com.au/pubpolls.html

tell us whether leaders had any real control over events that may have increased or reduced their popularity.

Calling a race in which one leader is ahead, falls behind, and makes up ground on the other is easy and simple. It feeds into the preoccupation with Prime Ministers that is becoming more pronounced in Australian politics. It does not recognise the fact that political parties are complex organisations within which leadership is a more difficult enterprise than one of simply holding off challengers by maintaining popularity, as measured by opinion polls. It does not recognise the fact that a variety of issues are being dealt with at any one time. It does not even recognise that the factors that affect polling ought to be discussed at the time at which a poll is being reported. Just as opinion polling creates a superficial understanding of leadership that is bad for democracy and government in Australia; it also produces a superficial approach to reporting Australian politics among journalists.

Gives equal weight to the views of ill-informed people as it does to those who understand the issues

Another problem with opinion polling is that it treats carefully generated opinions in the same way that it treats ill-considered and uninformed opinions. No distinction is made between the opinions of those who have spent time and effort in understanding and developing views on an issue or about a leader and those who haven't. This leads directly to a tendency to devalue actively seeking and considering information relevant to political issues. Compulsory voting[18] already forces those who know and care little about Australian politics to vote; extensive use of opinion polling takes this even further and accords equal value to the ill-informed and thoughtless as it does the informed and thoughtful. Politics is an area in which many people consider their opinion to be valuable irrespective of the effort they have put into developing that opinion. The extensive use of opinion polling does nothing to encourage people to believe that some views are more valuable than others.

The view that a considered opinion is better than an ill-considered opinion is not necessarily anti-democratic. Indeed, another approach to democracy, known generally as deliberative democracy,[19] has developed in order to overcome problems with representative democracy and the widespread use of opinion polls as a means to gauge public opinion.

Deliberative democracy may take a variety of forms. The simplest model is one in which a representative group of citizens is first provided with the information and support they need to consider pressing policy issues and are then brought together in a forum in which they can discuss their options and decide on the most appropriate policy. More complex models involve initial polling, the release of information packages, questionnaires, meetings of small groups of citizens, and then a series of meetings in which a larger group of citizens reaches some agreement as to the appropriate policy to be adopted in a specific situation.

Essentially, deliberative democracy is a process in which citizens are provided with the information and the opportunities for deliberation necessary for them to develop a more considered opinion. Deliberative democracy is a direct response to problems with the use of opinion polling as a means to bring considered and informative public opinion to members of the political executive and political parties.

Summary

We may well be stuck with the extensive use of polling and may consider it desirable when it involves members of political executives seeking information about the citizens they are meant to serve. As a method for reporting on Australian politics, however, it creates undesirable side effects about which we should be concerned. Support for polling is very much a reflection of the view that the people's will ought to be registered in an ongoing fashion and in a representative democracy. The No case relies, in part, on the problems that an obsession with popularity creates for those in positions of political leadership and, in part, on a different understanding of democracy from that which underpinned the Yes case.

To reach a conclusion on the question of whether extensive use of polling is good for Australian government and democracy requires considering the gains and losses that may accrue from the extensive use of polling. It may also require a more careful consideration of the meaning of democracy. The question that arises in this context concerns whether democracy requires the equal treatment of all people's opinions or whether it ought to give greater weight to the opinions of those who have put some effort into forming their opinion.

> **QUESTION**
>
> Can mechanisms associated with deliberative democracy provide more effective means of bringing public opinion to members of political executives than the present methods of opinion polling?

2: POLITICAL MARKETING

Another aspect of polling is increasingly referred to as 'political marketing'. Just as polling is important to the way that products are marketed, so, too, polling can be understood to perform the same function in relation to parties, candidates, and leaders. For those who are concerned about political marketing, the question that arises is whether there is anything new in this phenomenon. Once again, alternative positions on this question will be presented. The No case relies upon the view that politics has always been about people selling themselves as leaders and that this is even more pronounced in democracies. For the Yes case, television and new information and communication technologies are opening up spaces for political exposure, providing continual access to people, giving marketers greater control over content, and providing opportunities for candidates and leaders to associate themselves with innovative technologies and, hence, market themselves as relevant leaders.

Is there anything new about political marketing?

No case
Political leaders need to establish legitimacy
The argument that politics has always been about marketing[20] begins with the position that political leaders can only maintain their position by persuading enough people to support them. That is, people will obey those in positions of political power if they believe that they deserve to be there. A political leadership maintains its legitimacy to the extent that it can continue to maintain

the support of the people. Convincing people that you deserve to be in power is to sell yourself or your administration to the people. From this perspective, the ability to sell yourself and the ability to maintain a position of political leadership are identical.

They have always used various methods to get people to support them
The ability to convince people to follow has always been an essential attribute of a political leader. A variety of methods are available to those in positions of political power. Violence and intimidation must be included here, but persuasion is more likely to be an effective way to maintain power. Even brutal regimes that impose terror on a population rely on support from sections of the community, the armed forces in particular, to maintain their position. In the end, it is only by maintaining their legitimacy among powerful members, or the right members of a society, that political leaders can maintain their positions. So, persuasion and winning support through selling ideas or leadership is fundamental to all political systems.

BOX 12.3
ALP 'It's Time' campaign

The ALP's 'It's time' campaign in 1972 introduced the use of television, songs, slogans, and personalities to political campaigning in Australia. Australia had been governed since 1949 by the Liberal/Country Party Coalition. Central to the campaign was the slogan 'It's time for freedom, it's time for moving, it's time for freedom, yes it's time'.

Source: http://australianpolitics.com; http://www.whitlamdismissal.com/speeches/72-11-13_it's-time.shtml

This is even more pronounced in democracies
Democracies are obviously political systems in which the ability to sell oneself is essential to the acquisition of political power. Candidates can only win support if enough voters have been convinced that they have the attributes that make them worth supporting. These attributes might include a winning personality, a convincing set of ideas, or an ability to understand and promote a collective interest. But whatever these attributes are, they can only be acknowledged if the candidate is able to convince other people that they have them. They must be put on public display and be displayed in a convincing manner if people are going to be persuaded to give them support. That is, support can only be gained if a leadership contender is marketed properly.

Yes case
Television and the internet are spaces for different forms of persuasion
Political marketing is something new because television and the internet have given marketers a completely different way to influence voters. The sophisticated advertising techniques developed for television advertising produce a form of political communication that is nothing like persuading people to support your policies by making persuasive arguments.[21] Web sites, YouTube, FaceBook, MySpace, email lists, blogs, and the other spaces of the internet have created new connections to voters that require different approaches to gaining their support. Attending a public meeting in order to gain voter support, as politicians once did, is nothing like creating a favourable response from voters by producing a thirty-second commercial, podcasting, blogging, creating a web site, or making a video for uploading to the internet.

The internet al.so makes possible 24/7 niche political marketing
Another difference in the nature of internet-based political marketing is that it can be both continuous and oriented to niche markets. The importance of the internet's continuity is that successful election campaigns will be those that continuously use the internet to develop the party 'brand' in light of newly emerging issues and the results from the most recent opinion poll. The fact that most of the people who browse web sites for political information are different from most of those who use YouTube, MySpace and FaceBook, and other internet spaces, allows marketers to direct specific messages to particular types of voters. The internet is both continuous and multiple and this means that contemporary political marketing is nothing like the past.

Politicians can spin their own stories
New technology also enables politicians to present their arguments without having to rely on a journalist to ask the right questions and to present their answers in the right way. Of course, they can still provide a thirty-second sound bite to the television journalists; they can also present a ten-minute podcast of their position on any given issue from their personal or government web site, or on YouTube. But importantly, they control the content—no one can edit them. It can be rehearsed, even re-shot, if a politician is unhappy with the segment, and no journalist will interrupt them.

Politicians can identify themselves in terms of technology
People who log on anytime and anywhere will respond positively to politicians who show a similar level of connectivity. The internet is changing political marketing because politicians who present themselves as technologically savvy

will gain an edge on other opponents who can't use the new digital technologies. This was evident during the 2007 federal election campaign. Opposition Leader, Kevin Rudd, sold himself as part of a new generation. Members of the ALP had invested heavily in marketing though new technologies. They regularly uploaded to YouTube and produced two web sites for two different types of voters. The Liberal Party's only web site simply presented the Parliamentary party, its policies and its election promises, contained current and archived media releases, and requested voluntary and financial support from the public. For voters who understand the internet, the strongest message was in the design of the web site and not in its contents.

BOX 12.4
Kevin 07

While the ALP used a web site to provide information in the normal way, it also established KEVIN 07. Its title was only part of its novelty. KEVIN 07 also incorporated blogs produced by ALP candidates, an opportunity for people to comment online or by SMS, and an opportunity to purchase KEVIN 07 clothing and download wallpaper. KEVIN 07 was a presence on YouTube. Visitors could view over sixty video clips developed for the campaign. The day after the official policy launch, it was possible to view a ten-minute extract of Rudd's speech. This approach to political marketing was part of projecting Opposition Leader Kevin Rudd as the leader for the digital age and Prime Minister, John Howard, as out of touch with new technologies and, therefore, younger Australians.

Summary

Persuasion has always been part of politics. It is essential to political leaders gaining and retaining support from the people. The only difference between current political marketing and previous political marketing may be the availability and use of new information and communication technologies. From this perspective, nothing has changed apart from the technologies through which leaders sell themselves. The view that political marketing is new may derive from the view that new information and communication technologies are changing the nature of political marketing. From this perspective, political marketing can reach greater numbers in an almost infinite number of settings; leaders can convey their message anytime someone wants it and even construct a particular identity for general consumption. It can also provide leaders with greater opportunities for marketing 'spin'.

> **QUESTION**
>
> Does continual technological development ensure that political marketing will also continue to evolve?

CONCLUSION

Both opinion polling and political marketing are important contextual factors within which government and democracy in Australia operate. Opinion polling may have a beneficial effect on Australian government and democracy if it is viewed as a means by which members of political executives and policy-makers within parties attain a sense of what the people want. It may contribute to superficiality with respect to government and democracy, however, by undermining the quality of leadership and political journalism in Australia. Political marketing may reduce the quality of government and democracy in Australia by making elections into contests between rival advertising firms over their capacity to manipulate voters' emotions. Assuming, that is, that elections haven't always been contests of this kind.

FURTHER READING

Introductory texts

Jaensch, Dean, 1994, *Parliament, Parties and People: Australian Politics Today*, 2nd edn, Longman Cheshire: Melbourne.

Morgan, Gary, 1998, 'Polling and the Political System', in D. Lovell, I. McAllister, W. Maley & C. Kukathas (eds), *The Australian Political System*, 2nd edn, Longman: South Melbourne.

Specialist texts

Balough, Maggie, 1996, 'Changing Techniques: Asian Experiment May Alter the Way Journalists Measure Populace's Mood', *The Quill*, vol. 84, no. 1, pp. 20–3.

Fletcher, Winston, 1997, 'Marketing is not a Johnny Come Lately to Politics', *Marketing*, April 17, p. 5.

Frankovic, Kathleen, 1998, 'Public Opinion and Polling', in D. Graber, D. McQuail & P. Norris (eds), *The Politics of News, The News of Politics*, CQ Press: Washington DC.

Gawiser, Sheldon & G. Evans Witt, 1994, *A Journalist's Guide to Public Opinion Polls*, Praeger: Westport.

Hamel, Jacques, 2001, 'The Focus Group Method and Contemporary French Sociology', *Journal of Sociology*, vol. 37, no. 4, pp. 341–53.

Heith, Diane, 2000, 'The Polls: Polling for a Defence: The White House Public Opinion Apparatus and the Clinton Impeachment', *Presidential Studies Quarterly*, vol. 30, no. 4, pp. 783–90.

Hickey, Jennifer, 2000, 'Danger: Poll Ahead', *Insight*, 11 September, pp. 10–12.

Kavanagh, Dennis, 1995, *Election Campaigning: The New Marketing of Politics*, Blackwell: Oxford.

Kitchener, Jennifer, 1999, 'Business Journalism in the 1980s', in A. Curthoys & J. Schultz (eds), *Journalism, Print, Politics and Popular Culture*, University of Queensland Press: St Lucia.

Mattinson, Deborah, 1999, 'People Power in Politics: Qualitative Research for the 21st Century: Public Involvement in the Decision-Making Process', *Journal of the Market Research Society*, vol. 41, no. 1, pp. 87–96.

Merkle, Daniel, 1996, 'The Polls-Review: The National Issues Convention Deliberative Poll', *Public Opinion Quarterly*, vol. 60, pp. 588–619.

Mills, Stephen, 1999, 'Polling, Politics and the Press 1941–1996', in A. Curthoys & J. Schultz (eds), *Journalism, Print, Politics and Popular Culture*, University of Queensland Press: St Lucia.

Price, Vincent & Peter Neijens, 1998, 'Deliberative Polls: Toward Improved Measures of "Informed" Public Opinion?', *International Journal of Public Opinion Research*, vol. 10, no. 2, pp. 145–77.

Robertson, Lori, 2001, 'Polled Enough for Ya?', *American Journalism Review*, January/February, pp. 29–33.

Schultz, Julianne, 1999, 'The Many Paradoxes of Independence', in A. Curthoys & J. Schultz (eds), *Journalism, Print, Politics and Popular Culture*, University of Queensland Press: St Lucia.

Traugott, Michael, 2000, 'Presidential Address: Polling in the Public's Interest', *Public Opinion Quarterly*, vol. 64, pp. 374–84.

Weisberger, Bernard, 2000, 'Taking America's Temperature (History of the use of Public Opinion Polls for the Presidential Elections)', *American Heritage*, vol. 51, no. 7, pp. 58–61.

Zaller, John, 1992, *The Nature and Origins of Mass Opinion*, Cambridge University Press: Cambridge.

Web sites

Newspoll Market Research: http://www.newspoll.com.au
Roy Morgan Research: http://www.roymorgan.com.au
The Gallup Organisation: http://www.gallup.com
Galaxy Research: http://www.galaxyresearch.com.au/pubpolls.html

Notes

1. For more on opinion polling, see Bowman (2001, pp. 90–8).
2. For more information on face-to-face interviewing, see Bradburn & Sudman (1988, pp. 188–91).
3. For more details on telephone polling, see Goot (1988, pp. 126–9) and Oskamp (1991, p. 107).
4. Those interested in focus group research might find Morgan & Krueger (1998) and Greenbaum (2000) useful.
5. For more on phone polls, see Oskamp (1991, pp. 111–12).
6. For more information on the importance of the sample in polling, see Gallup (1944, p. 13), Bradburn & Sudman (1988, pp. 180–5), Milburn (1991, pp. 17–19), and Oskamp (1991, pp. 103–7).
7. For more on wording the questionnaire, see Bradburn & Sudman (1988, pp. 186–8), Milburn (1991, pp. 19–20), and Oskamp (1991 pp. 112–15).
8. See Goot (1993, pp. 133–56).
9. http://www.roymorgan.com.au
10. As quoted in Goot (1993, p. 135).
11. Ibid (p. 137).
12. For more on 'don't know' responses, see Bradburn & Sudman (1988, pp. 204–9) and Oskamp (1991, pp. 117–19).
13. The 'father' of opinion polling, George Gallup (1940 and 1944), put this argument most strongly. See http://www.ciadvertising.org/studies/student/99_spring/interactive/bklee/theory2/home.html
14. For more on opinion polls measuring popularity, see Beresford (1998, pp. 24–32), Bradburn & Sudman (1988, pp. 217–20), Goot (1996, pp. 24–9), and McNair (2003, p. 32).
15. An example of the use of deliberative polling to resolve this apparent contradiction can be found in Weeks (2000, pp. 360–72).
16. For more information concerning politicians following opinion polls, see Gallup (1944, pp. 7–8) and Goot (1998).
17. For more on opinion polling and the media, see Holcomb & Seawell (2001, pp. 13–15), Kohut (2000, pp. 66–7), Steinhorn (2000, p. 40), Carroll (2000, pp. 42–3), and McNair (2003, pp. 32).
18. For more on compulsory voting, see Ward & Stewart (2006, p.105) and Singleton et al. (2006, p. 184).
19. More on deliberative democracy can be found in Dryzek (2000) and Pettit (2001).
20. For more on political marketing, see Beresford (1998, pp. 24–32), Corner (1996, pp. 354–6), and McNair (2003, pp. 36–8).
21. For more on political advertising, see Edmondson (1986, pp. 27–32) and McNair (2003, pp. 36–8).

Globalisation

13

LEARNING OBJECTIVES

- To comprehend the different understandings of globalisation
- Be able to grasp the implications of different understandings of globalisation for government and democracy in Australia

INTRODUCTION

Our need to respond to the challenge of globalisation is used to justify many of the policies that are proposed by members of Cabinet. The problem with this is that we don't really know what someone is saying when they argue that a particular policy is needed because of globalization. We can't see, feel, touch, or taste globalisation. It is an idea or concept used to explain why some things have happened and others need to happen. We need to ask what this idea is. This is not an easy question to answer; we think that the issue may not be 'what is globalisation?,' but 'how has the idea of globalisation been used by members of political executives?' Instead of offering a definition of globalisation (or, better, stipulating a meaning for the concept), we begin this chapter by discussing two different understandings of globalisation.[1] In the first, globalisation is an irresistible force that is annihilating national and regional differences with respect to economics, politics, and culture, and is producing a global economic, political, and cultural order. The other understanding takes globalisation to be a manifestation of a hegemonic ideology. From this perspective, globalisation has been accepted as real, rather than *is* real, because it dominates our thinking about the present and the future, especially as these relate to economics and politics. From this point of view, globalisation is not a description of what is actually happening in the world, but is an idea that those in positions of power in our society believe to be true (and have convinced many others it is true). That they believe it to be true means that it shapes their and our ideas about politics and political possibilities.

The effects of these different understandings of globalisation on views about the possibilities for government and democracy in Australia are taken up in the final section of this chapter. First, we present globalisation as an economic, political and cultural process that limits what members of political executives can do and, as a result, prevents them from responding to citizens' demands when these are not consistent with the processes of globalisation. We then present the implications for government and democracy in Australia when globalisation is understood as a manifestation of a hegemonic ideology. In this case, the fact that those in positions of power in society believe globalisation to be true means that it becomes true, and when members of political executives believe it to be true, they do not respond to a variety of demands that citizens make, as they simply will not make sense to them.

1: DIFFERENT UNDERSTANDINGS OF GLOBALISATION

Introduction

While globalisation is treated as real by most writers, some commentators (such as Bell[2] and Hirst and Thompson[3]) dispute the facts associated with globalisation. They argue that the evidence did not support the position that globalisation was a new force reshaping the world. From this perspective, globalisation becomes real to the extent to which members of the political executive make it real. Members of political executives want to justify their policies and use the rationale of globalisation to do this. In short, globalisation was not a context for government and democracy, it was a device used by members of political executives to legitimise their policies. This casts globalisation in a very different light from a 'fact of life' that we might embrace or reject.

In the following discussion, we account for globalisation from these two perspectives. First, we explain the position that Australia is increasingly part of a global economic, political, and cultural system that is undermining its citizens' connection to and identification with specific national economies, political systems, and cultures. This will be referred to as the irresistible force position. The other view is that globalisation is not a 'fact of life' and that globalisation is being used (either knowingly or not) by influential figures in politics, business, and the media to justify the introduction of policies that they support. We refer to this view as the hegemonic ideology position, though globalisation is, from this perspective, only one manifestation of a hegemonic ideology, which is the free market or neo-liberal ideology. We explain both understandings because our intention is not to suggest that either position is true, but to indicate the ways that globalisation can be, and has been, understood.

An irresistible force (resulting in the integration of economics, politics, and culture into a global economy, politics, and culture)

Irresistible force
Central to this understanding of globalisation is that it is an irresistible force.[4] From this perspective, globalisation is a 'fact of life'. Not to accept and embrace globalisation is to turn your back on the future. People who think that they can resist globalisation do not understand the way the world is or are unwilling to make the types of changes necessary for the future. Young people who oppose

globalisation simply do not understand the facts of life that older people do. Older people who oppose globalisation are tolerated, because older people have never coped with change.

Trying to stop globalisation, from this perspective, is like trying to stop yourself from getting older. It can't be done. We may choose to grow old gracefully or not, but we cannot choose not to grow old. We can value some of the consequences of growing older (like being able to drink in hotels, drive cars, and vote) and regret others (like looking older and finding it harder to keep fit), but the real questions relate to how we deal with growing older. From this perspective, globalisation is something that people have to accept and of which they can take advantage.

Economic
International finance institutions
This view of globalisation usually begins with economics.[5] Probably the most important of these is the development of a largely unregulated international financial system. The end of World War II saw the introduction of the Bretton Woods system[6] that introduced controls over exchange rates. This was intended to introduce stability into the world economy by preventing major fluctuations in exchange rates. The end of the Bretton Woods system allowed for the development of currency markets, which determine exchange rates and, as a result, have a significant effect on domestic economic policy.

Mobile multinational corporations (MNC)
Another important economic feature of globalisation is a significant increase in the number and size of multinational, sometimes called trans-national, companies.[7] These are companies that operate in a number of different countries and usually locate parts of their production, distribution, marketing, and administration in more than one country. Their capacity to move these aspects of their companies to different countries (their mobility) is extremely important.

An increase in their number means that the production and distribution of goods and services is increasingly being carried out by internationally oriented companies that have a limited connection to a specific country. Many MNCs are larger, in economic terms, than some countries.[8] The value of internal transfers of goods and services within these MNCs often exceed that of countries that have relatively small economies, such as Australia.

Loosening of foreign ownership rules
One of the effects of the rise of multinational companies has been a tendency for national governments to loosen restrictions on foreign ownership of local

industries and national resources. Members of most political executives in most countries see great value in the presence of MNCs in their countries. Part of this value lies in the increases in employment that result from a decision by an MNC to locate an aspect of the production, distribution, marketing, or administration divisions (or a regional node of one of these) in a particular country.

Another desirable effect is the introduction of expertise, either by training local workers or importing foreign experts, which results from entry of an MNC. A final, perhaps related, effect is the way that local firms can learn from MNCs, especially by learning to use technology in the same way. This potential for 'technology transfer' is one reason that MNCs are welcomed into a country.

Assistance of new technologies (ICTs)

While they have been important in the cultural aspects of globalisation, digital information and communication technologies (ICTs) have also been an important factor in the economics of globalisation. This is partly because they have made the development and growth of MNCs much easier. A reason for this is that they allow an administrative centre of an MNC or a regional administrative node of an MNC to coordinate the various activities that occur within the company.

ICTs also allow the central administration of an MNC to relocate sub-elements of the company around the world, as long as basic communication infrastructure, mainly telephone lines, is available. Advances in ICTs have also assisted the economic aspects of globalisation by providing information about markets and economically significant events around the world, but particularly in the major economies. This information has important effects in international, regional, and national markets and, as it is a central part of news bulletins, affects the attitudes and behaviour of ordinary citizens.

Political
End of the Cold War

Globalisation is not, in this understanding, just an economic process. Politics is also globalising. One of the most important recent changes to international politics was the breakdown of the Soviet Union and the end of the Cold War.[9] The most important effect of this was that it contributed to the end of what were referred to as communist regimes. Whether they were actually communist is unclear, but the main feature of these authoritarian regimes was that they divided the world's population into those who participated in centrally controlled or planned economies and those who participated in market-based economies. The breakdown of the Soviet Union meant the removal of major impediments to economic, political, and cultural aspects of globalisation.

International political institutions (UN, G8, CHOGM, EU, NAFTA)[10]
One of the more important political effects of the breakdown of the Soviet Union was that it made the United Nations a more powerful and effective body. One of the problems that the United Nations[11] faced soon after it came into being, after World War II, was that it was a site of the struggle between members of political executives in the USA and their allies and those in the Soviet Union and their allies. The veto power that representatives of the USA's and Soviet Union's political executive had in the UN Security Council meant that it could not function effectively. The competition in the General Assembly between the USA and its allies and the Soviet Union and its allies made the United Nations relatively ineffectual. The demise of the Soviet Union has resulted in the United Nations becoming a more influential institution that is more willing to act as an international policing agency and to criticise and censure the behaviour of some governments.

Another part of political globalisation is international forums, such as the Group of Eight (G8). The G8 is an informal meeting of the heads of Canada, France, Germany, Italy, Japan, Russia, the United Kingdom, and the United States. These Heads of State meet to discuss broad economic and foreign policies.[12] The Commonwealth Heads of Government Meeting (CHOGM) is another international organisation whose members play a role in creating international pressures on members of political executives in particular countries to embrace democracy and free trade. These meetings are not yet at the point where they constitute significant international agencies but, within this understanding of globalisation, they are evidence of a continuing trend in the creation of international political institutions.

Regional international institutions, of which the European Union (EU) is the best example, are further evidence of the creation of international political institutions. The creation of the European Union (EU) represents a freeing up of the movement of goods, services, and people within its territory. As important is the fact that membership of the EU is only available to countries that agree to follow common political and economic policies. While the North Atlantic Free Trade Agreement is a basically economic agreement, it, too, is an important international institution. The Association of South East Asian Nations (ASEAN) and the Asia-Pacific Economic Cooperation Forum (APEC) have yet to prove effective international political organisations. But the existence of these and other international political institutions is evidence of the political aspects of globalisation.

International 'economic' institutions with political effects (IMF, World Bank, WTO (GATT))
Possibly more important than these international political institutions are the apparently 'economic' institutions that have had a profound political effect in many countries. Institutions, such as the International Monetary Fund (IMF)[13]

and the World Bank,[14] provide assistance to countries that face economic difficulties. Their role is to prevent major disruptions to the world economy. In fulfilling this function, they have applied pressure to members of political executives who have sought assistance to deregulate their markets and introduce other economic reforms. Similarly, the World Trade Organisation (WTO) only allows membership to those countries whose political executives agree to join a free global market. It also has the power to force political executives to reverse policies when they are proven to have breached the guidelines that must be agreed to before a nation becomes part of the WTO.

BOX 13.1
Pro-globalisation

Pro-globalisation refers to the encouragement of economic activity, open markets, competition, and the free flow of goods from which consumers are considered to be the principle beneficiaries. Those who advocate globalisation argue that it fosters growth, allows quick access to markets, and creates hundreds of millions of jobs around the world. Proponents of globalisation argue that it does not affect the sovereignty of a nation and creates strong incentives for governments to pursue sound economic policies. Groups that support globalisation include the Brookings Institute, the World Trade Organisation, the World Bank, the World Economic Forum, and the US Alliance for Trade Expansion.

Sources: http://www.imf.org; http://www.globalisationguide.org/sb02.html

Cultural
Advanced international communication technologies
Cultural aspects of globalisation[15] derive from the spread of digital information and communication technologies (ICTs). These technologies, especially the internet and 'pay' television, mean that people throughout the world have access to very similar sources of information and entertainment. They also allow a much wider range of possibilities for interaction between people than was available via the telephone. Opportunities for email and internet-based 'chat' mean that people can communicate with each other much more easily than they could previously.

International media organisations
The existence of these digital ICTs has enabled the development of international media organisations, of which Time-Warner-AOL and News Limited are

examples. Those who run these organisations, which of course are MNCs, seek to extend their markets in order to increase their profitability. They are also driven to seek programs, usually referred to as content, to distribute through their media organisations and they create international media networks to channel this international content. The fact that much of this content is produced in the United States does not undermine this position, as it may reflect the globalisation of US culture.

The emergence of the global

When the economic, political and cultural processes combine, in this understanding, they produce global effects, and global markets in commodities, services, and labour emerge. While these globalisation processes are important, so, too, is the dominance of free market policies and the legitimisation of a set of (Western) political ideas, practices, and institutions that are part of globalisation. Each of these will be discussed in this sub-section.

Global commodity markets

One of the features of the emergence of the global is the development of global commodity markets.[16] Central to this was an increase in the size and number of MNCs. These companies are constantly seeking new markets for their commodities, so they continually draw more and more people into global economic processes. The development of these global commodity markets is also facilitated by the development of digital ICTs.

These technologies assist globalisation in a number of ways. First, a global market in digital technologies has developed, which include mobile telephones, televisions, computers, computer software, electronic gaming devices, and satellite dishes. Second, digital ICTs enable companies to provide commodities to a global market (of which Amazon.com is one of the most famous). Third, they assist by exposing users of these technologies to advertising, and fourth, by producing demand for the products advertised during or after programs. A more important effect, however, results from product placement in which television or film actors, for example, use or consume particular products. Finally, the merchandising that accompanies many television programs, of which the Simpsons and Pokemon are examples, assists in the development of global commodity markets.

Global service markets

Another feature of the globalised world is the development of global service markets. One of the more important of these services is support for the users of the new information technologies. That these technologies are used worldwide and are a way in which support itself can be sought means that advanced information technologies are themselves producers of demand for services. Any service that can be delivered at a distance is also part of the global service market. These include data processing and analysis, financial planning, programming, and personal advice. The creation of international call centres, in which people provide assistance with respect to particular products or services, is another example of the way that services can be provided at a distance. These centres can be located anywhere in the world where people can be trained to provide the required service.

Global labour markets

International labour markets are another economic aspect of the emergence of the global;[17] this phenomenon is related to the emergence of powerful and highly mobile MNCs. Their mobility means that they are not limited to setting up one element of their company in a particular nation, and among a particular set of workers. Certainly, they are limited by a desire to maximise the benefits to be gained from existing factories or administrative nodes, but they are not permanently wedded to a particular site. This becomes particularly significant if factories or assembly plants have to be refitted for the production of later versions of an MNC's products. In these circumstances, those responsible for an MNC can calculate the costs associated with using a particular set of workers. This will reflect the wages they have to pay workers, but will also take into account the skills of the workforce and the extent to which they have participated in strikes or other forms of industrial action.

Global free market policies (reduction of market interference by political executives)

Possibly the most compelling evidence of the existence of globalisation can be found in the global shift towards market economies.[18] This is most dramatic in the countries of the former Soviet Union, but is occurring in almost all countries of the world. The leaders of the Chinese Communist Party have even adopted free market principles. The IMF, World Bank, and WTO have played a significant role in the adoption of market policies around the globe, but their role is only part of the story. The search for new markets by national and multinational producers and service providers is also contributing to this phenomenon. Advanced ICTs also contribute to the emergence of global markets, as they make cross-border transactions much easier. This phenomenon is one of the strongest arguments for the irresistibility of globalisation. The fact that no members of a political executive in any country seem able to resist adopting these policies evidences the reality and necessity of globalisation.

Global political ideas, practices, and institutions (democracy)
The move to market economies is an indication that particular economic and political ideas, practices, and institutions are attaining legitimacy around the globe. The widespread acceptance, especially by members of political executives, that markets are superior to any alternative form of economic organisation is simply one example of this. It is also evidenced in the continuing attempts to introduce democratic processes and institutions, especially in the countries of the former Soviet Union, and in Africa, Asia, and Central and South America. While some of the pressure to adopt these changes has come from the United Nations, the role of advanced ICTs and media organisations providing content in which democratic processes are the norm has also contributed to this momentum.

Summary
The development of global markets in commodities, services and labour; the adoption of free market policies; and the global spread of democratic ideas, practices, and institutions are expressions of the economic, political, and cultural aspects of globalisation. Some of the proponents of this understanding of globalisation would see the widespread adoption of free market policies and democratic ideas, practices, and institutions as common sense. Although others might be more sceptical about these ideas, they would understand the evidence of the widespread adoption of these policies, ideas, and practices, as proof that, in the words of *Star Trek's* the Borg, 'resistance to globalisation is futile'.

Hegemonic ideological position

While some people take globalisation to be real, others see it as an idea that is part of a hegemonic ideology. Before we explain this understanding of globalisation, we discuss the nature of a hegemonic ideology. The central point of this understanding of globalisation is that the 'irresistible force' understanding of globalisation is not supported by the evidence and has become a dominant understanding of globalisation because opinion leaders have treated it as true, acted on its truth and, as a result, have made it true. The result of this is that those who do not accept the understanding of globalisation as an irresistible force have come to be treated as naïve or misguided.

What is a hegemonic ideology?
An ideology[19] is a way of seeing the world, that is, it is a world view. The idea that ideology is important to the way that people behave begins with the view that the facts are not demonstrable, especially facts about the social world. Rather, what

people come to accept as true results from the way that they have been trained to see the world. An ideology becomes hegemonic[20] when it is the dominant way that people see the world, particularly the social world. This way of seeing the world is not true, in some fundamental sense, but the fact that everyone treats it as true means that the ways that they behave reflect this world view and it becomes true for them.

For example, if people, including women, see women as inferior and as only capable of managing the home, then the fact that women do not participate in paid work and politics could be understood to reflect or demonstrate the truth of this position. If this view is understood as a hegemonic ideology, on the other hand, the fact that women are not found in paid work and in politics is a reflection of the fact that women and men are trained to accept the absence of women in paid work and politics as natural and normal. When ideas about women change, however, this natural and normal state of affairs becomes unnatural and unjustifiable. At this point, the attitudes and practices that have resulted in women's exclusion from public life are seen to have resulted from prejudice and not the way things actually are.

Globalisation as hegemonic ideology
Evidence is weak
The view that there is nothing obvious, natural, or commonsense in the understanding of globalisation as an irresistible force begins with an attack on the claims that are central to this view of globalisation. Critics point out that the evidence of economic, political, and cultural globalisation is not as compelling as it is taken to be. Some globalising might have occurred, such as the development of a global finance market and the emergence of internationally networked ICTs (and the industries that supply and rely on them), but many economic, political, or cultural phenomena have not been globalised.

Markets, from this perspective, continue to be predominantly national and determined by national economic, political, and cultural processes.[21] International political agencies, from this perspective, can be understood as vehicles through which dominant countries maintain their dominance over economics, politics, and culture. Free trade is not the global reality as protection continues to be practised by members of political executives in all countries, including those allegedly leading the push for free trade. Members of political executives embrace free trade when it is in their interests to do so and refuse it when it is not. Members of political executives in the USA, Japan, and the EU continue to operate highly protected economies despite their continual claims as to the need for free trade.

Another problem with the irresistible force view is that, despite the apparent commitment to democratic ideas, practices, and institutions, the politics in many countries whose leaders claim to have adopted democratic ideas, practices, and institutions is unlike democracy as many of us in the West know it. At most, we might find more people wanting democracy, but this might depend on the places in which we look and at whom we look.[22]

Truth of the position is not apparent, yet there has been convergence—why?
The fact that economics, politics, and culture have not become truly global, because much less has changed than many people believe it has, raises the question as to why there is apparent widespread agreement as to the reality of globalisation. A related question concerns why members of political executives in many countries have adopted the rhetoric and some, but not all, of the practices of free trade. This is the point at which the idea of hegemonic ideology becomes important. For the explanation of the convergence of the rhetoric and policy that reflects the irresistibility of globalisation can be explained by looking at the attitudes of those in positions of intellectual, political, and economic power in the community.

Those in business, media, political executives, and major political parties have treated it as true
The understanding of globalisation as a manifestation of a hegemonic ideology leads us to look to those responsible for the ideas and practices adopted in Australian politics and society for an explanation of the dominance of this idea. While there have been some dissenting voices, the dominant views that emerge from business leaders, media commentators, members of political executives, and leaders of the major political parties reflect the irresistible force position. Others who have participated in the production and legitimisation of the irresistible force position include academics and unionists who have urged Australians to adjust to the new reality of a globalised world.

The fact that they are convinced that globalisation is real and irresistible has meant that business leaders and media commentators have continually called on those in political executives and the major parties to introduce policies that reflect the irresistible force position. In particular, business leaders and media commentators have called on policy-makers to deregulate markets and open the Australian economy to globalising economic, political, and cultural forces. Members of political executives and leaders of the major parties have already accepted the legitimacy of this position, so this means that they are ready and willing to introduce these policies and accept praise from business leaders and media commentators for doing so.

They have made it true
The fact that Australian business leaders, media commentators, members of political executives, and leaders of the major parties have adopted the irresistible force understanding of globalisation has meant that this idea has influenced policy-making since the 1990s. To an extent, this makes redundant the issue of whether the irresistible force conception of globalisation is true or not. Globalisation has become our truth and is something to which all Australians have had to adjust themselves. This is not all that has happened, however. The consistency with which these ideas were accepted and legitimised by those in business, the media, political executives, and the major political parties has resulted in the irresistible force understanding of globalisation becoming the only understanding available to most people.

Anything that diverges from this position is treated as irrational
The irresistible force understanding of globalisation, as we have been trying to demonstrate, is not the only understanding available. The power of this idea, however, has resulted in demonstrations against globalisation.[23] To some extent, those who protest against globalisation may well reinforce the truth of globalisation. It doesn't make much sense to protest against something that is not happening. Those people who demonstrate against globalisation can easily be presented as naïve, simple-minded, misguided and, in some cases, evil individuals, who stand in the way of sense and progress. The fact that some of them argue that globalisation is a choice and not a necessity is likely to be lost, especially in the news media, whose members must simplify the messages that members of these groups are trying to communicate.

Summary
The understanding of globalisation as a reflection of a hegemonic ideology is important because it brings the irresistible force understanding into question. When understood as part of a hegemonic ideology, globalisation is not an irresistible truth that rational people have to accept, but an understanding of the world that has been promoted, adopted, and made real by business leaders, media commentators, members of political executives, and leaders of the major political parties. In adopting this view of the world, members of political executives have introduced policies that are responses to globalisation and have made the irresistible force understanding of globalisation into both common sense and a reality. Not to accept this understanding is to be unrealistic and to act in a way that is counter to Australians' interests. Even protests against globalisation validate this understanding, as they confirm the reality of globalisation.

> **QUESTION**
>
> What are differences between the irresistible force understanding of globalisation and the hegemonic ideological position?

2: WHAT ARE THE IMPLICATIONS OF THE DIFFERENT UNDERSTANDINGS OF GLOBALISATION FOR GOVERNMENT AND DEMOCRACY IN AUSTRALIA?

Before we leave this discussion of globalisation, some discussion of the implications of these two understandings is required because they have profoundly different implications for government and democracy in Australia. If globalisation is an irresistible force, then members of political executives must respond to globalisation with the right economic and social policies. The consequence for democracy is that it limits the capacity of those in political executives to adopt different policies, even if those policies are supported by a majority of voters. Those who adopt the hegemonic ideology understanding of globalisation believe that political executives don't have to adopt economic and social policies that reflect globalisation. Consequently, they could respond to the wishes of a majority of voters who might not want the types of policies that are justified by the belief that globalisation is an irresistible force.

Irresistible force resulting in integration of national policies into a global economy, politics, and culture

A loss of autonomy or sovereignty
The main consequence for government of the irresistible force understanding of globalisation is that it results in a loss of autonomy for the members of political executives.[24] Members of autonomous political executives, in this understanding, used to set economic policy and, through this, control the nature of Australian society.[25] But now they can't do this. The fact that political executives were autonomous meant that they were free to set economic policy as they, and their voters, desired. This meant that they were free to interfere in domestic markets by providing services, subsidies, and protection. In seeing themselves as responsible for the nature of society, members of political executives would introduce policies that were designed to produce a way of life that people wanted. Political executives and institutions grew in size, function, and cost in order to create a particular way of life for Australian citizens. The justification for their ownership of important

BOX 13.2
Anti-globalisation

The term 'anti-globalisation' is a blanket-term for a variety of different protest groups. These include groups that promote environmentalism, seek to have Third World debt waived, support animal rights, reject child labour, and groups that oppose capitalism and multinational corporations. The targets of members of anti-globalisation movements include the World Trade Organisation, the International Monetary Fund, and multinational companies. Those who oppose globalisation argue that it leads to the exploitation of workers, accelerates the world's poor, and damages the environment. They also contend that it enables rich companies to become richer and results in an increased Americanisation of the world. Groups opposing globalisation include the South Centre, the International Forum on Globalisation, the Third World Network (based in Singapore), the International Labour Organisation, and Friends of the Earth.

Sources: http://www.bbc.co.uk; http://www.globalisationguide.org/sb02.html

economic and social institutions led, in some cases, to the creation of a welfare state. However, the point is that, before globalisation, members of autonomous political executives were free to respond to the wishes of voters.

The loss of autonomy of political executives

Those who view globalisation as an irresistible force argue that members of political executives have lost the control they once had and must set economic policy according to the requirements of global and globalising economic and political forces. Members of political executives are competing to attract mobile MNCs, trying to avoid the discipline of financial markets, and attempting to escape interference from political and quasi-political institutions. They are also required by international political and quasi-political institutions to adopt free market policies and reduce protection for domestically produced goods and services.

Members of political executives in a globalised world, in this understanding, are seeking to train a workforce that meets the needs of MNCs or who can participate in industries in which Australia has a comparative or competitive advantage. They must limit potential disruption from workers. They must reduce the size of the political executive itself, in order to lower taxation to attract MNCs and to make domestic businesses more competitive against overseas businesses. They must reduce the money supply and control inflation. Most importantly, they are not free to determine national economic and social policy and are not free to respond to wishes of voters (unless those wishes are consistent with the requirements of the global economic and political order). They may even need to tolerate higher levels of unemployment and underemployment than most voters would accept.[26]

Hegemonic ideological position

Globalisation as irresistible force is a powerful position

Those who see globalisation as a manifestation of a hegemonic ideology know that the irresistible force position is hard to displace. First, because it is the 'truth' for those in business, the media, political executives, and major parties (not to mention their advisers and their potential critics); and second, because alternative 'truths' aren't available as they seem to run counter to good sense. The alternative 'truths' begin with the position that members of political executives have autonomy. One implication of this position is that government does not have to be small. It also means that members of political executives can pursue competitive advantage[27] (which is the fostering or creation of industries that, through public investment and protection from competition, can ultimately compete with overseas firms or even MNCs located in Australia). The final, alternative 'truth' that becomes available with the adoption of the understanding of globalisation as a reflection of a hegemonic ideology is that members of the political executive can promote the type of society that citizens desire.

> **QUESTION**
>
> Which pressure groups premise their advocacy upon the irresistible force understanding of globalisation? Do any adopt the hegemonic ideological position?

CONCLUSION

The status of globalisation is paramount for any discussion of important issues in government and democracy, such as citizenship and identity, and the environment. Our answer to the question of whether globalisation is an irresistible force or a manifestation of a hegemonic ideology has profound implications for what we can expect from members of political executives and whether they can respond to the wishes of voters. Understanding globalisation as an irresistible force results in the view that members of political executives have little, if any, capacity to resist global forces. Taking globalisation to be a manifestation of a hegemonic ideology leads to the view that members of political executives can respond to the wishes of voters. We can't resolve the question of which understanding is superior by appealing to the facts because the view that globalisation is a manifestation of a hegemonic ideology begins with the assumption that complex facts, such as globalisation, are not facts at all; they are shared preconceptions.

FURTHER READING

Introductory texts

Hughes, Owen, 1998a, *Australian Politics*, 3rd edn, Macmillan: South Yarra.

Peacock, Andrew, 1980, 'New International Economic Order: Implications for Australia', in H. Mayer & H. Nelson (eds), *Australian Politics: A Fifth Reader*, Longman Cheshire: Melbourne.

Scott, Shirley, 1994, 'Australia and International Institutions', in J. Brett, J. Gillespie & M. Goot (eds), *Developments in Australian Politics*, Macmillan: South Melbourne.

Sheil, Christopher (ed.), 2001, *Globalisation: Australian Impacts*, UNSW Press: Sydney.

Wiseman, John, 1998, *Global Nation?: Australia and the Politics of Globalisation*, Cambridge University Press: Melbourne.

Specialist texts

Argy, Fred, 1998, *Australia at the Crossroads: Radical Free Markets or a Progressive Liberalism?*, Allen & Unwin: St Leonards.

Capling, Ann & Brian Galligan, 1992, *Beyond the Protective State: The Political Economy of Australia's Manufacturing Industry Policy*, Cambridge University Press: Cambridge.

Conley, Tom, 2001, 'The Domestic Politics of Globalisation', *Australian Journal of Political Science*, vol. 36, no. 2, pp. 223–46.

Frankel, Boris, 2001, *When the Boat Comes In: Transforming Australia in the Age of Globalisation*, Pluto Press: Annandale.

Galligan, Brian, Winsome Roberts & Gabriella Trifiletti, 2001, *Australians and Globalisation: The Experience of Two Centuries*, Cambridge University Press: Oakleigh.

Singh, Kavaljit, 1998, *The Globalisation of Finance: A Citizens Guide*, Zed Books: London.

Woodley, Gil, 2000, 'The "Battle for Seattle": Globalisation and its Discontents', *Social Alternatives*, vol. 19, no. 1, pp. 26–9.

Yeatman, Anna, 1992, 'Women's Citizenship Claims, Labour Market Policy and Globalisation', *Australian Journal of Political Science*, vol. 27, pp. 449–61.

Web sites

Australian politics: http://australianpolitics.com
Australian Stock Exchange: http://www.asx.com.au
Organisation of the Petroleum Exporting Countries: http://www.opec.org
Organisation for Economic Development: http://www.oecd.org
The International Monetary Fund: http://www.imf.org
The United Nations: http://www.un.org
The World Bank: http://www.worldbank.org
The World Trade Organisation: http://www.wto.org

Notes

1. For more information on the concept of globalisation, see Held, McGrew, Goldblat & Perraton (1999, pp. 1–31), Griffiths & O'Callaghan (2002, pp. 126–9), and Scholte (2000, pp. 89–110).
2. See Bell (1998, pp. 157–68) and Bell (1997, pp. 345–67).
3. See Hirst & Thompson (1999).
4. For more details concerning the inevitability of globalisation, see Watts (2000, pp. 17–23).
5. For information on how globalisation affects economies, see Held et al. (1999, pp. 149–235), Self (2000, pp. 138–44), Emy (1993, pp. 167–73), and Probert (1994, pp. 98–115).
6. For more information on the Bretton Woods system, see Held et al. (1999, pp. 199–201) and Griffiths & O'Callaghan (2002, pp. 20–2) or visit http://www.polsci.ucsb.edu/faculty/cohen/inpress/bretton.html
7. For more details on multinational corporations, see Held et al. (1999, pp. 236–82) and Griffiths & O'Callaghan (2002, pp. 199–201).
8. See, for example, Anderson, Sarah & John Cavanagh, 2000, 'The Rise of Corporate Global Power', Institute for Policy Studies. (Can be found at http://www.tni.org/archives/cavanagh/top200.pdf)
9. For more information on the Cold War and the implications of its conclusion, see Halliday (1994, pp. 191–215) and Griffiths & O'Callaghan (2002, pp. 35–8).
10. See Held et al. (1989, pp. 214–40).
11. For more details on the United Nations, see Held et al. (1999, pp. 62–70) and Griffiths & O'Callaghan (2002, pp. 316–20).
12. For more details on the G8, see http://www.g8.gc.ca/menu-en.asp.
13. For more details on the IMF, see Griffiths & O'Callaghan (2002, pp. 161–3).
14. For more details on the World Bank, see Griffiths & O'Callaghan (2002, pp. 333–5).
15. For more information concerning the cultural aspects of globalisation, see Held et al. (1999, pp. 327–75).
16. For more on world trade and global commodity markets, see Held et al. (1999, pp. 149–88) and Self (2000, pp. 132–8).
17. For more on global labour markets, see Lee (1997, pp. 173–89).

18	For more on market economies, see Self (2000, pp. 4–32).
19	For more on ideology, see Heywood (2007, pp. 1–23).
20	For more on hegemony, see Griffiths & O'Callaghan (2002, pp. 135–9).
21	For more on the criticisms of globalisation as it concerns economics, see Self (2000, pp. 154–8).
22	For more on the criticisms of globalisation's effect on democracy, see Self (2000, pp. 296–8).
23	For more on resistance to globalisation, see Woodley (2000, pp. 26–9) and Chin & Mittelman (1997, pp. 25–37).
24	For more on globalisation and its effects on state sovereignty, see Griffiths & O'Callaghan (2002, pp. 296–8), Hughes (1998a, pp. 471–5), and Cerny (1996, pp. 123–36).
25	See 'Introduction' in Kelly (1992).
26	These issues are a part of a set of policies that are referred to as the Washington Consensus; for more see Williamson (1990, pp. 7–20).
27	For more on the notion of a competitive advantage, see Emy (1993, pp. 186–90).

PART IV

Issues for Government and Democracy in Australia

Indigenous Australians

LEARNING OBJECTIVES

- Understand the most significant feature of the relationship between Indigenous Australians, government, and democracy in Australia in terms of policy failure
- Learn about government in Australia from policy failure with respect to Indigenous Australians
- Learn about democracy in Australia from policy failure with respect to Indigenous Australians

INTRODUCTION

A consideration of the relationship between Indigenous Australians and government and democracy in Australia offers a variety of insights into Australian politics. The most significant feature of this relationship is **policy failure**. In short, Indigenous Australians do not enjoy the same lifespan and quality of life as non-Indigenous Australians. This is despite the fact that members of Australian political executives have been actively trying to make a difference for at least the last thirty years. A variety of policies have been implemented in an attempt to reduce the gap between Indigenous and non-Indigenous Australians. These policies have failed. This failure may tell us something important about government and democracy in Australia.

> **policy failure**: We use this phrase to refer to a situation in which a public policy did not achieve the outcomes that its designers and advocates intended it to achieve.

This chapter has two main parts. In the first, we deal with what we might learn about government in Australia from policy failure with respect to Indigenous Australians. In the second, we deal with what we might learn about democracy in Australia from policy failure with respect to Indigenous Australians. But before these discussions are presented, we explain the idea of policy failure as it relates to Indigenous Australians.

PRELIMINARY DISCUSSION

Policy failure and Indigenous Australians

Indigenous Australians have shorter lives, less education, suffer more from diseases, and are more likely to be unemployed, malnourished, drug dependent, and sexually abused than other Australians.[1] This, for us, is policy failure. We can't prove that all members of all Australian political executives wanted to avoid this situation, but it has been a long time since any of them have said that they wanted Indigenous Australians to be in this position.

Even if we ignore policies before 1970, members of political executives during the last thirty years have claimed that they are committed to promoting the interests of Indigenous Australians. Policies adopted up until 1970, such as the forced removal of Indigenous children from their parents[2], damaged the lives of many Indigenous Australians. Policies adopted since then have done nothing to improve their lives.

Statistics show a clear difference between the life chances of Indigenous and non-Indigenous Australians and indicate policy failure.[3]

BOX 14.1
Quality of life for Indigenous Australians

The death rate for Indigenous Australians is five to six times higher than the death rate for the general population. Infant mortality is three to five times higher among Indigenous Australians than it is for non-Indigenous people. In 1998, 32 per cent of Indigenous Australians had completed Year 10 of school, whereas it was 73 per cent for the general population. In 2000, the imprisonment rate for Indigenous Australians was fourteen times higher than for non-Indigenous Australians, and Indigenous Australians constituted 19 per cent of the adult prison population. Life expectancy for Indigenous men was 56 years and for women 63 years, whereas for non-Indigenous Australians it was 76 years for men and 82 years for women. The 2006 census recorded 513,977 as the total population of Indigenous Australians.

Source: http://www.abs.gov.au/ausstats

1: WHAT DOES POLICY FAILURE TELL US ABOUT GOVERNMENT IN AUSTRALIA?

A number of aspects of government in Australia are highlighted if we approach the situation of Indigenous Australians as an indicator of policy failure. The most obvious of these is the lack of Indigenous Australians in Australian political executives. Other aspects of government highlighted by policy failure with respect to Indigenous Australians are the distance (both physical and cultural) between members of political executives and Indigenous Australians; the problems that members of political executives have with respect to a diverse group with divergent interests; and their lack of unity and consistency in relation to this issue (to which federalism has made a profound contribution). These aspects are discussed in later sections. Before they are discussed, though, Colin Tatz's more radical views on what policy failure with respect to Indigenous Australians tells us about Australian government and democracy deserves consideration.

Tatz: bypass the political, engage with the legal

Colin Tatz[4] has argued that Indigenous Australians ought not to look to members of Australian political executives for any meaningful support but should seek legal remedies and undertake actions in courts to attain justice. The fact that the *Mabo*[5] and *Wik*[6] decisions have done more for Indigenous Australians than any initiative emerging from Australian political executives supports Tatz's view. The introduction of the *Native Title Act* in 1993[7] suggests that members of political executives will only do something to assist Indigenous Australians when courts, particularly the High Court, take the initiative. Legal remedies are more reliable than legislation, however, especially when they derive from basic legal principles, as these remedies cannot be undermined or revised by later Cabinets, Ministers, or Parliaments.

Few members of political executives have been Indigenous Australians

The lack of Indigenous people in Australian political executives

Very few members of Australian political executives have been Indigenous Australians. While non-Indigenous middle-class, middle-aged men can make policy for other types of people, the question of whether non-Indigenous Australians can develop effective policies for Indigenous Australians remains open. The view that only those who belong to a particular group can make effective policies for people in their group is one explanation for policy failure with respect to Indigenous Australians. The fact that most politicians and public servants, especially senior public servants, have been non-Indigenous middle-class, middle-aged men may explain policy failure in this context.

Racism

The argument that we just presented suggests that we can make policy only for ourselves. If this is so, we might as well abandon policy-making as it always involves people making decisions for others. Policy failure with respect to Indigenous Australians, then, reflects the attitudes of those policy-makers who think of themselves as superior to or more advanced than Indigenous Australians and consequently make bad policy.[8] British colonists believed that they were superior to Indigenous Australians and treated them as primitive creatures. This explains past policy failure and may also explain more recent policy failure.[9]

Paternalism

A sense of superiority also played itself out in paternalism towards Indigenous Australians. Indigenous Australians were seen to be, and were treated as, children. Being treated in the way that a father treats his children—which is what paternalism means—could be beneficial. But if you are not a child, being treated like one won't be good for you. This lack of respect for Indigenous Australians and their cultures that produced this paternalism did not make 'fathering' a positive experience.

Although members of political executives usually see themselves as superior to those for whom they are responsible and it is a constant feature of their treatment of everyone, this sense of superiority is particularly powerful with respect to Indigenous Australians. The deep lack of respect it shows produces continued policy failure.

A note on the Aboriginal and Torres Strait Islander Commission
A variety of initiatives have been taken to achieve some presence of Indigenous Australians within Australian political executives. One of the most important of these was the creation of the Aboriginal and Torres Strait Islander Commission (ATSIC).[10] ATSIC was created in 1990 and abolished in 2004 by members of the Howard Cabinet. It represented the interests of Indigenous Australians and advised members of political executives at the national, state, and local levels on issues that concerned this group. It also sought to provide services to Indigenous Australians and monitor the services already provided for them. ATSIC had a governing board whose members were elected by regional councillors, who themselves had been elected by their Indigenous communities.

ATSIC was an important attempt to include Indigenous Australians in policy-making, or at least the monitoring of policies, with respect to Indigenous Australians. Its members often found themselves in a difficult relationship with members of Australian political executives and were subjected to criticism from a variety of people (including Indigenous Australians). ATSIC's role was undoubtedly a difficult one and criticism of its performance was to be expected. With a budget of over $1 billion, however, it represented an attempt to overcome policy failure by including Indigenous Australians in the federal political executive. Its abolition indicates that it was another example of policy failure.

Australian political executives distant from Indigenous Australians

Physical distance
Another explanation of policy failure with respect to Indigenous Australians is the distance that separates Indigenous Australians and those in Australian political executives. This distance can be understood in a variety of ways. It can refer to the fact that many Indigenous Australians live in remote regions of Australia, whereas most policy-makers are in urban centres. Indigenous Australians in urban areas encounter police officers and social workers and not policy-makers. Police officers and the public servants who deliver social services do not make policy.

Cultural distance
Physical distance is only one aspect of the gulf that separates non-Indigenous, middle-class policy-makers in Australian political executives from Indigenous Australians. Most Indigenous Australians have very different ways of life from policy-makers.

Most policy-makers are white and middle-class; Indigenous Austalians obviously are not white, and few are middle-class.

Intellectual distance

Physical and cultural distance explains only part of the gap between policy-makers and Indigenous Australians. Intellectual distance is also a problem. Developing effective policies, in this context, requires a capacity to imagine a different way of life from those with which we are familiar. Our argument here is that policy-makers are simply intellectually distant from Indigenous Australians and that this is part of an explanation for policy failure. Their inability to imagine or understand how Indigenous Australians live, including the demands made upon them and the contexts within which they make choices, means that members of Australian political executives cannot produce effective policies.[11]

Indigenous Australians have different interests, making policy-making difficult

Another explanation for policy failure is that Indigenous Australians are a diverse group of people who have a variety of needs and interests. In the first instance, the cultural differences between Aborigines and Torres Strait Islanders are sufficiently great that they create an immediate administrative problem. 'Aboriginal' and 'Torres Strait Islander' do not refer to people who all share the same interests, but refers to a variety of different cultures and ways of life.[12]

Tendency to prefer single policies

Policy-making tends to be more effective when those for whom policy is made are similar. Almost by definition, policy-making works best when the same policy has the same effect on everyone. This can't really happen, though. Requiring that all children start school at the same age, for example, might well put some children who are ready for school into classes with others who are not. Daylight saving might suit people in southern regions of Australia, but not those in northern regions. Effective policy-making in the face of the diversity that exists within and between Indigenous communities might be impossible, so we should expect policy failure.

Idiosyncratic on-the-ground strategies that reflect specific locations

Another source of problems in this context may arise from the actions of members of the Australian bureaucracy who are responsible for for the delivery of services to Indigenous Australians. Those in the field are unlikely to be closely monitored and have to develop strategies to achieve the results intended by policies. This may lead to individual interpretations of general policy and result in some divergences across and within regions. Tensions may then develop between those who make policy and those who work in the field and these tensions may cause problems with respect to effective policy-making and implementation.[13] People who work in the field have different values from policy-makers and this creates further problems with respect to effective policy-making.

Political executives have been neither united nor consistent

Changes in Cabinet and Ministries (inconsistent policies)
Another explanation of policy failure is the changes of policy resulting from changes of Cabinet and of the Ministers responsible for Indigenous Australians. The ALP and the LPA–NPA coalition have adopted quite different approaches to dealing with Indigenous Australians.[14] Changes in the Cabinet membership bringing the introduction of different policies contributes to policy failure. Each Minister responsible for Indigenous Australians has adopted an approach different from that of her or his predecessor, even when they are members from the same party. This contributes to policy failure.

Tensions between Cabinet and Ministers and departments (conflicting policy objectives)
Yet another contribution to policy failure comes from the tensions that can develop between the Minister and members of the department responsible for Indigenous Australians. While those in public service departments are supposed to carry out the wishes of their Minister, this does not always happen. In many instances, those in the departments have greater knowledge and experience with respect to the specific policy area than Ministers. While those in departments may use this knowledge and experience to influence Ministers to adopt the policies that they desire, they are not always successful in doing so. This can result in tensions developing between Ministers, who see themselves as responsible for policy, and those in departments, who see themselves as responsible for developing and implementing appropriate policy.

Federalism
Lack of clarity as to which political executive is responsible for Indigenous Australians
Federalism creates problems in this context because responsibility for the administration of Indigenous Australians is often a source of conflict between members of state and federal political executives.[15] The lack of clarity with respect to who is responsible for Indigenous Australians leads to confusion and competition

over responsibility, which contributes to policy failure. Tensions arise between different political executives. The 2007 Northern Territory intervention illustrates this problem. Members of Cabinet in the Northern Territory commissioned a report, entitled *Little Children are Sacred* (2007), which confirmed widespread sexual abuse of Indigenous children. The report was submitted to Ministers and was released at a media conference on 21 June 2007. While the authors of the report had hoped it would come to the attention of the federal government, they were unprepared for the response they received. Within a week of the report's launch, the Prime Minister and his Indigenous Affairs Minister declared a state of emergency, and organised a police and military response. Members of the Howard Cabinet had not consulted members of the Northern Territory's political executive or the authors of the report, Rex Wild and Pat Anderson. Some considered the response from members of the Howard Cabinet as an attempt to overcome long-term policy failure, while others understood it as a cynical grab for Indigenous land leases under the guise of protecting children (because the federal intervention involved compulsorily acquiring land on just terms).

BOX 14.2
Little Children are Sacred report 2007

Clare Martin, the then Chief Minister of the Northern Territory and other members of her Cabinet commissioned a board of inquiry, headed by Rex Wild QC and Patricia Anderson, to examine the extent, nature, and factors that contributed to the sexual abuse of Indigenous children, with a specific focus on the unreported incidents of sexual abuse. Members of the board of inquiry sought to identify obstacles to an effective response to the sexual abuse of Indigenous children. They considered the practices, procedures, and resources of Northern Territory government agencies with direct responsibilities in this area, specifically Family and Children's Services and Police, as well as the role of all tiers of government and non-government agencies in protection.

http://www.nt.gov.au/dcm/inquirysaac/pdf/bipacsa_final_report.pdf

Confusion with respect to implications of change to Constitution with respect to 'power to make laws with respect to peoples ... of any race'
Confusion over responsibility for Indigenous Australians was increased, rather than diminished, by the change to the wording of the Constitution which was approved in the 1967 referendum.[16] This gave the federal Parliament the power to make laws with respect to 'the people of any race for whom it is deemed necessary

BOX 14.3
A short history of the Department of Aboriginal Affairs

At Federation, the Commonwealth Parliament had no power to make laws for Indigenous Australians, so state Parliaments were responsible for Indigenous Australians who lived outside the ACT and the Northern Territory. Before 1967, the federal Parliament had jurisdiction only over Indigenous Australians living in the Australian territories. In 1967, a referendum authorised amendments to the Constitution that gave the Commonwealth Parliament power to legislate for Aboriginal Australians living in the states. The Department of Aboriginal Affairs was established in 1972. This department has now been incorporated into the Department of Families, Housing, Community Services and Indigenous Affairs (FaHCSIA).

Source: http://www.abs.gov.au/Websitedbs/c311215.
nsf/20564c23f3183fdaca25672100813ef1/0179c2b24398
e077ca2570a8000945d2!OpenDocument;
http://www.facsia.gov.au

to make special laws'.[17] There is considerable confusion as what this means and it did nothing to reduce the potential for confusion over who is responsible for Indigenous Australians.

Conflicts over resources, 'development', and blame

Conflict between members of state and federal political executives over responsibility for Indigenous Australians generally arises when this concerns control over resources or affects economic development. Indigenous Australians often assert land rights[18] over areas that are used for agriculture or mining; areas in which members of both the federal and state political executives have strong interests. The other situation in which conflict occurs is with respect to responsibility for problems in Indigenous communities. Members of both federal and state political executives are likely to deny responsibility for problems and attribute blame for flawed policies adopted by members of the other political executives, or to Indigenous Australians themselves.

Summary

Policy failure with respect to Indigenous Australians seems almost inevitable. Policies are not devised by Indigenous Australians and are generally created by people at a physical and cultural distance from them. Even if this were not true, the diversity of interests and values present within Indigenous communities makes policy-making a difficult activity. Changes in Cabinets and Ministers and tensions within Australian political executives, sometimes between Ministers and members of their departments, contribute to the problems associated with effective policy-making in this area. Federalism contributes both to the lack of consistency in policy-making and a lack of clarity with respect to who, among members of Australia's political executives, is responsible for Indigenous Australians (a situation that the 1967 Referendum did little to resolve).[19]

QUESTIONS

1. Is policy failure the best way to describe the relationship between Indigenous Australians and political executives?
2. Tatz suggests that Indigenous Australians should seek redress for injustices through the legal system rather than through political executives. Do you agree? Why/Why not?

2: WHAT DOES POLICY FAILURE WITH RESPECT TO INDIGENOUS AUSTRALIANS TELL US ABOUT DEMOCRACY IN AUSTRALIA?

Policy failure with respect to Indigenous Australians also offers a variety of insights into democracy in Australia. First, it reminds us that the will of only some people is represented in representative democracies. A more specific insight concerns the way that the voting systems, or systems of representation, which determine election outcomes at the state and federal levels, affect the composition of Parliaments and Cabinets. The operation of the two-party system also plays a significant role in determining the interests that Australian Parliaments and Cabinets reflect. The limited influence of those pressure groups whose members seek to represent Indigenous Australians contributes to policy failure. Finally, policy failure indicates the extent to which Indigenous Australians are alienated from and lack feelings of political efficacy with respect to the Australian political system, which inhibits their capacity to involve themselves successfully in policy-making.

Representative democracies reflect the will of only some people

The majority
While democratic theory often presents democracies as systems in which the will of the people is reflected in political decision-making, this never happens. Even decisions taken in participatory democracies won't equally reflect the will

BOX 14.4
A short history of Land Rights for Indigenous Australians

In the early 1970s, Australian Parliaments started to legislate to return some Crown land to Indigenous communities (*The Aboriginal Land Rights (Northern Territory) Act 1976* is one example). In 1993, federal laws changed to allow recognition of land rights of Indigenous Australians. Native title was first recognised under Australian law in 1992, when the High Court accepted a land claim by the late Eddie Mabo, a Torres Strait Islander. The High Court concluded that native title could exist where the members of a particular Indigenous community had maintained their traditional connection to the land and where their native title had not been extinguished by government action on the land.

The decision of the High Court led to the *Native Title Act 1993*, which created a consensus-based process for resolving problems caused by claims to native title. The Act, however, did not fully address the possibility that native title could co-exist with other rights on the same land. The Wik people of Cape York put a land claim to members of the High Court in 1996. Their claim required a decision as to whether native title might survive on pastoral leases. A majority of members of the High Court decided in favour of the Wik people, but they also held that the rights of pastoral lessees prevailed over any inconsistent rights that native titleholders may have. The *Yorta Yorta* decision, which expresses an even more conservative reading of the *Mabo* decision, was another setback to the pursuit of land rights for Indigenous Australians.

Source: http://www.ags.gov.au/publications/agspubs/legalpubs/legalbriefings/br11.htm

---

of every person. If no decision will accommodate the views of all people then the best that can be hoped for is that it reflects the views of a majority. Australians generally accept the view that the will of a majority of people ought to determine political outcomes. The fact that Indigenous Australians make up only a small percentage of voters means that their views will be constantly overridden without this undermining the view that Australians live in a democracy.

Those who determine the results in an election

The Westminster system also contributes to minimising the significance of the 'voice' of Indigenous Australians. Central to the Westminster system is the convention that the members of the party or coalition of parties that wins a majority of seats in the Lower House of Parliament determine the membership of Cabinet. The fact that a considerable number of the seats in Parliament are unlikely to change hands (i.e., are 'safe' seats) means that election campaigns are mainly fought over those seats that might change hands. The fact that the people in those seats will play a central role in determining an election outcome means that their views are central to the policies presented at an election. Many of the electorates that might change hands, or marginal seats, are found in the outer suburbs of major cities. These electorates contain few Indigenous Australians.

They are not particularly concerned about policy failure
Results from elections at all levels of government in Australia suggest that neither a majority of voters nor a majority of voters in marginal seats treat policy failure with respect to Indigenous Australians as a significant problem. This issue is never among the most important in an election and is never one that strategists within parties treat as significant to their electoral chances. Indeed, people in marginal electorates may be less concerned about policy failure than most of the candidates who stand for election and less sympathetic to the situation in which Indigenous Australians find themselves than most other voters.[20]

Voting system does not allow for representation of interests of Indigenous Australians

Single member geographical constituencies
While the sentiments of a majority of voters and voters in marginal electorates are important for explaining a lack of concern with respect to policy failure, a more important factor relating to policy failure is the electoral system[21] that governs the selection of Members of Parliament (and, consequently, members of Cabinet). Tasmania is the only exception to the rule that members of the Lower Houses of Australian Parliaments are elected from single member geographical constituencies. In other words, voters are grouped together because of their location and each of these groups of voters elects one person to represent them. No federal electorate contains a majority of Indigenous Australians.

Proportional representation
The other electoral system used in Australia is proportional representation. Once again, voters are grouped according to their location, but they select more than one representative. Proportional representation is used in the elections for the Australian Senate, and the Legislative Councils of New South Wales, Western Australia, and South Australia, while the Tasmanian House of Assembly uses a variation of proportional representation known as the Hare-Clarke system.[22] The greatest number of representatives that can be chosen by the members of an electorate is twelve. This occurs when federal Parliament has been dissolved in accordance with s 57 of the Constitution. To be elected in this situation, candidates for the Senate must receive 13 per cent of the votes in the state for which they seek

to be a representative.[23] The Northern Territory is the only state or territory in which Indigenous Australians are more than 13 per cent of the population (they comprise around 30 per cent).

Indigenous Australians will never represent Indigenous Australians
The fact that Indigenous Australians constitute around two per cent of the population[24] of Australia means that proportional representation is unlikely to result in the election of a candidate who represents Indigenous Australians. Single member geographical constituencies have a slightly greater chance of delivering representation of Indigenous Australians, but no electorates have been drawn up with the specific intention of ensuring a majority of Indigenous Australians in a particular electorate. This is possible in some regions of Australia, but seems almost impossible when electorates in any state cannot vary the number of voters by more than 10 per cent.[25] The only way to overcome this problem is to introduce seats in Parliament for which only Indigenous Australians vote.

Two-party system does not help representation of Indigenous Australians' interests

Dominated by middle-class, non-Indigenous men
Another factor that might explain policy failure with respect to Indigenous Australians is the fact that middle-class, non-Indigenous men dominate the major parties. This domination makes these parties unlikely to attract Indigenous Australians and give them meaningful roles in the party. There are, and have been, a number of exceptions to this rule,[26] but the internal cultures within the major parties continue to make them uncomfortable places for Indigenous Australians.

Threat to some supporters of the National Party of Australia
There seem to be strong grounds to suggest that the National Party of Australia contains and represents people whose interests are threatened by attempts to reflect the interests of Indigenous Australians in policies. This is a result of the fact that the National Party represents non-Indigenous Australians who live and work in rural areas.[27] Most Indigenous Australians live in these regions and it is on these regions that any rights granted to Indigenous Australians, especially land rights, will have the greatest impact.

Internal policy-making processes of ALP and LPA do not favour participation of Indigenous Australians
The Australian Labor Party and the Liberal Party of Australia do not represent as many people whose interests are directly threatened by any attempts to grant rights to Indigenous Australians as the National Party. But few Indigenous Australians

are members of the ALP and LPA, which suggests that participation in policy-making requires specific skills and a sense of political efficacy that Indigenous Australians don't have. Most members of these parties, and especially their leaders, want to win elections, which mean that they adopt policies that appeal to as many people as possible. Indigenous Australians are too small a minority for their interests to be central to policy-making within the ALP and LPA.

Pressure groups representing the interests of Indigenous Australians have not been effective

Lack of receptivity on the part of pressure points within political executives
One of the main problems with the attempt to pressure Ministers, Parliamentarians and public servants to adopt policies that are in the interests of Indigenous Australians is that they must be receptive to such pressure. Meeting with representatives of Cabinet, Parliament, the public service, and parties is one thing; getting them to adopt the policies that you want is another. The fact that pressure groups representing Indigenous Australians will compete for influence with those who represent agricultural and mining interests, means in effect that they will lose.

Diversity of needs, interests, and desires among Indigenous Australians creates problems for effective organisation and operation of interest groups
Indigenous Australians are not a homogeneous group, containing people with identical views and interests. This is another factor that reduces the effectiveness of any pressure group whose members claim to represent them. Tensions existing among different Indigenous communities can lead to a variety of pressure groups presenting different views as to effective policy. Different views as to the best strategies to achieve these policies are also likely to arise, and this will reduce the effectiveness of all the groups whose members seek to represent the interests of Indigenous Australians.

Feelings of political inefficacy

Not the same interest in voting
One reason that Indigenous Australians do not participate in policy-making processes is that they do not feel confident about their ability to participate effectively. Literacy rates are low and they are not willing, therefore, to participate or even vote.

Their votes won't be decisive in election campaigns, so they are not important to campaign strategies. Resources are unlikely to be devoted to encouraging them to vote and this means that they are under little pressure to participate. The fact

BOX 14.5
Apology to Australia's Indigenous Peoples

In 2007, Kevin Rudd made a commitment to the Australian people that if the Australian Labor Party formed the new Commonwealth government they would say sorry to the 'stolen generations'. At the commencement of the 42nd Parliament of the Commonwealth on 13 February 2008, the newly formed Rudd government honoured its pre-election promise. The apology has both practical and symbolic significance and provides a way for Indigenous and non-Indigenous Australians to move forward with a shared future. The following is an extract from the Prime Minister's speech with the full text available from the source below.

> I move that today we honour the Indigenous peoples of this land, the oldest continuing cultures in human history. We reflect on their past mistreatment. We reflect in particular on the mistreatment of those who were Stolen Generations—this blemished chapter in our nation's history. The time has now come for the nation to turn a new page in Australia's history by righting the wrongs of the past and moving with confidence to the future. We apologise for the laws and policies of successive Parliaments and governments that have inflicted profound grief, sufferings and loss on these our fellow Australians. We apologise especially for the removal of Aboriginal and Torres Strait Islander children from their families, their communities and their country. For the pain, suffering and hurt of these Stolen Generations, their descendants and for their families left behind, we say sorry. To the mothers and the fathers, the brothers and the sisters, for the breaking up of families and communities, we say sorry. For the indignity and degradation thus inflicted on a proud people and a proud culture, we say sorry. We the Parliament of Australia respectfully request that this apology be received in the spirit in which it is offered as part of the healing of the nation. For the future we take heart; resolving that this new page in the history of our great continent can now be written.
>
> Source: http://parlinfoweb.aph.gov.au/piweb/ TranslateWIPILink.aspx?Folder=HANSARDR&Criteria= DOC_DATE:2008-02-13%3BSEQ_NUM:3%3B

that they were not required to register to vote until 1984 indicates the lack of interest in putting the same pressure on them to participate in elections that is placed on other people who are entitled to vote.

Unlikely to see avenues for effective participation

Any pressure on Indigenous Australians to vote is unlikely to have a significant effect as they won't believe that greater involvement in Australian politics is likely to result in policies that better reflect their views and interests. Non-Indigenous, middle-class people dominate most of the formal and informal institutions within the Australian political system, so they appear unlikely to be receptive to the interests of Indigenous Australians. The problem of expressing interests and views to people who do not share your culture or values may well appear insurmountable. The abolition of ATSIC reinforced this perception.

Past experience is unlikely to see involvement as worthwhile
The relationship between Indigenous Australians and Australian political institutions has generally been negative and they have little motivation to interact with and to attempt to influence decisions within formal and informal institutions. They compete for attention with more powerful groups who are not attuned to their needs. This contributes to their feelings that any involvement is not worthwhile.

Summary

The profound disengagement of Indigenous Australians from democratic processes results from a variety of factors. They don't have the numbers to affect election results and they lack influence within the major political parties, so they are unlikely to play a direct role in policy-making. Pressure groups whose members seek to promote their interests will find it difficult to put pressure on members of Australian political executives to alter or adopt new policies with respect to Indigenous Australians. And their experiences with government and democracy in Australia may well lead Indigenous Australians to believe that there is little point in seeking to influence policy.

QUESTIONS

1   How relevant is democracy for Indigenous Australians?
2   What are some of the main factors for the disengagement of Indigenous Australians from democratic processes?

CONCLUSION

None of the relevant statistics suggest that Indigenous Australians are enjoying lives of equal quality and length to non-Indigenous Australians. Indeed, most statistics indicate a considerable gap in the life experiences of Indigenous and non-Indigenous Australians. If we treat this as evidence of policy failure, then it highlights a variety of features of government and democracy in Australia. While we may not go as far as Tatz and argue that Australian political institutions offer Indigenous Australians no hope, we must concede that members of Australian political executives will find it difficult to develop policies that are likely to improve the situation in which Indigenous Australians find themselves. The more important problems, however, are that voters are not putting pressure on members of Australian political executives to solve these problems and that Indigenous Australians do not view Australian democracy as being able to reflect their interests.

FURTHER READING

Introductory texts

Altman, Jon & Melinda Hinkson (eds), 2007, *Coercive Reconciliation*: *Stabilise, Normalise, Exit Aboriginal Australia*, Arena Publications: North Carlton.

Brunton, Ron, 1998, 'The Human Wrongs of Indigenous Rights', in D. Lovell, I. McAllister, W. Maley & C. Kukathas (eds), *The Australian Political System*, 2nd edn, Longman: South Melbourne.

Burgmann, Meredith, 1983, 'Aborigines: The Struggle Continues', in R. Lucy (ed.), *The Pieces of Politics*, 3rd edn, Macmillan: South Melbourne.

Butt, Peter, Robert Eagleson & Patricia Lane, 2001, *Mabo, Wik and Native Title*, 4th edn, Federation Press: Leichhardt.

Goot, Murray & Tim Rowse, 2007, *Divided Nation?: Indigenous Affairs and the Imagined Public*, Melbourne University Press: Carlton.

Lavarch, Michael, 1998, 'What Price Native Rights?', in D. Lovell, I. McAllister, W. Maley & C. Kukathas (eds), *The Australian Political System*, 2nd edn, Longman: South Melbourne.

Specialist texts

Arther, Bill, 1994, 'Cultural Autonomy, Economic Equity and Self-Determination within Nation-States: Australian Aborigines in Remote Regions', *Australian Aboriginal Studies*, no. 2, pp. 28–35.

Brady, Veronica, 1992, *Towards Reconciliation: National Council for Reconciliation*, Indian Ocean Centre for Peace Studies: Nedlands.

Brock, Peggy, 2001, 'Aboriginal Women, Politics and Land', in P. Brock (ed.), *Words and Silences: Aboriginal Women, Politics and Land*, Allen & Unwin: Crows Nest.

Broome, Richard, 1996, 'Historians, Aborigines and Australia: Writing the National Past', in B. Attwood (ed.), *In the Age of Mabo: History, Aborigines and Australia*, Allen & Unwin: St Leonards.

Danley, John, 1991, 'Liberalism, Aboriginal Rights, and Cultural Minorities', *Philosophy and Public Affairs*, vol. 20, no. 2, pp. 168–85.
Fletcher, Christine, 1992, *Aboriginal Politics: Intergovernmental Relations*, Melbourne University Press: Carlton.
Fletcher, Christine (ed.), 1994, *Aboriginal Self-Determination in Australia*, Aboriginal Studies Press for the Australian Institute of Aboriginal and Islander Studies: Canberra.
Gilbert, Kevin, 1993, *Aboriginal Sovereignty: Justice, the Law and Land* (includes draft treaty), 3rd edn, Burrambinga Books: Canberra.
Goodall, Heather, 1992, '"The Whole Truth and Nothing But…": Some Intersections of Western Law, Aboriginal History and Community Memory', in B. Attwood & J. Arnold (eds), *Power, Knowledge and Aborigines*, La Trobe University Press (in association with the National Centre for Australian Studies, Monash University): Bundoora.
Gray, Geoffrey & Christine Winter (eds), 1997, *The Resurgence of Racism: Howard, Hanson and the Race Debate*, Department of History, Monash University: Clayton.
Healey, Justin (ed.), 2002, *Aboriginal Land Rights*, Spinney Press: Rozelle.
Ivison, Duncan, Paul Patton & Will Sanders (eds), 2000, *Political Theory and the Rights of Indigenous Peoples*, Cambridge University Press: Melbourne.
Keon-Cohen, Bryan (ed.), 2001, *Native Title in the New Millennium: A Selection of Papers from the Native Title Representative Bodies Legal Conference*, 16–20 April 2000: Melbourne, Victoria, Aboriginal Studies Press and Native Title Research Unit: Canberra.
Lattas, Andrew, 1990, 'Aborigines and Contemporary Australian Nationalism: Primordiality and the Cultural Politics of Otherness', *Journal of Cultural and Social Practice*, no. 27, April, pp. 50–69.
Morris, Barry, 1988, 'The Politics of Identity: From Aborigines to the First Australia', in J. Beckett (ed.), *Past and Present: The Construction of Aboriginality*, Aboriginal Studies Press for the Australian Institute of Aboriginal Studies: Canberra.
Mowbray, Martin, 1990, 'Mainstreaming as Assimilation in the Northern Territory', *Australian Aboriginal Studies*, no. 2, pp. 20–6.
Reynolds, Henry, 1996, *Aboriginal Sovereignty: Reflections on Race, State and Nation*, Allen & Unwin: St Leonards.
Reynolds, Henry, 1999, *Why Weren't We Told: A Personal Search for the Truth About Our History*, Viking: Ringwood.
Reynolds, Henry, 2003, *The Law of the Land*, Penguin: Camberwell.
Rowse, Tim, 1987, '"Were You Ever Savages?" Aboriginal Insiders and Pastoralist's Patronage', *Oceania*, vol. 58, no. 1, pp. 139–44.

Rowse, Tim, 2002, *Indigenous Futures: Choice and Development for Aboriginal and Islander Australia*, UNSW Press: Sydney.

Saunders, Cheryl, 2000, 'The Implications of Federalism for Indigenous Australians', in Y. Ghai (ed.), *Autonomy and Ethnicity: Negotiating Competing Claims in Multi-Ethnic States*, Cambridge University Press: Cambridge.

Wild, Rex & Pat Anderson, 2007, *Little Children are Sacred*, Report of the Northern Territory Board of Inquiry into the Protection of Aboriginal Children from Sexual Abuse.

Web sites

Australians for Native Title: http://www.antar.org.au/

Australian politics: http://australianpolitics.com

Bringing them Home, Report of the National Inquiry into the Separation of Aboriginal and Torres Strait Islander Children from Their Families: http://www.austlii.edu.au/au/special/rsjproject/rsjlibrary/hreoc/stolen/

Council for Aboriginal Reconciliation: http://www.austlii.edu.au/au/orgs/car/

Documents of Reconciliation: http://www.austlii.edu.au/au/orgs/car/docrec/index.htm

Australian Declaration Towards Reconciliation: http://www.austlii.edu.au/cgi-bin/sinodisp/au/journals/AILR/2001/7.html?query=Declaration%20of%20Reconciliation

Department of Families, Housing, Community Services and Indigenous Affairs: http://www.facsia.gov.au

Message Stick—ABC Indigenous online: http://www.abc.net.au/message/

National Archives of Australia: http://www.naa.gov.au

Reconciliation and Social Justice Library: http://www.austlii.edu.au/au/special/rsjproject/rsjlibrary/

Notes

1. For more on the social problems facing Indigenous Australians, see Robbins & Summers (1997, pp. 527–8), Stewart & Ward (1994, pp. 298–9), and Cunneen (1990, pp. 37–50).
2. The people removed are sometimes referred to as the stolen generation. See http://www.humanrights.gov.au/social_justice/bth_report/index.html. The 'stolen generation' issue was raised by the National Inquiry into the Separation of Aboriginal and Torres Strait Islander Children from their Families (1997). This report received a variety of responses. Some were critical of its methods and findings; see Brunton (1998) and Manne (2001).
3. The Australian Bureau of Statistics is a good source of information about the life situations of Indigenous Australians. The Bureau has been publishing reports on this each year since 1997. The latest available when this book went to print is the *Health and Welfare of Australia's Aboriginal and Torres Strait Islander Peoples* (2005). See also Aboriginal Studies, ANU (Virtual Library) (http://www.ciolek.com/WWWVL-Aboriginal.html), and Australian Institute of Aboriginal and Torres Strait Islander Studies (http://www.aiatsis.gov.au).

4   See Tatz (1979, pp. 49–65; 1981, pp. 131–42).
5   For more information on the *Mabo* decision, see Kukathas (in Galligan et al.) (1997, pp. 168–74), Robbins & Summers (2006, pp. 523–4), Ward & Stewart (2006, p. 47), Mansell (1993, pp. 168–239), and Lovell et al. (1998, pp. 688–91).
6   For more information on the *Wik* decision, see Robbins & Summers (2006, pp. 533–4) and Lovell et al. (1998, pp. 639–40 and 692–700).
7   Visit http://www.comlaw.gov.au/ComLaw/Legislation/ActCompilation1.nsf/0/A7856C855CFC19A9CA256F710050F3BE/$file/NativeTitle1993.pdf to view the *Native Title Act* of 1993.
8   For more on racism in Australia, see Rowse (1994, pp. 192–3), Bennett (1989, pp. 46–61), and Thomas (2001, pp. 21–32).
9   This discussion is based on the idea that assimilationist policies are not designed to foster assimilation to a hybrid form of society to which all people are to be assimilated. That is, it is based on the idea that assimilation is to the dominant, in this case European, culture.
10 For more on ATSIC see Robbins & Summers (2006, pp. 523–4), Ward & Stewart (2006, p. 295), and Rowse (1994, pp. 191–2).
11 See Rowse (1992).
12 See Dudgeon & Oxenham (1990).
13 For more on policy formation and implementation, see Bridgman & Davis (1998) and Bennett (1989, pp. 85–108).
14 For more on the political parties' different approaches to Indigenous affairs, see Bennett (1989, pp. 22–9) and Brennan (1989, pp. 66–8).
15 See Robbins & Summers (2006, pp. 523–4), Bennett (1989, pp. 64–82), and Hanks (1984, pp. 24–37).
16 For more on the referendum of 1967, refer to Robbins & Summers (2006, p. 527), Bennett (1989, pp. 10–12), and Hanks (1984, pp. 19–24).
17 This was not the only change to the Constitution resulting from this referendum. Section 127 was removed completely. This section read, 'In reckoning the numbers of the people of the Commonwealth, or of a State or other parts of the Commonwealth, aboriginal natives shall not be counted'.
18 For more on land rights, refer to Robbins & Summers (2006, p. 537), Bennett (1989, pp. 29–37), and Lovell et al. (1998, pp. 638–9).
19 The factors that affect policy-making in this context are not unique to Indigenous Australians. The fact that those in Australian political executives are predominantly older, white, middle-class men who live in urban areas means that many of the policies they develop affect people who are quite different from them and with whom they have limited contact. The specific policy area with which members of Australian political executives are dealing may not involve significant levels of diversity, but some do, and this diversity can create problems for successful policy-making and implementation. Those for whom policy is made are unlikely to feel that their interests are either understood or reflected in the decisions taken by policy-makers. Changes in Cabinets and Ministers and internal tensions within Australian political executives are also not unique to attempts to make and implement policy for Indigenous Australians. Federalism also creates a variety of problems for successful policy-making and implementation across a wide variety of areas.
20 See Jackman (1998) who suggests that Members of Parliament are more likely to be sympathetic towards Indigenous Australians than other Australians.
21 For more on the electoral system and its effects on Indigenous Australians, see Robbins & Summers (2006, pp. 540–1), Bennett (1989, pp. 111–31), and Tatz (1979, pp. 19–25).
22 For more on the Hare-Clarke system, see http://www.electoral.tas.gov.au/pages/ElectoralInformationMain.html

23 For more on proportional representation, visit the Australian Electoral Commission at http://www.aec.gov.au/About_AEC/Media_releases/2001/FEB_Proportional_01.htm
24 See http://www.abs.gov.au
25 See http://www.aph.gov.au/library/handbook/elections/index.htm
26 Senator Aden Ridgeway took his seat in the Australian Senate for the Australian Democrats on 1 July 1999. He was only the second Aboriginal person to sit in the Federal Parliament, the first being Neville Bonner who entered Parliament in 1971. For more details, visit http://www.aec.gov.au/Voting/indigenous_vote/index.htm
27 See http://www.abs.gov.au

15

Ethnic Diversity

LEARNING OBJECTIVES

- Be able to differentiate ethnic diversity and 'real ethnic diversity'
- Be able to identify the stages of immigration policy and ethnic diversity in Australia
- Identify ways in which members of the political executive affect real ethnic diversity in contemporary Australia
- Outline the ways that real ethnic diversity affects democracy and representational democracy
- Consider whether government and democracy can be effective in a society where real ethnic diversity exists

INTRODUCTION

Australia is one of the most ethnically diverse countries in the world.[1] In this context, the questions of whether and how government and democracy in Australia should reflect this **ethnic diversity** become important. Early policies were intended to reduce ethnic diversity by assimilating all Australians to European, more specifically British-Australian, culture.[2] Recent policies have been designed to preserve ethnic diversity. These policies support and foster **multiculturalism**. Multiculturalism has attracted considerable criticism from a variety of sources. Some of this criticism results from the view that a **multicultural society** is a divided society in which no collective interest can be defined and pursued.

Two questions will be posed in this chapter, highlighting some of the issues that ethnic diversity raises for government and democracy in Australia. The first question relates to whether government can be effective in a society in which real ethnic diversity exists. The second is whether democracy can be effective in a society in which real ethnic diversity exists. These questions are dealt with in the second and third parts of this chapter. In the first part, we offer reasons to believe that ethnic diversity is important and will continue to be important for government and democracy in Australia.

Before the issues are discussed, however, the phrase '**real ethnic diversity**' deserves explanation. Real ethnic diversity is used to refer to significant differences between people of different ethnic communities. While their ethnic differences are important, people of English, Irish, Welsh, Scottish, South African, New Zealand, and North American descent are not really ethnically diverse. Real ethnic diversity is used to refer to differences between those of British culture and those of Southern and Eastern European, Asian, African, and Middle Eastern cultures.

ethnic diversity: We say that a society has, or exhibits, ethnic diversity when it contains people who have important cultural differences and does so without evidence of significant tension between the members of the different cultural groups. We are likely to refer to countries in which tension between cultures exists as ethnically divided. We are unlikely to refer to a society with two distinct cultures as ethnically diverse.

multiculturalism: Used to refer to policies adopted by members of political executives that support members of ethnic communities retaining the separation and distinctiveness of their community.

multicultural society: Used to refer to a society in which distinct ethnic communities exist and persist because the existence of ethically different communities is accepted and their differences valued.

1: THE IMPORTANCE OF ETHNIC DIVERSITY FOR GOVERNMENT AND DEMOCRACY IN AUSTRALIA

Ethnicity has always been an important issue for government in Australia. The judgment that Australia was an empty land (i.e., *terra nullius*) represented a failure on the part of people of one ethnic group to recognise practices of

real ethnic diversity: We use this phrase in this book to refer to significant ethnic differences, such as the differences that can be observed between British-Australians, Indigenous Australians, Italian-Australians, Vietnamese-Australians, and Sudanese-Australians. We treat the differences between Anglo-Australians, American-Australians, Canadian-Americans and New Zealanders as insignificant ethnic differences.

occupation of other ethnic groups.[3] Immigration policies reflect views about ethnicity and about appropriate levels and types of ethnic diversity in Australia. However, immigration policy is only one manifestation of political responses to ethnic diversity, for members of Australian political executives must also decide whether they will recognise and preserve, perhaps even increase, ethnic diversity in Australia. While it is possible for members of political executives to prevent increasing ethnic diversity, it does seem likely to increase in Australia. But even the existing levels of ethnic diversity will ensure that it remains significant for government and democracy in Australia, even if it does not increase.

This part is divided into three sections. The first is a discussion of immigration policy and ethnicity in Australia. The second is an examination of the different approaches to ethnic diversity that can be found in government policies towards ethnic diversity. In the final section, we argue that ethnic diversity in Australia is likely to increase. This part is intended to provide a background for the following discussions and to support the view that ethnic diversity is an important issue for government and democracy in Australia.

BOX 15.1
Ethnic diversity in Australia

The 2006 Census in Australia identified an 8.2 per cent growth in overseas-born Australian residents since 2001, and that 71 per cent of the Australian population were born in Australia. Some of the major groups that make up those born overseas are from the UK (4.3 per cent), New Zealand (2 per cent), Italy (1 per cent), China (1.0 per cent) and Vietnam (0.8 per cent). Just under twenty two percent of the population speaks languages other than English at home. Most commonly, Cantonese, Italian, Greek, Mandarin and Arabic are spoken. In the 2006 Census, 410,000 people identified themselves as either Aboriginal or as a Torres Strait Islander, which represented 2.3 per cent of the Australian population and an 11 per cent increase since the 2001 Census.

Source: 2006 Census QuickStats: Australia
http://www.censusdata.abs.gov.au/

Immigration policy and ethnic diversity in Australia

The White Australia Policy

One of the best-known periods in which immigration and ethnicity were central to policy-making was the period of the so-called White Australia Policy.[4] This policy was intended to preserve Australia as a home for white people (Indigenous Australians did not count). A justification for this policy was that a society in which significant ethnic diversity existed could not function. Australia was to have a white, or British, culture because it had been colonised by the British. People of other cultures were excluded because their presence would make a British-Australian society unstable.

Post-World War II immigration

The White Australia Policy stayed in place until the end of World War II.[5] After the war, political executives wanted to increase Australia's population, partly because of a sense of military vulnerability and partly to attract workers who could contribute to industrial development (as workers and consumers). This was a period of both declining immigration from Britain and an increase in immigration from other parts of Europe. Most of these immigrants came from Southern Europe, especially Italy and Greece. These immigrants have had a lasting effect on Australian society and have increased the level of ethnic diversity in Australia.

Immigration from the Asian region

Another period that merits attention in this brief discussion of immigration and ethnic diversity in Australia is the mid-1970s. Significant numbers of Asian refugees came to Australia during this period. Many of them were fleeing the effects of the Vietnam War[6] (in which Australian soldiers fought). Immigration from Asia has continued to be a significant part of immigration to this country and, for reasons that will be discussed below, this is unlikely to change. Immigration from Asia has certainly contributed to increasing ethnic diversity in Australia.

Muslim and African immigration

Into the new millennium, Australian governments have increased immigration to provide for Australia's growing economy and skills shortage. This has been done in the context of a robust Australian nationalism that has intensified in the post 11 September 2001 period. This is particularly the case in Australia, where 300,000 Muslims currently reside. The question of real ethnic diversity came into sharper focus in Australia in the context of the Sydney Cronulla beach riots that took place on 11 December 2005, where mainly white Australian males attacked those of Middle Eastern appearance. In October 2007, the Australian government halted Sudanese immigration for one year suggesting that Sudanese immigrants could not attain the education and language skills required fast enough to integrate effectively into the Australian way of life.

BOX 15.2
Patterns of immigration since 1788

European migration began with the transportation of convicts in 1788. Free settlers started arriving in the 1790s. The 1820s saw a marked increase in the migration of free people from the United Kingdom. Chinese immigrants were the largest non-British group who settled in Australia at this time. Increasing numbers of Afghanis and Japanese began to immigrate during the second half of the nineteenth century. Post-war Australian political executives introduce an immigration program that reflected a variety of agreements with other nations and international organisations. Formal migration agreements were signed with representatives of the United Kingdom, the Netherlands, Norway, France, Belgium, and Denmark. Other agreements involved assisted passage from Italy, West Germany, Turkey, and Yugoslavia and informal agreements with Austria, Greece, and Spain. The 1950s and 1960s also saw intakes from Hungary, Czechoslovakia, Chile, and Poland. The end of the Vietnam War in 1975 resulted in a significant influx of migrants from Indochina. Australia's population has changed from an Indigenous population, through a predominantly Anglo-Celtic one by 1900, to its present mix of 74 per cent Anglo-Celtic, 19 per cent other European, and 4.5 per cent Asian.

Source: http://www.immi.gov.au/media/publications/statistics/immigration-update/update_june07.pdf; http://www.immi.gov.au/media/publications/statistics/Federation/Federation.pdf

Policies with respect to ethnic diversity

Assimilation

The desire for **assimilation** dominated immigration policy in the pre-War period and this was extended to those immigrants who arrived after World War II. In being assimilated, these 'new Australians', as they were known, were to lose, perhaps abandon, the culture of the countries from which they came and acquire the values and outlooks of British-Australians. They were not encouraged to maintain their cultures or supported in their attempts to do so.[7]

assimilation: When used to refer to the treatment of immigrants, this word describes an attempt to encourage immigrants to become similar to members of the dominant ethnic group in a society.

Integration

Ozolinos[8] has argued that assimilationist policies were followed by policies that promoted integration. **Integration**, according to Ozolinos, was a policy that allowed, and even encouraged, migrants to maintain their own culture. That Ozolinos treats this policy as neither assimilation nor multiculturalism, suggests that migrants were encouraged to maintain their ethnic distinctiveness as far as this did not threaten their capacity to function as normal (British) Australians. Most policy-makers probably assumed that some sort of natural process would result in all Australians acting and feeling like British-Australians.

> **integration**: In the context of discussions of immigration, this word is used to refer to policies or practices that lead to all people being treated alike and having the same life opportunities.

Multiculturalism

Multiculturalism[9] represents the next identifiable policy towards ethnic diversity. Multiculturalism lies at the other end of a policy continuum that has assimilation at one end and integration somewhere in between. Thinking of this in terms of a policy continuum makes some sense, as policies are not simply of one sort or another. Multiculturalism resembles integration, in that ethnic diversity is preserved. Multicultural policy goes further, however, in that ethnic diversity is not only tolerated and supported in the short-term, but is maintained; migrants and their descendants are encouraged to preserve and foster those attributes that made their culture unique. In this context, Australians would identify themselves in terms of their ethnic inheritance, and hyphenated terms, like British-Australian, Italian-Australian, and Chinese-Australian, would mark a series of ethnic differences in Australian society.

Bilateralism

An important feature of most policies that have been adopted with respect to ethnic diversity is that they have generally received support from both of the major parties.[10] There are a variety of reasons for this **bilateralism**. One is that major parties contain people who disagree about the desirability of preserving and promoting ethnic diversity. To make it into a public issue would create tensions, if not splits, within the parties. Another reason is that members of the major political parties don't want to reveal that they are more sympathetic towards ethnic diversity than most Australians.[11] Finally, people who identify with particular ethnic communities vote. If a major party rejected multiculturalism, or immigration, they would alienate these voters.

> **bilateralism**: We use this word to describe a situation in which two entities, such as parties, or members of political executives, agree to work together or to accept a particular policy. Members of political executives from two countries sign 'bilateral' trade or diplomatic agreements that commit them to particular trading or defence arrangements.

Pressures towards increasing ethnic diversity

Inability to maintain and increase population without immigration
Ethnic diversity is unlikely to diminish in Australia, at least in the short-term, for a number of reasons. The most important of these is that immigration will continue because few members of political executives support the decline in population that an end to immigration would produce.[12] Most members of political executives believe that immigration is good for the Australian economy. They believe that skilled immigrants increase the competitiveness of Australian firms and all immigrants increase the size of local markets for goods and services. Symbolism also contributes to the desire to increase Australia's population. British-Australians have long battled with feelings of vulnerability that derive from a sense of themselves as a small group of British people inhabiting a large continent in the middle of nowhere. A decline in population would feed these feelings of vulnerability.[13]

Declining attractiveness of Australia to Britons
Immigration is necessary to maintain,[14] if not increase, Australia's population, but this does not necessarily mean that it will increase ethnic diversity. It only does when immigration occurs in a context of declining interest in immigration from potential immigrants in Britain. Immigration of Britons from New Zealand, Zimbabwe, and South Africa may reduce real ethnic diversity, but Australia is more attractive to people in our region than it is to people outside our region. This suggests that increasing real ethnic diversity is inevitable.

International obligations and expectations
Regulation and limitation of immigration is possible, and some Australians support this as a way to reduce ethnic diversity. Political instability and environmental crises in the Asian region, however, mean that influxes of refugees remain likely. Australia is a signatory to conventions that oblige us to accept these refugees.[15] Members of political executives may want to limit the number of people who qualify as refugees, but they will find it impossible to reject all refugees. This source of increased ethnic diversity may slow, but will only stop when major conflicts in the region stop.

Family reunions
Many immigrants have relatives in the countries from which they have come. At least some of these relatives will choose to join their family members in Australia. Family reunions are not always allowed and increasing scrutiny may be given to this source of immigration. But this is likely to remain a source of immigrants and will help to increase real ethnic diversity.

BOX 15.3
The dictation test (White Australia Policy)

In 1901, under pressure from miners and factory workers in Queensland, New South Wales, and Victoria, the new Australian Parliament passed an act to restrict Chinese and Pacific Islander people from migrating to Australia. Known as the 'White Australia Policy', the *Immigration Restriction Act 1901* included a dictation test for all applicants. The immigration official could choose a passage in any European language and ask the applicant to translate it into English. Those who couldn't were refused entry. This test was abolished in 1958.

Source: http://www.immi.gov.au

Summary

While real ethnic diversity may become more pronounced in Australia, this is not inevitable. Immigration policies could be reintroduced that prevent non-British immigrants or all immigrants from coming to the country. The mechanism used to achieve this may have to be more subtle than the dictation test, but it can be done. Preventing immigration would result in a decline in Australia's population, and most members of Australian political executives could not support it for this reason. However, stopping immigration is only one way to prevent increased ethnic diversity in Australia. Reintroducing assimilationist or integrationist policies and refusing to abide by the policy of multiculturalism is another method. Whether any of the policies designed to reduce ethnic diversity will be adopted and will succeed is unclear. Even if they don't, though, a discussion of whether government and democracy in Australia can be effective in a society in which real ethnic diversity exists tells us something about government and democracy in Australia.

QUESTIONS

1. How can we distinguish between ethnic diversity and real ethnic diversity?
2. What type of policies have Australian governments implemented in immigration with respect to ethnic diversity?

2: CAN GOVERNMENT BE EFFECTIVE IN A SOCIETY IN WHICH REAL ETHNIC DIVERSITY EXISTS?

In this part, we present alternative positions on the question of whether Australian government can be effective in a society in which real ethnic diversity exists. Five reasons to support each position are presented in separate sections. Two important questions are implicit to the reasons we present. The first concerns the proper role of government, and the second concerns the consequences that will result from acknowledging and promoting real ethnic diversity in Australia. Those who project a limited role for government are likely to believe that real ethnic diversity will not affect government in Australia. Those who believe that

BOX 15.4
Current immigration policy

Migrants will be accepted if they fit one of three main categories selected for migration to Australia. Migrants must either possess desirable skills, be seeking to reunite with their family, or deserve to migrate for humanitarian reasons. To qualify for the skills stream, applicants must have desired skills and be nominated by an employer, or have business skills and a specified amount of money to bring into Australia. To qualify under the family and relationships category, applicants must be sponsored by an Australian permanent resident. This category usually includes people seeking to reunite with a spouse or fiancée. Parents and children can also qualify under the 'balance of family test'.

In the 2006–2007 program, 13,000 people were allowed into Australia for humanitarian reasons, with 6,000 of these places going to refugees. A total of 7,000 places have been made available to the SHP (Special Humanitarian Program) to meet onshore protection needs. This enables them to stay in Australia for one to three years, after which time they can reassess the situation in their country of origin. The remainder of humanitarian places is allocated to people who can show that their human rights have been violated and that they have the support of an Australian permanent resident.

The statistics for immigration in preceding decades follow:

- 1945–60   1.6 million
- 1960s   1.3 million
- 1970s   960,000
- 1980s   1.1 million
- 1990s   900,000
- 2000–06   656,800

Source: http://www.immi.gov.au

recognising and fostering real ethnic diversity will not threaten the stability of Australian society are also likely to believe that real ethnic diversity will not affect government in Australia. Those who believe that government should play an extended role in society or that real ethnic diversity will create social instability are likely to believe that real ethnic diversity will render government in Australia unstable and ineffective.

Yes case

Introduction

The first two points of the Yes case reflect different versions of the view that the role of government is, or should be, limited. If governing is understood to be managing an economy or if it is seen to involve a minimal set of responsibilities, then there is no reason to believe that government will be affected by real ethnic diversity. The next three reasons put forward in support of the view that government can be effective in a society in which real ethnic diversity exists reflect a procedural view of governing. A government that follows the right processes, from this perspective, will not be undermined by real ethnic diversity. The processes through which members of political executives deal with competing demands for resources and resolve social conflicts allow them to work effectively in a society in which real ethnic diversity exists.

Governing is managing an economy

Elections are mainly about the economic management skills of the key figures of the major parties. Economic management is the issue that has the greatest importance for most commentators and participants in Australian politics. The importance of economic indicators to media reports on politics either reflects or has made economic management skills essential to governing. Indeed, many people want nothing more from members of political executives than that they manage the Australian economy well.[16]

Australians are more interested in sound economic management than in preserving real ethnic diversity. Real ethnic diversity has no obvious effect on whether Australia has a productive and sound economy. If real ethnic diversity has any economic significance, it arises in the context of the question of whether immigration is good for the Australian economy. Most of the evidence suggests that immigration is good for an economy.[17] The fact that developing a sound and productive economy has nothing to do with real ethnic diversity means that it is not an issue for government. If real ethnic diversity harmed the Australian economy then it might become an issue. Real ethnic diversity seems to have few economic effects, however, which means that it poses no obstacle to effective government.

Governing involves minimal responsibilities

Even if governing is more than managing an economy, it remains something that ought to be limited in its nature. Members of political executives should be careful not to become too involved in people's lives, as this will reduce their capacity to promote their own interests. Political executives should defend us against external threat, negotiate with representatives of other governments, protect life and property, ensure that markets operate fairly, guarantee a minimal level of education, protect people from starvation, and ensure that no one suffers unduly as a result of mental or physical incapacities.

Dealing with the issues raised by real ethnic diversity and its effects are not the responsibilities of governments. Real ethnic diversity may produce problems with which members of political executives must deal, but they deal with the problems and not their causes. Real ethnic diversity reflects people's individual choices about how they live their lives. Members of political executives should neither promote nor discourage any choice that does not threaten social stability. Promoting real ethnic diversity would exceed the proper role of government. Members of political executives need not concern themselves with real ethnic diversity, which means that it will not undermine the effectiveness of government.

Governing is treating people fairly

The principle that must govern the way that members of political executives act is that they must treat people fairly. This requires treating them as equals and ensuring that no one receives better treatment than others because of their ethnicity. While this principle reflects democratic principles, it also results from Weber's view that members of modern political executives maintain their authority because they follow correct procedures.[18] Treating all people in the same way is a method for reducing tension in society. Using the same rules for all people can also be understood as a basic principle of modern government. This does not mean that everyone gets the same things, only that everyone is treated in the same way.

From this perspective, the members of political executives should be indifferent to a person's ethnicity. They should not discriminate between members of different ethnic communities, but treat all people in the same manner. Government can be effective in a society in which real ethnic diversity exists, from this perspective, because members of political executives should be blind to ethnic diversity. This reflects the general principle that governments serve individuals. It also reflects proper practice within a modern government. Finally, it reflects good practice on the part of members of political executives, who do not want to cause social tension by unequal treatment of members of different ethnic communities.

Governing is distributing resources

Another way to understand governing is the way that resources are distributed, such as services, taxation, and other charges on business and the community. Members of political executives assess claims for resources to decide which claims are legitimate and deserve support. Some of these claims come from individuals who identify with particular groups. The claims of members of these groups will be assessed through the normal criteria used to determine priorities among different claimants on government resources.

An ethnic community is simply a word for one type of group. Members of a particular ethnic community may suffer from a common problem and may, as a result, be given additional resources. This creates no significant problems, as long as these allocative decisions are reached according to proper processes. Dealing with claims on resources is what members of political executives do (those who belong to one ethnic group may complain about allocations to another ethnic group, but this does not make government impossible or ineffective).

Governing is dealing with conflict

Another way to understand the role of political executives is that they are people responsible for stopping conflicts from threatening social stability. Societies are collections of people who, either individually or as members of groups, come into conflict with each other. To govern is to act as a social safety valve, which comes into play when tensions within society become so great that social cohesion begins to break down. Political processes replace violence as a means for resolving the tensions that emerge within a society.

Ethnic diversity is often a source of tension within a society. This is manifested in racism on the part of British-Australians toward Australians with a different ethnicity. It is also reflected in traditional rivalries between different ethnic communities. More importantly, it may be produced by persistent inequalities that result from some groups dominating resources. Modern governments, such as Australia's, are created to deal with these types of problems. The members of political executives can be expected to have the skills and, failing this, the coercive capacity to control any conflict caused by ethnic diversity.

Summary

Depending on your view of governing, real ethnic diversity either does not constitute an issue with which members of political executives have to deal, or does not represent an issue with which they can deal. If governing is understood as economic management then members of political executives do not have to deal with real ethnic diversity, as it has no negative economic consequences. Even if government is understood to be more than an economic manager, real ethnic diversity does not cause significant social disruption and falls outside the responsibilities of members of political executives. Also, if we treat governing or modern governing, as maintaining legitimacy through treating individuals fairly, then this also is not affected by real ethnic diversity. If real ethnic diversity is simply a source of claims for resources, then members of political executives can deal with these claims in the way that they deal with all claims for resources. In the same way, if real ethnic diversity is a source of social conflict, then members of political executives can institute normal processes for resolving this conflict.

No case

Five reasons to accept the view that Australian government cannot be effective in a society in which real ethnic diversity exists are presented in this section. The first of these is that governments cannot deal with the complex issues to which real ethnic diversity gives rise. The second reason is that real ethnic diversity undermines the community that members of Australian political executives are seeking to build. The third reason is that the uncommitted resources available to members of political executives are insufficient to allow them to support real ethnic diversity. The fourth reason is that governments are not able to respond to demands from non-dominant groups without losing support from dominant groups. The final reason presented here is that Australian political executives are so dominated by British-Australians that they are unable to reflect and respond to the needs and interests of members of non-British ethnic communities.

Governing is impossible in a society in which real ethnic diversity exists

Governing an entire population is not easy. It would be impossible if the specific needs and interests of each individual affected by a policy had to be taken into account when that policy was developed. To treat each person as an individual who requires individualised treatment is impossible. Members of political executives have to develop and apply policies that will be effective for most people most of the time. While some individual differences can be taken into account at the point at which a policy is applied, policy-makers within political executives cannot respond to individual differences when making policy. They develop broad principles and processes that work for most people or for particular categories of people. This is difficult enough and requires that differences between people are ignored and replaced by broad categories which function as the basis for and objects of policy-making. In the end, the targets of policies are generalisations that are simplified representations of real people.

Real ethnic diversity means that the population is divided into people with very different life experiences, needs, and wants. The cultural and intellectual differences that characterise real ethnic diversity mean that members of political executives have to deal with a number of different types of people about whom generalisations are difficult, if not impossible, to make. Members of specific ethnic communities have different values and treat different sorts of behaviour as acceptable, which means that they have different ideas as to what should be legal and illegal. Their different cultures mean that members of different ethnic communities will have different views on what makes an appropriate education for example. In addition, their different views on the nature of proper medical treatment will result in different health-care needs.

Governing is about community-building

Political executives play many roles. One of these is to represent the people and to reflect the national interest. While this is a symbolic role, it is an important one. It is important because it provides citizens with a sense that they contribute to and participate in a group, which gives them feelings of connection and purpose. Members of political executives always claim to be serving the collective interest (whether at a national, state, or local level) and present their policies as reflecting and serving this interest. They do this to justify their positions, but also to provide people with a sense of purpose and give them the feeling that they are contributing to promoting a collective interest. This has very positive effects on those individuals and the community.[19]

Real ethnic diversity, however, undermines people's ability to see themselves as members of a single community. Fundamental diversity in values means that no community exists that could be served by members of political executives. Any attempt to create a community would result in a particular (culturally specific) set of values being promoted over others and this would undermine real ethnic diversity. The connections between ethnic communities would be minimal, as feelings of connection with people in other ethnic communities would not arise. When it came to external affairs, continuing relationships between local ethnic communities and their 'mother' country will inhibit the ability of members of Australian political executives to speak with a single voice in international affairs.

Members of political executives lack resources to respond to real ethnic diversity

Taxation rates in Australia are relatively low, compared with other OECD[20] countries.[21] A result of this is that members of Australian political executives have limited resources at their disposal. They also have significant and expensive ongoing commitments. This means that they can do little more than maintain existing services. They will find it difficult to devote, or divert, resources to new areas and activities. Indeed, more energy is devoted to reducing government expenditure, than to increasing it.

Providing adequate support for real ethnic diversity is likely to prove an expensive activity. The different services and funding that supporting real ethnic diversity would require makes it too expensive. Australians won't accept increased levels of taxation to fund support for real ethnic diversity. Supporting real ethnic diversity, therefore, is beyond the resources of members of Australian political executives.

Members of political executives will support the dominant ethnic community and alienate members of other ethnic communities

Where one exists, members of political executives will support a dominant ethnic community. Members of a dominant ethnic community have the economic, social, and political power that gives its members a far greater ability to create irresistible pressure[22] on members of political executives. Dominant groups always wield considerable power in a democracy. This may be because they reflect the fact that their community is larger than other groups; or, it may reflect the influence that members of this community have over voters and over members of political executives.

Members of political executives cannot respond to all claims and will respond to the dominant ethnic community. This creates a problem in a society marked by real ethnic diversity. A dominant ethnic community is more likely to gain access to members of political executives and is more likely to have its claims viewed as legitimate (we will discuss this further below). A result of this will be that the members of the dominant group will receive greater support than members of other groups, and members of non-dominant groups will recognise that they are not receiving equal support. In this case, real ethnic diversity results in feelings of alienation on the part of those in non-dominant ethnic communities.

Australian government is British

The predisposition of members of political executives to serve the dominant ethnic community leads us to an inescapable fact about members of Australian political executives. This is that, besides being male and middle class, they are also predominantly British-Australians. This reflects the fact that British-Australians are the most numerous in Australia. It also reflects the fact that the processes of government and democracy in Australia reflect British culture. They are a culturally specific set of practices that exclude people of other cultures, or make their participation more difficult.

Members of Australian political executives are less likely to see demands from members of non-British communities as legitimate. To support real ethnic diversity, members of political executives must understand and identify with people from a variety of ethnic communities. Members of the ethnic communities whose values and attitudes are being reflected and supported are best placed to do this. Australian political executives are dominated by middle-class, British-Australian men and reflect the values and attitudes of middle-class, British-Australian men. A result of this is that members of Australian political executives can neither understand nor promote real ethnic diversity.

Summary

Some of the arguments put forward in this section reflect a view that governments are limited in what they can achieve by their composition and by the resources available to them. While some of these limitations, such as with respect to resources and the ethnicity of members of Australian political executives, may be overcome, they are likely to persist. The other reasons to believe that members of Australian political executives cannot be effective in a society in which real ethnic diversity exists reflect general limits with respect to the capacity of all political executives. Policy-makers cannot deal with complexity, will respond to members of the dominant ethnic community, and are community-builders. Each of these prevents members of Australian political executives from understanding and supporting real ethnic diversity.

Summary of both cases

One set of issues that need to be resolved, if the question addressed in this part can be answered, concerns the responsibilities and nature of members of political executives. The Yes case relies on a limited understanding of governing. The No case relies on an extended view of the responsibilities of those who govern. Another issue that arises in this context concerns our views about the consequences of real ethnic diversity. The No case relies on the view that real ethnic diversity undermines community and produces conflict with which members of Australian political executives cannot deal. The Yes case reflects the view that real ethnic diversity is not disastrous for the community and produces conflicts with which members of Australian political executives can deal. While these are not the only general issues that arise in this context, they represent important issues to consider in answering the question of whether government can be effective in a society in which real ethnic diversity exists.

QUESTION

Which argument about whether the role of government can be effective if real ethnic diversity exists is more convincing? Why?

3: CAN DEMOCRACY BE EFFECTIVE IN A SOCIETY IN WHICH REAL ETHNIC DIVERSITY EXISTS?

Real ethnic diversity is also an issue for democracy generally and, more particularly, representative democracy in Australia. In this part, we present reasons supporting the alternative answers to the question of whether democracy and representative democracy can be effective in a society in which real ethnic diversity exists. One of the more fundamental issues arising from this question is whether democracy is a culturally specific set of values and practices. The main issue concerns whether real ethnic differences can be represented through the institutions and processes of representative democracy.

Yes case

This section contains two separate propositions. The first is that democracy can be effective in a society in which real ethnic diversity exists. The second is that so too can representative democracy. The argument that democracy can be effective in a society in which real ethnic diversity exists is based on the contention that democracy is about expressing difference and tolerance and that both of these are consistent with the existence of real ethnic diversity. The argument that representative democracy can also be effective in such a society allows for the representation of different sorts of people and their participation.

Democracy is about expressing differences

One of the characteristics of a democracy is that all citizens can participate in decisions that affect their society. What defines someone as a citizen can vary, but in a democracy, all citizens can participate in collective decision-making. Central to democratic theory is the view that citizens will not be identical and will not share the same views and interests. In democratic decision-making, citizens are expected to express their different views on what to do about an issue or problem and to have their interests taken into account.[23] In short, in democracies all citizens can express their different views and defend their particular interests. The final decision may not suit everyone, but the process through which a final decision is achieved must allow everyone to participate in making this decision.

Real ethnic diversity is compatible with democracy because real ethnic diversity simply marks particular sets of views and interests. Indeed, it marks only some overlaps in views and interests. For members of ethnic communities will not be identical and will be affected by generational and other differences. To the extent that members of ethnic communities share certain views, democratic processes allow, even necessitate, that they express these views. Democracies provide a variety of avenues through which people express their different points of view to ensure that policy-makers are aware of these points of view. Real ethnic diversity does not undermine the effectiveness of democracy, as it reflects different views and interests.

Democracy is about tolerance

'I disapprove of what you say, but I will defend to the death your right to say it.'

While Voltaire may not have been the author of this declaration,[24] the sentiments expressed in it are fundamental to a democracy. Democratic processes will only work if citizens accept and defend the right to express controversial, and even objectionable, views. People must feel free to express their point of view and this is only possible when they know that their views will be treated with some respect. This means that all citizens must be willing to allow others to speak and, if they can, to listen to them. To live according to Voltaire's principle, all citizens must put a great deal of effort into remaining open to alternative views to their own.

If real ethnic diversity indicates anything, it is profound differences in views and probably interests. Under some circumstances, this might be a threat to social cohesion. People who cannot tolerate and respect different values and ways of life can do violence, and even murder. A society in which real ethnic diversity exists is one in which people with very different values and ways of life must co-exist. Democracy, then, is perfectly suited to such a society, for the tolerance of others that a democracy needs to work will enhance and maintain the social cohesion that real ethnic diversity might undermine. Democracy may be the only approach to collective decision-making that will prevent the breakdown of a society marked by real ethnic diversity.

Representative democracy allows for the representation of different sorts of people

In a representative democracy,[25] representation is of sub-groups of the general population. In Australian politics, the groups are often defined by their location. But location is only a part of the story, as representatives will rely on the support of a particular type of voter within their locality.[26] The relationship between a representative and the people with whom they feel a connection is at the centre of the representation in a representative democracy. Representatives, then, will derive much of their support from a particular constituency, or type of voter. Collective decisions emerge from negotiations between representatives of the different types of voters found in the community.

If representatives represent specific interests, then representative democracy is suited to a society that contains real ethnic diversity. This is so even without proportional representation or other methods that allow specific representation of distinct ethnic communities. Real ethnic diversity is likely to result in ethnic communities being concentrated in particular electorates. While these ethnic communities may not dominate a specific area, the representatives of these electorates cannot afford to ignore the interests of a group of people who are likely to constitute a significant number of voters. Representative democracy provides a mechanism for representing diversity, and ethnic diversity is simply one form of diversity.

Representative democracy allows participation by different sorts of people

Not only do representative democracies provide for the representation of divergent views and interests, they also provide opportunities for people to participate in policy-making. Elections represent one of a number of opportunities that citizens have to influence policy. As we have seen in the discussion of pressure groups, representative democratic systems can be thought of as a series of points at which voters can seek to influence policy-making. They can do this as individual citizens or as members of pressure groups. The most important point to note, in this context, is that the points within the policy-making process are receptive to pressure from all voters and pressure groups.

This means that members of those ethnic communities that might not have a sufficiently powerful electoral voice will not be excluded from policy-making processes. Their representatives may meet with Ministers and public servants to express the views and interests of their community. Members of these ethnic communities may join a political party or form groups that exert pressure on political parties, members of political executives, and voters. In this way, they can affect policy-making in a representative democracy.

Summary

Both democracy and representative democracy can be effective in a society in which real ethnic diversity exists. Indeed, the accommodation of difference and the tolerance for alternative points of view and practices that are central to democratic theory suggest that a democracy is the only effective political system for a society in which real ethnic diversity exists. Representative democracy allows both for the representation of different types of people and for participation in policy-making from different types of people, which means that it too is suited to a society marked by real ethnic diversity.

No case

The arguments that neither democracy nor representative democracy can be effective in a society in which real ethnic diversity exists will be presented in this section. These arguments derive from the view that democracy is not a universal and culturally neutral way of conducting collective decision-making. Rather, democracy is a culturally specific set of values and practices that are not compatible with the values of members of all ethnic communities. The argument that representative democracy cannot be effective in a society in which real ethnic diversity exists is based upon two propositions. The first, more general, proposition is that the skills required to participate in representative democracy in Australia are not available to members of all ethnic communities in Australia. The second, more specific, proposition is that most representatives in Australia are British-Australians who cannot represent people of other ethnicities.

Democracy reflects a set of culturally specific values

Democratic theory is based, or premised, on the idea that people have very different, potentially irreconcilable, views on issues that affect society. While conversation might lead to a unanimous decision, we can assume that it won't. Many people will agree, but some will not. We must respect different points of opinion in a democracy, however, because they reflect the fact that every issue can be seen from different perspectives and these may not be able to be reconciled. Tolerance of alternative views to ours requires us to accept that people think very differently and to respect other people's points of view.

Some ethnic communities may be unified by values that are inconsistent with the values of tolerance and respect for difference essential for democracy. This means that tension exists between the two sets of values. To ask members of some ethnic communities to adhere to these values may be to ask them to abandon fundamental aspects of what makes them part of their ethnic community. Tolerance and respect for difference are important values in the British-Australian ethnic community. To project these values onto others and to expect them to share these values amounts to expecting them to change their culture. This is incompatible with the preservation of real ethnic diversity, which requires respect for all cultures.

'Democracy' is a set of culturally specific practices

The creation of a public space for debate about the type of society people want to live in is crucial in a democracy. To be part of this public space, people must have the ability and willingness to behave in public discussions. While they are rarely explicit, a variety of 'rules' govern public spaces. We have to speak in the 'right' way. We also need to engage in debate with restraint because those who participate do so in a way that allows them to be acknowledged. Knowing how to behave in public discussions is not innate (we are not born with it). We have to know how to behave in a democracy.

The practices associated with participating in a democracy might appear to reflect normal behaviour, but this is simply the appearance they acquire for most Australians (who have been socialised to accept these practices as normal and legitimate). These ways of behaving and relating to others are not normal, or comfortable, for people raised in other cultures. The fact that all citizens must be addressed in the same manner and deserve to be listened to may not be obvious to those raised in hierarchical societies in which particular people, more often than not older men, are expected to dominate and can rely on having their orders followed without question. Traditional hostilities between people of different ethnicities, which may well help to define their ethnicities, may also prevent members of all ethnic communities from engaging in public discussions that are essential for democracy.

Representative democracy is complicated

Representative democracies are complex. Voters have to elect representatives who present policies that cover an overwhelming range of issues. These representatives are usually supported by parties, which are complicated organisations, and this makes voting even more difficult. The voting systems used in Australia create further complexities, as compulsory preferential voting for single member geographical constituencies and proportional representation are very different ways to aggregate voters' preferences.

Understanding the issues that arise in an election and the parties' policies with respect to those issues requires a capacity to access and understand the news media. While a number of quality publications are available for some of the ethnic communities in Australia, they are not available within all ethnic communities. Voting effectively is only possible if we understand what we are voting for (or against). Many British-Australians do not fully understand the electoral systems that operate here, so we can assume that people from other cultures are also unlikely to do so. But British-Australians are likely to feel more comfortable with voting than members of other ethnic communities, whose lack of comfort with voting may affect their ability to vote effectively.

Representative democracy in Australia is mostly middle-class British men

Any survey of Australian parliamentarians leads almost inevitably to the conclusion that only a certain type of person is represented. Members of Parliament are usually male, predominantly middle-class, and almost exclusively British-Australians. This reflects British-Australians' great self-confidence about participating in elections. It also reflects the fact that the major parties preselect male, middle-class British-Australian men as candidates. A move within the ALP to ensure that 50 per cent of those preselected for winnable seats are women is an indication that processes internal to parties are responsible for the limited representation produced within Australian Parliaments.

The message communicated by the make-up of Australian Parliaments is clear. You will have great difficulty in gaining preselection and going on to win a seat in Parliament, if you are not male, middle-class, and a British-Australian. The last of these characteristics is likely to make members of ethnic communities feel alienated from representative democracy in Australia. There are exceptions to the predominance of British-Australians, but these exceptions merely remind us of the dominance of male, middle-class, British-Australians. This causes members of ethnic communities to resist full engagement in representative democratic processes, which is required for true representation.

Summary
An incompatibility between the values and practices associated with a democracy and real ethnic diversity is a reason to believe that democracy cannot be effective in a society in which real ethnic diversity exists. Even if problems with respect to the compatibility of democracy and real ethnic diversity can be overcome, the problems that representative democracy creates for participation by members of ethnic communities remain significant. Understanding the issues and the electoral systems that are part of an election creates real problems for some members of ethnic communities. However, possibly the greatest obstacle to participation in elections is the predominance of British-Australians.

QUESTION

How important is real ethnic diversity for democracy and representational democracy in Australia?

CONCLUSION

Increased ethnic diversity seems an inevitable part of Australia's social and political future as a decline in Australia's population, and possibly economy, is not a situation that many members of Australian political executives could support. Even concerted efforts to reduce immigration may not reduce the degree of ethnic diversity in Australia. A return to assimilationist policies, and even the passage of time, might reduce real ethnic diversity in Australia. If real ethnic diversity persists, however, the questions that arise from this are whether government and democracy can be effective in this type of society. The presumption, thus far, appears to be that real ethnic diversity does not render Australian government and democracy ineffective. Indeed, there are good reasons to believe this. There are also good reasons to believe that government and democracy cannot be effective in a society in which real ethnic diversity exists.

FURTHER READING

Introductory texts

Batainah, Heba & Mary Walsh, 2008, 'From Multiculturalism to Citizenship', in C. Aulich & R. Wettenhall (eds), *Howard's Fourth Term*, University of New South Wales Press: Sydney.

Birrell, Robert, 1998, 'The Dynamics of Multiculturalism in Australia', in D. Lovell, I. McAllister, W. Maley & C. Kukathas (eds), *The Australian Political System*, 2nd edn, Longman: South Melbourne.

Bullivant, Brian, 1998, 'The Pluralist Crises Facing Australia', in D. Lovell, I. McAllister, W. Maley & C. Kukathas (eds), *The Australian Political System*, 2nd edn, Longman: South Melbourne.

Jayasuriya, Laksiri & Kee Poo Kong, 1999, *The Asianisation of Australia?: Some Facts about the Myths*, Melbourne University Press: Carlton.

Jupp, James, Barry York & Andrea McRobbie, 1989, *The Political Participation of Ethnic Minorities in Australia*, Australian Government Publishing Service: Canberra.

Jupp, James, 2007, *From White Australia to Woomera: The Story of Australian Immigration*, 2nd edn, Cambridge University Press: Port Melbourne.

Kukathas, Chandran, 1998, 'The Fraternal Conceit', in D. Lovell, I. McAllister, W. Maley & C. Kukathas (eds), *The Australian Political System*, 2nd edn, Longman: South Melbourne.

Kymlicka, Will, 2002, 'Multiculturalism', in *Contemporary Political Philosophy: An Introduction*, 2nd edn, Oxford University Press: Oxford.

Lovell, David, Ian McAllister, William Maley & Chandran Kukathas (eds), 1998, *The Australian Political System*, 2nd edn, Longman: South Melbourne.

Wong, Loong, 1992, 'Ethnicity, the State and the Public Agenda', in M. Muetzelfeldt (ed.), *Society, State and Politics in Australia*, Pluto Press Australia in association with Deakin University Press: Sydney.

Specialist texts

Castles, Stephen, Bill Cope, Mary Kalantzis & Michael Morrissey, 1992, *Mistaken Identity: Multiculturalism and the Demise of Nationalism in Australia*, Pluto Press: Sydney.

Dolby, Nadine, 2000, 'Race, Nation, State: Multiculturalism in Australia', *Arena Magazine*, vol. 45, pp. 48–51.

Grosz, Elizabeth, 2002, 'A Politics of Imperceptibility: A Response to "Anti-Racism, Multiculturalism and the Ethics of Identification"', *Philosophy and Social Criticism*, vol. 28, no. 4, pp. 663–72.

Hjerm, Mikael, 2000, 'Multiculturalism Reassessed', *Citizenship Studies*, vol. 4, no. 3, pp. 357–77.

Jupp, James & John Nieuwenhuysen, with Dawson, Emma, 2007, *Social Cohesion in Australia*, Cambridge University Press: Port Melbourne.

Martinello, Marco, 1998, 'Wieviorka's View on Multiculturalism: A Critique', *Ethnic and Racial Studies*, vol. 21, no. 5, pp. 911–16.

Povinelli, Elizabeth, 2002, *The Cunning of Recognition: Indigenous Alterities and the Making of Australian Multiculturalism*, Duke University Press: Durham.

Stratton, John & Jen Ang, 1998, 'Multicultural Imagined Communities: Cultural Difference and National Identity in the USA and Australia', in D. Bennett (ed.), *Multicultural States: Rethinking Difference and Identity*, Routledge: London.

Van den Berg, Rosemary, 2002, *Nyoongar People of Australia: Perspectives on Racism and Multiculturalism*, Brill: Leiden.

Vasta, Ellie, 1996, 'Dialectics of Domination: Racism and Multiculturalism', in E. Vasta & S. Castles (eds), *The Teeth are Smiling: The Persistence of Racism in Multicultural Australia*, Allen & Unwin: St Leonards.

Wieviorka, Michel, 1998, 'Is Multiculturalism the Solution?', *Ethnic and Racial Studies*, vol. 21, no. 5, pp. 881–910.

Zappalá, Gianni, 1998, 'The Micro-Politics of Immigration Service Responsiveness in an Australian "Ethnic Electorate"', *Ethnic and Racial Studies*, vol. 21, no. 4, pp. 683–702.

Zubrzycki, Jerzy, 1997, 'Multiculturalism, Social Cohesion and National Identity', *Without Prejudice*, no. 10, pp. 7–10.

Web sites

Department of Immigration and Citizenship: http://www.immi.gov.au
Federation of Ethnic Communities' Councils of Australia: http://www.fecca.org.au
Migration Information Source: http://www.migrationinformation.org
Refugee Council of Australia: http://www.refugeecouncil.org.au

Notes

1. See, for example, http://www.immi.gov.au/media/publications/multicultural/pdf_doc/people_of_australia.pdf.
2. Finding a word to describe this culture was difficult. We have chosen 'British' in the hope that this will serve the purpose.
3. See our discussion of hegemonic ideology in chapter 13.
4. For more on the White Australia Policy, see Parkin & Hardcastle (1997, pp. 488–9).
5. For more on Australia's immigration after World War II, see Parkin & Hardcastle (1997, p. 489) and Ozolinos (1994, pp. 203–7).
6. For more on Australia's immigration after the Vietnam War, see Parkin & Hardcastle (1997, pp. 491–3) and Ozolinos (1994, pp. 212–14).
7. For more on assimilation, see Maddox (2005, pp. 381–2).
8. See Ozolinos (1994, p. 206).
9. For more on multiculturalism, see Maddox (2005, pp. 394–403), Parkin & Hardcastle (1997, pp. 490–1), Ozolinos (1994, pp. 207–9), and Rubinstein (1996, pp. 118–30).
10. For more on immigration and the major political parties, see Parkin & Hardcastle (1997, pp. 498–500) and Maddox (2005, p. 400).
11. See Jackman (1998).
12. For population statistics, visit the Australian Bureau of Statistics at http://www.abs.gov.au
13. For more on the sense of vulnerability, see Jupp (1993, pp. 234–5).
14. For more on Australia's population policies, see Jupp (2002, pp. 162–78).
15. For more on obligations to accept refugees, see Gilding (2006, pp. 395–6) and Jupp (2002, pp. 182–4).
16. For more on economic rationales for immigration, see Bailey (1995, pp. 16–40).
17. Most members of political executives appear convinced that immigration is good for the economy. See http://www.immi.gov.au/media/media-releases/2007/d07014.htm and Jupp (2002, pp.141–60).
18. See http://www.sociosite.net/topics/weber.php
19. For more on communities and ethnic politics, see Heywood (2002b, pp. 169–73).
20. Organisation for Economic Co-operation and Development: http://www.oecd.org.
21. The Australian Bureau of Statistics provides information on this.
22. For more on pluralist theory, see Heywood (2002, pp. 78–9), Jaensch (1994, pp. 181–5), Matthews (1997, pp. 286–8), and Emy & Hughes (1991, pp. 549–71).
23. For more on citizenship and participation, see Heywood (2002, pp. 414–15), Rubinstein (1996, pp. 115–17), and Jupp (1996, pp. 102–8).
24. See http://www.classroomtools.com/voltaire.htm
25. For more on representative democracy, see Maddox (2005, pp. 210–16).
26. Functional representation provides a different process of representation (in which citizens are organised according to their social function—such as teachers, doctors, manufacturing workers, those with primarily domestic responsibilities). Functional representation is part of the electoral system in Hong Kong.

Citizenship and Australian Identity

16

LEARNING OBJECTIVES

- Be able to define citizenship, Australian identity, and Australian values
- Distinguish between legal, civic, national, naturalised and political citizenship
- Understand the contemporary context of developments in Australian citizenship
- Be able to outline the different positions of the members of Howard Cabinets, the Australian Citizenship Council, and Galligan & Roberts (2004) *Australian Citizenship*
- Identity key issues on citizenship and Australian identity relating to government and democracy

INTRODUCTION

citizenship:'Citizenship' is used to refer to a legal status accorded to persons who satisfy nationality requirements. In Western societies, this usually includes equality before the law, freedom of speech, the right to own property, and the right to vote and stand for election.

identity:We use this word to refer to what we think makes us identifiable as a particular person. It usually refers to the things that we believe in, value, and regularly do.

In this chapter, we examine Australian **citizenship** and **identity**. Although citizenship is not mentioned in the Constitution, it has been central to government and democracy in Australia, particularly after World War II and especially in the 1990s and 2000s. Many events have shaped Australian citizenship from the time of Federation in 1901 through Australia's *Citizenship Act* of 1948, to the Australian *Citizenship Act* of 2007, which outlines new procedures for becoming an Australian citizen. The introduction of the new Citizenship Test and present developments in Australian citizenship have meant that citizenship is a contemporary political issue that helps us to understand the complex interplays between government and democracy in Australia.

This chapter is divided into three parts. The first provides context for the following parts by discussing the resurgence of interest in citizenship at the end of the twentieth and the beginning of the twenty-first centuries. After briefly situating what has happened, we define citizenship and outline different types of citizenship as these have different effects on government and democracy in Australia. Questions about citizenship are directly related to Australian identity and Australian values. Part Two presents the approaches to citizenship advocated by three important players in the debates about citizenship: members of the Howard Cabinets of the period, those in the Australian Citizenship Council (ACC), and Australian political scientists Brian Galligan and Winsome Roberts. Part Three presents the 'yes' and 'no' cases on the question of whether civic citizenship should provide the basis for social cohesion in Australia. The question has direct implications for government and democracy in Australia.

1: PRELIMINARY DISCUSSION

Citizenship was widely discussed in the lead up to Australia's Centenary of Federation 2001. In February 2000, the Australian Citizenship Council, an independent body advising the government, released a report entitled *Australian Citizenship for the New Century* and presented it to the then Minister for Immigration and Multicultural Affairs, The Hon Philip Ruddock MP. The report was an attempt to identify the ideas about citizenship that were common to all Australians. In their report, members of the Council examined the question of what a citizen is and distinguished between small 'c' and big 'C' citizenship. Big 'C' citizenship referred to a legal approach to citizenship. Small 'c' citizenship referred to a civic approach citizenship (p. 7). These approaches do not exhaust those that can be taken to understanding and practising citizenship and at least two more approaches—national and political citizenship—are available. (We will provide short explanations for each of these approaches in the next part of this chapter.)

In their report, members of the Australian Citizenship Council stressed that national identity had to be understood as national *civic* identity. They presented citizenship as a crucial unifying symbol for Australia and advocated broadening the legal understanding of citizenship, which is associated with migrants, refugees, and asylum seekers gaining a particular legal status. They defined this broader concept of citizenship, small 'c' citizenship, as one in which people were committed to a set of values that are reflected in their political institutions and not to a national or ethnic group. A civic approach to citizenship, they argued, provided a more effective way to unite all people; those who were born in Australia (and did not make an official pledge to citizenship), with those who were not born in Australia and with permanent residents who were not citizens (p. 10). Citizenship was understood as a unifying concept that encompassed all people who lived in Australia (p. 11).

In 2006, members of the Howard Cabinet released a discussion paper, *Australian Citizenship: Much More than a Ceremony*, which had been preceded by a year during which leading members of the political executive spoke publicly about Australian values. In the context of the international war on terror and the US–Australia alliance, members of the Howard Cabinet wanted to promote citizenship as a basis for social cohesion. In the same period, the Department of Immigration and Multicultural Affairs (DIMA) had become the Department of Immigration and Citizenship (DIAC). Citizenship was presented as a privilege and not a right in the discussion paper and, therefore, as something that had to be earned by those who wanted to become part of Australia. Members of the Howard Cabinets did not seek to exclude people from non-British cultures but 'to include everybody, to integrate everybody into the national fabric'.[1]

What is citizenship?

The concept of citizenship first emerged in the Greek 'polis' or city state. The polis was not a place. It existed wherever the people came together to discuss and decide on their responses to issues that faced all or most citizens (and which were, therefore, public issues).[2] Citizenship is fundamentally about the relationship between people and between the people and those who govern them. Public or political association differs from other associations, like families, schools, clubs, interest groups, and political parties, because the latter are essentially private and economic associations.

Being a citizen means being part of a political community. 'It is what a person *does* rather than what they *get* that makes them a citizen.'[3] Ideas of citizenship emerged from two traditions; one that emphasised the rights of the individual, and the other emphasising the individual's participation in public affairs and public discussion. Traditional class-based politics has declined and people have stopped treating contests over the distribution and redistribution of resources as a competition between classes. They now see it as a competition between individuals seeking to be recognised as deserving resources as particular members of a community. This has created a need for new ways to identify ourselves in contemporary representative democracies. The crucial political task is to be recognised as both part of a community and an individual deserving particular resources.[4] There are many understandings of citizenship that differ fundamentally and each of these relates to, and is part of, a very different type of political community and society.

Five of these understandings of, or approaches to, citizenship are legal: civic, national, naturalised, and political. We provide a brief explanation of each of these in the following section, as we think that this will help readers to understand some of the issues we raise and discussions we present in the remainder of this chapter. We cannot hope to provide complete explanations and do not consider the following as anything more than an attempt to give some content to ideas that we rely upon in the discussions that follow.

Legal citizenship

In this minimal understanding, citizens have a particular legal status that is defined by an act of Parliament (for us, the *Australian Citizenship Act 2007*). This Act gives citizens a variety of rights. These include the right to vote, hold a passport, seek election to Parliament, register children born overseas as Australian by descent, get help from Australian officials in embassies or consulates in other countries, and be employed by the Australian Defence Force or Australian Public Service. The Act also requires citizens to perform certain duties. These include serving on a jury, and defending Australia, if they are required to do so.

Civic citizenship

People express civic citizenship when they commit themselves to universal democratic principles and the institutions they produce. These include universal rights and the values and practices necessary for participation in representative democracies. These principles and institutions are not culturally specific; citizens commit themselves to them because they are right. While my principles and institutions might be the same as those adopted by people in other counties, I remain committed to my principles and institutions because they make sense. The similarity of our institutions simply reflects of the fact that we have the same principles. In many ways, this is the most rational of all conceptions. This is because my reasoning, or thoughtful commitment to our principles as right, provides the ground for my commitment to our community.

National citizenship

This approach to citizenship begins with the community into which we are born and suggests that being born into a community means that someone can practise citizenship. Those who are born into a community understand and identify with that community in a way that no one else can. Their public practices of citizenship, as a result, reflect and emerge from their identification with their nation or community and will stabilise and enhance it. They know what to do and what 'we' (nation/community) are trying to do, so they are able to work with and identify with others who were born here. (In this conception, Australia is a British-Australian nation, so Indigenous Australians cannot be born into it.)

Naturalised citizenship

This conception of citizenship is a companion to national citizenship, in that it requires national citizenship to make sense. If national citizenship is about people who were born here, then naturalised citizenship concerns people who have migrated to Australia. In this approach, citizenship is granted to people who have become sufficiently like us that they can be thought of as almost Australian-born, or national, citizens. One way to think of this conception is to think of citizenship as granted to people for whom being Australian has become 'natural'. It is already natural to people who are born here, so the people who qualify for citizenship within this conception are those who have been 'naturalised'.

Political citizenship

In this approach to citizenship, people become who they are as members of a political community. Citizens must do much more than merely vote in elections and must engage in public life; that is, they must become more than a mere consumer of services in a representative democracy. This approach is like national citizenship, except that it is not an ethnic or cultural community through which one identifies, but a political one. I emerge into a community of people with whom I participate in a public life. My participation in that collective life (i.e., citizenship) is who I am in that group and determines how I must function as part of that group. That is, to be a member of a political community, or political citizen, is to be a publicly active member of that community. In this conception, not to participate in a political community is to be no one.

BOX 16.1
Australian Citizenship Pledge

From this time forward, under God*
I pledge my loyalty to Australia and its people
Whose democratic beliefs I share,
and whose rights and liberties I respect, and
whose laws I will uphold and obey.

* People may choose whether or not to use the words 'under God'.

Australian identity and values

In the early 1990s, then Prime Minister Paul Keating advocated a republic because fewer Australians were of British origin. He believed that our future was in our own region and that our identity was not derived from anywhere else, but was uniquely our own. While Australia's was a blend of British and American political systems, its political institutions and people had developed their own distinctiveness and become uniquely Australian. In 2007, the then Prime Minister John Howard and other members of his Cabinet promoted discussion of citizenship in contemporary Australia and revised legislation dealing with citizenship. Members of the Howard Cabinets saw citizenship as a way to develop **social cohesion**.

social cohesion: A society is said to be 'cohesive' when its members feel a sense of connection to each other. The more they have in common, or the more points of connection they feel to others, the more social cohesion is said to exist.

To be Australian is to believe in mateship, a fair go, treating everyone equally (or egalitarianism), Parliamentary democracy, and the rule of law. While 'Australianness' is associated with characters like the bushman, soldier, ordinary bloke, etc, being Australian is intimately connected to Australia and its place in the world. Developments in Australian citizenship and the official shift away from multiculturalism under members of the Howard Cabinets have highlighted the differences between Australians who are born here and those who are naturalised, as well as the relationship of these two groups of citizens to non-citizens.

A report commissioned by members of the last Howard Cabinet, *Becoming an Australian Citizen*, was intended to link Australian values to citizenship. In this report, Australian values are identified as respect for the equal worth, dignity and freedom of the individual, freedom of speech, freedom of religion and secular government, freedom of association, support for Parliamentary democracy and the rule of law, equality of men and women, equality of opportunity, peacefulness, tolerance, mutual respect, and compassion for those in need.[5] Critics of such an account of Australian values claim they are simply the values of all people who live in Western liberal democracies and are not uniquely Australian. One response to this criticism is to claim that universal understandings of liberal democratic values have been modified and made distinctive as a result of their interaction with Australian identity and values.

BOX 16.2
The Australian People

Population

21 million

Indigenous

483,000 (2.3 per cent of the population)

Birthplace

Born overseas 22%

Of those born overseas:
United Kingdom 19.4%
New Zealand 8.8%
China 4.7%
Italy 4.5%
Vietnam 3.6%

Median Age

37 years

Religion

Christianity 63.9%
Buddhism 2.1%
Islam 1.7%
Hinduism 0.7%
Judaism 0.4%

Source: Australian Government, 2007, *Becoming an Australian Citizen.* p. 10. Available at http://www.citizenship.gov.au/test/resource-booklet/citz-booklet-full-ver.pdf, last accessed 13 June 2008.

2: CITIZENSHIP IN CONTEMPORARY AUSTRALIA

In the previous part of the chapter, the context of contemporary Australian citizenship was outlined through a discussion of different types of citizenship and issues relating to Australian identity and values. In this part, we overview three different perspectives on Australian citizenship as a way of demonstrating that there are a range of positions that can be taken. These are the positions of leading members of Cabinets under Prime Minister John Howard (1996–2007);

the position of members of the Australian Citizenship Council (ACC), and that of Brian Galligan and Winsome Roberts.

Howard Cabinets' position (1996–2007)

Citizenship and the question of Australian values, as well as the question of Australian identity, have become increasingly prominent in the contemporary political landscape. In August 2005, the then Prime Minister John Howard hosted an Islamic Summit. Later that day, then Treasurer Peter Costello was interviewed about the Cabinet's position on the ABC television program *Lateline*. He was asked whether the position of members of Cabinet was that Muslims who migrate to Australia but don't accept Australian values should leave. Costello said that Australia was a country founded on democracy and that Australia was a secular state, with laws made by the Australian Parliament. 'If those are not your values, if you want a country which has Sharia law or a theocratic state, then Australia is not for you. This is not the kind of country where you would feel comfortable if you were opposed to democracy, Parliamentary law, independent courts, and so I would say to people who don't feel comfortable with those values there might be other countries where they'd feel more comfortable with their own values or beliefs'.[6]

A day after the Islamic Summit, another member of the Howard Cabinet, the Minister for Education, Dr Brendan Nelson, said that Muslims who don't accept Australian values and teach them to their children should 'clear off'. Dr Nelson was soon meeting with the Australian Federation of Islamic Councils to discuss programs for children in Islamic schools, as well as other children, to fully understand Australian values. 'We don't care where people come from; we don't mind what religion they've got or what their particular view of the world is. But if you want to be in Australia, if you want to raise your children in Australia, we expect those children to be taught and to accept Australian values and beliefs'.[7] Dr Nelson wanted Australian history and culture and the Australian values of mateship and a fair go understood. He recounted the tale of John Simpson Kirkpatrick using his donkey to carry wounded soldiers in the battlegrounds of Gallipoli as representing what is truly Australian. The Prime Minster, John Howard, said that community concern would be raised by Muslims who do not pledge their primary loyalty to Australia.[8]

September 2006 saw the Minister for Immigration and Citizenship release a discussion paper entitled *Australian Citizenship: Much More than a Ceremony*. In the discussion paper, Australian citizenship was presented as a privilege not a right. The document also outlined important questions about the merits of introducing a formal citizenship test for people who come to Australia. Leading figures in the Howard Cabinet argued that it was crucial for immigrants to learn English-language skills that would allow them to communicate effectively in the education and employment sectors. They also said that it was important that migrants come to understand the Australian way of life, shared our values, and demonstrated a commitment to contributing to Australia's community and values. They argued that a formal citizenship test would best achieve this.

Australian Citizenship: Much More than a Ceremony contained a recommendation for a formal citizenship test that would assess an applicant's knowledge of Australia and their commitment to Australian values. The *Australian Citizenship Act 2007*, which replaced the earlier *Australian Citizenship Act 1948*, introduced a test for those wishing to become citizens. The citizenship test comprises twenty questions. The information necessary to answers these questions is contained in *Becoming an Australian Citizen*, which was released by the Minister for Immigration and Citizenship in 2007. The *Australian Citizenship Act 2007* commenced in July 2007 and the first citizenship test was put into practice on 1 October 2007.

QUESTION

What do contemporary developments in Australian citizenship tell us about the former Howard Cabinets?

BOX 16.3
Citizenship in Australia 1997–2007

- Discovering Democracy Program, 1997
- *Contemporary Australian Citizenship*, Issues Paper by the Australian Citizenship Council, February 1999
- *Australian Citizenship for a New Century*, A Report by the Australian Citizenship Council, February 2000 (commissioned for the Government)
- *Australian Citizenship: A Common Bond*, Government response to the Report of the Australian Citizenship Council, May 2001
- *Australian Citizenship: Much More than a Ceremony—Consideration of the Merits of Introducing a Formal Citizenship Test*, Discussion Paper, September 2006
- *Australian Citizenship Act 2007* (July)
- *Becoming an Australian citizen*, Australian Government, 2007

Australian Citizenship Council position (2000)

Members of the Australian Citizenship Council (ACC) were interested in how citizenship could best serve Australians in the lead up to the centenary of Federation in 2001 and focused upon citizenship as an idea that could unify Australians. Spokespeople for the ACC argued that citizenship was more than a legal status and should be expanded to include the widely held, but rarely articulated, civic values that formed the basis for Australia's democratic society. They recommended the promotion of an 'Australian Compact' of seven shared values to add meaning to Australian citizenship. The ACC's Chairman at the time, Sir Ninian Stephen, argued that Australian citizenship requirements were 'about right and working well', so the compact was not a test and was not intended to make it harder for people to become citizens.[9]

According to spokespeople for the ACC, treating citizenship as merely a legal status was a relatively recent development and was associated with the process of 'naturalisation' undergone by the six million immigrants who came to Australia after the Second World War in a process of planned migration. The inclusion of these migrants through their embracing of Australian citizenship was very successful. The paradox is that citizenship continues to have less relevance to those born in Australia, who are referred to as nationals, because they are given citizenship automatically and do not choose it; so, their citizenship is not that important to them as a prominent marker of their being Australian.

The wider concept of citizenship advocated by spokespeople for the ACC was based upon membership of the Australian community and adherence to civic values. These were taken to promote unity whether or not a person was formally recognised to be an Australian citizen. This position reflected increased interest in how citizenship can be brought to reflect the civic values that form the basis of Australia's democratic society and used as a powerful unifying force. The position of members of the ACC was that aim was important in Australia's increasingly multicultural society because traditional national symbols had become less relevant to Australia as it moved into the twenty-first century.

In their contributions to debates about citizenship, members of the ACC promoted a conception of civic citizenship that went beyond the limited legal approach. They sought a broader meaning comprised of ideals of civic life that constitute core values in a society of people with many different beliefs and ways of life deriving from diverse national and ethnic backgrounds, and who may be affected by their strong identification with the particular regions of their origins. Members of the ACC sought to distinguish between their understanding of citizenship and those conceptions that required a desire to serve the community in everyday life or which demanded an emotional attachment to places and things in Australia. They also contended that the nation of Australia was different from the polity of the United States because Americans understood their citizenship in terms of their being committed to specific political beliefs and institutions.

Members of the ACC also criticised attempts to base Australian citizenship upon a national identity. Their argument was that national identity 'cannot be definitively captured and does not stand still'.[10] Australia's national identity changed, in their view, because of changes in Australian society and in Australia's position in international affairs. They expressed concern that national identity had become 'an argumentative matter,'[11] and that making claims about national identity was divisive, and did not provide a basis for a common bond. They encouraged Australians to move beyond the idea of a single identity, which they saw as an imagined identity that excluded many Australians, and suggested that they commit themselves to core civic values. This entailed moving beyond national identity to national *civic* identity, in which Australians set out the values that they have come to share in conducting their civic, or public, lives.

QUESTION

The ACC advocate a civic understanding of citizenship because national identity claims are divisive. Do you agree?

Galligan & Roberts's position (2004)

Galligan and Roberts are highly regarded Australian political scientists who have produced important work on Australian citizenship. They have argued that official discourse on Australian citizenship is limited because it reduces citizenship to shared political institutions, abstract values, and the toleration of difference. They contend that this does not do justice to the complexity of Australian citizenship, which is not limited to the institutional arrangements of a liberal democracy in a federal republic but also reflects a particular heritage and history. Australian citizenship is complex because it is a Federation that was formed with little external pressure and which began as part of the British Empire and was changed by the more than six million immigrants who came to Australia after the Second World War. Galligan and Roberts argued that this has made Australia into a **pluralistic society** and not a truly multicultural society, and claim that this distinction is important, but often overlooked. For them,

pluralistic society: A society is said to be pluralistic when it is made up of people with different ethnicities, religions, or values. Pluralism, on the other hand, is used to refer to an approach to government in which public policies are the reflection of the pressure that private and independent pressure groups exert on members of political executives.

Australian citizenship is experienced and grounded in everyday life and local communities and nationality is a contrived and imposed attribute.

Citizenship, for Galligan and Roberts, is lived and experienced. It cannot be reduced to a legal definition or political institution. It is about loyalty and shared beliefs, to which the *Australian Citizenship Act 2007* and pledge of commitment refer, that is evidenced in a feeling of deep connection to a personal and political association that is greater than the sum of its individual members. In countries like Australia, people's preoccupation with their individual rights dominates other concerns. This means that patriotism and love of the country must be developed if the public good is to be acknowledged alongside personal interests and entitlements. This is particularly necessary in Australia, they argue, where the dominant understandings of civic citizenship focus entirely upon shared political institutions and the celebration of cultural diversity. The viability of political communities, Galligan and Roberts contend, requires strengthening national culture and heritage and developing loyalty and patriotism.

For Galligan and Roberts, Australian citizenship blends the particular aspects of being Australian with the universal institutional aspects of liberal democracy. Citizenship is not created through our imaginations or attempts at conscious construction. It emerges through our use of the English language, our natural and human environment, and the inter-generational and inter-cultural blending of the traditions and histories of individuals, families, and ethnic groups.[12] Galligan and Roberts criticise what they refer to as 'hollowed out citizenship', in which Australian citizenship is understood in civic terms, with citizens sharing only a set of political institutions and values. Provided there is agreement about these values and individuals agree to tolerate others, they argue, each citizen must define what being Australian means for her or himself.

While Galligan and Roberts consider national culture to be crucial, they do not define citizenship exclusively in terms of the nation state and have previously argued that Australian citizenship entails multiple loyalties.[13] Until 1949, Australians have understood themselves primarily as British subjects, rather than Australian citizens: yet this does not mean that they did not develop a distinctive style of Australianness throughout this period. Galligan and Roberts contend that Australia is not 'a nation without nationalism,'[14] but a country of constrained nationalism because of its federal system and its British heritage. They criticize advocates of multiculturalism who focus on cultural pluralism and reduce nationalism to institutions that are overlaid by a thin unifying structure. They reject Kalantzis's 'new civic pluralism', in which Australia is presented as a nation of the future because Australians have a post-nationalist sense of common purpose and a sense of being a nation without expressing nationalism.[15] They claim that Kalantzis overstates the significance of cultural and linguistic diversity and neglects a more basic grounding in the English language.

QUESTION

Why are Galligan and Roberts (2004) critical of civic citizenship?

Summary

This part of the chapter outlined the different perspectives on citizenship by leading figures of Howard Cabinets, the Australian Citizenship Council, and by Australian political scientists Galligan and Roberts. While on some levels those in Howard Cabinets and the ACC agreed about general values, leading members of Howard Cabinets advocated a strong sense of national identity and integration, rather than multiculturalism. Galligan and Roberts argued that Australia is a pluralistic society and that it is politically naive to expect Australians not to be proud of their own distinctive identity. Australian nationalism is a positive force for citizenship that should not be submerged by multiculturalism.

BOX 16.4
The Australian Citizenship Test 2007

The Australian Citizenship Test commenced on 1 October 2007 and was intended to assist people who want to become Australian Citizens. The resource book *Becoming an Australian Citizen* provides information on Australian history, traditions, values, and national symbols. To pass the test applicants must correctly answer 12 of the 20 questions, which have been selected from a pool of 200 questions. Leading figures in Howard Cabinets argued that the test is an important way to ensure that migrants are able to participate fully in the Australian way of life, thereby ensuring social cohesion and successful community integration.

Source: http://www.citizenship.gov.au/test/index.htm

3: CITIZENSHIP AND DEMOCRACY

In the previous section, we examined three prominent, and different, views on what should constitute Australian citizenship in the context of recent developments in citizenship law and policy. The position adopted by members of Howard Cabinets carried great weight because Cabinet members are responsible for the legislation, regulations, and policies that affect citizenship in Australia. Groups like the ACC are also important, as they include people with expertise in the field and their members consult with the wider community to identify differences in their approaches to citizenship. They also provide information as to how Australia compares to other countries with respect to citizenship law and policy. Galligan and Roberts (2004) present citizenship as a reflection of the unique feeling associated with being Australian and the source of Australian nationalism. In the next section, we address the question of whether civic citizenship should provide the basis for social cohesion in Australia and outline the yes and no cases in response to this question.

Should civic citizenship provide the basis for social cohesion in Australia?

Yes case

A civic understanding is better than a legal one for producing cohesion
The shift from citizenship understood in strictly legal terms to a deeper understanding of citizenship that incorporates civic values was advocated by members of Howard Cabinets (1996–2007) and the ACC. They argued that something more than legal citizenship would provide Australia with a level of social cohesion that included everybody who lives here, and not just those who are defined as citizens under the *Citizenship Act*. Their goal was to develop ideals of civic value as core public values because they saw Australian society as marked by a coexistence of different beliefs and ways of life, many nationalities and ethnicities, and many people who strongly identify with the region of the world that they had come from. Civic values, in their view, provided the least divisive way to give all Australians a sense that they were part of one community.

Civic does not rely on the dubious, unreliable, and dangerous notion of national identity
The civic understanding of citizenship rejects the claim that there is an Australian identity and opposes understandings of citizenship based upon nationalism. In many ways, the civic (read commercial and economic) understanding of citizenship wants to promote social cohesion within Australia without reference to nationalistic citizenship, which it generally sees as divisive. The ACC wants to eliminate claims based on national identity for social cohesion and, instead, wants to posit a national civic identity that is comprised of the beliefs and practices of our polity in very general terms as part of our fundamental understanding of citizenship.

The values that underpin civic citizenship are universal, not Australian, and can change
If you ask many Australians to define Australian values, they will identify mateship and a 'fair go' as quintessentially Australian. Those who adopt a civic understanding of citizenship deny that these values and many others are specifically Australian and argue instead that the values most Australians aspire to are universal Western liberal democratic values that can be found in any liberal democratic country. Citizenship does not become a basis for nationalism when these values are understood as civic, rather than Australian, and we can look to other countries to help us to improve the quality of government and democracy in Australia.

Civic citizenship works in a multicultural society, like Australia—principles are abstract and universal, not ethnic, and so will not cause tension in Australia. Those who advocate the civic understanding of citizenship do so because they argue that Australia is a multicultural society and adopting the values of civic citizenship will help us to maintain a healthy and effective multicultural society. Multiculturalism requires a recognition of the legitimacy of all voices in a community and a means for allowing people with different values to speak to each other. This requires the recognition of and respect for alternative opinions and the rights of others and a willingness to engage in debate and not violence. Civic citizenship is one means, and possibly the only one, to achieve peace and order in a society in which people from very different cultures must work together

Summary
Advocates of civil citizenship believe that this approach to citizenship is the best for promoting social cohesion, given the nature of Australian society and the international context in which we find ourselves. Civic values are free from nationalist values and claims to national identity that will prove unacceptable in a multicultural society. Culturally specific ideas of nation represent a significant problem for a multicultural society and this means that it is crucial that we do not value one nationality over others. The civic values that are essential to liberal democracies explains how aspects of Australian society work to prevent nationalistic clashes by providing a means for social cohesion based on a shared commitment to the values associated with liberal democracies.

No case
A civic understanding does not engage with the feelings of Australians born here who are the dominant majority
The first reason to believe that civic citizenship will not work in Australia is because it does not engage with the experiences of those who were born here.

Citizenship is taken for granted by those born in Australia (as it is elsewhere) because they do not sit citizenship tests and are not tested for proficiency in English and knowledge of Australian history, traditions, symbols, and values. They become citizens automatically upon their birth only, not because they share the values associated with civic citizenship.

A civic understanding does not engage with feelings of early post-war immigrants whose naturalisation registers their commitment to this country

While Australians who are born here take pride in their Australian identity and see it as central to their being citizens, so too do naturalised Australians who migrated here from Europe and other parts of the world. Many of these people came here post-World War II, establishing two or three generations of Australians who consider themselves just as Australian as natural-born Australians. The latter retain their cultures, but remain proudly Australian. None of these feelings derive from a commitment to the values associated with civic citizenship.

A civic understanding does not reflect Australia's pluralistic society

Civic citizenship is not appropriate for the people who believe that Australia is a pluralistic society, rather than a multicultural society. This pluralistic society, in their view, emerges from processes in which people come from diverse backgrounds to establish an Australian culture. Understanding and practising Australian citizenship, for them, requires going beyond multiculturalism to being Australian. Becoming a citizen in Australia, then, involves accepting and seeking to become 'Australian'.[16] Australia is not a multicultural society, 'rather migrating people have become Australianised.' Civic citizenship prevents the emergence of an Australian society, because, as its advocates acknowledge, there is nothing particularly Australian about these values.

A civic understanding undermines the sense of self of those who feel different as Australians and are proud of being Australian

Most advocates of multiculturalism and civic understandings of citizenship are uncomfortable with the idea and pursuit of a national identity. This suggests that they treat other forms of identity as acceptable, but reject national pride among Australians. Instead of recognising that Australians have a right to be proud of their nationality, they want Australians to forget that they are Australian when we act as citizens. They seem to be asking us to respect a range of identities while admonishing us for thinking that being Australian is the best thing to be.[7]

Adoption of a civic understanding marginalises or neglects political citizenship

Australian history provides considerable evidence that a preoccupation with civic citizenship results in a failure to promote political citizenship. The adoption of principles and practices associated with civic citizenship produces and requires minimal involvement in public life and this puts political citizenship off the agenda. This means that a permanent limitation of Australian citizenship arises once civic citizenship becomes the dominant approach. The suggestion that political citizenship advocates a shift beyond representative democracy to direct democracy doesn't even get on the agenda, and citizenship is no longer understood to include a responsibility to participate in government and democracy in Australia.

Summary

Those who reject civic citizenship as the basis for achieving social cohesion in Australia do so for a number of reasons. They believe that this conception of citizenship does not reflect or embrace the feelings of people who were born here or migrants who have developed such a deep commitment to Australia that they have become 'naturalised' Australians. Those who reject civic citizenship as the basis for achieving social cohesion also believe that Australian society is pluralistic, and not multicultural, and that civic citizenship is not suited to a pluralistic society. Finally, they contend that Australians should practise a conception of citizenship that allows them to be proud of who they are.

CONCLUSION

The resurgence of interest in citizenship at the end of the twentieth and the beginning of the twenty-first centuries provides an important background to recent developments concerning citizenship in Australia. These events provide an historical context, whereas the different approaches to citizenship provide an intellectual, or conceptual, context for this discussion. The main question that arises concerns which conception of citizenship is best suited to government and democracy in Australia. Before we provided the alternative answers to the question of whether the civic citizenship approach is best for achieving social cohesion in Australia, we discussed the approaches to citizenship advocated by three important players in the debates on this issue: members of the Howard Cabinets of the period; those in the Australian Citizenship Council (ACC); and Australian political scientists Brian Galligan and Winsome Roberts. Then we presented the 'yes' and 'no' cases on the question of whether civic citizenship is best for social cohesion in Australia.

Australian citizenship has been a central issue for government and democracy in Australia since Federation. The war in Iraq, international terrorism, and an increasingly globalised economy has caused us to ask questions about our citizenship, Australian identity, and the values we share. The issues surrounding debates on Australian citizenship go right to the heart of the question of what it is to be an Australian and, more generally, what it means to be an Australian citizen. This book was produced soon after Kevin Rudd formed the first Rudd Cabinet, so we do not know how they will approach the issues of citizenship and multiculturalism. However, there is no doubt that developments in citizenship law and policy and the influence of this on Australian identity and values will have ongoing implications for government and democracy in Australia.

FURTHER READING

Introductory texts

Arendt, Hannah, 1958, *The Human Condition*, Chicago University Press: Chicago.

Burgmann, Verity, 2003, *Power, Profit and Protest: Australian Social Movements and Globalisation*, Allen & Unwin: Crows Nest.

Clancy, Mike, 2007, *Howard's Seduction of Australia: Where to Now?*, Fast Books: Watsons Bay.

Davidson, Alastair, 1997, *From Subject to Citizen: Australian Citizenship in the Twentieth Century*, Cambridge University Press: Melbourne.

Galligan, Brian & Winsome Roberts, 2004, *Australian Citizenship*, Melbourne University Press: Carlton, Victoria.

Hudson, Wayne & John Kane (eds), 2000, *Rethinking Australian Citizenship*, Cambridge University Press: Cambridge.

Stokes, Geoffrey (ed.), 1997, *The Politics of Identity in Australia*, Cambridge University Press: Melbourne.

Specialist texts

Aitkin, Don, 2005, *What was it all for? The Reshaping of Australia*, Allen & Unwin: Crows Nest.

Altman, Dennis, 2006, *51st State?*, Scribe Publications: Carlton North.

Benhabib, Seyla, 2002, *The Claims of Culture: Equality and Diversity in the Global Era*, Princeton University Press: Princeton.

Brett, Judith, 2005, 'Relaxed and Comfortable: The Liberal Party's Australia', *Quarterly Essay*, 19, pp. 1–80.

Elder, Catriona, 2007, *Being Australian: Narratives of National Identity*, Allen & Unwin: Crows Nest.

Faulks, Keith, 2000, *Citizenship*, Routledge: London & New York.

Hamilton, Clive & Sarah Maddison, 2007, *Silencing Dissent: How the Australian Government is Controlling Public Opinion and Stifling Debate*, Allen & Unwin: Crows Nest.

Hannay, Alastair, 2005, *On the Public*, Routledge: London & New York.

Hartcher, Peter, 2007, 'Bipolar Nation: How to Win the 2007 Election', *Quarterly Essay*, 25, pp. 1–60.

Howe, Brian, 2007, *Weighing Up Australian Values*, University of New South Wales Press: Sydney.

Ingram, David, 2004, *Rights, Democracy, and Fulfillment in the Era of Identity Politics: Principled Compromises in a Compromised World*, Rowman & Littlefield Publishers: Maryland.

Jupp, James, 2007, *From White Australia to Woomera: The Story of Australian Immigration*, 2nd edn, Cambridge University Press: Melbourne.

Kenny, Michael, 2004, *The Politics of Identity*, Polity: Cambridge.

Marr, David, 2007, 'His Masters Voice: The Corruption of Public Debate under Howard', *Quarterly Essay*, 26, pp. 1–84.

McKnight, David, 2005, *Beyond Left and Right: New Politics and the Culture Wars*, Allen & Unwin: Crows Nest.

Mouffe, Chantal, 1993, *The Return of the Political*, Verso: London & New York.

Mouffe, Chantal, 2000, *The Democratic Paradox*, Verso: London & New York.

Mouffe, Chantal, 2005, *On the Political*, Routledge: London & New York.

Skinner, Quentin & Bo Strath (eds), 2003, *States and Citizens: History, Theory, Prospects*, Cambridge University Press: Cambridge.

Walsh, Mary, 2005, 'The Republican Debate', in C. Aulich & R. Wettenhall (eds), *Howard's Second and Third Governments*, University of New South Wales Press: Sydney.

Weiss, Linda, Elizabeth Thurbon & John Mathews, 2007, *National Insecurity: The Howard Government's Betrayal of Australia*, Allen & Unwin: Crows Nest.

WEBSITES

http://www.citizenship.gov.au

Notes

1. John Howard quoted on a Sydney radio station in Megalogenis (2006) 'All the same, only different—Election 2007,' *The Australian*, 16 December.
2. See Arendt (1958, p. 198).
3. See Galligan & Roberts (2004, p. 1).
4. See Davidson (1997, p. 248).
5. Australian government (2007), *Becoming an Australian Citizen*, pp. 5–7.
6. For the full transcript of this interview see 'Respect Australian values or leave: Costello,' http://www.abc.net.au/lateline/content/2005/s1444603.htm, broadcast 23 August 2005.
7. For the full transcript of this interview with Brendan Nelson, see Grattan, Michelle, 'Accept Australian values or get out,' http://www.theage.com.au, 25 August 2005.
8. Ibid.
9. See *Australian Citizenship for a New Century: A Report by the Australian Citizenship Council*, February (2000, p. 2).
10. Ibid, (p. 10).
11. Ibid.
12. See Galligan & Roberts (2004, p. 5).
13. See Galligan, Roberts & Trifiletti (2001).
14. See Galligan & Roberts (2004, pp. 120–39).
15. See Kalantzis, Mary (2000), pp. 99–110.
16. It has been suggested that under John Howard's Prime Ministership, Australian national consciousness was 'inflamed' and that Australians rediscovered their authentic identity against claims of multiculturalism. See Soutphommasane, Tim, (2007), pp. 133–40, especially p. 134.
17. See Galligan & Roberts (2004, p. 79).

The Environment and Climate Change

17

LEARNING OBJECTIVES

- Be able to explain why government and democracy in Australia cannot deliver environmental sustainability
- Consider how government and democracy might deliver environmental sustainability in Australia
- Be able to identify the difference between the Howard political executive and the Rudd political executive's response to climate change

INTRODUCTION

This chapter deals with one of the most important issues facing government and democracy in Australia. Environmental protection is important because of real changes in the environment and because Australians seem to be more aware and concerned about environmental problems and the impact of climate change. This issue merits attention in a book on Australian politics and provides another way to reflect on aspects of government and democracy in Australia.

This chapter is in two parts. The first is a discussion of the proposition that government and democracy in Australia cannot deliver environmental sustainability. In the second part, we illustrate the discussion presented in the first part by discussing the different positions on ratifying the Kyoto Protocol adopted by members of the Howard and Rudd Cabinets. Members of a series of Howard Cabinets refused to authorise ratification of the Kyoto Protocol, which supports the view that government and democracy in Australia cannot deliver environmental sustainability. One of the first decisions taken by members of the first Rudd Cabinet was to authorise ratification of the Kyoto Protocol, which was done on 3 December 2007.

1: PROPOSITION: GOVERNMENT AND DEMOCRACY IN AUSTRALIA CANNOT DELIVER ENVIRONMENTAL SUSTAINABILITY

We begin this part by presenting reasons that someone might believe that government and democracy in Australia cannot deliver environmental sustainability. While we might have devoted this sub-section to an explanation of what someone might mean in making this statement, we felt that it was clear enough. The only term that might not be clear is 'environmental sustainability'.[1] Following John Barry,[2] we use environmental sustainability to refer to a situation in which the way that people live and the way that they want to live provide satisfaction for themselves and for all future generations. We use it to refer to change of both practice and attitude, which mean that people attain what they value without causing environmental problems in either the present or the future.[3] In the second sub-section, we introduce reasons for refuting the pessimism expressed in the proposition and comment on some of the reasons we put forward to justify it.

Dominance of developmental orientation

In this sub-section, we look at different reasons to believe that government and democracy in Australia cannot deliver environmental sustainability. The first reason is that government and democracy in Australia are governed by a developmental orientation that is counter to that required for environmental sustainability. The second reason is that government and democracy in Australia are dominated by a preoccupation with short-term outcomes that prevent the long-term thinking required for environmental sustainability. Third, government and democracy in Australia cannot produce the sort of coherent policy-making across a variety of policy areas that is necessary for achieving environmental sustainability. Finally, govern-ment and democracy in Australia cannot deliver environmental sustainability because any attempt to do so will result in divisions that will produce policy deadlock.

Introduction (development v. environmental sustainability)

The first argument that might explain why someone would believe that government and democracy in Australia cannot deliver environmental sustainability is that environmental sustainability runs counter to the developmental orientation that dominates Australian government and democracy.[4] A developmental orientation, some might suggest preoccupation, was a central part of colonisation. It has long been central to the understanding that non-indigenous Australians have had of the function of government and the role of human society. Even if a developmental orientation had not been central to non-indigenous thinking about government, those who have an interest in promoting development have occupied dominant positions in Australian political executives and the major parties, and this orientation is represented by powerful pressure groups.

BOX 17.1
Soil degradation in Australia

At the end of the 1990s, about 5.7 million hectares of Australia were assessed as having a high potential to develop salinity problems through shallow or rising water tables. There are several forms of soil degradation in Australia: acidity, soil erosion, and salinity. While Australian soils have naturally high levels of salt, increased problems with soil degradation have resulted from land-clearing, large-scale agriculture, over-grazing, and the introduction of invasive species, such as rabbits and goats. Soil degradation can affect inland waters, estuaries, and inshore marine environments, and threatens some 630,000 hectares of natural vegetation.

Source: http://www.abs.gov.au/ausstats/abs@.nsf/94713a d445ff1425ca25682000192af2/1ca94df590adff7fca2569 f300250a31!OpenDocument

BOX 17.2
Rainfall and water availability

The main source of water in Australia is rainfall and Australia has a long-term average rainfall of 472 millimetres (mm), giving it the lowest rainfall of any continent except Antarctica. The average total rainfall throughout Australia in 2006 was 493mm, slightly higher than the average, although much of this water fell inland and many of the most populated areas in Australia experienced rainfall well below the average. This continued in 2007, particularly in the agriculturally significant area of the Murray-Darling Basin. October 2007 was the sixth year of lower than average rainfalls, with the November 2001 to October 2007 period being the Basin's equal driest six-year period on record.

Source: ABS, *Australia's Environment: Issues and Trends*, 4613.0, 2007, p. 6

Historical/cultural attitude to the land

For Australia's colonisers, colonisation to use or exploit natural resources was humanity's mission (Europeans were merely leading the way).[5] This is why they took Australia to be *terra nullius*. The practices of Indigenous Australians would not have looked like the occupation of a territory. The absence of agriculture and human settlements, which Europeans treated as evidence of progress, meant that they could interpret Australia as an unoccupied land.

For the colonists and those who followed them, occupying the land was not mere passive adaptation to the existing environmental circumstances; it required changing those circumstances to make them productive. They sought to exploit the resources available in order to satisfy their needs and, ultimately, to create surpluses to export to markets overseas. Occupation was exploitation in their minds and the responsibility of members of political executives was to promote the exploitative occupation of the land.[6]

Ongoing reliance on primary industries (non-renewable resources)

The quality of life of Australians has always been linked with the development of primary industries. Agriculture requires that the land be cleared and otherwise made suitable for imported plant species and changes to the land were also necessary to foster the growth of imported animals. The other dominant forms of primary industry, such as the extraction of minerals and the use of timber from forests, also had profound and, in those days, welcomed effects on the land.

While primary industries remain central to Australian history and culture, creating and promoting secondary industries have also been important. How important they are has varied over time, but the health of manufacturing industries has also been important in deciding whether members of a political executive have done their jobs well. Their success in increasing Australia's productivity is an indication of the ability of members of Cabinet to govern.

Power of developmental interests in political executives

Another reason to believe that government and democracy in Australia cannot deliver environmental sustainability is that political executives are dominated by those who have an interest in development.[7] The central role of the Treasurer and the Treasury in political executives is a reflection of this. Ministers and public servants whose departments cover primary and secondary industries usually play important roles in Australian political executives. Ministers and departments responsible for environmental protection are much less likely to play leading roles in political executives.

In major parties

The major parties also reflect the importance of development to government and democracy in Australia. The formation, membership, and ideology of the National and Labor Parties are directly linked to promoting development. The National Party is the party of farmers, miners, and others involved in industries in the non-metropolitan regions. The Labor Party is the party of workers, who rely on their employment in primary and secondary industries for their income. The Liberal Party is the party of business, and to promote the interests of businesspeople is to promote development.[8] The emergence and persistence of the Greens reflects the failure of existing political parties to represent people who think that environmental sustainability should be the highest priority of members of Australia's political executives.[9]

The most powerful pressure groups in Australian politics represent farming, mining, and business interests. This simply reflects both the support within political executives for these interests and Australians' acceptance that they are important interests. The revenue derived from the export of agricultural products, oil, and minerals means that their importance for society is consistent with the power of the pressure groups that represent people involved in these activities. Their voices, speaking the language of development, will drown out those who speak for environmental sustainability

Summary

The dominance of a developmental orientation explains why someone might believe that government and democracy in Australia cannot deliver environmental sustainability. Few Australians will embrace environmental sustainability as a primary goal and accept the fundamental reorientation of Australia's society and economy that it requires. Even if they did, those whose highest priority is to promote development dominate Australia's political executives and major parties and they are supported in this by powerful pressure groups.

Preoccupation with the short-term

Members of political executives think short-term

One of the reasons that members of Cabinets think short-term is due to the frequency of elections. In Australia, Lower Houses of Parliament sit for three or four years. Even if all Parliaments sat for a full term, and most don't, members of Lower Houses face reelection every three or four years. Members of Cabinet, especially Prime Ministers and Premiers, are judged on their performance while in office, so they have to concentrate on achieving results quickly, producing a preoccupation with short-term achievements.

Public servants may not be driven by electoral cycles in the same way, but they are affected by them. Their Ministers want regular delivery of outcomes that demonstrate their competence and leadership skills. Those public servants who seek promotion are under even greater pressure to produce results that justify their promotion. A result of these pressures is that public servants also adopt a short-term perspective, even when they do not wish to.[10]

Journalists think short-term

Journalists and, indeed, all members of media organisations are preoccupied with the short-term. Most journalists submit, or file, stories each day. This means that they need something new to report every day. A spectacular event is the most desirable of daily events, especially for televised news programs. Achieving environmental sustainability is likely to be a long slow process, with many setbacks and little spectacle. It will offer few of the moments that journalists most like to report. What environmental sustainability is and how it can be achieved are also complex ideas, when simpler events are easier to report, so this also makes it harder to cover in a news context.

People think short-term

We expect members of political executives to deliver immediate results, at least in part, because we measure time in terms of our own lives. Achievements that may take decades, even centuries, to produce are unlikely to interest people who will be dead before they are attained. We are also prone to preferring that future generations make the sacrifices necessary to achieve environmental sustainability.

Reducing our access to resources or making them significantly more expensive won't appeal to those whose lives will be affected now.[11]

One of the most significant aspects of people's short-term thinking is their focus on their employment. Working brings in money that can be used to satisfy our needs and desires and those of our dependants [12] Our identities are also deeply enmeshed with our work. Most people see us, and most of us see ourselves, in terms of the work that we do or the work we are seeking. Losing our jobs to protect the environment simply does not make sense. Even if we are rewarded for doing so, the rewards are unlikely to compensate us fully and they do nothing with respect to the problem of losing our identity in the workplace.

Summary

A short-term focus may simply reflect people's limited life spans. Members of Cabinet have even shorter political 'life spans', so they look no further ahead than the next election. Electoral pressures do not affect public servants as directly, but a short-term orientation is likely to be important for promotion. Similarly, journalists and members of media organisations rely on the immediacy of stories to create news. Members of political executives also respond to the short-term orientation of voters, who will resist sacrifices that they think will reduce the quality of their lives.

No capacity for coherent policy-making for all policy areas

Another reason to believe that government and democracy in Australia cannot deliver environmental sustainability is that members of political executives cannot generate coherent policies covering all of the policy areas that have to be coordinated to achieve environmental sustainability. Policy-making is incremental, involving small decisions that build upon each other. Only non-incremental, total policy coordination can deliver environmental sustainability and government and democracy in Australia cannot deliver this.[13]

Policy-making is incremental

Those who study public policy distinguish between 'rational-comprehensive' policy-making and incremental policy-making. In rational-comprehensive policy-making, overall goals are generated and appropriate policies are identified and implemented. In incremental policy-making, limited goals are set, past experience is used to guide the choice of policies, and the policies that are adopted must be accepted by the people who have to implement them.[14] While rational-comprehensive policy-making is suited to delivering environmental sustainability, incremental policy-making is not. The latter is what policy-makers in Australia actually do (and for good reasons).

Political executives are segmented

The responsibilities of members of bureaucracies are complex and extensive. No single agency could successfully fulfill all of them, and bureaucracies are divided into departments that have separate staff and responsibilities. Each department is responsible for a separate policy area, which makes developing and implementing the comprehensive policies required for environmental sustainability impossible. In the first instance, this is because each department will do things a little differently, but also because the heads of each department will want to maintain their authority and control. Departments also contain specialists trained in the particular field for which their department is responsible. They develop specific areas of interest, which limits their capacity to participate in developing and implementing the range of policies required to deliver environmental sustainability.

A federal structure significantly increases the degree of segmentation of bureaucracies. Departments are reproduced at both the state and federal levels and this means that discrete policy areas are administered at two levels. Developing and implementing policies that result in environmental sustainability is difficult in a unitary system (one that has a single dominant government), but close to impossible in a Federation. Members of local governments must also implement policies that support environmental sustainability, adding to the complexity of achieving it.[15]

Summary

To claim that government and democracy cannot deliver environmental sustainability because policy-making is incremental and because bureaucracies are segmented and hard to coordinate is not intended as a criticism of members of Australian political executives. Indeed, these effects may be necessary to the functioning of modern political executives, or at least modern bureaucracies. The problem, however, is that each of these segments has a role to play, but no one within each of them has the capacity or means to imagine all of the segments working together to deliver environmental sustainability.

Attempts to introduce environmental sustainability likely to result in deadlock

Another reason to contend that government and democracy in Australia cannot deliver environmental sustainability is that any attempt to do so would result in political deadlock.[16] Delivering environmental sustainability is impossible because the level of cooperation it requires cannot be achieved. Politics emerges out of conflict. At best, political processes reduce the problems that conflict might otherwise create, such as violence or social breakdown.[17] Government and democracy in Australia are designed to reduce the worst effects of division, but not to overcome division.

Division in Parliament

Parliamentary democracy in Australia is based upon the management of conflict. Division is represented by the existence of two Houses. It is also represented in the design of our Houses of Parliament, which indicates a confrontation of people and ideas. Two sides face each other across the House, with the front benches devoted to the leaders of the party and the backbenches occupied by their loyal (and sometimes not so loyal) supporters. The divisions within Parliament are generally organised by political parties. Even though one party will control the Lower House, the opposition has various means by which it will attempt to block, slow down, or otherwise frustrate any initiatives that come from the majority party or coalition. Opposition control over the Upper House provides an even more effective means for slowing or preventing the passage of legislation promoted by the members of Cabinet.

Division in political executives

Division is also a persistent feature of political executives. Rivalries and hostilities between members of different departments are common. This sometimes reflects their different values and can also reflect their different expertise. Sometimes division among members of different departments is simply a reflection of different personalities. The same factors explain divisions that arise between senior public servants and their ministers, though the different nature of the positions of minister and public servant will also contribute to division. Departments are also divided.[18] Once again, these divisions reflect differences in values, resources, strategies for achieving goals, and personalities.

Division in a federal system

A federal system is not just segmented; it is divided.[19] The creation of two levels of government produces two sets of political executives containing people seeking power. The purpose of a federal system is to ensure that power is divided between them. Conflict concerning who has power over a particular policy area is inevitable. Problems will result if members of the federal political executive see themselves as having the authority to implement an extensive policy program designed to deliver environmental sustainability. This denies the reality that the Australian Constitution gives members of state political executives much of the power over the specific policy areas affected by environmental sustainability, and they will not surrender this willingly. Members of political executives at both levels will use confusion about power, which results from the division of power in our Federation, to deny their responsibility for a problem, including environmental problems.

Division also occurs between the political executives who govern each of the states; traditional interstate rivalries, attempts to demonstrate effective leadership, a desire to increase revenue, or party rivalries, result in division between members of different state political executives. The problem is that delivering environmental sustainability requires a level of cooperation between members of state political executives that government and democracy in Australia have never produced.

Division between and within parties

The division reflected and produced by parties creates division in Parliament, between and within political executives, and in a federation. The most significant of the divisive effects of parties occur during referenda. No referendum proposal will succeed if one of the major parties opposes it. This shows that party division, especially between major parties, will frustrate attempts to achieve significant changes to Australian politics and society

While their leaders work hard to create the appearance of party unity, this is always an illusion. Parties contain many strong-minded people with different values and different views as to how problems can be solved. They also contain ambitious people competing for a limited number of positions. Major parties are networks of state-based organisations presided over by people who like to be in control. Also, some members of parties simply do not respect or like each other and will oppose policies simply because they are supported by these people.

Division among and within pressure groups

In liberal-pluralist theory, democracy only exists when all pressure groups affect policy-making. Every group's pressure must have some effect on the policies adopted by members of political executives or legislation passed in Parliament. This is important, in this context, because any attempt to deliver environmental sustainability will activate a variety of pressure groups. Some of them will oppose environmental sustainability or specific policies that promote it.

Division also arises because members of the different groups that push for environmental sustainability do not understand it in the same way. They also have different views as to how environmental sustainability can be achieved. Consequently, different groups will create pressure to introduce different policies. Some may refuse to accept that it can be delivered through the processes normally associated with government and democracy in Australia. Egos will also play a role in creating divisions, especially among the leaders of the different environmental pressure groups. In this context, the question arises as to why the Greens (WA) is not part of the Australian Greens.[20]

Summary

The divisions that prevent members of political executives from introducing policies that deliver environmental sustainability have been exacerbated by disputes among scientists as to whether the evidence demonstrates the existence of global warming. But even if all scientists were in agreement, government and democracy in Australia cannot deliver environmental sustainability because of divisions in Parliament, political executives, Federations, political parties, and pressure groups. Delivering environmental sustainability will require a fundamental change in the way people live and this will activate and accentuate these divisions.

QUESTION

Does a strong development orientation mean that environmental sustainability can't be achieved?

2: COMMENTS ON THE PROPOSITION

While the reasons to believe that government and democracy in Australia cannot deliver environmental sustainability presented above might be plausible, they do not validate the proposition. This part begins with a couple of general points that suggest that government and democracy's inability to deliver environmental sustainability in Australia is not as inevitable as we made it appear. In this section, we make points specific to each of the arguments presented above.

General points

Changing values

The first point that must be made about the proposition is that it concerns the future. The fact that government and democracy *have not* delivered environmental sustainability does not mean that they *cannot* do so. Values in the Australian community are changing, and voters were highly sensitive to environmental issues in the 2007 federal election. Concern about the environment is becoming a normal part of Australian politics and Australians seem less convinced by development and the 'progress' it is supposed to bring. Anti-globalisation activism is another indication that Australians' values have changed.[21]

A greater capacity for collective action to achieve environmental sustainability

Another problem with the proposition is that its proponents underestimate the capacity of members of political executives to organise and act when a crisis, such as a war, emerges. Inaction on the parts of members of political executives may reflect the divisions among scientists as to the extent of the threat to the world's environment. Delivering environmental sustainability is like winning a war. Once the extent of the crisis is fully understood, and we are close to this now, everyone involved in government and democracy in Australia will cooperate and make the sacrifices and other changes necessary to deliver environmental sustainability.

Normalisation of environmental issues has occurred

One of the most important developments in Australian politics since the mid-1990s, was that environmental issues became a normal part of our political agenda. This indicates a change in people's values, which makes them more willing to act collectively to achieve environmental sustainability. As Pakulski, Tranter, and Crook suggest,[22] Australians have moved from perceiving environmental problems as a series of crises to viewing them as part of an ongoing problem that requires continuing management.

BOX 17.3
The Kyoto Protocol

By signing the 1997 Kyoto Protocol, representatives of most countries agreed to reduce greenhouse gas emissions so that emissions would be 5 per cent lower in 2010 than they were in 1990. This Protocol was an outcome of the Convention on Climate Change 1992 of which Australia was a party. The premise of the Protocol is that no one country can affect climate change alone. The Protocol is intended to stabilise emissions at a level that would prevent dangerous human-induced interference with the climate. To be binding, the Protocol needs to be ratified by 55 countries that account for at least 55 per cent of the total carbon dioxide emissions of developed countries.

Source: http://www.climatechange.gov.au/international/kyoto

Specific points

A new economy
New industries
The argument that the dominance of a development orientation prevents government and democracy in Australian from delivering environmental sustainability assumes an inconsistency between development and environmental sustainability. This assumption is not necessarily valid. Sustainable development is available through new technologies and a change in our way of life. The importance of tourism for the Australian economy creates increasing pressure to preserve our environment in order to attract tourists. While eco-tourism represents an important niche market, it is one form of development that demands environmental sustainability.[23]

New economic measures
The main reason that development and environmental sustainability are thought to be inconsistent is that normal economic measures don't accurately represent the cost of development.[24] The result is that they do not register the regressive aspects of some forms of development. Sustainable development becomes possible when the costs and benefits of development are accurately measured.

Evidence of long-term thinking
Green movements
The growth of green and environmental movements suggests not only that values are changing, but that more Australians are engaging in long-term thinking. Most Australians are now aware that natural resources are not infinite[25] and that pollution is destroying the environment for present and future generations.[26] Green pressure groups and political parties have made Australians more aware of the consequences of their actions for the environment. Globalisation means that we are also aware of environmental problems in other countries. Green pressure groups and parties also alert us to global environmental problems. In short, short-term thinking has become increasingly difficult due to the rise of national and international green pressure groups and parties.[27]

'Post-materialist' values[28]
This increased capacity for long-term thinking reflects the increased importance of 'post-materialist' values.[29] Post-materialists focus on the quality of their lives. Increasing numbers of Australians feel dissatisfied with the quality of their lives and this makes them more receptive to accepting the values associated with

environmental sustainability. Many advocates of environmental sustainability argue that it requires a way of life that offers greater peace of mind.

Problems with specialisation and lack of coordination can be overcome

Environmental science degrees

One of the reasons that members of political executives cannot coordinate policy-making across the variety of policy areas to achieve environmental sustainability is their training. Education systems produce specialists, rather than people whose thinking has the breadth and depth necessary for achieving environmental sustainability. The creation of environmental science degrees means that universities can begin to produce specialists in the broad and long-term thinking required to deliver environmental sustainability. Students would need to understand both the science and politics of environmental sustainability.

General environmental education[30]

All Australians needs to know more about environmental sustainability if it is to be delivered. Primary and secondary schooling must provide citizens with an understanding of, and an ability to participate in, measures introduced to deliver environmental sustainability. Many schools have embraced this and we expect this trend to continue. Almost every specialty has some effect on the environment, so an appreciation of what is required for environmental sustainability must be part of every specialist's training. This has not yet happened, but it is crucial if government and democracy in Australia is to deliver environmental sustainability.

Greater capacity for coordination

The increased power of the departments of Prime Minister and Cabinet and Treasury (and their equivalents in the states) is another reason to believe that government and democracy in Australia can achieve the necessary coordination. The importance of party leaders means that Prime Ministers will be expected to exert the control required to coordinate policies across a range of policy areas. Increased use of digital technologies will also assist those in central agencies to monitor and control other members of political executives. So, the closer we move to e-government, the more that coordination across political executives becomes possible.

Attempts to introduce environmental sustainability likely to result in deadlock

Divisions will disappear in the face of real crisis

Australian politics might be riddled with divisions that produce deadlock, but this does not mean that government and democracy in Australia cannot deliver environmental sustainability. Australians will understand and treat deadlock as an indulgence when the significance and immediacy of the environmental problems we face become even more evident. Much of the division in politics can be traced to ego, rather than real differences in values, so deadlock is not inevitable.

Summary

While a number of points can be made in defence of the proposition discussed in this part, none of them can be validly defended on a number of grounds noted above; none need to be accepted without question. Another basis for rejecting the proposition is that the claim that government and democracy in Australia will never deliver environmental sustainability assumes that we will keep making the same mistakes. More people are aware of our past mistakes and more are committed to overcoming the obstacles to achieving environmental sustainability.

QUESTION

Does the failure to achieve environmental sustainability mean that it is too difficult to achieve in the future?

BOX 17.4
UN Framework Convention on Climate Change

The United Nations Framework Convention on Climate Change Conference occurred on 3–14 December 2007 at the International Convention Centre in Bali, Indonesia.

This two-week conference included the Conference of the Parties to the UNFCCC, its subsidiary bodies, and the meeting of the parties to the Kyoto Protocol. Ministerial sessions in the second week concluded the conference. It was attended by over 10,000 people from over 180 countries.

The conference culminated in the Bali roadmap, which begins new negotiations that will conclude in 2009 and will provide impetus for a new international agreement on climate change when the Kyoto Protocol expires in 2012.

Source: http://unfccc.int/meetings/cop_13/items/4049txt.php

3: TWO AUSTRALIAN CABINETS AND INTERNATIONAL COVENANTS ON GREENHOUSE GAS EMISSIONS

Our discussion of the proposition dealt with in the first part of this chapter addressed general issues only. This book was completed in early 2008, which was not long after members of the newly appointed Rudd Cabinet authorised the ratification of the Kyoto Protocol. Because of its importance, this one action suggests that government and democracy in Australia can deliver environmental sustainability. To authorise the ratification of Kyoto was to reject the policies adopted by members of all Howard Cabinets, who showed little interest in environmental sustainability[31] and whose policies confirmed the view that government and democracy in Australia cannot deliver environmental sustainability.

Members of Howard Cabinets refused to authorise ratification of the Kyoto Protocol because they believed this would harm Australia's economy and voters did not want to sacrifice jobs or their quality of life. Members of the Rudd Cabinet authorised ratification for a number of reasons, including that it was necessary for the national economy. What Australians do about their greenhouse gas emissions is important, as Australians allow more greenhouse gases to enter the environment than most other countries.

Howard Cabinet's refusal to ratify the Kyoto Protocol

Members of Howard Cabinets would not authorise ratification of the Kyoto Protocol at the first opportunity in 1997 or subsequently. The Environment Minister in 1997, Senator Robert Hill, was told not to sign the Protocol if two demands were not met. The first was that the Protocol allowed Australians to increase its greenhouse gas emissions. And the second was that the target set for Australia had to be based on a calculation that included the emissions resulting from land clearing in 1990 (1990 emissions were used to work out by how much the people of each country had to reduce their emissions). Senator Hill did not sign the Kyoto Protocol, despite the fact that, at this time, Australian's target was 8 per cent greater than our emissions were in 1990.

Protecting the environment damages the economy
The response to the Kyoto Protocol from members of Howard Cabinets was a continuation of the policy adopted by members of the Hawke (Labor) Cabinet, who decided that they would not authorise ratification of any international agreement for reducing emissions if this 'harmed' the economy. Members of Hawke or Howard

BOX 17.5
Kyoto Protocol targets for selected Annex B countries

Country	Target %
Iceland	110
Australia	108
Norway	101
New Zealand	100
Russian Federation	100
Ukraine	100
Canada	94
Japan	94
Poland	94
United States	93
European Union	92

Source: Hamilton 2007, p. 78.

Cabinets never defined 'harm', and almost any change to the economy can be used to refuse to reduce our emissions. Representatives of the coal, oil, and electricity industries, supported by those representing cement and aluminium manufacturers and other mining interests, had considerable influence over members of Howard Cabinets. Many of these lobbyists had direct access to the most powerful Ministers. Members of Howard Cabinets always said that successfully managing the national economy was the most important of their roles, so everything else, including the environment, took second, or a lower, place.

Different developed countries have different responsibilities

Another argument that members of the Howard Cabinet put forward to justify their refusal to authorise ratification of the Kyoto Protocol was that it was based on the view that all developed countries had the same responsibilities. They argued that Australia's increasing population and our access to relatively inexpensive coal-produced electricity meant that Australia had to be treated differently. These factors did not affect European nations, whose representatives wanted uniform cuts for all developed nations. So members of the Howard Cabinet rejected uniformity and argued for 'differentiation', which meant targets that reflected growth in population and GDP.

Developing countries should pull their weight

Another reason that members of Howard Cabinets opposed ratifying the Kyoto Protocol was that it did not contain binding emissions targets for developing countries. They argued that it was unfair to impose binding targets to reduce emissions on people in developed nations when those in developing nations would eventually produce more emissions than those in developed nations. Accepting the targets set for them, they claimed, would disadvantage people in developed nations. They rejected the argument that those in developed countries should lead the way.

We don't need a coordinated response from all governments

The close relationship between senior members of the Howard Cabinet and US President George W. Bush was another factor in the refusal to ratify the Kyoto Protocol. A meeting between John Howard and George W. Bush in 2001 resulted in a proposal for a global focus on new technology, as opposed to national targets. Their alternative was the AP6, the Asia–Pacific Partnership on Clean Development and

---

BOX 17.6
The Intergovernmental Panel on Climate Change (IPCC)

The World Meteorological Organisation (WMO) and the United Nations Environment Program (UNEP) established the Intergovernmental Panel on Climate Change (IPCC) in 1998, as a response to global debate of climate change. Members of the IPCC evaluate the scientific, technical and socio-economic information that is relevant to understanding human-induced climate change. The IPCC makes its assess-ments based on published and peer reviewed scientific literature and produces comprehensive reports assessing the status of global climate change. The IPCC's Fourth Report was released a month before the UNFCCC conference in Indonesia on 3–14 December 2007 and provided the basis for agreement as to the scientific impact of global climate change. The report indicated that, unless action is taken, average global temperatures would increase 1.1°C–6.4°C by the end of the 21st century.

Source: www.ipcc.ch/

Climate, which would make industry partnerships central to reducing greenhouse gas emissions, rather than targets for cutting emissions and other forms of long-term planning. Members of the Howard Cabinet argued that the AP6 agreement would be better that the Kyoto Protocol. This was because the Kyoto protocol did not affect the world's largest emitters, whereas AP6 would bind the US (the world's number one emitter), China (No. 2), India (No. 4), Japan (No. 5), and South Korea (No. 9), which together were responsible for more than 50 per cent of all emissions.

The first Rudd Cabinet

Ratifying the Kyoto Protocol is in Australia's national interest
On 3 December 2007, the newly elected Australian government ratified the Kyoto Protocol in its first official act, demonstrating its commitment to dealing with climate change. Ratification of the Kyoto Protocol was authorised in the first Executive Council. Australia became a signatory to the Kyoto Protocol in March 2008. Members of the first Rudd Cabinet committed themselves to ensuring that Australians meet their Kyoto Protocol obligations. These included setting a target to reduce emissions by 60 per cent on 2000 levels by 2050, establishing a national emissions trading scheme by 2020, and meeting 20 per cent of our energy needs through renewable energy sources by 2020.

Without the environment, we won't have an economy
Rather than treating environmental sustainability as a threat to the economy, members of the first Rudd Cabinet argued that it was necessary for a healthy economy. In his speech to the UN Framework Convention on Climate Change, Prime Minister Rudd spoke of climate change as 'an emerging reality' and referred to the dying of Australia's inland rivers, more intense and frequent bushfires, and the potential risks to the Great Barrier Reef, Kakadu, and Australian rainforests. All of these threaten the Australian economy.

Developed countries must demonstrate leadership
Members of the first Rudd Cabinet argued that people in developed countries were obliged to accept reductions before they were imposed on those in developing countries. They accepted that climate change is due largely to the emissions of the developed countries who were and are the major contributors to the current situation. They also argued that those in developed countries should assist developing countries through technology transfer and financial support. Without leadership and support from people in developed countries, those in developing countries would continue their rapid deforestation, which adds to greenhouse gas omissions and leads to fewer trees to absorb carbon dioxide.

International cooperation is essential
In his speech to the UN Framework Convention climate change conference, Prime Minister Kevin Rudd argued that climate change transcended the old ideological, political, and developmental divides, and said that the future of the planet was at dire risk if the community of nations did not cooperate. Members of the first Rudd Cabinet supported ratifying the Kyoto Protocol because they saw it as an expression of international cooperation. Their decision to ratify the Protocol was an important step, in part because it increased the pressure to sign the Protocol that was being exerted on those who had not done so, especially those delegates who represented the US.

Summary

We discussed the different positions adopted by members of Howard Cabinets and the first Rudd Cabinet on ratifying the Kyoto Protocol. The position adopted by members of the Howard Cabinet is consistent with the claim that government and democracy in Australia cannot deliver environmental sustainability. While the position adopted by members of the first Rudd Cabinet does not prove that government and democracy in Australia can deliver environmental sustainability, it provides some support for those who think it can.

QUESTIONS

1. What are the main differences between members of Howard Cabinets and of the first Rudd Cabinet on ratifying the Kyoto Protocol?
2. Should Australia have ratified the Kyoto Protocol in 2007? Why/why not?

CONCLUSION

Delivering environmental sustainability is one of the main challenges that Australians will face over the next decade. Members of Parliaments, political executives, and parties will come under increasing pressure to deliver environmental sustainability. Whether they can respond to this pressure with policies that deliver environmental sustainability remains an open question. Certainly, many obstacles will confront those who seek environmental sustainability. Pressure seems likely to build within the system, however, and those who contend that government and democracy in Australian cannot deliver environmental sustainability may have to revise their views. They will feel vindicated by the policies adopted by members of Howard Cabinets, but some might feel less confident after members of the first Rudd Cabinet authorised ratification of the Kyoto Protocol. Time, assuming that we have enough of it, will tell whether government and democracy in Australia can deliver environmental sustainability.

FURTHER READING

Introductory texts

Carter, Neil, 2006, *The Politics of the Environment. Ideas, Activism, Policy*, 2nd edn, Cambridge University Press: Cambridge.

Dovers, Stephen, 2006, *Environment and Sustainability Policy*, The Federation Press: Sydney.

Goodin, Robert, 1992, *Green Political Theory*, Polity Press: Cambridge.

Hay, Peter, 2002, *Main Currents in Western Environmental Thought*, UNSW Press: Sydney.

Papadakis, Elim, 1993, *Politics and the Environment: The Australian Experience*, Allen & Unwin: St Leonards.

Stewart, Jenny & Grant Jones, 2003, *Renegotiating the Environment: The Power of Politics*, Federation Press: Sydney.

Thomas, Ian, 2007, *Environmental Policy: Australian Practice in Context of Theory*, The Federation Press: Crows Nest.

Walker, Ken, 1994, *The Political Economy of Environmental Policy: An Australian Introduction*, UNSW Press: Kensington.

Specialist texts

Connell, D., 2007, *Water Politics in the Murray-Darling Basin*, Federation Press: Sydney.

Dobson, Andrew & Paul Lucardie (eds), 1993, *The Politics of Nature: Explorations in Green Political Theory*, Routledge: London.

Gillespie, Alexander & William Burns (eds), 2000, *Climate Change in the South Pacific: Impacts and Responses in Australia, New Zealand, and Small Island States*, Kluwer Academic Publishers: Dordrecht.

Gray, John, 1993, *Beyond the New Right: Markets, Government and the Common Environment*, Routledge: London.

Hamilton, Clive, 2007, *Scorcher: The Dirty Politics of Climate Change*, Black Inc. Agenda: Melbourne.

Lowe, Ian, 2007, 'Reaction Time: Climate Change and the Nuclear Option,' in *Quarterly Essay*, 27, pp. 1–88.

Mathews, Freya (ed.), 1996, *Ecology and Democracy*, Frank Cass: London.
McLaughlin, Andrew, 1993, *Regarding Nature: Industrialism and Deep Ecology*, State University of New York Press: Albany.
Pearse, Guy, 2007, *High & Dry: John Howard, Climate Change and the selling of Australia's future*, Penguin: Australia.

Web sites

An Inconvenient Truth: http://www.aninconvenienttruth.com.au/truth
Australian politics: http://australianpolitics.com
Australian Conservation Foundation: http://www.acfonline.org.au
Australian Department of Climate Change: http://www.climatechange.gov.au
Australian Department of the Environment, Water, Heritage and the Arts: http://www.environment.gov.au
Friends of the Earth Australia: http://www.foe.org.au
Intergovernmental Panel on Climate Change: http://www.ipcc.ch/
Greenpeace: http://www.greenpeace.org
The Wilderness Society: http://www.wilderness.org.au

Notes

1. For more on sustainability and sustainable development, see Dobson (2007, pp. 12–13, 29).
2. See Barry (1996, p. 117).
3. Please note that this is not a definition of the term. It is a stipulation of the meaning that this term will have for this discussion. Definitions require final statements of the meaning of terms that are rarely possible and usually politically charged. In some instances, those who promote the dominant definition of a concept dominate a society.
4. For more on the dominant paradigm of development, see Papadakis (1997, 1, pp. 201–4), Lumley (1999, pp. 35–49), and Aplin (2000, pp. 273–87).
5. How far back the link between being human and exploiting nature goes is a subject matter for debate. A starting-point for anyone interested in this debate is Harrison (1999). In this article, Harrison disputed the claim that the link comes from the Bible.
6. For more on anthropocentric and ecocentric outlooks, see Dobson (2007, pp. 20, 42–6, 52) and Eckersley (1992, pp. 26–31).
7. McGinnis (1994) has suggested that the mentality of 'the bureaucrat' is dominated by the myth of the human ability to control nature.
8. A former Liberal Premier of South Australia, David Tonkin (1984), denies the validity of the assumption that Liberal Party policy is simply an expression of the interests of those in the business community. Given that Tonkin suggests that those inside and outside the party hold this view suggests that it is a common understanding of the relationship between the Liberal Party and the business community.
9. For more details on political parties and their policy positions concerning the environment, see Papadakis (1997, pp. 204–6; 457–9), Jensen-Lee (2001, pp. 142–4), Christoff (1994, pp. 358–60), O'Neill (2000, pp. 165–82), Hamilton (2007, pp. 55–81), and Pearse (2007, pp. 127–287).
10. For more information concerning the careers of public servants and New Public Management, see Hughes (1998b, pp. 52–80).

11 For more on environmental reasons for limiting access to resources, see Dobson (2007, pp. 53–62).
12 For more information concerning the relationship between capitalism (markets) and the environment, see Eckersley (1995, pp. 7–45) and Rosewarne (1993, pp. 53–71).
13 For more on the type of governments required for environmental sustainability, see Dobson (2007, pp. 105–15), Midlarsky (1998, pp. 341–59), Hardin (1968, pp. 1243–8), and Walker (1994, pp. 285–99).
14 This discussion is my own interpretation of Doyle & Kellow (1995, pp. 137–42) and is not an interpretation for which they should be held responsible.
15 For more on the dangers of over-specialisation, see Saul (1992, pp. 473–7) and Saul (2002, pp. 30–1; 61–2).
16 This is sometimes referred to as political gridlock. See Silvia (1999) and Feldman, Peretz & Jendrucko (1994).
17 See Crick (2005, pp. 18–37).
18 See Weller & Davis (1996) and Mellors (1996).
19 Silvia (1999, p. 167) has argued that 'gridlock is a cyclical product of party competition in a federal system'.
20 For more on the divisions between environmentalists, see Dobson (2007, pp. 2–3).
21 For more on the attitudes of Australians towards environmental issues, see Lothian (1994, pp. 78–96).
22 Pakulski, Tranter & Crook (1998), though compare this with Jensen-Lee (2001).
23 For more on development that is consistent with environmental sustainability, see Christoff (1995, pp. 2–18) or visit http://www.gdrc.org/uem/eco-tour/eco-tour.html
24 See, for example, Lumley (1999) and Coombs (1990).
25 For more on the limits of growth theory, see Dobson (1994, pp. 106–7).
26 For more on the importance of the ideas surrounding the future generations, see Dobson (2007, pp. 156–7).
27 For more information on green movements and globalisation, see Newman (1995, pp. 122–7), Hurrell & Kingsley (1992, pp. 1–47), and O'Brien et al. (2000, pp. 109–57).
28 For discussions of post-materialist values and voting, see Western & Tranter (2001) and Gow (1990).
29 For more on post-materialism, see Dobson (2007, pp. 5, 7).
30 An interesting discussion of these issues can be found in Luke (2001).
31 Hamilton (2007, p. 78)

18 National Security and Terrorism

LEARNING OBJECTIVES

- To understand why some people might claim that rights should be restricted to curb the threat of terrorism
- Identify those rights that are threatened by anti-terrorism legislation
- Be able to recognise and understand the concepts of security that underpin the debate over whether people's rights should be restricted in response to the threat of terrorism

INTRODUCTION

The attack on the World Trade Center on 11 September 2001 began a process in which Westerners revised their views as to how secure they were. And the deaths of 200 people, most of them Australian, that resulted from the bombing of a nightclub in Bali on 12 October 2002[1] shattered our sense that we had little to fear from **terrorism**. Before these attacks, we thought that terrorism was something that other people had to worry about. Some Australians were aware that there had been a terrorist attack here: the 1978 bombing outside Sydney Hilton Hotel, where a Commonwealth Heads of Government Meeting was taking place, in which three people died and seven were injured.[2] We were aware of terrorism in Northern Ireland and some of us had heard about the 'Unabomber',[3] who had sent bombs to US universities and airlines intermittently between 1975 and 1995, and Timothy McVie and Terry Nicholls, who destroyed a federal government building in Oklahoma City and killed 168 people.[4] But terrorism was a rare event for most Australians. We were a long way from attacks in the UK,[5] Spain,[6] the Middle East,[7] and South America.[8] Regardless of what was happening elsewhere, Australians felt safe.

The impact of live television coverage of the attack on the World Trade Center, repeated exposure to images of the World Trade Center towers collapsing, and the Bali bombing changed many Australians' views on terrorism and their vulnerability to attack. The effect of the television coverage of the terrorist attacks in the US and the graphic images coming from Bali should not be underestimated. The attack on the World Trade Center occurred during the evening. The millions of people who were watching television at the time found their programs being suddenly interrupted with live footage of the World Trade Center being attacked and collapsing. It was surreal. Smoke billowed from two of the tallest buildings in the world and those familiar parts of the New York skyline were no longer there. Another country had actually attacked the US! Terrorists hijacked foreign aircraft, assassinated foreign political leaders, exploded bombs in crowded areas in other countries where Australians were rarely found; but they did not (or so we thought) fly aircraft into buildings we recognised or attacked us in one of our favourite holidays 'playgrounds'.

Shock and horror became anxiety, and Australians turned to members of their political executive to demand that their security be guaranteed. Spokespeople for the major political parties committed them to supporting the US President's 'War on Terror' and promised to find any political terrorists abroad or at home who might threaten Australian security. Members of the federal political executive responded by amending the *Criminal Code Act 1995* (CCA) and introducing the *Australian Anti-Terrorism Act 2005* (AATA). These made the following possible:

- life imprisonment for individuals who 'facilitated' a terrorist act, even if the attack did not take place;
- life imprisonment for providing financial support to a terrorist organisation even if they did not know it was a terrorist organisation;
- control orders that restrict a person's movement for a year before these orders must be reviewed;
- preventative detention orders that prevent those detained from telling friends and family anything more than that they are 'safe', but not contactable.

These legislative amendments give rise to the proposition that will be discussed in the first part of this chapter. This proposition is that we cannot protect people's rights and freedom and provide for their security.[9] In discussing this, we present reasons why someone might make such a claim and then comment on these reasons. This leads us, in the second part of the chapter which is to pose and answer the question: 'What conceptions of security characterise the different responses to restricting people's rights to achieve security?' We argue that those who accept the sacrificing of rights to security and those who reject this do so because they conceive of security differently. Our intention is to explain the two conceptions of security that lead some people to believe that sacrificing rights can produce security and others to believe that security does not exist in a society in which people have sacrificed their rights. It is up to individual readers to decide which concept of security better reflects their values and views about the kind of society in which they want to live.

1: PROPOSITION: WE CANNOT PROTECT PEOPLE'S RIGHTS AND PROVIDE FOR THEIR SECURITY

The sense of vulnerability among Australians that resulted from the attack on the World Trade Center and the Bali bombing produced widespread support for the introduction of measures to counter terrorism. The proposition that we cannot protect people's rights and provide for their security is implicit in contemporary debates about how members of Australian political executives should respond to the threat of terrorism. In the first section of this discussion, we present reasons that support this view. In doing so, we have presented reasons why someone might believe that rights and security are incompatible, rather than explain the particular uses of the ideas of 'rights' and 'security' that make sense of this contention. Conceptions of security are discussed later in this chapter. In the second section, we discuss each of these reasons and, in some cases, question their validity.

The proposition

Those who believe that we cannot protect people's rights and provide for their security do so for at least four reasons. First, granting the right and freedom to associate freely is thought to provide opportunities for the conspiracy and collaboration necessary for terrorism. Second, they contend that protecting the right to privacy prevents authorities from intercepting emails and telephone messages sent by terrorists. Third, a free press is thought to undermine the secrecy that would enable members of political executives to deal effectively with terrorism and would give unwanted publicity to a group's cause. Finally, the 'rule of law' or 'due process' undermines a political executive's ability to obtain information about actual or potential threats.

BOX 18.1
Joseph 'Jack' Thomas

The case of Joseph 'Jack' Thomas raises questions about how members of political executives, in an effort to secure civilians, should be able to obtain information from suspected terrorists and constrain their behaviour after being found innocent. In March 2006, Thomas was charged with receiving funds from Al Qaeda. He was sentenced to five years jail.

This case is important because, during the trial, the lawyers defending Thomas argued that interrogators had placed him under great pressure, perhaps even tortured him, to obtain the evidence they were using to support his conviction. The judge who tried the case ruled that the evidence was gathered properly and could be used to justify a conviction, but this decision was overruled on appeal and Thomas's conviction was quashed.

The Australian government responded by having a magistrate place a control order on Thomas. This required that he have access to only one landline and one mobile phone approved by the Australian Federal Police; that he be fingerprinted; and that he remain in the country. It also forbade him from being outside between midnight and 5 am, having contact with people identified as terrorists, making telephone calls without prior approval, and using public telephones. Thomas sought to have the control order ruled invalid by the High Court, but he was unsuccessful.

Sources: Transcript of Attorney General Philip Ruddick's response on the ABC *AM* program to Thomas's original conviction, http://www.abc.net.au/am/content/2006/s1578987.htm; transcript of the ABC *Four Corners* interview with Thomas, http://www.theaustralian.news.com.au/story/0,20867,20199530-601,00.html; transcript of the High Court decision, http://www.austlii.edu.au/cases/cth/high_ct/2007/33.htm

> **QUESTION**
>
> What means should members of political executives be able to employ to protect their citizens? Should suspected terrorists be treated differently to other criminal suspects?

The right to free association assists terrorists

The first reason to believe that the recognition of rights is incompatible with security is that granting people the right to associate with whomever and wherever they want allows radical elements to conspire and collaborate to disrupt government and democracy in Australia. Protecting this right protects private meetings, in which terrorists can discuss their plans, and public meetings, in which extremist positions can be promoted. For example, temples can provide a sanctuary for radical priests in which they can foster hatred towards Westerners among their followers. Internet chat rooms and online discussion groups also provide opportunities to promote extremist positions and gather supporters. This was the reason why a control order was placed on Joseph 'Jack' Thomas, even after he was found not to have received funds from the terrorist network, Al Qaeda.

The right to privacy aids terrorists

The second reason to believe that rights are incompatible with security is that granting the right to privacy prevents authorities from intercepting emails and telephone messages sent by members of terrorist organisations. Terrorists can communicate with each other more freely than they would if surveillance and the interception of messages could not be carried out quickly and easily. If the authorities cannot monitor and intercept all communications at all times, then they cannot ascertain the risks facing the community and work to provide protection.

A free press hinders counter-terrorism and helps terrorists

The third reason to propose a contradiction between respecting rights and providing security is that a free press would reveal plans to neutralise a terrorist threat and give unwanted publicity to a group. Members of political executives will be more effective in countering terrorism, if they can work in secret. If a free press obtained and publicised such plans, then terrorists would gain a significant advantage. Further, publicising terrorist attacks helps spread the feelings of insecurity that terrorists are trying to produce. A free press is also likely to contain those who would give spokespeople for terrorist organisations the opportunity to explain and defend their actions. This would help them to spread their message and gather support for their groups.

The 'rule of law', and the right to 'due process', makes it harder to prosecute terrorists

The fourth reason that supports the view that security cannot be achieved in a society in which rights are protected is that the 'rule of law' and 'due process' can undermine a government's ability to obtain information about actual or potential threats. The 'rule of law' (which requires treating all citizens according to the same rules) is not suited to the unique threat that terrorism poses. Terrorists are not 'normal' people. In fact, to recognise them as citizens would be a perversion of the concept. They do not recognise the rights of others to go about their lives in peace, so they should not receive the same treatment as those who recognise these rights. Terrorists should not be presumed innocent: always given access to lawyers, allowed to know about and to cross-examine witnesses, and have charges against them proven 'beyond reasonable doubt'. Finally, if a society is to be made secure, then suspected terrorists should be detained until they can prove that they do not pose a threat to the citizenry.

Summary

The proposition that we cannot protect people's rights and provide for their security is an important one for government and democracy in Australia. It reflects a sense of vulnerability that may lead some Australians to accept the loss of their rights. They might surrender their right to associate freely because this right enables terrorists to conspire and collaborate. They might sacrifice their right to privacy to allow members of political executives to monitor and intercept all communications, and therefore those between suspected terrorists. They may abandon a free press because the news media might reveal plans to counter terrorism, increase insecurity by publicising terrorist attacks, and help terrorists to promote their causes and groups. Finally, Australians might sacrifice the 'rule of law' and 'due process' in order to allow members of political executives to detain, prosecute, and imprison terrorists more easily and effectively.

Comments on the proposition

The reasons that support the proposition merit further consideration for an adequate discussion. First, we suggest that restricting the right to association furthers the terrorists' aim of disrupting Australian society. Second, we acknowledge that surveillance is integral to counter-terrorism strategies, but we emphasise the threat to civil liberties that it represents. Third, we offer reasons to reject the claim that a free press will threaten security. Fourth, we explain why denying 'rule of law' and 'due process' to terrorists might pose a greater threat to security than any terrorist's actions.

Limiting the right to free association plays into terrorists' hands
While granting the right to freely associate provides opportunities for conspiracy and collaboration, its restriction also helps the terrorists to achieve their aim of disrupting the lives of ordinary citizens. Terrorists aim to disrupt society to such an extent that members of political executives give in to the terrorists' demands. After all, democratic political institutions are supposed to secure peace and public order, so that people can interact freely and civil society can flourish. If the right to free association is surrendered, the terrorists win. First, because society has been disrupted, and second, because the public interactions that are at the heart of democracy and representative democracy itself will be impossible. A result will be that citizens will question the way that they are governed and wonder whether they live in a democracy.

Civil liberties will be threatened
While the gathering of intelligence is an integral element of any counter-terrorism strategy, it must be viewed in the light of the possibility that unrestricted intelligence gathering will be abused and civil liberties threatened. Evidence gathered through surveillance can be used selectively to embarrass opponents, not just to oppose terrorists, and to present information or provide images that can be taken out of context or misconstrued. The 'Children Overboard' affair illustrates this potential. In this case, members of Federal Cabinet presented images that were alleged to be

---

BOX 18.2
Children Overboard

In October 2001, images of people on a boat off the coast of northwestern Australia were shown on the front pages of major Australian newspapers and on television news programs. Members of the political executive, including the Prime Minister and Minister for Immigration, said that they showed 'illegal immigrants' throwing their children into the water after scuttling their own boat. They did so, Australians were told, in order to force their rescue and to ensure that they were taken to the Australian mainland as refugees. These claims were later found to be false. Members of Cabinet defended themselves by claiming that they were not told that the images did not show children being thrown overboard in a deliberate strategy to force their rescue and acceptance as refugees. Many commentators rejected their claim that they had not been told.

Source: Marr, David & Marian Wilkinson 2004, *Dark Victory*, 2nd edition, Sydney: Allen & Unwin; http://truthoverboard.com/

those of adult asylum seekers throwing children from their boat in order to force the Australian Navy to pick them up and take them to Australia. These images were intended to promote an anti-asylum seeker attitude among Australians and increase support for Cabinet policy to prevent as many asylum seekers as possible from getting asylum in Australia.

Members of a political executive may release selected extracts from the data that has been collected to support a claim that a person poses a potential threat. This is a particular concern when people can be detained for posing a threat to society. In the case of suspected terrorist, Mohammad Haneef, for example, the Australian Federal Police were found to have selectively released evidence in order to create the impression that Haneef had acknowledged living in England with people who were later charged with terrorism.

The free press is no real danger

The argument that the threat to security posed by a free press requires limiting its freedom exaggerates the threat that a free press represents. A free press reports on events that include acts of terrorism and measures to counter terrorism. They do so because citizens wish to know what is happening in their society and many of them will feel less secure when they know that information about terrorist attacks is being withheld. Citizens will also want to form their own views about the violence done. They will not merely accept that the acts that members of political executives call 'terrorism' are, indeed, terrorism.

There is no reason to believe that news reporting would undermine a government's counter-terrorism strategy. Another important point is that for a political executive to retain its legitimacy, it is imperative that it accounts for itself to the Members of Parliament and, ultimately, to the people. This cannot happen without a free press, as the people have to be informed if accountability, and representative democracy itself, can be said to exist.

Finally, the threat posed by the removal or demotion of the rule of law and due process may be a greater threat to our sense of security than terrorism. The example of Mohammad Haneef indicates that members of political executives whose actions are not controlled by the 'rule of law' and 'due process' may use their position to undermine our feelings of security. Those who are recognisably different from the white, Christian, and British-Australian majority who dominate the Australian government and society are most likely to feel particularly vulnerable when not protected by the rule of law and due process. Anyone who has dark skin and practices Islam or Hinduism will be treated with suspicion.

Summary

A number of reasons support the argument that, after 9/11 and the Bali bombing, we cannot protect people's rights and provide for their security. The right to free

BOX 18.3
Dr Mohammad Haneef

Dr Mohammad Haneef is an Indian citizen and qualified doctor who had worked in England and then at the Gold Coast Hospital on a temporary skilled visa since September 2006. In the aftermath of an attack on the Glasgow International Airport on 30 June 2007, Haneef purchased a one-way airfare ticket to India. He was arrested at Brisbane Airport on suspicion of collaborating with terrorists and held for twelve days under Australia's anti-terrorism legislation without being charged. Subsequently, he was charged with providing support to a terrorist organisation. If convicted, Haneef faced a maximum of 15 years imprisonment.

The bases for his arrest were that he did not have a satisfactory explanation for his returning to India with a one-way ticket, that two of the people directly involved in the attack on Glasgow Airport were his cousins, and that he had given one of them his SIM card. Haneef told members of the Australian Federal Police (AFP) that his father-in-law had purchased the one-way airfare ticket so that Haneef could visit his wife, who had just given birth to their daughter, but members of the AFP would not accept his explanation.

Officers of the AFP later claimed in court that Haneef had acknowledged having lived with two of the suspects in Britain. The AFP's own record of the interview, however, showed that he said he had lived in a boarding house in London with several other doctors, and not the suspects.

Officers of the AFP, acting upon advice from Scotland Yard, also claimed that Haneef had left his SIM card with one of the suspects and that the SIM card was found in the vehicle used in the bombing. This evidence also proved to be false and the Director of Public Prosecution withdrew the charge.

Despite the collapse of the case against him and the success of Haneef's appeal in the Federal Court to have his work visa reinstated, the Immigration Minister continued to argue that he was not a person of good character and should not remain in Australia. Thus, his passport was returned, his work visa was cancelled, and he left the country. His 12-day incarceration without charge was another important aspect of this case, as it is an illustration of the way that terrorists can be dealt with differently by being denied rule of law and the due process that it requires.

Sources: *The Australian*, 2007, 'DPP finds Haneef investigation flawed', 12 October, http://www.theaustralian.news.com.au/story/0,25197,22575449-2702,00.html; *The Age*, 2007, 'Government appeals Haneef judgement', 5 September. http://www.theage.com.au/news/national/government-appeals-haneef-judgement/2007/09/05/1188783314174.html; *The Hindu*, no date, 'Transcripts of Australian Police interviews with Dr. Mohammad Haneef', http://www.hindu.com/nic/0058/haneef.htm; Jackson, Liz, 2007, 'Transcript of the "Four Corners" program, The Trials of Dr Haneef', 1 October. http://www.abc.net.au/4corners/content/2007/s2048086.htm; *The Age*, 2007, 'Transcript support Haneef', 23 August, http://www.theage.com.au/articles/2007/08/22/1187462354555.html

association allows terrorists to organise easily. A right to privacy prevents members of political executives from gathering the information they need to combat terrorism. A free press increases feelings of insecurity by publicising terrorist attacks and undermining counter-terrorism measures by revealing them. Finally, the rule of law and due process restricts rapid and effective responses to terrorist threats.

These reasons do not make the proposition unquestionably true, however. Restricting the right to free association disrupts society, and this is what terrorists want. While intelligence gathering that is not restricted by the recognition of rights is necessary for counter-terrorism, it can be abused. A free press reinforces the legitimacy of the institutions of representative democracy because it is essential for accountability. Likewise, denying the rule of law and due process to terrorists undermines feelings of security among all Australians, and particularly those who look different, practise non-Christian religions, or who have different political views from those of British-Australians.

QUESTIONS

1. Which rights are threatened by anti-terrorism legislation?
2. What concepts of security characterise the different responses to restrictions placed upon people's rights in Australia?

2: DIFFERENT UNDERSTANDINGS OF SECURITY

We do not believe that a way exists to verify the proposition that we cannot protect people's rights and provide for their security. Our reason is that we believe that those who accept the proposition conceive of security differently from those who question the arguments made in defence of the proposition. In this second part of the chapter, we suggest that those who believe that rights must be sacrificed to protect security conceive of security as *territorial* security. Those unconvinced by the arguments put forward to justify this position understand security in terms of *human* security. We contend that the choice will depend, at least in part, upon the type of society we want.

Territorial security[10]

The arguments that support the proposition that we cannot protect people's rights and provide for their security make sense when 'security' refers to the capacity of members of a political executive to maintain almost complete control over society. The traditional conception of a nation state is of a territory controlled by members of the political executive. Their control is manifested by their capacity to protect their territories from external and internal threats.

Terrorists seek to undermine the control over their territory that members of a political executive can exercise. They seek to create disorder in the societies they attack. A society can only be protected by members of political executives who will do whatever is necessary to protect their territory. To preserve the integrity of their territories, they will focus on creating their defence forces, intelligence services, policing capacities, and diplomatic services. This way of thinking about security makes considerable sense. The civil wars in north east Africa (Somalia) and in central Africa (Rwanda) highlight the profound insecurity that people experience when no institutions exist that can make those territories secure.

When security is used to refer to a capacity to protect territory, then comprehensive counter-terrorism measures are vital. These can include constant video surveillance, phone tapping, the interception of email and ordinary mail, detaining people without charging them with any offence, interrogating people without giving them access to legal representation, banning texts critical of members of the political executive and their policies, exchanging intelligence with members of political executives in other states, and pre-emptive attacks against alleged terrorists in other countries. The effects of these measures on people's rights are irrelevant, as the issue of security does exist when members of a political executive cannot ensure the safety of those who live in their territory.

The Australian *Anti-Terrorism Act 2005* and amendments to the *Criminal Code Act 1995* (CCA) exemplify the consequences of this conception of security. Australian citizens can be sentenced to life imprisonment for helping the activities of terrorists, whether or not any doubts existed as to the legitimacy of these groups. Australians can also be detained for questioning without friends and relatives knowing their whereabouts and without legal representation. Under s 104.16d of the CCA, Australians can be placed under a control order for up to a year before their case need be reviewed.

Members of Australia's political executives have also actively courted members of political executives in the region to ensure that conflicts near Australia do not affect our territory. They have exchanged intelligence with members of the political executive in Indonesia regarding the terrorist group Jemaah Islamiyah and participated in joint anti-terrorist exercises. Australian bureaucrats and police officers have also played a leading role in a multinational taskforce that went to the Solomon Islands in July 2003 to quell ethnic tensions between Guales and Malaitans.

Legislative changes are not the only ways in which government and democracy in Australia has been affected by the territorial conception of security. During the 2007 Asian Pacific Economic Cooperation (APEC) summit, inner city Sydney was effectively closed down, large numbers of police and soldiers patrolled the area, and restrictions were placed upon the movements of Sydney's residents. These actions reflect the priority among members of Australia's political executive in providing and maintaining control over territory that is essential for security. At the conclusion of the summit, members of Australia's political executives accepted that they had infringed people's rights. The then Prime Minister, John Howard, thanked the security services for their efforts and said:

> Could I say to the people of Sydney, I'm sorry that you've been inconvenienced. It's not the fault of our visitors, it's not the fault of either the New South Wales Government or the Federal Government, it's the fault of those people who resort to violence in order disrupt gatherings of this kind.

Source: http://www.news.com.au/dailytelegraph/story/0,22049,22389333-5001021,00.html

Human security[11]

Those who understand security as human security are unlikely to accept the restrictions introduced during APEC 2007, which is justified by the position that we cannot protect people's rights and provide for their security. Those who adopt this conception of security focus their attention on the feelings of the people being governed. Attention, then, is directed to threats that individuals experience. These relate to their economy, the resources they have available to them, their natural and built environment, and the population of their country. Insecurity arises in the face of environmental degradation, rapid population growth, and increasing poverty and military conflict in their region.

Specifically, this conception of security highlights the interconnectedness of human existence and the meaninglessness of territorial borders. Pollution flows downstream or overhead and does not respect lines on maps that are supposed to indicate independent territories. Scared and starving people, too, ignore borders when there is nowhere else for them to go, or to go safely. Thus, refugees fleeing civil war in Sudan and elsewhere have strained resources and created feelings of insecurity among those in neighbouring countries.

Faced with the possibility of great human suffering, those who adopt this conception seek to preserve the norms, rules, institutions, and values that allow people to feel economically, politically, socially, and environmentally secure. Human security exists when people's rights, such as those enshrined in the *United Nations International Covenant on Economic, Social and Cultural Rights*, are respected. Human security also requires institutions that are designed to promote civil society, such as freely elected legislatures, independent judiciaries, a respected police force, and a stable economy.

Considerable opposition to counter-terrorism measures that are seen to impinge upon people's rights has emerged in Australia. The Law Council of Australia, for example, has repeatedly challenged Australia's anti-terrorism legislation.[12]

Opposition to counter-terrorism measures is based upon the view that people will feel insecure, even when they are protected from being physically harmed by members of terrorist groups, if they fear those who are in positions of political power. Those who conceive of security as human security view a capacity on the part of members of their political executive to arrest, interrogate, and incarcerate its citizens as a source of insecurity. They contend that members of political executives, even when they have been elected, constitute a much greater threat to security than terrorists. They also suggest that measures to counter terrorism that are biased against particular groups are more likely to incite violence and threats to security, rather than make people more secure. They also believe that greater accountability of the intelligence and police services to Parliament will help people to feel more secure.

Summary

Both conceptions of security make sense. One conception makes it possible for people to sacrifice rights for security, whereas the other one makes this impossible. Understanding both conceptions of security can help us to appreciate the different ways that terrorism can affect our rights. The *territorial* conception of security focuses upon the potential instability and disruption that terrorism can cause and the need for members of the political executive to do whatever it takes to maintain order. In this case, of course, maintaining control within a territory is more important than protecting rights. Those who conceive of security as human security highlight the fact that people who fear those who govern them are not secure. In this case, rights are regarded as essential for security.

The issue is a difficult one, but we must take up a position on the fundamental question of whether we must sacrifice our rights in order to be secure. Our positions on this issue are likely to reflect our personal values and ideas about what makes a society a 'good society'. Those of us who think that to feel secure we need to feel that our territory is being protected by members of political executives will accept the proposition that we cannot protect people's rights and provide for their security. Alternatively, those who believe that security relates to people's rights will claim that losing the protection of their rights makes people feel vulnerable and under threat from the members of their political executives.

> **QUESTION**
>
> What is the difference between human security and territorial security?

CONCLUSION

A decade ago, the Australian political landscape was similar to today, with one particular exception: the issue of terrorism. The attack on the World Trade Center buildings in New York and the bombing of a nightclub in Bali have forced security and defence into the forefront of issues for government and democracy in Australia. The Australian Security Intelligence Organisation (ASIO) and Australia's other intelligence arms, which once kept a very low profile, now actively and very publicly recruit analysts and intelligence officers in newspapers and universities. Television networks and newspapers, too, play their part in reminding us that the spectre of terrorism looms over us and poses a grave threat to our security.

After discussing the emergence of terrorism as an important issue for contemporary Australian politics, we discussed the proposition that we cannot protect people's rights without risking their security. This is both an important question that Australians will continue to confront and a way to open up issues that are significant for government and democracy in Australia. First, we sought to identify reasons to believe that rights must be sacrificed to security. Second, we discussed these reasons and commented upon their persuasiveness. Finally, we drew attention to the fact that those who accept that rights must be sacrificed to security and those who do not accept that this is possible, have different conceptions of security.

FURTHER READING

Introductory texts

Lutz, James M. & Brenda Lutz, 2004, *Global Terrorism*. London: Routledge.
Martin, Gus, 2006, *Understanding Terrorism: Challenges, Perspectives, and Issues*, 2nd edn, Sage Publications: Thousand Oaks.
Wilkinson, Paul, 1977, *Terrorism and the Liberal State*. London: Macmillan.

Specialist texts

Ayson, Robert & Desmond Ball, (eds), 2006, *Strategy and Security in the Asia Pacific*. Allen & Unwin: Crows Nest.

Chase, Alston, 2003, *Harvard and the Unabomber: The Education of an American Terrorist*. W.W. Norton: New York.

Curley, M. & Thomas, H., 2004, 'Human Security and Public Health in Southeast Asia: The SARS outbreak', *Australian Journal of International Affairs*, vol. 58, no. 1, pp. 17–32.

Dershowitz, Alan M., 2002, *Why Terrorism Works: Understanding the Threat, Responding to the Challenge*. Yale University Press: New Haven.

Downer, Alexander, 2005, 'Securing Australia's Interests: Australian Foreign Policy Priorities.' *Australian Journal of International Affairs*, vol. 59, no. 1, pp. 7–12.

Fitzpatrick, Joan, 2003, 'Speaking Law to Power: The War Against Terrorism and Human Rights.' *European Journal of International Law*, vol. 14, no. 2, pp. 241–64.

Greener-Barcham, Beth, K. & Manuhuia Barcham, 2006, 'Terrorism in the South Pacific? Thinking Critically about Approaches to Security in the Region.' [Paper presented at the Victoria University and New Zealand Police-hosted National Counter-Terrorism Capability Seminar, Wellington, 15–16 August 2005.] *Australian Journal of International Affairs*, vol. 60, no. 1, pp. 67–82.

Hertz, John, H., 1957, 'Rise and Demise of the Territorial State.' *World Politics*, vol. 9, no. 4, pp. 473–93.

Hocking, Jenny, 2003, ASIO, *Counter-Terrorism and the Threat to Democracy*, UNSW Press: Sydney.

Howard, Lawrence, (ed) 1992, *Terrorism: Roots, Impact, Responses*, Praeger: New York.

King, Gary & Christopher J.L. Murray, 2001–02, 'Rethinking Human Security.' *Political Science Quarterly*, vol. 116, no. 4, pp. 585–610.

Mathews, Jessica T., 1989, 'Redefining Security.' *Foreign Affairs*, vol. 68, no. 2, pp. 162–77.

McCulloch, J. and Tham, J-C., 2005, 'Secret state, Transparent Subject: The Australian Security Intelligence Organisation in the age of terror.' *Australian and New Zealand Journal of Criminology*, vol. 38, no. 3, pp. 400–15.

McAllister, Ian, 2005, *Representative Views: Mass and Elite Opinion on Australian Security*. Report prepared for the Australian Strategic Policy Institute, June 2005. Available at http://www.aspi.org.au/htmlver/21935_RepViews/_lib/pdf/ASPI_Arepresentative_views.pdf, last accessed 12 June 2008.

McMaster, Don, 2002, 'Asylum-Seekers and the Insecurity of a Nation.' *Australian Journal of International Affairs*, vol. 56, no. 2, pp. 279–90.

Michaelson, Christopher, 2005, 'Antiterrorism Legislation in Australia: A Proportionate Response to the Terrorist Threat.' *Studies in Conflict and Terrorism*, vol. 28, no. 4, pp. 321–39.

Smith, Paul J., (ed), 2005, *Terrorism and Violence in Southeast Asia: Transnational Challenges*. M.E. Sharpe: Armonk.

Thomas, N. Nicholas & W.T. Tow, 2002, 'The Utility of Human Security: Sovereignty and Humanitarian Intervention,' *Security Dialogue*, vol. 33, no. 2, pp.177-92.

Whittaker, David J., (ed.) 2001, *The Terrorism Reader*. Routledge: New York.

Williams, Clive, 2002, 'Australian Security Policy, Post-11 September,' *Australian Journal of International Affairs*, vol. 56, no. 1, pp. 13–21.

Web sites

Australian National Security: http://www.nationalsecurity.gov.au

Department of Foreign Affairs and Trade: http://www.dfat.gov.au/globalissues/terrorism.html

UN Action to Counter Terrorism: http://www.un.org/terrorism/terrorism-hr.html

Australian Security Policy Institute: http://www.aspi.org.au; http://www.indo.com/bali121002/index.html

Notes

1. See Smith (2005, pp. 981–1021) for details on the Bali Bombing.
2. For more on the Hilton Bombing, see http://www.abc.net.au/gnt/history/Transcripts/s1202891.htm
3. For details about the Dr Theodore Kaczynski (the so-called 'Unabomber'), see Chase (2003).
4. For further discussion of Timothy McVeigh, see 'A Covenant with Death' *The Economist*, 2001, vol. 359. no. 8221, p. 33; Crothers, Lane, 2002, 'The Cultural Foundations of the Modern Militia Movement,' *New Political Science*, vol. 24, no. 2, pp. 221–34; Gleick, Elizabeth, 1995, 'Who are they?' Time.com, 1 May. Available at http://www.time.com/time/magazine/article/0,9171,982868,00.html, last accessed 13 June 2008.
5. For details of terrorism in the UK, see Whittaker (2001, 89–107).
6. See Whittaker (2001, 125–138) and Martin (2006: 298–9) for details on terrorism in Spain.
7. See Lutz & Lutz (2004: 107–11) and Whittaker (2001, 41–53) for information on terrorism in the Middle East.
8. For details about terrorist activities in South America, see Lutz & Lutz (2004, 132–5) and Whittaker (2001, 165–82).
9. For a wide-ranging discussion of the proposition, see Dershowitz (2002, 166–222), Michaelsen (2005), Fitzpatrick (2003), and Wilkinson in Howard (1992, 155–66).
10. The concept of territorial security is elaborated upon in Hertz (1957), King & Murray (2001–02) and reflected in Downer (2005).
11. Further details on the concept of human security can be found in Thakur, Ramesh in Ayson & Ball (2006: 121–37), Curley & Thomas (2004), Mathews (1989) and Thomas & Tow (2002).
12. For examples of the Law Council of Australia's submission and correspondence on the matter, see Law Council of Australia, 2004, Submission to the Senate Legal and Constitutional Committee's inquiry into the Anti-Terrorism Bill (No. 2) 2004, 15th July, available at http://www.lawcouncil.asn.au/get/submissions/2399855020.pdf, last accessed 13 June 2008; Law Council of Australia, 2007, Review of the Power to Proscribe Organisations as Terrorist Organisations, 7th March, avaiable at http://www.lawcouncil.asn.au/get/submissions/2435648490.pdf, last accessed 13 June 2008.

Conclusion

An understanding of government and democracy in Australia must begin with an appreciation of the nature and role of those institutions that are central to providing overall coordination and direction for Australian society, as these institutions are at the very heart of government in Australia. To understand more about how these institutions function, we need to consider not only the rules laid down in the Constitution, but also the effects of the practices and informal institutions of representative democracy. Each of the institutions of government (Parliament, the political executive, the High Court, the Head of State, and the bureaucracy) are affected by federalism, the electoral system, parties, and pressure groups. A change to any of these elements of aspects of representative democracy would have profound implications for the institutions that are involved in governing this country. Of course, the reverse is also true with respect to parties and pressure groups, as their operation will be affected by their interaction with formal political institutions (they will also affect each other).

An understanding of the formal and informal institutions and practices of government and democracy in Australia necessitates, in our view, that the context within which they operate is taken into account. The news media and opinion polling and political marketing are significant aspects of that context. Globalisation is also an important contextual factor, though its importance may depend upon its ideological significance and not its actual effects. The factors discussed in this text are also not the only aspect of the context of government and democracy in Australia that deserve attention. The nature of the Australian economy, religion in Australia, and the international political environment are also important contextual factors that have been discussed in Part III.

Together, Parts I, II, and III cover most of the important features of government and democracy in Australia. But to have left the book there, in our view, would not do justice to government and democracy in Australia or to a book on politics. Politics is about issues. It is about resolving difficult problems that have no simple solution and it is about providing or finding direction for communities. Both democratic and representative democratic politics is about giving voice to and dealing with the different views and values of members of the community. By examining issues raised by Indigenous Australians, ethnic diversity, citizenship, environmental sustainability, and security and terrorism, we may gain a sense of the possibilities and limitations inherent in government and democracy in Australia.

The limitations encountered in the discussions of the issues dealt with in Part IV are particularly important, as they may represent reasons for reforming the institutions of Australian government. Any reform to these institutions will have important effects on the operation of parties and pressure groups. Dealing with the issues discussed in Part IV may also necessitate reform to aspects of the democratic system. Changes to electoral systems and to federalism itself may result in very different dynamics developing within Australian politics. These new dynamics may have profound consequences for the way that government and democracy in Australia work.

We are hopeful that the discussion arising from these issues will provoke and sustain an interest in the politics of the day, and the potential consequences of changes in procedure and style that have already occurred under a new government.

Bibliography

Abbott, Keith, 1996, *Pressure Groups and the Australian Federal Parliament*, Australian Government Publication Service: Canberra.

Abbott, Tony, 1998, 'Republic is More Trouble than it's Worth', in D. Lovell, I. McAllister, W. Maley & C. Kukathas (eds), *The Australian Political System*, 2nd edn, Longman: South Melbourne.

Adams, Phillip & Lee Burton, 1997, *Talkback: Emperors of Air*, Allen & Unwin: St Leonards.

Aitkin, Don, 2005, *What was it all for? The Reshaping of Australia*, Allen & Unwin: Crows Nest.

Aldred, Ken, Kevin Andrews & Paul Filing (eds), 1994, *The Heart of Liberalism*, Albury Papers: Mitcham.

Altman, Dennis, 2006, *51st State?*, Scribe Publications: Carlton North.

Altman, Jon & Melinda Hinkson (eds), 2007, *Coercive Reconciliation: Stabilise, Normalise, Exit Aboriginal Australia*, Arena Publications: North Carlton.

Anderson, Sarah & John Cavanagh, 2000, 'The Rise of Corporate Global Power', Institute for Policy Studies. http://www.tni.org/archives/cavanagh/top 200.pdf

Aplin, Graeme, 2000, 'Environmental Rationalism and Beyond: Toward a More Just Sharing of Power and Influence', *Australian Geographer*, vol. 31, no. 3, pp. 273–87.

Arendt, Hannah, 1958, *The Human Condition*, Chicago University Press: Chicago.

Argy, Fred, 1998, *Australia at the Crossroads: Radical Free Markets or a Progressive Liberalism?*, Allen & Unwin: St Leonards.

Arther, Bill, 1994, 'Cultural Autonomy, Economic Equity and Self-Determination within Nation-States: Australian Aborigines in Remote Regions', *Australian Aboriginal Studies*, no. 2, pp. 28–35.

Atkinson, Alan, 1993, *The Muddle-Headed Republic*, Oxford University Press: Melbourne.

Attwood, Bain & Andrew Markus, 2007, *The 1967 Referendum: Race, Power and the Australian Constitution*, 2nd edn, Aboriginal Studies Press: Canberra.

Australian Bureau of Statistics, 2007, *Australia's Environment: Issues and Trends* 4613.0, 4th edn, ABS: Belconnen.

Australian Bureau of Statistics, *Census 2006*.

Australian Bureau of Statistics & Australian Institute of Health and Welfare, 2001, *The Health and Welfare of Australia's Aboriginal and Torres Strait Islander Peoples*, Australian Bureau of Statistics: Canberra.

Australian Citizenship Council, 2000, *Australian Citizenship for a New Century: A Report by the Australian Citizenship Council*, Australian Citizenship Council: Canberra.

Australian Government, 2007, *Becoming an Australian Citizen*. Available at http://www.citizenship.gov.au/test/resource_booklet/citz-booklet-full-ver.pdf, last accessed 13 June 2008.

Ayson, Robert & Desmond Ball (eds), 2006, *Strategy and Security in the Asia Pacific*, Allen & Unwin: Crows Nest.

Bailey, Stephen J., 1995, *Public Sector Economics*, Macmillan: London.

Ball, Terence & Richard Dagger, 2006, *Political Ideologies and the Democratic Ideal*, Pearson Longman: New York.

Balough, Maggie, 1996, 'Changing Techniques: Asian Experiment May Alter the Way Journalists Measure Populace's Mood', *The Quill*, vol. 84, no. 1, pp. 20–3.

Barns, Greg, 2003, *What's Wrong with the Liberal Party?*, Cambridge University Press: Port Melbourne.

Barr, Trevor, 2000, *Newmedia.com.au: The Changing Face of Australia's Media and Communications*, Allen & Unwin: St Leonards.

Barry, John, 1996, 'Sustainability, Political Judgement and Citizenship: Connecting Green Politics and Democracy', in B. Doherty & M. de Geus (eds), *Democracy and Green Political Thought: Sustainability, Rights and Citizenship*, Routledge: New York.

Batainah, Heba & Walsh, Mary, 2008, 'From Multiculturalism to Citizenship', in C. Aulich and R. Wettenhall (eds), *Howard's Fourth Term*, University of New South Wales Press: Sydney.

Bates, J.N., 1998, 'The Future of Parliamentary Scrutiny of Delegated Legislation: Some Judicial Perspectives', *Statute Law Review*, vol. 19, no. 3, pp. 155–76.

Bean, Clive, 1997, 'Parties and Elections', in B. Galligan, I. McAllister & J. Ravenhill (eds), *New Developments in Australian Politics*, Macmillan: South Melbourne.

Bean, Phillip, 2002, *Drugs and Crime*, Willan Publishing: Devon.
Bell, Stephen, 1997, 'Globalisation, Neoliberalism and the Transformation of the Australian State', *Australian Journal of Political Science*, vol. 32, no. 3, pp. 345–67.
Bell, Stephen, 1998, 'Economic Restructuring in Australia: Policy Settlements, Models of Economic Development and Economic Rationalism', in P. Smyth & B. Cass (eds), *Contesting the Australian Way: States, Markets and Civil Society*, Cambridge University Press: Melbourne.
Benhabib, Seyla, 2002, *The Claims of Culture: Equality and Diversity in the Global Era*, Princeton University Press: Princeton.
Bennett, Scott, 2006, 'The politics of the Australian federal system', *Research Brief*, no. 4. Available at http://www.aph.gov.au/library/pubs/rb/2006-07/07rb04.pdf, last accessed 11 June 2008.
Bennett, Scott, 1989, *Aborigines and Political Power*, Allen & Unwin: Sydney.
Beresford, Quentin, 1998, 'Selling Democracy Short: Elections in the Age of the Market', *Current Affairs Bulletin*, vol. 74, no. 5, pp. 24–31.
Birrell, Robert, 1998, 'The Dynamics of Multiculturalism in Australia', in D. Lovell, I. McAllister, W. Maley & C. Kukathas (eds), *The Australian Political System*, 2nd edn, Longman: South Melbourne.
Blackshield, Tony, 1994, 'Reinterpreting the Constitution', in J. Brett, J. Gillespie & M. Goot (eds), *Developments in Australian Politics*, Macmillan: South Melbourne.
Blackshield, Tony, Michael Coper & George Williams (eds), 2001, *The Oxford Companion to the High Court*, Oxford University Press: South Melbourne.
Blundell, Richard & Ian Preston, 1998, 'Consumption Inequality and Income Uncertainty', *Quarterly Journal of Economics*, no. 113, pp. 603–38.
Bogdanor, Vernon, 1995, *The Monarchy and the Constitution*, Clarendon Press: Oxford.
Bolton, Geoffrey, 1998, 'Who Should be in Parliament?', *Legislative Studies*, vol. 12, no. 2, pp. 76–9.
Boreham, Paul, Geoffrey Stokes & Richard Hall, 2000, *The Politics of Australian Society*, Pearson Education: Frenchs Forest.
Borland, Jeff & Roger Wilkins, 1996, 'Earnings Inequality in Australia', *The Economic Record*, vol. 72, no. 216, pp. 7–23.
Botsman, Peter, 2000, *The Great Constitutional Swindle: A Citizen's View of the Australian Constitution*, Pluto Press: Annandale.
Bottomore, Thomas, 1971, *Elites and Society*, Penguin: Harmondsworth.
Bowman, Karlyn, 2001, 'Knowing the Public Mind', *Wilson Quarterly*, Autumn, pp. 90–8.

Bowman, Leo, 1994, 'How Journalists' Cultural Dispositions Affect News Selections', *Australian Journalism Review*, vol. 16, no. 2, pp. 25–30.
Bradburn, Norman & Seymour Sudman, 1988, *Polls and Surveys: Understanding What They Tell Us*, Jossey-Bass Publishers: San Francisco.
Brady, Veronica, 1992, *Towards Reconciliation: National Council for Reconciliation*, Indian Ocean Centre for Peace Studies: Nedlands.
Bray, John, 1997, 'A Web of Influence', *The World Today*, August/September, pp. 206–8.
Brennan, Deborah, 1994, 'Social Policy', in J. Brett, J. Gillespie & M. Goot (eds), *Developments in Australian Politics*, Macmillan: South Melbourne.
Brennan, Frank, 1989, 'Is a Bipartisan Approach Possible?', *Legal Service Bulletin*, vol. 14, no. 2, pp. 66–8.
Brennan, Geoffrey & Alan Hamlin, 1998, 'Rationalising Parliamentary Systems', in D. Lovell, I. McAllister, W. Maley & C. Kukathas (eds), *The Australian Political System*, 2nd edn, Longman: South Melbourne.
Brett, Judith, 2003, *Australian Liberals and the Moral Middle Class: From Alfred Deakin to John Howard*, Cambridge University Press: Port Melbourne.
Brett, Judith, 2005, 'Relaxed and Comfortable: The Liberal Party's Australia', *Quarterly Essay*, 19, pp. 1–80.
Brett, Judith, James Gillespie & Murray Goot (eds), 1994, *Developments in Australian Politics*, Macmillan: Melbourne.
Bridgeman, Peter & Glyn Davis, 1998, *Australian Policy Handbook*, Allen & Unwin: St Leonards.
Brock, Peggy, 2001, 'Aboriginal Women, Politics and Land', in P. Brock (ed.), *Words and Silences: Aboriginal Women, Politics and Land*, Allen & Unwin: Crows Nest.
Broome, Richard, 1996, 'Historians, Aborigines and Australia: Writing the National Past', in B. Attwood (ed.), *In the Age of Mabo: History, Aborigines and Australia*, Allen & Unwin: St Leonards.
Brunton, Ron, 1998, *Betraying the Victims: The Stolen Generation Report*, Institute for Public Affairs: Melbourne.
Brunton, Ron, 1998, 'The Human Wrongs of Indigenous Rights', in D. Lovell, I. McAllister, W. Maley & C. Kukathas (eds), *The Australian Political System*, 2nd edn, Longman: South Melbourne.
Bullivant, Brian, 1998, 'The Pluralist Crises Facing Australia', in D. Lovell, I. McAllister, W. Maley & C. Kukathas (eds), *The Australian Political System*, 2nd edn, Longman: South Melbourne.
Burgmann, Meredith, 1983, 'Aborigines: The Struggle Continues', in R. Lucy (ed.), *The Pieces of Politics*, 3rd edn, Macmillan: South Melbourne.

Burgmann, Verity, 2003, *Power, Profit and Protest: Australian Social Movements and Globalisation*, Allen & Unwin: Crows Nest.

Burmester, Henry, 1989, 'Federalism, the State and International Affairs: A Legal Perspective', in B. Galligan (ed.), *Australian Federalism*, Longman Cheshire: Melbourne.

Butt, Peter, Robert Eagleson & Patricia Lane, 2001, *Mabo, Wik and Native Title*, 4th edn, Federation Press: Leichhardt.

Capling, Ann & Brian Galligan, 1992, *Beyond the Protective State: The Political Economy of Australia's Manufacturing Industry Policy*, Cambridge University Press: Cambridge.

Carroll, Maurice, 2000, 'Does the Reliance of the News Media on Polls Distort Reporting? No: Pollsters Have a Responsibility to Seek Truth, Gather Information and Report the Results', *Insight*, December 25, pp. 41–3.

Carter, John, 1993, *Parliamentary Government in Australia: A Students' Guide to the Commonwealth Parliament*, 2nd edn, Parliamentary Education Office: Canberra.

Carter, Neil, 2006, *The Politics of the Environment. Ideas, Activism, Policy*, 2nd edn, Cambridge University Press

Cass, Deborah, 1998, 'Through the Looking Glass: The High Court and the Right to Political Speech', in A. Thacker (ed.), *Women and the Law: Judicial Attitudes as They Impact on Women*: Proceedings of a Conference Held on 9–10 June, 1993 at Melbourne, Deakin University Press: Geelong.

Castles, Stephen, Bill Cope, Mary Kalantzis & Michael Morrissey, 1992, *Mistaken Identity: Multiculturalism and the Demise of Nationalism in Australia*, Pluto Press: Sydney.

Cerny, Phillip, 1996, 'What Next for the State', in E. Kofman & G. Youngs (eds), *Globalisation Theory and Practice*, Printer: London.

Chaples, Ernie, 1997, 'The Australian Voters', in R. Smith (ed.), *Politics in Australia*, Allen & Unwin: St Leonards.

Chase, Alston, 2003, *Harvard and the Unabomber: The Education of an American Terrorist*, W.W. Norton: New York.

Chin, Christine & James Mittelman, 1997, 'Conceptualising Resistance to Globalisation', *New Political Economy*, vol. 2, no. 1, pp. 25–37.

Chishti, Muhamad, W.J. Martin & Jack Jacoby, 1997, *Information Technology Enabled Organisational Change: A Survey of Australian Practices*, RMIT Business: Melbourne.

Christoff, Peter, 1994, 'Environmental Politics', in J. Brett, J. Gillespie & M. Goot (eds), *Developments in Australian Politics*, Macmillan: South Melbourne.

Christoff, Peter, 1995, *Exploring Ecological Modernisation*, Paper Delivered at APSA Conference, Melbourne, September, pp. 2–21.

Clancy, Mike, 2007, *Howard's Seduction of Australia: Where to now?* Fast Books: Watsons Bay.
Coaldrake, Peter, 1992, 'Public Servants Serving the Public?: The Drive For Regionalism in the Queensland Public Sector', *Canberra Bulletin of Public Administration*, no. 70, October, pp. 102–4.
Coleman, Peter, 1985, 'Australia's Leftists Clip Hawke's Wings', *The Wall Street Journal*, Eastern edition, 11 March, p. 1.
Conley, Tom, 2001, 'The Domestic Politics of Globalisation', *Australian Journal of Political Science*, vol. 36, no. 2, pp. 223–46.
Connell, D, 2007, *Water Politics in the Murray-Darling Basin*, Federation Press: Sydney.
Considine, Mark, 1992, 'Alternatives to Hierarchy: The Role and Performance of Lateral Structures Inside Bureaucracy', *Australian Journal of Public Administration*, vol. 51, no. 3, pp. 309–20.
Considine, Mark, 1994, *Public Policy: A Critical Approach*, Macmillan: South Melbourne.
Considine, Mark, 1996, 'Market Bureaucracy: The Changing Form of Social Administration in Australia', in A. Farrar & J. Inglis (eds), *Keeping it Together: State and Civil Society in Australia*, Pluto Press: Leichhardt.
Cook, Ian, 1999, *Liberalism in Australia*, Oxford University Press: Melbourne.
Coombs, H.C., 1990, *The Return of Scarcity: Strategies for an Economic Future*, Cambridge University Press: Cambridge.
Copley, Gregory R., Andrew Pickford & Barry Patterson, 2007, *Australia 2050: An Examination of Australia's Condition*, Sid Harta Publishers: Hartwell.
Corner, John, 1996, 'Election Campaigning: The New Marketing of Politics', *Parliamentary Affairs*, vol. 49, no. 2, pp. 354–6.
Costar, Brian, 2006, 'Electoral Systems', in D. Woodward, A. Parkin & J. Summers (eds), *Government, Politics, Power and Policy in Australia*, 5th edn, Longman: South Melbourne.
Cothers, Lane 2002, 'The cultural foundations of the modern militia movement', *New Political Science*, vol. 24, no. 2, pp. 221–34.
—— 2001, 'A covenant with death', *The Economist*, no. 359 (8221): pp. 33–4.
Cox, Eva, 2000, 'Creating a more Civil Society: Community Level Indicators of Social Capital', *Just Policy*, 19–20 September, pp. 100–7.
Craig, John, 1993, *Australian Politics: A Source Book*, 2nd edn, Harcourt Brace: Sydney.
Cranston, Ross, 1987, *Law, Government and Public Policy*, Oxford University Press: Melbourne.
Craven, Gregory, 1986, *Secession: The Ultimate States Right*, Melbourne University Press: Carlton.

Craven, Gregory, 1988, 'Would the Abolition of the States be an Alteration of the Constitution under Section 128?', *Federal Law Review*, vol. 18, no. 12, pp. 85–121.
Craven, Gregory, 1999, 'Judicial Activism in the High Court—A Response to John Toohey', *University of Western Australia Law Review*, vol. 28, no. 2, July, pp. 214–24.
Crick, Bernard, 1986, *In Defence of Politics*, 2nd edn, Penguin: Ringwood.
Crisp, L.F., 1965, *Australian National Government*, Longman Cheshire: Australia, pp. 1–39.
Cullen, Peter, 1998, 'Lobbying Parliamentarians: Does it Make a Difference?', in D. Lovell, I. McAllister, W. Maley & C. Kukathas (eds), *The Australian Political System*, 2nd edn, Longman: South Melbourne.
Cunneen, Chris, 1990, 'Aborigines and Law and Order Regimes', *Journal for Social Justice Studies*, Special Editions Series, Contemporary Race Relations, vol. 3, pp. 37–50.
Cunningham, Helen (ed.), 1997, *Fragile Bastion: Judicial Independence in the Nineties and Beyond*, Judicial Commission of New South Wales: Sydney.
Cunningham, Stewart & Terry Flew, 1997, 'Media Policy', in D. Woodward, A. Parkin & J. Summers (eds), *Government, Politics, Power and Policy in Australia*, 5th edn, Longman: South Melbourne.
Curley, Melissa & Nicholas Thomas, 2004, 'Human Security and Public Health in Southeast Asia: The SARS Outbreak,' *Australian Journal of International Affairs*, vol. 58, no. 1, pp. 17–32.
Danley, John, 1991, 'Liberalism, Aboriginal Rights, and Cultural Minorities', *Philosophy and Public Affairs*, vol. 20, no. 2, pp.168–85.
Daverall, Kate, Rebecca Huntley, Penny Sharpe & Jo Tilly, 2000, *Party Girls: Labor Women Now*, Pluto Press: Annandale.
Davidson, Alastair, 1997, *From Subject to Citizen: Australian Citizenship in the Twentieth Century*, Cambridge University Press: Melbourne.
Davis, Glyn, John Wanna, John Warhurst & Patrick Weller, 1993, *Public Policy in Australia*, 2nd edn, Allen & Unwin: Sydney.
Davis, Glyn, 1997a, 'The Core Executive', in B. Galligan, I. McAllister & J. Ravenhill (eds), *New Developments in Australian Politics*, Macmillan: South Melbourne.
Davis, Glyn, 1997b, 'Executive Government: Cabinet and the Prime Minister', in D. Woodward, A. Parkin & J. Summers (eds), *Government, Politics, Power and Policy in Australia*, 5th edn, Longman: South Melbourne.
Dershowitz, Alan M., 2002, *Why Terrorism Works: Understanding the Threat, Responding to the Challenge*, Yale University Press: New Haven.
Dobson, Andrew, 1994, 'Environmentalism', in M. Foley (ed.), *Ideas That Shape Politics*, Manchester University Press: Manchester.
Dobson, Andrew, 2007, *Green political thought*, 4th edn, Routledge: London.

Dobson, Andrew & Paul Lucardie (eds), 1993, *The Politics of Nature: Explorations in Green Political Theory*, Routledge: London.

Dolby, Nadine, 2000, 'Race, Nation, State: Multiculturalism in Australia', *Arena Magazine*, vol. 45, February–March, pp. 48–51.

Dovers, Stephen, 2006, *Environment and Sustainability Policy*, The Federation Press: Sydney.

Downer, A., 2005, 'Securing Australia's Interests: Australian Foreign Policy Priorities', *Australian Journal of International Affairs*, vol. 59, no. 1, pp. 7–12.

Doyle, John, 1998, 'Do Judges Make Policy? Should They?', *Australian Journal of Public Policy*, vol. 57, no. 1, pp. 89–98.

Doyle, Timothy & Aynsley Kellow, 1995, *Environmental Politics and Policy Making in Australia*, Macmillan: South Melbourne.

Dryzek, John, 2000, *Deliberative Democracy and Beyond: Liberals, Critics, Contestations*, Oxford University Press: Oxford.

du Gay, Paul, 2000, *In Praise of Bureaucracy: Weber, Organisation, Ethics*, Sage: London.

Dudgeon, Patricia & Darlene Oxenham, 1990, *The Complexity of Aboriginal Diversity*, University of Queensland: St Lucia.

Eckersley, Robyn, 1992, *Environmentalism and Political Theory: Toward an Ecocentric Approach*, UCL Press: London.

Eckersley, Robyn (ed.), 1995, *Markets, the State and the Environment: Towards Integration*, Macmillan: South Melbourne.

Economou, Nick, 1998, 'Interest Groups and Governments: The Case of Environmental Policy-making', in D. Lovell, I. McAllister, W. Maley & C. Kukathas (eds), *The Australian Political System*, 2nd edn, Longman: South Melbourne.

Edmondson, Brad, 1986, 'The Political Sell', *American Demographics*, vol. 8, no.11, pp. 27–32.

Eggerking, Kitty, 1996, 'Introducing the Media and Indigenous Australians Project', *Australian Journalism Review*, vol. 18, no. 1, pp. 21–4.

Elder, Catriona, 2007, *Being Australian: Narratives of National Identity*, Allen & Unwin: Crows Nest.

Emy, Hugh V., 1978, *The Politics of Australian Democracy: Fundamentals in Dispute*, 2nd edn, Macmillan: South Melbourne.

Emy, Hugh, 1993, *Remaking Australia: The State, the Market and Australia's Future*, Allen & Unwin: St Leonards.

Emy, Hugh, 1997, 'The Mandate and Responsible Government', *Australian Journal of Political Science*, vol. 32, no. 1, pp. 65–78.

Emy, Hugh, 1998, 'States, Markets and the Global Dimension: An Overview of Certain Issues in Political Economy', in P. Smyth & B. Cass (eds), *Contesting the Australian Way: States, Markets and Civil Society*, Cambridge University Press: Melbourne.

Emy, Hugh V. & Owen E. Hughes, 1991, *Australian Politics: Realities in Conflict*, 2nd edn, Macmillan: South Melbourne.

Evans, Harry, 1998, 'Can Parliament be Reformed?', in D. Lovell, I. McAllister, W. Maley & C. Kukathas (eds), *The Australian Political System*, 2nd edn, Longman: South Melbourne.

Evans, Harry, 1999, 'The Cost of the Commonwealth Parliament: Amalgamations, Values and Comparisons', *Australian Journal of Public Administration*, vol. 58, no. 1, pp. 106–11.

Evans, Tim, 2006, *Compulsory Voting in Australia*. Available at http://www.aec.gov.au/pdf/voting/compulsory_voting.pdf, last accessed 12 June 2008.

Everard, Jerry, 2000, *Virtual States: The Internet and the Boundaries of the Nation State*. Routledge: London.

Ewart, Jacqui, 1997, 'Journalists, Readership and Writing', *Australian Studies in Journalism*, no. 6, pp. 83–103.

Farr, Ian, 1992, 'Regional Coordination at Local Level', *Canberra Bulletin of Public Administration*, no. 70, October, pp. 83–7.

Farrell, David, 1998, 'The Study of Electoral Systems', in D. Lovell, I. McAllister, W. Maley & C. Kukathas (eds), 1998, *The Australian Political System*, 2nd edn, Longman: South Melbourne.

Faulkner, John & Stuart Macintyre, 2001, *True Believers: The Story of the Federal Parliamentary Labor Party*, Allen & Unwin: Crows Nest.

Faulks, Keith, 2000, *Citizenship*, Routledge: London & New York.

Feldman, David L., Jean H. Peretz & Barbara D. Jendrucko, 1994, 'Policy Gridlock in Waste Management: Balancing Federal and State Concerns', *Policy Studies Journal*, vol. 22, no. 4, pp. 589–604.

Fenna, Alan, 1998, *Introduction to Australian Public Policy*, Longman: South Melbourne.

Fenna, Alan, 2001, *Essentials of Australian Government*, Tertiary Press: Croydon.

Fitzpatrick, Joan, 2003, 'Speaking Law to Power: The War against Terrorism and Human Rights', *European Journal of International Law*, vol. 14, no. 2, pp. 241–64.

Fletcher, Christine, 1992, *Aboriginal Politics: Intergovernmental Relations*, Melbourne University Press: Carlton.

Fletcher, Christine (ed.), 1994, *Aboriginal Self-Determination in Australia*, Aboriginal Studies Press for the Australian Institute of Aboriginal and Islander Studies: Canberra.

Fletcher, Christine, 1998, 'Rediscovering Australian Federalism by Resurrecting Old Ideas', in D. Lovell, I. McAllister, W. Maley & C. Kukathas (eds), 1998, *The Australian Political System*, 2nd edn, Longman: South Melbourne.

Fletcher, Don & Rosemary Whip, 2000, 'One Nation and the Failure of Political Leadership', in Michael Leach, Geoff Stokes & Ian Ward (eds), *The Rise and Fall of One Nation*, University of Queensland Press: St Lucia.

Fletcher, Winston, 1997, 'Marketing is not a Johnny Come Lately to Politics', *Marketing*, April 17, p. 5.

Flint, David, 2001, *How News is Made in Australia*, Australian Broadcasting Authority Conference, Radio Television and the New Media, 3–4 May: Canberra.

Forde, Susan, 1997, 'Characteristics and Values of Alternative Press Journalists', *Australian Studies in Journalism*, no. 6, pp. 104–26.

Frankel, Boris, 2001, *When the Boat Comes In: Transforming Australia in the Age of Globalisation*, Pluto Press: Annandale.

Frankovic, Kathleen, 1998, 'Public Opinion and Polling', in D. Graber, D. McQuail & P. Norris (eds), *The Politics of News, The News of Politics*, CQ Press: Washington DC.

Gadir, S., 1982, 'Media Agenda Setting in Australia: The Rise and Fall of Public Issues,' *Media Information Australia*, no. 26, November, pp. 13–23.

Gaebler, Ted, 1996, 'Reinventing Government', in P. Weller & G. Davis (eds), *New Ideas, Better Government*, Allen & Unwin: St Leonards.

Galligan, Brian, 1987, *Politics of the High Court*, University of Queensland Press: St Lucia.

Galligan, Brian (ed.), 1989, *Australian Federalism*, Longman Cheshire: Melbourne.

Galligan, Brian, 1989, 'Federal Theory and Australian Federalism: A Political Science Perspective' in B. Galligan (ed.), *Australian Federalism*, Longman Cheshire: Melbourne.

Galligan, Brian, 1993, 'Federalism and Policy Making', in A. Hede & S. Prasser (eds), *Policy Making in Volatile Times*, Hale and Iremonger: Sydney.

Galligan, Brian, 1995, *A Federal Republic: Australia's Constitutional System of Government*, Cambridge University Press: Melbourne.

Galligan, Brian & Winsome Roberts, 2004, *Australian Citizenship*, Melbourne University Press: Carlton, Victoria.

Galligan, Brian, Winsome Roberts & Gabriella Trifiletti, 2001, *Australians and Globalisation: The Experience of Two Centuries*, Cambridge University Press: Oakleigh.

Gallup, George, 1940, *The Pulse of Democracy*, Simon & Schuster: New York.

Gallup, George, 1944, *A Guide to Public Opinion Polls*, Princeton University Press: Princeton.

Gawiser, Sheldon & G. Evans Witt, 1994, *A Journalist's Guide to Public Opinion Polls*, Praeger: Westport.

Gibbs, Harry, 1987, 'The Separation of Powers: A Comparison. The Legislative, Executive and Judicial Arms of Government and Powers Invested in Them by the Constitution', *Federal Law Review*, vol. 17, no. 3, pp. 151–61.

Gilbert, Kevin, 1993, *Aboriginal Sovereignty: Justice, the Law and Land* (includes draft treaty), 3rd edn, Burrambinga Books: Canberra.

Gilding, Michael, 2006, 'Class and Elite Analysis,' in A. Parkin, J. Summers & D. Woodward (eds), *Government, Politics, Power and Policy in Australia*, 8th edn, Pearson Education: Frenchs Forest.

Gillespie, Alexander & William Burns (eds), 2000, *Climate Change in the South Pacific: Impacts and Responses in Australia, New Zealand, and Small Island States*, Kluwer Academic Publishers: Dordrecht.

Gillespie, James, 1994, 'New Federalism', in J. Brett, J. Gillespie & M. Goot (eds), *Developments in Australian Politics*, Macmillan: South Melbourne.

Gleik, Elizabeth, 1995, 'Who are they?' *Time.com*, 1 May. Available at http://www.time.com/time/magazine/article/0,9171,982868,00.html, last accessed 13 June 2008.

Goodall, Heather, 1992, '"The Whole Truth and Nothing But…": Some Intersections of Western Law, Aboriginal History and Community Memory', in B. Attwood & J. Arnold (eds), *Power, Knowledge and Aborigines*, La Trobe University Press (in association with the National Centre for Australian Studies, Monash University): Bundoora.

Goodin, Robert, 1992, *Green Political Theory*, Polity Press: Cambridge.

Goot, Murray, 1988, 'Trust the Polls', in I. McAllister & J. Warhurst (eds), *Australia Votes: The 1987 Federal Election*, Longman Cheshire: Melbourne.

Goot, Murray, 1993, 'Polls as Science, Polls as Spin: Mabo and the Miners', *Australian Quarterly*, vol. 65, no. 4, pp. 133–56.

Goot, Murray, 1994, 'Class Voting, Issue Voting and Electoral Volatility', in J. Brett, J. Gillespie & M. Goot, (eds), 1994, *Developments in Australian Politics*, Macmillan: Melbourne.

Goot, Murray, 1996, 'Engendering the Gap: The Polls, the Press and the NSW Premier', *Australian Studies in Journalism*, vol. 5, pp. 17–42.

Goot, Murray, 1998, 'Australia's "Stolen Children": Which Poll Would a Poll-Following Prime Minister Have Followed?', *International Journal of Public Opinion Research*, vol. 10, issue 4, pp. 349–64.

Goot, Murray & Tim Rouse, 2007, *Divided Nation: Indigenous Affairs and the Imagined Public*, Melbourne University Publishing: Melbourne.

Gordon, Michael & Georgina Windsor, 1997, 'Wik Made Simple: A User's Guide', *The Weekend Australian*, Saturday, 22 November, p. 26.

Gow, David John, 1990, 'Economic Voting and Postmaterialist Values', in C. Bean, I. McAllister & J. Warhurst (eds), *The Greening of Australian Politics: The 1990 Federal Election*, Longman Cheshire: Melbourne.

Graber, Doris, Denis McQuail & Pippa Norris, 1998, 'Introduction: Political Communication in a Democracy', in D. Graber, D. McQuail & P. Norris (eds), *The Politics of News, The News of Politics*, CQ Press: Washington DC.
Grattan, Michelle (ed.), 2000, *Australian Prime Ministers*, New Holland: Frenchs Forest.
Grattan, Michelle, 2005, 'Accept Australian Values or Get Out', *The Age*, 25 August.
Gray, Gary, 1998, 'The Political Climate and Election Campaigning', in D. Lovell, I. McAllister, W. Maley & C. Kukathas (eds), 1998, *The Australian Political System*, 2nd edn, Longman: South Melbourne.
Gray, Geoffrey & Christine Winter (eds), 1997, *The Resurgence of Racism: Howard, Hanson and the Race Debate*, Department of History, Monash University: Clayton.
Gray, John, 1993, *Beyond the New Right: Markets, Government and the Common Environment*, Routledge: London.
Greenbaum, Thomas L., 2000, *Moderating Focus Groups: A Practical Guide for Group Facilitation*, Sage: Thousand Oaks.
Greener-Barcham, Beth & Manahuia Barcham, 2006, 'Terrorism in the South Pacific? Thinking Critically about Approaches to Security in the Region', Paper presented at the Victoria University and New Zealand Police-hosted National Counter-Terrorism Capability Seminar, Wellington, 15–16 August 2005, *Australian Journal of International Affairs*, vol. 60, no. 1, pp. 67–82.
Griffiths, Martin & Terry O'Callaghan, 2002, *International Relations: The Key Concepts*, Routledge: London.
Grosz, Elizabeth, 2002, 'A Politics of Imperceptibility: A Response to "Anti-Racism, Multiculturalism and the Ethics of Identification"', *Philosophy and Social Criticism*, vol. 28, no. 4, pp. 663–72.
Gruen, Fred & Michelle Grattan, 1998, 'Managing the Pressure Groups', in D. Lovell, I. McAllister, W. Maley & C. Kukathas (eds), *The Australian Political System*, 2nd edn, Longman: South Melbourne.
Hagan, Stephanie & Graham Maddox, 1984, 'The Australian Democrats and the Two-Party System', *The Australian Quarterly*, vol. 56, no. 1, pp. 30–40.
Hague, Rod & Martin Harrop, 2004, 'Constitutions and the Legal Framework,' in *Comparative Government and Politics*, Palgrave Macmillan: Houndmills.
Halliday, Fred, 1994, *Rethinking International Relations*, Macmillan: Basingstoke.
Hamel, Jacques, 2001, 'The Focus Group Method and Contemporary French Sociology', *Journal of Sociology*, vol. 37, no. 4, pp. 341–53.
Hamer, David, 1994, *Can Responsible Government Survive in Australia?*, Centre for Research in Public Sector Management, University of Canberra: Belconnen.
Hamer, David, 2004, *Can Responsible Government Survive in Australia*, 2nd edn, Centre for Research in Public Sector Management, University of Canberra: Belconnen.

Hamilton, Clive, 2007, *Scorcher: The Dirty Politics of Climate Change*, Black Inc. Agenda: Melbourne.

Hamilton, Clive & Sarah Maddison, 2007, *Silencing Dissent: How the Australian Government is Controlling Public Opinion and Stifling Debate*, Allen & Unwin: Crows Nest.

Hanks, Peter, 1984, 'Aborigines and Government: The Developing Framework', in P. Hanks & B. Keon-Cohen (eds), *Aborigines and the Law: Essays in Memory of Elizabeth Eggleston*, Allen & Unwin: Sydney.

Hannay, Alastair, 2005, *On the Public*, Routledge: London & New York.

Hardin, Garrett, 1968, 'The Tragedy of the Commons', *Science*, vol. 162, no. 3859, pp. 1243–8.

Harris, C.P., 1992, 'Regionalism and Economic Development: Propping Up or Strategic Choice—1', *Canberra Bulletin of Public Administration*, no. 70, October, pp. 91–8.

Harrison, Peter, 1999, 'Subduing the Earth: Genesis 1, Early Modern Science, and the Exploitation of Nature', *The Journal of Religion*, vol. 79, no. 1, pp. 86–99.

Hartcher, Peter, 2007, 'Bipolar Nation: How to Win the 2007 Election', *Quarterly Essay*, 25, pp. 1–60.

Hartley, Dean & Margaret Melrose, 1999, *Poverty, Riches and Social Citizenship*, Macmillan: Basingstoke.

Haward, Marcus, 1997, 'Parliament', in R. Smith (ed.), *Politics in Australia*, Allen & Unwin: St Leonards.

Hawker, Geoffrey, 1994, 'Executive Government' in J. Brett, J. Gillespie & M. Goot (eds), *Developments in Australian Politics*, Macmillan: South Melbourne.

Hay, Peter, 2002, *Main Currents in Western Environmental Thought*, UNSW Press: Sydney.

Hayden, Bill, 1998, 'End of Ideology Will Lead to More Pragmatic Age', in D. Lovell, I. McAllister, W. Maley & C. Kukathas (eds), *The Australian Political System*, 2nd edn, Longman: South Melbourne.

Head, Brian, 1989, 'Federalism, the State and Economic Policy', in B. Galligan (ed.), *Australian Federalism*, Longman Cheshire: Melbourne.

Head, Brian W., 2007, 'Community Engagement: Participation on Whose Terms?', *Australian Journal of Political Science*, vol. 42, no. 3, pp. 441–54.

Healey, Justin (ed.), 2002, *Aboriginal Land Rights*, Spinney Press: Rozelle.

Heith, Diane, 2000, 'The Polls: Polling for a Defence: The White House Public Opinion Apparatus and the Clinton Impeachment', *Presidential Studies Quarterly*, vol. 30, no. 4, pp. 783–90.

Held, David, 1989, *Political Theory and the Modern State*, Polity Press: Oxford.

Held, David, Anthony McGrew, David Goldblatt & Jonathan Perraton, 1999, *Global Transformations: Politics, Economics and Culture*, Polity Press: Cambridge.

Henderson, Gerard, 1994, *Menzies' Child: The Liberal Party of Australia 1944–1994*, Allen & Unwin: St Leonards.

Henningham, John, 1996, 'Journalists' Perceptions of Newspaper Quality', *Australian Journalism Review*, vol. 18, no. 1, pp. 13–19.

Henningham, John, 1998, 'The Australian Journalist', in M. Breen (ed.), *Journalism: Theory and Practice*, Macleay Press: Paddington.

Henry, Nicholas, 1995, *Public Administration and Public Affairs*, Prentice Hall: Eaglewood Cliffs.

Hertz, John H., 1957, 'Rise and Demise of the Territorial State', *World Politics*, vol. 9, no. 4, pp. 473–93.

Heywood, Andrew, 2002, 'Constitutions, the Law and Judiciaries,' in *Politics*, 2nd edn, Palgrave: Basingstoke.

Heywood, Andrew, 2007, *Political Ideologies: An Introduction*, 4th edn, Palgrave: Basingstoke.

Hickey, Jennifer, 2000, 'Danger: Poll Ahead', *Insight*, 11 September, pp. 10–12.

Hill, Lisa, 2002, 'On the Reasonableness of Compelling Citizens to "Vote": The Australian Case', *Political Studies*, vol. 50, no. 1, pp. 80–102.

Hinich, Melvin & Michael Munger, 1997, *Analytical Politics*, Cambridge University Press: Cambridge.

Hirst, Paul & Grahame Thompson, 1999, *Globalization in Question: The International Economy and the Possibilities of Governance*, 2nd edn, Polity Press: Cambridge.

Hjerm, Mikael, 2000, 'Multiculturalism Reassessed', *Citizenship Studies*, vol. 4, no. 3, pp. 357–77.

Hobbes, Thomas, 1985 [1651], *Leviathan*, Penguin Books: London.

Hocking, Jenny, 2003, *ASIO, Counter-Terrorism and the Threat to Democracy*, UNSW Press: Sydney.

Hogan, Michael, 1981, 'Separation of Church and State: Section 116 of the Australian Constitution', *Australian Quarterly*, vol. 53, no. 2, pp. 214–28.

Hogan, Michael, 1997, 'The Structures of Inequality', in R. Smith (ed.), *Politics in Australia*, Allen & Unwin: St Leonards.

Holcomb, John & Buie Seawell, 2001, 'Weighing Public Perception', *Quill Magazine*, April, pp. 13–15.

Hollander, Robyn & Patapan, Haig, 2007, 'Pragmatic Federalism: Australian Federalism from Hawke to Howard', *Australian Journal of Public Administration*, vol. 66, no. 3, pp. 280–97.

Howard, Lawrence (ed.), 1992, *Terrorism: Roots, Impact, Responses*, Praeger: New York.

Howe, Brian, 2007, *Weighing Up Australian Values*, University of New South Wales Press: Sydney.

Hudson, Wayne & John Kane (eds), 2000, *Rethinking Australian Citizenship*, Cambridge University Press: Cambridge.

Hughes, Owen, 1998a, *Australian Politics*, 3rd edn, Macmillan Education: South Yarra.

Hughes, Owen, 1998b, *Public Management & Administration: An Introduction*, 2nd edn, Macmillan Education: South Yarra.

Hughes, Robert Allan & Geoffrey Leane, 2001, *Australian Legal Institutions: Principles, Structure and Organisation*, FT Law and Tax: South Melbourne.

Hunter, Rosemary, 1999, 'Equality and Inequality in Australia', in D. Glover & G. Patmore (eds), *New Voices for Social Democracy: Labour Essays 1999–2000*, Pluto Press: Melbourne.

Hurrell, Andrew & Benedict Kingsley (eds), 1992, *The International Politics of the Environment: Action, Interests and Institutions*, Clarendon Press: Oxford.

Ingram, David, 2004, *Rights, Democracy, and Fulfillment in the Era of Identity Politics: Principled Compromises in a Compromised World*, Rowman & Littlefield Publishers: Maryland.

Ivison, Duncan, Paul Patton & Will Sanders (eds), 2000, *Political Theory and the Rights of Indigenous Peoples*, Cambridge University Press: Melbourne.

Jackman, Simon, 1998, 'Pauline Hanson, the Mainstream, and Political Elites: The Place of Race in Australian Political Ideology', *Australian Journal of Political Science*, vol. 22, no. 2, pp. 167–86.

Jackson, Michael, 1997, 'Democratic Theory and Practice', in R. Smith (ed.), *Politics in Australia*, Allen & Unwin: St Leonards.

Jaensch, Dean, 1992, *The Politics of Australia*, Macmillan: South Melbourne.

Jaensch, Dean, 1994, *Parliament, Parties and People: Australian Politics Today*, 2nd edn, Longman Cheshire: Melbourne.

Jaensch, Dean, 1995, *Election!: How and Why Australia Votes*, Allen & Unwin: St Leonards.

Jaensch, Dean, 1997, 'The Australian Constitution,' *The Politics of Australia*, Macmillan Education: South Yarra.

Jaensch, Dean & David Scott Mathieson, 1998, *A Plague on Both Your Houses: Minor Parties in Australia*, Allen & Unwin: St Leonards.

Jamrozik, Adam, 1991, *Class, Inequality and the State: Social Policy and the New Middle Class*, Macmillan: South Melbourne.

Jayasuriya, Laksiri & Kee Poo Kong, 1999, *The Asianisation of Australia?: Some Facts about the Myths*, Melbourne University Press: Carlton.

Jensen-Lee, Catherine, 2001, 'The Future of Environmental Issues on the Mainstream Political Agenda', *Australian Journal of Social Issues*, vol. 36, no. 2, pp. 139–51.

Johnston, Carla, 1998, *Global News Access: The Impact of New Communication Technologies*, Praeger: Westport.

Jones, Frank L., 1983, 'Sources of Gender Inequality in Income: What the Australian Census Says', *Social Forces*, vol. 62, no. 1, pp. 134–52.

Jun, Jong S., 1986, *Public Administration: Design and Problem Solving*, Macmillan: New York.

Jupp, James, 1993, 'Perspectives on the Politics of Immigration', in J. Jupp & M. Kabala (eds), *The Politics of Australian Immigration*, Australian Government Publishing Service: Canberra.

Jupp, James, 1996, 'Citizenship, Social Justice and Ethnic Diversity', in S.R. Davis (ed.), *Citizenship in Australia: Democracy, Law and Society*, Constitutional Centenary Foundation: Carlton.

Jupp, James, 2002, *From White Australia to Woomera: The Story of Australian Immigration*, Cambridge University Press: Port Melbourne.

Jupp, James, 2007, *From White Australia to Woomera: The Story of Australian Immigration*, 2nd edn, Cambridge University Press: Port Melbourne.

Jupp, James & John Nieuwenhuysen with Emma Dawson, 2007, *Social Cohesion in Australia*, Cambridge University Press: Port Melbourne.

Jupp, James, Barry York & Andrea McRobbie, 1989, *The Political Participation of Ethnic Minorities in Australia*, Australian Government Publishing Service: Canberra.

Kalantzis, Mary, 2000, 'Multicultural Citizenship', in Hudson, Wayne & Kane, John (eds), *Rethinking Australian Citizenship*, Cambridge University Press: Melbourne

Kamenka, Eugene, 1989, *Bureaucracy*, Blackwell: Oxford.

Karene, Witcher S., 1991a, 'Australia Leader Beats Challenge from Treasurer', *Wall Street Journal*, 4 June, p. 12.

Karene, Witcher S., 1991b, 'Former Ally Unseats Australia's Hawke in Close Party Ballot for Prime Minister', *Wall Street Journal*, 20 December, p. 12.

Kavanagh, Dennis, 1995, *Election Campaigning: The New Marketing of Politics*, Blackwell: Oxford.

Keating, Michael S., 1995, 'The Evolving Role of Central Agencies: Change and Continuity', *Australian Journal of Public Administration*, vol. 54, no. 4, pp. 579–83.

Kelly, Paul, 1992, *The End of Certainty*, Allen & Unwin: St Leonards.

Kelly, Paul, 1995, *November 1975: The Inside Story of Australia's Greatest Political Crisis*, Allen & Unwin: St Leonards.

Kenny, Michael, 2004, *The Politics of Identity*, Polity: Cambridge.

Keon-Cohen, Bryan (ed.), 2001, *Native Title in the New Millennium: A Selection of Papers from the Native Title Representative Bodies Legal Conference*, 16–20 April 2000: Melbourne, Victoria, Aboriginal Studies Press and Native Title Research Unit: Canberra.

King, Gary & Murray, Christopher J.L, 2001–02, 'Rethinking Human Security', *Political Science Quarterly*, vol. 116, no. 4, pp. 585–610.

Kirby, Michael, 1997, 'What is it Really Like to be a Justice of the High Court of Australia?: A Conversation between Law Students and Justice Kirby', *Sydney Law Review*, vol. 19, pp. 514–28.

Kirkpatrick, Rod, 1998, 'Shield of the People? The Provincial Press and the Fourth Estate', *Australian Journalism Review*, vol. 20, no. 1, pp. 82–103.

Kitchener, Jennifer, 1999, 'Business Journalism in the 1980s', in A. Curthoys & J. Schultz (eds), *Journalism, Print, Politics and Popular Culture*, University of Queensland Press: St Lucia.

Klotz, Robert, 1997, 'Positive Spin: Senate Campaigning on the Web', *PS: Political Science and Politics*, vol. 30, no. 3, pp. 482–6.

Kohut, Andrew, 2000, 'Polls Speed Down Slippery Slope, But They Don't Have To', *CJR*, November/December, pp. 66–7.

Krieken, Robert van, 2000, 'From Milirrpum to Mabo: The High Court, Terra Nullius and Moral Entrepreneurship', *UNSW Law Journal*, vol. 23, no. 1, pp. 63–77.

Kukathas, Chandran, 1997, 'Cultural Rights in Australia', in B. Galligan, I. McAllister & J. Ravenhill (eds), *New Developments in Australian Politics*, Macmillan, South Melbourne.

Kukathas, Chandran, 1998, 'The Fraternal Conceit', in D. Lovell, I. McAllister, W. Maley & C. Kukathas (eds), *The Australian Political System*, 2nd edn, Longman: South Melbourne.

Kymlicka, Will, 2002, 'Multiculturalism', in *Contemporary Political Philosophy: An Introduction*, 2nd edn, Oxford University Press: Oxford.

Lane, P.H., 1996, 'The Changing Role of the High Court', *The Australian Law Journal*, vol. 70, March, pp. 246–51.

Lattas, Andrew, 1990, 'Aborigines and Contemporary Australian Nationalism: Primordiality and the Cultural Politics of Otherness', *Journal of Cultural and Social Practice*, no. 27, April, pp. 50–69.

Lavarch, Michael, 1998, 'What Price Native Rights?', in D. Lovell, I. McAllister, W. Maley & C. Kukathas (eds), *The Australian Political System*, 2nd edn, Longman: South Melbourne.

Lee, Eddie, 1997, 'Globalization and Labour Standards: A Review of the Issues', *International Labour Review*, vol. 136, no. 2, pp. 173–89.

Lehmann, Geoffrey, 1983, 'The Income Tax Judgements of Sir Garfield Barwick', *Monash University Law Review*, vol. 9, no. 3, pp. 115–56.

Lindell, Geoffrey & Bob Bennett (eds), 2001, *Parliament: The Vision in Hindsight*, Federation Press: Annandale.

Loo, Eric, 1998, 'Journalistic Representation of Ethnicity', in M. Breen (ed.), *Journalism: Theory and Practice*, Macleay Press: Paddington.

Lothian, Andrew, 1994, 'Attitudes of Australians Towards the Environment: 1975 to 1994', *Australian Journal of Environmental Management*, vol. 1, September, pp. 78–99.

Louth, Jonathon and Lisa Hill, 2005, 'Compulsory Voting in Australia: Turnout With and Without It', *Australian Review of Public Affairs*, vol. 6, no. 1, pp. 25-37. Available at http://www.australianreview.net/journal/v6/n1/louth_hill.pdf, last accessed 13 June 2008.

Lovell, David, Ian McAllister, William Maley & Chandran Kukathas (eds), 1998, *The Australian Political System*, 2nd edn, Longman: South Melbourne.

Lowe, Ian, 2007, 'Reaction Time: Climate Change and the Nuclear Option,' in *Quarterly Essay*, 27, pp. 1–88.

Lucy, Richard, 1993, *The Australian Form of Government: Models in Dispute*, 2nd edn, Macmillan: South Melbourne.

Luke, Timothy, 1991, 'Touring Hyperreality: Critical Theory Confronts Informational Society', in P. Wexler (ed.), *Critical Theory Now*, The Falmer Press: London.

Luke, Timothy, 2001, 'Education, Environment and Sustainability: What are the Issues, Where to Intervene, What Must Be Done?' *Educational Philosophy and Theory*, vol. 33, no. 2, pp. 187–202.

Lumley, Sarah, 1999, 'Interpreting Economics, Rhetoric and Sustainable Development: Some Implications for Policy Determination', *Australian Geographer*, vol. 30, no. 1, pp. 35–49.

Lutz, James M. & Brenda J. Lutz, 2004, *Global Terrorism*, Routledge: London.

Macpherson, C.B., 1966, *The Real World of Democracy*, Oxford University Press: Oxford.

Macquarie Reference Series, 1998, *Government in Australia: Key Events in Politics, Law and the Economy*, Macquarie Library: Sydney.

Maddox, Graham & Tod Moore, 1997, 'In Defence of Parliamentary Sovereignty', in Michael Coper & George Williams (eds), *Power, Parliament and the People*, Federation Press: Sydney.

Maddox, Graham, 1992, 'Political Stability, Independents and the Two Party System', *Current Affairs Bulletin*, vol. 69, no. 1, pp. 20–7.

Maddox, Graham, 2005, *Australian Democracy: In Theory and Practice*, 5th edn, Longman Cheshire: Melbourne.

Malthus, Thomas, 1992 [1798], *An Essay on the Principle of Population*, Cambridge University Press: Cambridge.

Manne, Robert, 1998, 'Why I Am Not a Republican', in D. Lovell, I. McAllister, W. Maley & C. Kukathas (eds), *The Australian Political System*, 2nd edn, Longman: South Melbourne.

Manne, Robert, 2001, *In Denial: The Stolen Generations and the Right*, Schwartz Publishing: Melbourne.

Mansell, Michael, 1993, 'Australians and Aborigines and the Mabo Decision: Just Who Needs Whom the Most?', *The Sydney Law Review*, vol. 15, no. 2, pp. 168–239.

Marr, David, 2007, 'His Masters Voice: The Corruption of Public Debate under Howard', *Quarterly Essay*, 26, pp. 1–84.

Marr, David & Marian Wilkinson, 2004, *Dark Victory*, 2nd edn, Allen & Unwin: Sydney.

Marsden, Stephanie, 1999, *Talkback Trash and Treasure: Wit, Wisdom and Wireless*, Rand Publications Marketing: Carlton North.

Marsh, Ian, 1995, *Beyond the Two Party System: Political Representation, Economic Competitiveness, and Australian Politics*, Cambridge University Press: Melbourne.

Marsh, Ian, 1997, 'Interest Group Analysis', in D. Woodward, A. Parkin & J. Summers (eds), *Government, Politics, Power and Policy in Australia*, 5th edn, Longman: South Melbourne.

Marsh, Ian, 1998, 'Major Party Membership, Organisation and Roles', in D. Lovell, I. McAllister, W. Maley & C. Kukathas (eds), *The Australian Political System*, 2nd edn, Longman: South Melbourne.

Martin, Gus, 2006, *Understanding Terrorism: Challenges, Perspectives, and Issues*, 2nd edn, Sage Publications: Thousand Oaks.

Martinello, Marco, 1998, 'Wieviorka's View on Multiculturalism: A Critique', *Ethnic and Racial Studies*, vol. 21, no. 5, pp. 911–16.

Mason, Anthony, 1998, 'Courts and Community Values', in D. Lovell, I. McAllister, W. Maley & C. Kukathas (eds), *The Australian Political System*, 2nd edn, Longman: South Melbourne.

Mathews, Freya (ed.), 1996, *Ecology and Democracy*, Frank Cass: London.

Mathews, Jessica T., 1989, 'Redefining Security', *Foreign Affairs*, vol. 68, no. 2, pp. 162–77.

Matthews, Trevor, 1980, 'Australian Pressure Groups', in H. Mayer & H. Nelson (eds), *Australian Politics: A Fifth Reader*, Longman Cheshire: Melbourne.

Matthews, Trevor, 1997, 'Interest Groups', in R. Smith (ed.), *Politics in Australia*, Allen & Unwin: St Leonards.

Mattinson, Deborah, 1999, 'People Power in Politics: Qualitative Research for the 21st Century: Public Involvement in the Decision-Making Process', *Journal of the Market Research Society*, vol. 41, no. 1, pp. 87–96.

McAllister, Ian, 2005, *Representative Views: Mass and Elite Opinion on Australian Security*. Report prepared for the Australian Strategic Policy Institute, June 2005. Available at http://www.aspi.org.au/htmlver/21935_RepViews/_lib/pdf/ASPI_Arepresentative_views.pdf, last accessed 12 June 2008.

McAllister, Ian, 1992, *Political Behaviour: Citizens, Parties and Elites in Australia*, Longman Cheshire: Melbourne.

McCulloch, Jude & Joo-Cheong Tham, 2005, 'Secret State, Transparent Subject: The Australian Security Intelligence Organisation in the Age of Terror', *Australian and New Zealand Journal of Criminology*, 38(3): 400–15.

McGinnis, Michael, 1994, 'Myth, Nature and the Bureaucratic Experience', *Environmental Ethics*, vol. 16, no. 4, p. 425.

McGuinness P.P., 1998, 'Practical Protest Against the Compulsory Vote', in D. Lovell, I. McAllister, W. Maley & C. Kukathas (eds), *The Australian Political System*, 2nd edn, Longman: South Melbourne.

McKenna, Mark, 1994, 'Tracking the Republic', in D. Headon, J. Warden & B. Gammage (eds), *Crown or Country: The Traditions of Australian Republicanism*, Allen & Unwin: St Leonards.

McKnight, David, 2005, *Beyond Left and Right: New Politics and the Culture Wars*, Allen & Unwin: Crows Nest.

McLaughlin, Andrew, 1993, *Regarding Nature: Industrialism and Deep Ecology*, State University of New York Press: Albany.

McLean, Iain, 1989, *Democracy and New Technology*, Polity Press: Cambridge.

McMaster, Don, 2002, 'Asylum-seekers and the Insecurity of a Nation', *Australian Journal of International Affairs*, vol. 56, no. 2, pp. 279–90.

McNair, Brian, 2003, *An Introduction to Political Communication*, Routledge: London.

McNutt, Patrick, 2002, *The Economics of Public Choice*, 2nd edn, Edward Elgar: Cheltenham.

Megalogenis, George, 2006, 'All the same, only different—Election 2007,' *The Australian*, 16 December.

Mellors, John, 1996, 'Managing and Leading in the Next Century', *Australian Journal of Public Administration*, vol. 55, no. 3, pp. 83–9.

Melucci, Alberto, 1980, 'The New Social Movements: A Theoretical Approach', *Social Science Information*, vol. 19, no. 2, pp. 199–226.

Melucci, Alberto, 1985, 'The Symbolic Challenge of Contemporary Movements', *Social Research*, vol. 52, no. 4, pp. 789–816.

Melucci, Alberto, 1992, 'What Is "New" in the "New Social Movements"?', *Sociologia*, vol. 26, nos. 2–3, pp. 271–300.

Melucci, Alberto, 1995a, 'Conflict and Rule: Social Movements and Political Systems', *Sociologica*, vol. 10, no. 28, pp. 225–33.

Melucci, Alberto, 1995b, 'The New Social Movements Revisited: Reflections on a Sociological Misunderstanding', in L. Maheu (ed.), *Social Movements and Social Classes: The Future of Collective Action*, Sage: London.

Merkle, Daniel, 1996, 'The Polls-Review: The National Issues Convention Deliberative Poll', *Public Opinion Quarterly*, vol. 60, pp. 588–619.

Michaelson, Christopher, 2005, 'Antiterrorism Legislation in Australia: A Proportionate Response to the Terrorist Threat', *Studies in Conflict and Terrorism*, vol. 28, no. 4, pp. 321–39.

Midlarsky, Manus I., 1998, 'Democracy and the Environment: An Empirical Assessment', *Journal of Peace Research*, vol. 35, no. 3, pp. 341–61.

Milburn, Michael, 1991, *Persuasion and Politics: The Social Psychology of Public Opinion*, Brooks/Cole Publishing: Pacific Grove.

Mills, C. Wright, 1959, *Political Elites*, Oxford University Press: Oxford.

Mills, Stephen, 1999, 'Polling, Politics and the Press 1941–1996', in A. Curthoys & J. Schultz (eds), *Journalism, Print, Politics and Popular Culture*, University of Queensland Press: St Lucia.

Moffitt, Athol, 2000, 'Judges, Royal Commissioners and the Separation of Powers', *Quadrant*, vol. 45, no. 5, pp. 36–9.

Moore, Tod & Graham Maddox, 1995, 'Rights, Jurisdiction and Responsible Government: The Spectre of Capital Television', *Journal of Commonwealth and Comparative Politics*, vol. 33, no. 3, pp. 400–15.

Moore, Tod, Sandra Bourke & Graham Maddox, 1998, 'Australia and the Emergence of the Modern Two-Party System', *Australian Journal of Politics and History*, vol. 22, no. 1, pp. 17–31.

Morgan, David L. & Richard A. Krueger, 1998, *The Focus Group Kit*, Sage: Thousand Oaks.

Morgan, Gary, 1998, 'Polling and the Political System', in D. Lovell, I. McAllister, W. Maley & C. Kukathas (eds), *The Australian Political System*, 2nd edn, Longman: South Melbourne.

Morris, Barry, 1988, 'The Politics of Identity: From Aborigines to the First Australia', in J. Beckett (ed.), *Past and Present: The Construction of Aboriginality*, Aboriginal Studies Press for the Australian Institute of Aboriginal Studies: Canberra.

Moser, Mary Anne with Douglas MacLeod, (eds), 1996, *Immersed in Technology: Art and Virtual Environments*, MIT Press: Cambridge, Mass.

Mouffe, Chantal, 1993, *The Return of the Political*, Verso: London & New York.

Mouffe, Chantal, 2000, *The Democratic Paradox*, Verso: London & New York.

Mouffe, Chantal, 2005, *On the Political*, Routledge: London & New York.

Mowbray, Martin, 1990, 'Mainstreaming as Assimilation in the Northern Territory', *Australian Aboriginal Studies*, no. 2, pp. 20–6.

Mulgan, Richard, 1998, 'The Australian Senate as a "House of Review"', in D. Lovell, I. McAllister, W. Maley & C. Kukathas (eds), *The Australian Political System*, 2nd edn, Longman: South Melbourne.

National Inquiry into the Separation of Aboriginal and Torres Strait Islander Children from their Families, 1997, *Bringing Them Home*, Human Rights and Equal Opportunity Commission: Sydney.

Newman, Peter, 1995, 'Globalisation and Sustainability', in J. Phillimore (ed.), *Local Matters: Perspectives on the Globalisation of Technology*, Institute for Science and Technology Policy, Murdoch University: Perth.

Nicholson, Pip, 1996, 'Appointing High Court Judges', *Australian Quarterly*, vol. 68, no. 3, pp. 69–87.

Nicholson, Pip, 1998, 'Appointing High Court Judges: Need for Reform?', in D. Lovell, I. McAllister, W. Maley & C. Kukathas (eds), *The Australian Political System*, 2nd edn, Longman: South Melbourne.

Norris, Keith & Ben McLean, 1999, 'Changes in Earnings Inequality, 1975 to 1998', *Australian Bulletin of Labour*, vol. 25, no. 2, pp. 23–31.

O'Brien, Robert, Anne Marie Goetz, Jan Aarte Scholte & Marc Williams, 2000, *Contesting Global Governance: Multilateral Economic Institutions and Global Social Movements*, Cambridge University Press: Cambridge.

O'Neill, Michael, 2000, 'Preparing for Power: The German Greens and the Challenge of Party Politics', *Contemporary Politics*, vol. 6, no. 2, pp. 165–84.

Osborne, David & Ted Gaebler, 1993, *Reinventing Government: How the Entrepreneurial Spirit is Transforming the Public Sector*, Plume: New York.

Oskamp, Stuart, 1991, *Attitudes and Opinions*, Prentice Hall: Englewood Cliffs.

Ozolinos, Uldis, 1994, 'Immigration and Immigrants', in J. Brett, J. Gillespie & M. Goot (eds), *Developments in Australian Politics*, Macmillan: South Melbourne.

Page, Barbara, 1997, 'Cabinet', in R. Smith (ed.), *Politics in Australia*, Allen & Unwin: St Leonards.

Painter, Martin, 1997, 'Federalism', in R. Smith (ed.), *Politics in Australia*, Allen & Unwin: St Leonards.

Painter, Martin, 1998, *Collaborative Federalism: Economic Reform in Australia in the 1990s*, Cambridge University Press: Cambridge.

Pakulski, Jan, Bruce Tranter & Stephen Crook, 1998, 'The Dynamics of Environmental Issues in Australia: Concerns, Clusters and Carriers', *Australian Journal of Political Science*, vol. 33, no. 2, pp. 235–52.

Papadakis, Elim, 1993, *Politics and the Environment: The Australian Experience*, Allen & Unwin: St Leonards.

Papadakis, Elim, 1997a, 'The Environment', in B. Galligan, I. McAllister & J. Ravenhill (eds), *New Developments in Australian Politics*, Macmillan: South Melbourne.

Papadakis, Elim, 1997b, 'Environmental Policy', in D. Woodward, A. Parkin & J. Summers (eds), *Government, Politics, Power and Policy in Australia*, 5th edn, Longman: South Melbourne.

Parker, R.S., 1989, 'The Politics of Bureaucracy', in G.R. Curnow & B. Page (eds), *Politicization and the Career Service*, Canberra College of Advanced Education & NSW Division of the Royal Australian Institute of Public Administration, Canberra.

Parkin, Andrew, 1997, 'Towards a Republic?', in D. Woodward, A. Parkin & J. Summers (eds), *Government, Politics, Power and Policy in Australia*, 5th edn, Longman: South Melbourne.

Parkin, Andrew & Geoff Anderson, 2007, 'The Howard Government: Regulatory Federalism and the Transformation of Commonwealth–State Relations', *Australian Journal of Political Science*, vol. 42, no. 2, pp. 295–314.

Parkin, Andrew & Leonie Hadcastle, 1997, 'Immigration and Ethnic Affairs Policy,' in A. Parkin, J. Summers & D. Woodward (eds), *Government, Politics, Power and Policy in Australia*, 6th edn, Pearson Education: Frenchs Forest, pp. 486–509.

Parkin, Andrew & John Summers, 2002, 'The Constitutional Framework', in D. Woodward, A. Parkin & J. Summers (eds), *Government, Politics, Power and Policy in Australia*, 7th edn, Longman: South Melbourne.

Parry, Geraint, 1969, *Political Elites*, Allen & Unwin: London.

Patapan, Haig, 1999, 'Separation of Powers in Australia', *Australian Journal of Political Science*, vol. 34, no. 3, pp. 391–407.

Patapan, Haig, 2000, *Judging Democracy: the New Politics of the High Court of Australia*, Cambridge University Press: Oakleigh.

Patching, Roger, 1998, 'The Preparation of Professional Journalists', in M. Breen (ed.), *Journalism: Theory and Practice*, Macleay Press: Paddington.

Paul, J.B., 1998, 'Paul Kelly on the Dismissal', in D. Lovell, I. McAllister, W. Maley & C. Kukathas (eds), *The Australian Political System*, 2nd edn, Longman: South Melbourne.

Peacock, Andrew, 1980, 'New International Economic Order: Implications for Australia', in H. Mayer & H. Nelson (eds), *Australian Politics: A Fifth Reader*, Longman Cheshire: Melbourne.

Pearse, Guy, 2007, *High & Dry: John Howard, Climate Change and the Selling of Australia's Future*, Penguin: Australia.

Pearson, Mark & Jeffrey Brand, 2001, *Sources of News and Current Affairs: Stage One: The Industry*, Bond University for the Australian Broadcasting Authority: Sydney.

Perry, James L. & Kenneth L. Kraemer, 1983, *Public Management: Public and Private Perspectives*, Mayfield Publishing Company: Palo Alto.

Perry, Michael, 1998, *The Idea of Human Rights: Four Inquiries*, Oxford University Press: New York.

Peters, B. Guy, 1995, *The Politics of Bureaucracy*, Longman: New York.

Pettit, Philip, 2001, 'Deliberative Democracy and the Case for Depoliticising Government', *University of New South Wales Law Journal*, vol. 24, no. 3, pp. 724–36.

Pfetsch, Barbara, 1998, 'Government News Management', in D. Graber, D. McQuail & P. Norris (eds), *The Politics of News, The News of Politics*, CQ Press: Washington DC.

Pitkin, Hanna, 1967, *The Concept of Representation*, University of California Press: California.

Povinelli, Elizabeth, 2002, *The Cunning of Recognition: Indigenous Alterities and the Making of Australian Multiculturalism*, Duke University Press: Durham.

Price, Matt, 2002, 'Fake Docket Sinks Heffernan—PM Demands Friend Quit Over Kirby Affair', *The Australian*, Tuesday 19 March, p. 1.

Price, Vincent & Peter Neijens, 1998, 'Deliberative Polls: Toward Improved Measures of "Informed" Public Opinion?', *International Journal of Public Opinion Research*, vol. 10, no. 2, pp. 145–77.

Probert, Belinda, 1994, 'Globalisation, Economic Restructuring and the State', in S. Bell & B. Head (eds), *State, Economy and Public Policy in Australia*, Oxford University Press: Melbourne.

Public Accounts Committee, 1999, *Report on the Role of the Government in an Online Environment*, Report no. 42, State Law Publisher: Perth.

Pusey, Michael, 1991, *Economic Rationalism in Canberra*, Cambridge University Press: Cambridge.

Rash, Wayne, 1997, *Politics on the Net: Wiring the Political Process*, WH Freeman: New York.

Rawls, John, 1972, *A Theory of Justice*, Oxford University Press: Oxford.

Renfrow, Patty, 1995, *An Assessment of the Senior Executive Service in the Australian Public Service: A Survey of its Officers*, Australian Government Publishing Service: Canberra.

Republic Advisory Committee, 1993, *An Australian Republic: The Options: An Overview*, Australian Government Publishing Service: Canberra.

Reynolds, Henry, 1996, *Aboriginal Sovereignty: Reflections on Race, State and Nation*, Allen & Unwin: St Leonards.

Reynolds, Henry, 1999, *Why Weren't We Told: A Personal Search for the Truth About Our History*, Viking: Ringwood.

Reynolds, Henry, 2003, *The Law of the Land*, Penguin: Camberwell.

Richardson, Jeremy J., 1993, *Pressure Groups*, Oxford University Press: Oxford.

Robbins, Jane & John Summers, 2006, 'Indigenous Affairs Policy,' in A. Parkin, J. Summers & D. Woodward (eds), *Government, Politics, Power and Policy in Australia*, 8th edn, Pearson Education: Frenchs Forest.

Robertson, Lori, 2001, 'Polled Enough for Ya?', *American Journalism Review*, January/February, pp. 29–33.
Rosewarne, Stuart, 1993, 'Selling the Environment: A Critique of Market Ecology', in S. Rees, G. Rodley & F. Stilwell (eds), *Beyond the Market: Alternatives to Economic Rationalism*, Pluto Press: Leichhardt.
Rosewarne, Stuart, 2001, 'Review article, Women, Work and Inequality', *Journal of Australian Political Economy*, no. 47, June, pp. 123–35.
Rousseau, Jean-Jacques, 1973 [1762], *The Social Contract and Discourses*, J.M. Dent and Sons Ltd: London.
Rowse, Tim, 1987, '"Were You Ever Savages?" Aboriginal Insiders and Pastoralist's Patronage', *Oceania*, vol. 58, no. 1, pp. 139–44.
Rowse, Tim, 1992, *Remote Possibilities: The Aboriginal Domain and the Administrative Imagination*, Australian National University: Darwin.
Rowse, Tim, 1994, 'Aborigines: Citizens and Colonial Subjects', in J. Brett, J. Gillespie & M. Goot (eds), *Developments in Australian Politics*, Macmillan: South Melbourne.
Rowse, Tim, 2002, *Indigenous Futures: Choice and Development for Aboriginal and Islander Australia*, UNSW Press: Sydney.
Rubinstein, Colin, 1996, 'Australian Citizenship and Multiculturalism', in S.R. Davis (ed.), *Citizenship in Australia: Democracy, Law and Society*, Constitutional Centenary Foundation: Carlton.
Sargent, John, 1992, 'Regionalism and Economic Development: Propping up or Strategic Choice—2', *Canberra Bulletin of Public Administration*, no. 70, October, pp. 98–101.
Saul, John Ralston, 1992, *Voltaire's Bastards: The Dictatorship of Reason in the West*, Penguin Books: Toronto.
Saul, John Ralston, 2002, *On Equilibrium*, Penguin Books: Toronto.
Saunders, Cheryl, 2000a, 'The Implications of Federalism for Indigenous Australians', in Y. Ghai (ed.), *Autonomy and Ethnicity: Negotiating Competing Claims in Multi-Ethnic States*, Cambridge University Press: Cambridge.
Saunders, Cheryl, 2000b, 'The Separation of Powers', in Brian Opeskin & Fiona Wheeler (eds), *The Australian Federal Judicial System*, Melbourne University Press: Melbourne.
Saunders, Peter, 1995, 'Equity Benchmarks and the Trend to Inequality', *Australian Quarterly*, vol. 67, no. 4, pp. 59–76.
Saunders, Peter, 2002, *The Ends and Means of Welfare: Coping with Economic and Social Change in Australia*, Cambridge University Press: Port Melbourne.
Scholte, Jan Art, 2000, *Globalisation: A Critical Introduction*, Palgrave: Houndsmill.

Schultz, Julianne, 1998, *Reviving the Fourth Estate: Democracy, Accountability and the Media*, Cambridge University Press: Cambridge.

Schultz, Julianne, 1999, 'The Many Paradoxes of Independence', in A. Curthoys & J. Schultz (eds), *Journalism, Print, Politics and Popular Culture*, University of Queensland Press: St Lucia.

Scott, Shirley, 1994, 'Australia and International Institutions', in J. Brett, J. Gillespie & M. Goot (eds), *Developments in Australian Politics*, Macmillan: South Melbourne.

Self, Peter, 2000, *Rolling Back the Market: Economic Dogma and Political Choice*, Macmillan: Basingstoke.

Sharman, Campbell, 1980, 'Federalism', in H. Mayer & H. Nelson (eds), *Australian Politics: A Fifth Reader*, Longman Cheshire: Melbourne.

Sharman, Campbell, 1994, 'Political Parties', in J. Brett, J. Gillespie & M. Goot (eds), *Developments in Australian Politics*, Macmillan: South Melbourne.

Sharman, Campbell, 1997, 'Defining Executive Power: Constitutional Reform for Grown-ups', *Australian Journal of Public Administration*, vol. 56, no. 2, pp. 107–14.

Sheil, Christopher (ed.), 2001, *Globalisation: Australian Impacts*, UNSW Press: Sydney.

Shelly, Robert, 2001, 'Institutionalising Deliberative Democracy', *Alternative Law Journal*, vol. 26, no. 1, pp. 36–40.

Shiell, Annette & Peter Spearritt, 1993, *Australians and the Monarchy*, Monash University: Melbourne.

Silvia, Stephen J., 1999, 'Reform Gridlock and the Role of the Bundesrat in German Politics', *West European Politics*, vol. 22, no. 2, pp. 167–8.

Simmons, John, 1992, *The Lockean Theory of Rights*, Princeton University Press: Princeton.

Simons, M., 1999, *Fit to Print: Inside the Canberra Press Gallery*, UNSW Press: Sydney.

Singh, Kavaljit, 1998, *The Globalisation of Finance: A Citizens Guide*, Zed Books: London.

Singleton, Gwynneth, Don Aitkin, Brian Jinks & John Warhurst, 2003, *Australian Political Institutions*, 7th edn, Pearson Education: Frenchs Forest.

Singleton, Gwynneth, Don Aitkin, Brian Jinks & John Warhurst, 2006, *Australian Political Institutions*, 8th edn, Pearson Education: Frenchs Forest.

Skinner, Quentin & Bo Strath (eds), 2003, *States and Citizens: History, Theory, Prospects*, Cambridge University Press: Cambridge.

Skorupski, John, 1989, *John Stuart Mill*, Routledge: London.

Smith, Martin J., 1993, *Pressure, Power and Policy: State Autonomy and Policy Networks in Britain and the United States*, Harvester Wheatsheaf: London.

Smith, Martin J., 1995, *Pressure Politics*, Baseline Books: Charlton.
Smith, Paul J. (ed), 2005, *Terrorism and Violence in Southeast Asia: Transnational Challenges*, M.E. Sharpe: Armonk.
Smith, Rodney, 1994, 'Parliament', in J. Brett, J. Gillespie & M. Goot (eds), *Developments in Australian Politics*, Macmillan: South Melbourne.
Smith, Rodney, 1997a, 'The Party System', in R. Smith (ed.), *Politics in Australia*, Allen & Unwin: St Leonards.
Smith, Rodney, 1997b, 'The News Media', in R. Smith (ed.), *Politics in Australia*, Allen & Unwin: St Leonards.
Smith, Rodney, 2001, *Australian Political Culture*, Longman: Australia.
Smith, Rodney, Ian Cook & Ariadne Vromen, 2006, *Keywords in Australian Politics*, Cambridge University Press: Melbourne.
Solomon, David, 1984, *The People's Palace: Parliament in Australia*, Thomas Nelson: Melbourne.
Solomon, David, 1988, *Australia's Government and Parliament*, 7th edn, Thomas Nelson: Melbourne.
Solomon, David, 1992, *The Political Impact of the High Court: How the High Court has Shaped Australian Politics, from Federation to Today*, Allen & Unwin: Sydney.
Solomon, David, 1997, 'The High Court', in D. Woodward, A. Parkin & J. Summers (eds), *Government, Politics, Power and Policy in Australia*, 5th edn, Longman: South Melbourne.
Solomon, David, 1998a, 'The Political Impact of the High Court', in D. Lovell, I. McAllister, W. Maley & C. Kukathas (eds), *The Australian Political System*, 2nd edn, Longman: South Melbourne.
Solomon, David, 1998b, 'What's Wrong with the High Court Playing a Significant Political Role', in D. Lovell, I. McAllister, W. Maley & C. Kukathas (eds), *The Australian Political System*, 2nd edn, Longman: South Melbourne.
Solomon, David, 1998c, *Coming of Age: Charter for a New Australia*, University of Queensland Press: St Lucia.
Solomon, David, 1999, *The Political High Court: How the High Court Shapes Politics*, Allen & Unwin: St Leonards.
Soutphommasane, Tim, 2007, 'Surrendering nationalism,' *Griffith Review*, Winter, pp. 133–40.
Spender, D., 1995, *Nattering on the Net: Women, Power and Cyberspace*, Spinifex: North Melbourne.
Starck, Kenneth, 1994, 'The Case for Intercultural Journalism', *Australian Journalism Review*, vol. 16, no. 2, pp. 11–24.
Steinhorn, Leonard, 2000, 'Does the Reliance of the News Media on Polls Distort Reporting? Yes: A Horse-Race Poll Becomes the Issue and it is Nothing but Manufactured News', *Insight*, December 25, pp. 40 and 43.

Steketee, Mike, 1998, 'The Press Gallery at Work', in D. Lovell, I. McAllister, W. Maley & C. Kukathas (eds), *The Australian Political System*, 2nd edn, Longman: South Melbourne.

Stewart, Jenny & Grant Jones, 2003, *Renegotiating the Environment: The Power of Politics*, Federation Press: Sydney.

Stewart, Jenny & Megan Kimber, 1996, 'The Transformation of Bureaucracy? Structural Change in the Commonwealth Public Service 1983–93', *Australian Journal of Public Administration*, vol. 55, no. 3, pp. 37–48.

Stewart, Randal & Ian Ward, 1994, *Politics One*, 2nd edn, Macmillan: South Melbourne.

Stewart, Randal & Ian Ward, 2006, *Politics One*, 3rd edn, Palgrave Macmillan: South Yarra.

Stilwell, Frank, 2000, *Changing Track: A New Political Economic Direction for Australia*, Pluto Press: Annandale.

Stock, Jenny T., 2006, 'Greens, Democrats, Minor Parties and Independents,' in A. Parkin, J. Summers & D. Woodward, (eds), *Government, Politics, Power and Policy in Australia*, 8th edn, Pearson Education: Frenchs Forest.

Stockwell, Stephen, 1999, 'Beyond the Fourth Estate: Democracy Deliberation and Journalism Theory', *Australian Journalism Review*, vol. 21, no. 1, pp. 37–49.

Stokes, Geoffrey, 1997 (ed), *The Politics of Identity in Australia*, Cambridge University Press: Melbourne.

Stone, Wendy, 2000, 'Social Capital and Social Security: Lessons from Research', *Family Matters*, vol. 57, Spring–Summer, pp. 10–13.

Stratton, John & Jen Ang, 1998, 'Multicultural Imagined Communities: Cultural Difference and National Identity in the USA and Australia', in D. Bennett (ed.), *Multicultural States: Rethinking Difference and Identity*, Routledge: London.

Summers, John, 2006, 'Parliament and Responsible Government,' in A. Parkin, J. Summers & D. Woodward (eds), *Government, Politics, Power and Policy in Australia*, 8th edn, Pearson Education: Frenchs Forest.

Tatz, Colin, 1979, *Race Politics in Australia: Aborigines, Politics and Law*, University of New England Publishing Unit: Armidale.

Tatz, Colin, 1981, 'Aborigines: The Struggle for Law', in P. Hiller (ed.), *Class and Inequality in Australia: Sociological Perspectives and Research*, Harcourt Brace Jovanovich Group: Sydney.

Theophanous, Andrew, 1994, *Understanding Social Justice: An Australian Perspective*, 2nd edn, Elika Books: Carlton South.

Thomas, Cora, 2001, 'From "Australian Aborigines" to "White Australians"', *Australian Aboriginal Studies*, no. 1, pp. 21–35.

Thomas, Ian, 2007, *Environmental Policy: Australian Practice in Context of Theory*, The Federation Press: Crows Nest.

Thomas, Nicholas & William T. Tow, 2002, 'The Utility of Human Security: Sovereignty and Humanitarian Intervention', *Security Dialogue*, vol. 33, no. 2, pp. 177–92.

Thompson, Elaine, 1994, *Fair Enough: Egalitarianism in Australia*, UNSW Press: Sydney.

Thompson, Elaine, 2001, 'The Constitution and the Australian System of Limited Government, Responsible Government and Representative Democracy: Revisiting the Washminster Mutation', *University of New South Wales Law Journal*, vol. 24, no. 3, pp. 657–69.

Tiffen, Rodney, 1994, 'Media Policy', in J. Brett, J. Gillespie & M. Goot (eds), *Developments in Australian Politics*, Macmillan: South Melbourne.

Tonkin, David, 1984, 'The Liberal Party and Business', in G. Brandis, T. Harley & D. Markwell (eds), *Liberals Face the Future*, Oxford University Press: Melbourne.

Touraine, Alain, 1985, 'An Introduction to the Study of Social Movements', *Social Research*, vol. 52, no. 4, pp. 749–87.

Touraine, Alain, 1992, 'Beyond Social Movements?', *Theory, Culture & Society*, vol. 9, no. 1, pp. 125–45.

Touraine, Alain, 2004, 'The Subject and Societal Movements', in J.R. Blau (ed.), *The Blackwell Companion to Sociology*, Blackwell: Malden, MA.

Traugott, Michael, 2000, 'Presidential Address: Polling in the Public's Interest', *Public Opinion Quarterly*, vol. 64, pp. 374–84.

Trend, David (ed.), 2001, *Reading Digital Culture*, Blackwell: Oxford.

Twomey, Anne & Glenn Withers, 2007, *Australia's Federal Future: Delivering Growth and Prosperity*, a report prepared for the Council for the Australian Federation. Available at http://www.dpc.vic.gov.au/CA256D800027B102/Lookup/FederalistPaperAustralia'sFederalFuture/$file/Federalist%20Paper%20Australia's%20Federal%20Future.pdf, last accessed 11 October 2006.

Twomey, Anne, 1997, 'State Constitutions in an Australian Republic', *Monash University Law Review*, vol. 23, no. 2, pp. 312–30.

Uhr, John, 1993, 'Instituting Republicanism: Parliamentary Vices, Republican Virtues?', in S. Lawson & G. Maddox (eds), 'Australia's Republican Question', *Australian Journal of Political Science*, vol. 28, special issue, pp. 27–39.

Uhr, John, 1997, 'Parliament', in B. Galligan, I. McAllister & J. Ravenhill (eds), *New Developments in Australian Politics*, Macmillan: South Melbourne.

Uhr, John, 1998a, 'The Constitutional Convention and Deliberative Democracy', *University of New South Wales Law Journal*, vol. 21, no. 3, pp. 875–81.

Uhr, John, 1998b, *Deliberative Democracy in Australia: The Changing Place of Parliament*, Cambridge University Press: Melbourne.

Uhr, John, 2002, 'What's So Responsible about Responsible Government?', in D. Burchell & A. Leigh (eds), *The Prince's New Clothes: Why do Australians Dislike Their Politicians?*, UNSW Press: Sydney.

Van den Berg, Rosemary, 2002, *Nyoongar People of Australia: Perspectives on Racism and Multiculturalism*, Brill: Leiden.

Vasta, Ellie, 1996, 'Dialectics of Domination: Racism and Multiculturalism', in E. Vasta & S. Castles (eds), *The Teeth are Smiling: The Persistence of Racism in Multicultural Australia*, Allen & Unwin: St Leonards.

Vromen, Ariadne & Katherine Gelber, 2005, *Powerscape: Contemporary Australian Political Practice*, Allen & Unwin: Crows Nest.

Walker, Ken J., 1994, 'The Environmental Crises: A Critique of Neo-Hobbesian Responses', in R. Goodin (ed.), *The Politics of the Environment*, Edward Elgar Publishing: Aldershot.

Walker, Ken, 1994, *The Political Economy of Environmental Policy: An Australian Introduction*, UNSW Press: Kensington.

Walker, Kris, 1997, 'It's a Miracle! High Court Unanimity on Free Speech', *Alternative Law Journal*, vol. 22, no. 4, pp. 179–81.

Wallington, Tabatha & Ian Barns, 2001, 'Democratising Environmental Assessment: The Relevance of Deliberative Democracy for Environmental Decision Making in Western Australia', in G. Lawrence, V. Higgins & S. Lockie (eds), *Environment, Society, and Natural Resource Management: Theoretical Perspectives from Australasia and the Americas*, Edward Elgar: Cheltenham.

Walsh, Mary, 2005, 'The Republican Debate', in C. Aulich & R. Wettenhall (eds), *Howard's Second and Third Governments*, University of New South Wales Press: Sydney.

Wanna, John, 1997, 'Public Sector Management', in D. Woodward, A. Parkin & J. Summers (eds), *Government, Politics, Power and Policy in Australia*, 5th edn, Longman: South Melbourne.

Ward, Ian, 2006, 'The Media, Power and Politics', in A. Parkin, J. Summers & D. Woodward (eds), *Government, Politics, Power and Policy*, 8th edn, Pearson Education: Frenchs Forest.

Ward, Ian & Ian Cook, 1992, 'Televised Political Advertising, Media Freedom, and Democracy', *Social Alternatives*, vol. 11, no. 1, pp. 21–6.

Warhaft, Sally, 2004, *Well May We Say: The Speeches That Made Australia*, Black Inc: Melbourne.

Warhurst, John, 1993, 'Changing Relationships: Interest Groups and Policy-making in the 1990s', in A. Hede & S. Prasser (eds), *Policy Making in Volatile Times*, Hale and Iremonger: Sydney.

Warhurst, John, 1998, 'In Defence of Single-Issue Interest Groups', in D. Lovell, I. McAllister, W. Maley & C. Kukathas (eds), *The Australian Political System*, 2nd edn, Longman: South Melbourne.

Warhurst, John, 2006, 'Interest Groups and Political Lobbying,' in A. Parkin, J. Summers & D. Woodward (eds), *Government, Politics, Power and Policy in Australia*, 8th edn, Pearson Education: Frenchs Forest.

Warhurst, John & Andrew Parkin, 2000, *The Machine: Labor Confronts the Future*, Allen & Unwin: St Leonards.

Watts, Rob, 2000, 'Politics and Social Action in an Era of Globalisation', *Just Policy/Advocacy and Social Action*, September, pp. 17–23.

Webb, Martyn, 2001, 'When No Means No: The Failure of the Australian November 1999 Republican Referendum and its Roots in the Constitutional Convention of 1998', in A. Murray (ed.), *Trusting the People: An Elected President for an Australian Republic*, Optima Press: Perth.

Weber, Max, 1996, 'Bureaucracy', in J.M. Shafritz & J. Steven Ott (eds), *Classics of Organization Theory*, Harcourt Brace: Fort Worth.

Webster, F., 1994, 'What Information Society?', *The Information Society*, vol. 10, no. 1, pp. 1–23.

Weeks, Edward, 2000, 'The Practice of Deliberative Democracy; Results from Four Large-Scale Trials,' *Public Administration Review*, vol. 60, no. 4, pp. 360–72.

Weisberger, Bernard, 2000, 'Taking America's Temperature. (History of the use of Public Opinion Polls for the Presidential Elections)', *American Heritage*, vol. 51, no. 7, pp. 58–61.

Weiss, Linda, Elizabeth Thurbon & John Mathews, 2007, *National Insecurity: The Howard Government's Betrayal of Australia*, Allen & Unwin: Crows Nest.

Weller, Patrick, 1985, *First Among Equals: Prime Ministers in Westminster Systems*, Allen & Unwin: Sydney.

Weller, Patrick, 1996, 'Commonwealth–State Reform Processes: A Policy Management Review', *Australian Journal of Public Administration*, vol. 55, no. 1, pp. 95–110.

Weller, Patrick, 1998, 'Prime Ministers, Political Leadership and Cabinet Government', in D. Lovell, I. McAllister, W. Maley & C. Kukathas (eds), *The Australian Political System*, 2nd edn, Longman: South Melbourne.

Weller, Patrick, 2003, 'Cabinet Government: An Elusive Ideal', *Public Administration*, vol. 81, no. 4, pp. 710–22.

Weller, Patrick, 2004, 'Parliamentary Democracy in Australia', *Parliamentary Affairs*, vol. 57, no. 3, pp. 630–45.

Weller, Patrick & Glyn Davis (eds), 1996, *New Ideas, Better Government*, Allen & Unwin: St Leonards.

Weller, Patrick & Dean Jaensch, 1980, *Responsible Government in Australia*, Drummond: Richmond.

Western, Mark C. & Bruce Tranter, 2001, 'Postmaterialist and Economic Voting in Australia: 1990–98', *Australian Journal of Political Science*, vol. 36, no. 3, pp. 439–58.
Whalan, D.J., 1991, 'Scrutiny of Delegated Legislation by the Australian Senate', *Statute Law Review*, vol. 12, no. 2, pp. 87–108.
Whitehouse, Gillian, 2001, 'Recent Trends in Pay Equity: Beyond the Aggregate Statistics', *The Journal of Industrial Relations*, vol. 43, no. 1, March, pp. 66–78.
Whittaker, David J. (ed.), 2001, *The Terrorism Reader*, Routledge: New York.
Wieviorka, Michel, 1998, 'Is Multiculturalism the Solution?', *Ethnic and Racial Studies*, vol. 21, no. 5, pp. 881–910.
Wild, Rex & Pat Anderson, 2007, *Little Children are Sacred*, Report of the Northern Territory Board of Inquiry into the Protection of Aboriginal Children from Sexual Abuse. Available at http://www.nt.gov.au/dcm/inquirysaac/pdf/bipacsa_final_report.pdf, last accessed 12 June 2008.
Wilkinson, Paul, 1977, *Terrorism and the Liberal State*, Macmillan: London.
Wilkinson, Paul, 1992, 'Observations on the Relationship of Freedom and Terrorism', in L. Howard (ed.), *Terrorism: Roots, Impact, Responses*, Praeger: New York.
Williams, Clive, 2002, 'Australian Security Policy, Post-11 September', *Australian Journal of International Affairs*, vol. 56, no. 1, pp. 13–21.
Williams, George, 2000, *A Bill of Rights for Australia*, UNSW Press: Sydney.
Williams, George, 2001, 'Distrust of Representative Government: Australian Experiments with Direct Democracy', in Marian Sawer & Gianni Zappala (eds), *Speaking for the People: Representation in Australian Politics*, Melbourne University Press: Carlton.
Williamson, John, 1990, 'What Washington Means by Policy Reform', in J. Williamson (ed.), *Latin American Adjustment: How Much has Changed*, Institute for International Economics: Washington.
Winter, Ian (ed.), 2000, *Social Capital and Public Policy in Australia*, Australian Institute of Family Studies: Melbourne.
Winterton, George, 1994a, 'The Constitutional Implications of a Republic', in M. Stephenson & C. Turner (eds), *Australia: Republic or Monarchy?*, University of Queensland Press: St Lucia.
Winterton, George, 1994b, *Monarchy to Republic: Australian Republican Government*, 2nd edn, Oxford University Press: Melbourne.
Wiseman, John, 1998, *Global Nation?: Australia and the Politics of Globalisation*, Cambridge University Press: Melbourne.
Wong, Loong, 1992, 'Ethnicity, the State and the Public Agenda', in M. Muetzelfeldt (ed.), *Society, State and Politics in Australia*, Pluto Press Australia in association with Deakin University Press: Sydney.

Woodley, Gil, 2000, 'The "Battle for Seattle": Globalisation and its Discontents', *Social Alternatives*, vol. 19, no. 1, pp. 26–9.

Yeatman, Anna, 1992, 'Women's Citizenship Claims, Labour Market Policy and Globalisation', *Australian Journal of Political Science*, vol. 27, no. 3, pp. 449–61.

Zaller, John, 1992, *The Nature and Origins of Mass Opinion*, Cambridge University Press: Cambridge.

Zappalá, Gianni, 1998, 'The Micro-Politics of Immigration Service Responsiveness in an Australian "Ethnic Electorate"', *Ethnic and Racial Studies*, vol. 21, no. 4, pp. 683–702.

Zines, Leslie, 1997, *The High Court and the Constitution*, 4th edn, Butterworths: Sydney.

Zubrzycki, Jerzy, 1997, 'Multiculturalism, Social Cohesion and National Identity', *Without Prejudice*, no. 10, June, pp. 7–10.

Index

Aboriginal and Torres Strait Islander Commission (ATSIC)   271
Aboriginal people *see* Indigenous Australians
accountability   28, 30, 101–2, 127–8
adjudication   61
advertising and news media   211
agenda setting   211
agents, elected representatives   140
anarchism   100, 173
anti-globalisation   259
Asia-Pacific Economic Cooperation Forum (APEC)   250
assimilation   292
Association of South East Asian Nations (ASEAN)   250
Australia Act 1986   19
Australian Citizenship Council   322–3
Australian Citizenship Pledge   318
Australian Citizenship Test (2007)   325
Australian Democrats   169
Australian Labor Party   161, 166–7, 168, 173–6, 239, 279–80, 337
Australian People Census 2006   319
autonomy, loss of   258–60

backbench   49, 97
balance of power   29
bias, media   216
bicameral   22
bilateralism   293
budgets   114
bureaucratic mentality   102–3, 105–6
bureaucracy   96–108
   accountability problems   101–2
   cost   100
   definition   96
   historical and political aspects   106
   impedes the capitalist economy   10
   less efficient than markets   101
   less is better than more   99–103
   people's freedom   101
   problems of large   100–2
   problems with   104–5
   as a rational authority   96–9
   reorientation of   105–6

Cabinet   xxxi–xxxii
   ministers   195
   and pressure groups   193–5, 198
   Prime Minister as head of   44–5
candidates   22, 43, 89, 92, 142–6, 149, 150, 152, 153, 161, 164, 172, 174, 178, 191, 238, 239, 278, 279, 309
capitalism   259
career paths and parties   160, 163, 191
Caucus   46
census   319
children overboard   362
citizenship   314–30
   Australian Citizenship Council   322–3
   Australian Citizenship Pledge   318
   Australian Citizenship Test (2007)   325
   in contemporary Australia   319–25
   definition   314, 315–17
   and democracy   325–9
   Galligan & Roberts's position (2004)   323–4
   Howard Cabinet position (1996–2007)   320–1
Citizenship in Australia (1997–2007)   321
civic citizenship   316–17, 326–9
civil liberties   362
climate change   164, 347
Cold War   249

collective action   344
colonial politics   167
committees of federal Parliament   33
common law   59
Commonwealth Heads of Government Meeting (CHOGM)   250
Commonwealth/state powers   10
community-building   301, 303
competition
    and efficiency   120
    and pressure groups   187–8
compulsory voting   xxvii, 22, 134, 135, 143, 144, 145, 153, 169, 210, 237, 308
    preferential   144, 145, 153, 154, 169, 308
conservative, Australian as   116
constituencies
    multiple member   142–3
    single member   142
Constitution   4
    alteration to   11–12
    Australian   8–12, 18
    definition   5
    and High Court   64
    how did it emerge in Australia?   5–6
    and Indigenous Australians   274–5
    and judiciary   62–3
    relevance to democracy in contemporary Australia   15–17
    relevance to government in contemporary Australia   12–14
    what is does/doesn't say   7–8
    written   122–3
Constitutional change   116–16
Constitutional Convention   5, 91
Constitutional crisis (1975)   82–5, 88
Constitutional Monarchy   87
conventions   5, 7
corruption   6, 136, 171
Council of Australian Governments (COAG)   40, 115
court system, Australian   59–61
cross-benches   27
cultural distance   271

debates, parliament   171
decision-making process   xxxii–xxxiv, 58, 68, 124, 136, 138–9, 191, 195, 232, 276, 304, 305, 307
democracy   xxxii–xxxiv, 69–73
    and citizenship   325–9

    direct   xvii, xxxi, 138–9, 147, 156, 329
    and environmental sustainability   334–43
    and ethnic diversity   289–95, 304–9
    and federal system   124–9
    and freedom   xxx, 101, 318–19
    and Indigenous Australians   276–80
    and news media   207–8
    opinion polling   232–8
    participatory   138
    and political parties   160–1
    and pressure groups   189–90
    see also representative democracy
democratic principle (federal elections)   149
democratic theory   136–8
    representative   138–40
development v. environmental sustainability   335–6
developmental interests in political executives   337
developing countries and greenhouse gas emissions   349–50, 351
direct democracy   xvii, xxxi, 138–9, 147, 156, 329
division
    federal system   341–2
    parliament   341
    political executives   341
    and pressure groups   342–3
    within parties   342
division of powers   6–7, 115
double dissolution   10, 82

economic globalisation   248–9
eco-tourism   345
efficiency and competition   120
egalitarianism   318
election results   148
elections
    candidate deposits   152
    federal, should Australians vote in   147–55
    Prime Minister as focus of   43
    and political parties   161
    safe/marginal seats   150–1, 155
    see also voting
electoral system and the two-party system   169
elite rule   136
environmental education   346
environmental issues   344

environmental sustainability   172, 344–7,
        351, 352
    deadlock   340–3
    v. development   335–6
    government and democracy   334–43
ethnic diversity   289–310
    in Australia   290
    definition   289
    government and democracy   289–95,
        296–303, 304–9
    and immigration policy   291–2
    and political executives   301–2
    policies with respect to   292–3
    policy-making   339–40
    preoccupation with the short-term   338–9
    pressures towards increasing   294
    real   289, 290, 296–303
ethnicity   140, 289
European Union (EU)   250
euthanasia legislation   194
executive power   xvi, xvii, 39, 78, 79, 80, 81

face-to-face interviewing   227–8
factions   162
Family First Party   178
family reunions   294
federalism   5, 6, 114–29
    and democracy   124–9
    and government   118–23
    and Indigenous Australians   273–5
    permanence in Australia   116–17
financial assistance to states   11
first-past-the-post system   143
fiscal imbalance   128
focus groups   228
foreign ownership rules   248–9
fourth estate theory   207–8
franchise   166
Franklin River   184
free press   363
free speech   64, 122
freedom and democracy   xxx, 101, 318–19
front bench   97

Galligan & Roberts's position (2004)   323–4
global commodity markets   252
global free market policy   253
global labour markets   253
global political ideas, practices and
        institutions   254

global service markets   252–3
globalisation   246–61
    anti-globalisation   259
    cultural   251–2
    different understandings of   247–57
    economic   248–9
    emergence   252–4
    as hegemonic ideology   255–7
    hegemonic ideological position   254–8,
        260
    irresistible force   247–8, 260
    government and democracy   258–60
    political   249–51
    pro-globalisation   251
Goods and Services Tax (GST)   29
government   xxxi–xxxii, 69–73
    by elites   136–7
    and environmental sustainability   334–43
    and ethnic diversity   289–95, 296–303
    and federal system   118–23
    and news media   207–8
    opinion polling   232–8
    and policy failure   269–76
    and political parties   160–1
    responsible   5, 6
Governor-General   9, 77–93
    appointing the   87
    Constitutional crisis   82–5, 88
    electing a   86–92
    importance of   82–6
    preliminaries for   77–80
    resignation   78
    What you see, what you get   80–2
greenhouse gas emissions   348–52
Greens   337
Group of Eight (G8)   250
groups
    opposed interests on policies   188
    shared/competing interests   187–8

Haneef, Mohammad   363, 364
Hawke, Bob   46, 50
Head of State   9–12, 77, 86–7
    appointment of   90–2
    election of   89–92
    Referendum (1999)   91
hegemonic ideology   254–6
High Court   11, 57
    and Australian society   64
    and Constitution   64

decisions 64
judges and politics 72, 73
and judicial activism 65–8
political visibility 69–73
and pressure groups 197
Hollingworth, Peter 78
House committees 33
Houses of Parliament
deadlock 83–4
definition 83
disagreement between 10–11
House of Representatives 9–10
counting votes 144
election results 148
marginal seats 152
voting to elect members 145
Howard Cabinet 320–1, 348–51
human security 367–8

identity 314
Australian 318
national 326
ideology
hegemonic 246, 247, 254–7, 260–1
political 174–5
immigration
from the Asian region 291
Muslim and African 291–2
patterns since 1900 292
and population 294
post-World War II 291
immigration policy
current 296–7
and ethnic diversity 291–2
independent party representatives 151–2
independents in the Federal Parliament 178
Indigenous Australians 268–83
apology to 281
and Cabinet/Ministries 273
conflicting policy objectives 273
conflicts over resources 275
and Constitution 274–5
cultural distance 271–2
and democracy in Australia 276–82
Federalism 273–5
and government in Australia 269–76
and inconsistent policies 273
intellectual distance 272
land rights 277

Little Children are Sacred report 2007 274
paternalism 270–1
physical distance 271
and policy failure 268, 271–3
policy-making 272, 279–80
political inefficacy 280–2
and political executive 270–5
and pressure groups 280
quality of life 269
racism 270
and two-party system 279–80
and voting 280–1
voting system 278–9
individuals with shared/competing
interests 187–8
informal votes 137
information and communication technologies
(ICTs) 249, 251
integration 293
intellectual distance 272
Intergovernmental Panel on Climate Change
(IPCC) 350
international 'economic' institutions with
political effects 250–1
international financial institutions 248
International Monetary Fund (IMF)
250, 253
international political institutions 250
Internet 217–21, 240
interviewing
face-to-face 227–8
telephone 228

Joint committees 33
judicial activism
and High Court 65–8
judiciary 57–73
questions of visibility 615

Keating, Paul 50
Kerr, Sir John 84
Kevin 07 241
Kirby, Michael 72
Kyoto Protocol 344, 348–51

land, historical/cultural attitude to 336
land rights and Indigenous Australians 277
laws, passing 30
leaders, electing/rejecting xxxii–xxxiii
legal citizenship 316

legislation
    passing (from bill to act)   23
    preliminary discussion   22–3
legislature   28
Liberal Party of Australia   163, 168, 173–6, 279–80, 337
liberalism   175, 187
liberal-pluralism   186, 187
Little Children are Sacred report 2007   274
lobby groups   229
lobbying   183, 186, 214–15
long-term thinking   335, 345, 346

Mabo   64, 65, 68
mandate   88
marginal seats   150–1, 155, 235, 278
media *see* news media
ministers
    Cabinet   195
    definition   97
    role of   49
minor party representatives   151–2
mobile multinational corporations (MNC)   248, 253, 259, 260
moral obligation (federal elections)   149
motion of no confidence   27
multicultural society   289
multiculturalism   289, 293
multiple member constituencies   142
MX missiles   46

national citizenship   317
national identity   326
National Farmers' Federation (NFF)   193
National Party of Australia   167, 168, 279, 337
natural resources   336, 345
naturalised citizenship   317
neo-liberalism   104, 106
new public management   99, 106–7
news media   205–22
    ABC and SBS   212
    and advertising   211
    agenda setting   211
    audience's limits   211
    commercial   212
    concentration of ownership   212–13
    ideal role   208–10
    Internet   217–21
    importance government and democracy   207–8
    internationally syndicated organisations   215–16, 251–2
    male, white, middle-class organisations   216
    nationally networked organisations   215–16
    and news   211
    organisations   212–16
    ownership in Australia   213
    press galleries   214
    and pressure groups   185–6
    and the Prime Minister   41
    routinised organisations   213–15
    why they do not fulfill and ideal role   210–15
non-renewable resources   336–7
North American Free Trade Agreement (NAFTA)   250

opinion polling   227–38
    agencies   236
    government and democracy   232–8
    important aspects   229–31
    types of   227–9

Parliament   9–12
    conflicting voices in   85–6
    debates   171
    division in   341
    and Head of State   90
    Is it a waste of time?   24–35
    and pressure groups   197
    socially important debates   29
    'Welcome to Country' ceremony   25
Parliamentary committees   31–2
Parliamentary debates   24, 25, 28, 171
party organisation   479
party powerbrokers   48
paternalism   270–1
personal benefits (federal elections)   150
phone polls   228–9
physical distance   271
pluralistic society   323, 328
policy   xxv, 28
    advisers   xxv, 49–50, 195
    decided as a result of pressure   188–9
    failure   268
policy-making
    and ethnic diversity   339–40
    and Indigenous Australians   272, 279–80

and opinion polling 232, 233
and political parties 161
political blogs 220–1
political citizenship 317
political deadlock xiii, 10, 83–5, 87, 89, 90, 93, 340–3, 346–7
political executive
   definition 39
   division in 341
   and ethnic diversity 301–2
   hegemonic ideology 256
   Indigenous Australians 270–5
   information from 207
   lack of responsiveness 190
   loss of autonomy 259–60
   members 39–40
   and opinion polling 233
   power of developmental interests 337
   and pressure groups 197–8, 280
   segmented 340
   think short-term 338
   and two-party system 171
political globalisation 249–51
political inefficacy 280–2
political institutions xxxii, 191
   international 250
political marketing 238–41
political parties 28, 117, 159–78
   Australia, government and democracy 160–1
   career paths 163
   differences between the two parties 173–7
   and division 342
   and elections 161
   factions 162
   hegemonic ideology 256
   involvement in causes 164
   male domination 164–5
   meetings 164
   and opinion polling 233
   policy-making 161
   power struggles 162–3
   and pressure groups 196
   two-party system 165–9
political spin 149, 153, 155, 240
political strategising (organisation) 162
political system 160, 165–9
political visibility of High Court 69–73
politicians, state 117

polling agencies 236
popular will, reflection of 126–7
population and immigration 294
post-materialism 345–6
poverty 184, 367
power struggles 162–3
preferential voting 22
   compulsory 144, 145, 153, 154, 169, 308
   optional 144
Premier and pressure groups 194–5
press gallery 33–4, 214
press secretaries 214
pressure groups 182–99
   and Cabinet 193–5, 198
   democracy in action 189–90
   and division 342–3
   effective pressure 192–8
   emergence of 184–5
   importance in a representative democracy 186–92
   and Indigenous Australians 280
   influence 183–6, 192–8
   lobbying 183, 185
   news media 185–6, 214–15
   and political executives 197–8, 280
   outside of Cabinet 195–8
   protests 185
   reflects weight of opinion 189
primary industry, ongoing reliance on 336–9
Prime Minister
   centre of election contests 43
   head of Cabinet 44–5
   head of party 43–4
   importance of 42–53
   informal power 45–7
   and the media 41, 42, 47
   and pressure groups 194
privatisation 101
pro-globalisation 251
proportional representation 142–3, 278–9
protection 114
protests 185
proportional representation 22, 85, 142, 145, 146, 152, 169, 172, 278–9, 306, 308
public opinion 228, 229, 237
public policy (monetary and fiscal) 28
public service 49–50
   and pressure groups 196

quality of life 269

racism   270
rainfall and water availability   336
rational-comprehensive policy-making   339
real ethnic diversity   289, 290, 296–303
referenda   146–7
referendum   12
Referendum (1999)   91
representation of communities   125–6
representation of individuals   124–5
representative democracy   160–78
   and ethnic diversity   305, 308–9
   importance of pressure groups   186–92
   and Indigenous Australians   276–8
   Westminster–style   190–1
   and white middle-class men   308–9
representative democratic theory   138–40
representatives, boundaries and numbers of   141–2
republic referendum   9, 91
Rudd Ministry   51–2, 351–2
rule of law   57, 58

safe seats   155, 277
save the Franklin campaign   184
secession in Western Australia   125
security, national   357–69
Senate   9
   censure over Iraq   27
   counting votes   145
   election results   148
   group voting tickets   145
   voting to elect members   146
Senate committees   33
Senior Executive Service (SES)   98
separation of powers   4, 5
single member constituencies   142, 143, 144, 145, 169, 278, 279, 308
social benefits (federal elections)   151
social cohesion   xxx, 229, 305, 314, 315, 318, 325, 326–9, 330
society, Australian   171
soil degradation in Australia   335
sovereignty, loss of   258–60
state governments   6, 8, 11, 12, 13, 62, 66–7, 69, 123
suffrage   166
supply   114

Tasmanian Dam case   67–8
Tatz, Colin   270

technology   249
terra nullius   64, 336
territorial security   365–7
terrorism   357–69
Thomas, Joseph 'Jack'   359
two-party system
   and Australian politics   170–2
   definition   160
   and the electoral system   169
   and Indigenous Australians   279–80
   intellectual/philosophical foundations   168
   meaning of   165–6
   origins   166–7
   stability of   168

Uniform Income Taxation cases   66–7, 68
unions   166
United Nations   250

values, Australian   318–19, 327
vertical fiscal imbalance   115
vote weighting   143
voting   134–56
   in Australia   134–5
   compulsory   xxvii, 22, 134, 135, 143, 144, 145, 153, 169, 210, 237, 308
   democratic theory   136–8
   House of Representatives   144, 145
   and Indigenous Australians   280–1
   informal votes   137
   people deciding and controlling their destiny   137–8
   practices   141–55
   preference expressed for a single member geographical constituency   143–4
   preferential, compulsory   144
   preferential, optional   144
   representative democratic theory   138–40
   Senate   145
   should Australians vote in federal elections?   147–55
   system and Indigenous Australians   278–9
   theories   136–41

water availability and rainfall   336
web site visitor polls   228–9
'Welcome to Country' ceremony   25
Western Australia, secession in   125

Westminster system　xxv, 6, 11
Westminster–style democracies　190–1
White Australia Policy　291, 295
white middle-class men
　　and Indigenous Australians　279
　　Internet　219–20
　　news media　216
　　and Parliament　24–5
　　and representative democracy　308–9
Whitlam government　84
Wik　64, 68
women and Parliament　25
World Bank　250, 253
World Trade Organization (WTO)　251, 253